T0320004

A Comparative History of Central Bank Behavior

A Comparative History of Central Bank Behavior

Consistency in Monetary Policy in the US and UK

John H. Wood

Reynolds Professor of Economics, Emeritus, Wake Forest University, USA

Cheltenham, UK • Northampton, MA, USA

Published by
Edward Elgar Publishing Limited
The Lypiatts
15 Lansdown Road
Cheltenham
Glos GL50 2JA
UK

Edward Elgar Publishing, Inc.
William Pratt House
9 Dewey Court
Northampton
Massachusetts 01060
USA

A catalogue record for this book
is available from the British Library

Library of Congress Control Number: 2022944521

This book is available electronically in the **Elgar**online
Economics subject collection
http://dx.doi.org/10.4337/9781803926605

MIX
Paper from
responsible sources
FSC
www.fsc.org   FSC® C013056

ISBN 978 1 80392 659 9 (cased)
ISBN 978 1 80392 660 5 (eBook)

Printed and bound in Great Britain by TJ Books Limited, Padstow, Cornwall

Contents

Preface

Central bankers are people too. This is the most recent of several books I've written which illustrate their consistency over time in being guided by the imperfect information available to them and the interests upon whose political support they have depended, particularly governments and financial institutions, with the occasional participation of the public when the damages of the so-called experts become too great to bear.

Acknowledgment

My greatest debts are to my excellent colleagues in the Economics Department and those in the economics profession generally who take the above principles seriously and are willing to subject ideas and institutions to criticism.

1. Governments and their banks

WHOSE MONETARY POLICY?

This book is about the making of monetary policy, especially the people behind those policies, in the United States and the United Kingdom during crises in the last two centuries. Central banks are sometimes called independent, although one might ask *"Of what?"* No one is independent of *everything* – of all interests, ideas, and pressures. More precisely, the claim normally (and erroneously) amounts to denials of high-spending governments' desires or abilities to substitute bank credit for unpopular taxes.

Standard presentations of central banks devoted to financial stability neglect their actual performances as accomplices of government spending and supporters of national debts, which have been the actual primary reasons for their existence. The normal state of government finances has been borderline crisis or worse. The debts of ancient governments and debasements of their coinages are legend. Wartime inflation, then as now, was common. Aristophanes' *Frogs* in which Charon demands twice his usual price to take Dionysus down to Hades was a comment on inflation during the Peloponnesian War. The Roman Emperor Diocletian's *Edict on Maximum Prices* in AD 301 was an attempt to curb inflation by price ceilings, which turned out to be no more effective than the many other price controls that have been tried from time to time, down to President Nixon's attempted controls during the Great Inflation of the 1970s (Jones 1974, p. 190; Southern 2001, p. 160; Blinder 1979).

In the eighteenth century, with the development of commerce including expensive luxuries, Adam Smith ([1776] 1937, p. 861) wrote that sovereigns, like the other great proprietors in their dominions, spent large parts of their revenues on the expanding indulgences:

> How can it be supposed that [the sovereign] should be the only rich man in his dominions who is insensitive to pleasures of this kind? ... His ordinary expence becomes equal to his ordinary revenue, and it is well if it does not ordinarily exceed it ... and when extraordinary exigencies require extraordinary expenses, he must necessarily call upon his subjects for an extraordinary aid.

In fact,

> The parsimony which leads to accumulation has become almost as rare in republican as in monarchical governments. The Italian republics, the United Provinces of the Netherlands, are all in debt. The canton of Berne is the single republic in Europe which has amassed any considerable treasure.

"The taste for pageantry prevails as much in the apparently sober senate-house of little republics as in the dissipated court of the greatest king," Smith continued. For all of them, "the want of parsimony in time of peace imposes the necessity of contracting debt in time of war."

Much of the difference between government and household spending may be found in the expected future costs and benefits of current behavior. Households can look forward to future rewards from current savings; not so politicians and government officials, whose rewards are concentrated in the present and near future in popularity, power, and re-elections. One might have expected fiscal irresponsibility to be less in small representative governments because of the closer proximity of their overseers/taxpayers, only to be disappointed, Smith observed. Voters of all kinds press for immediate advantages (Buchanan and Wagner 1977, pp. 93–111). Even the smallest government units must borrow for necessary projects such as schools, roads, and overdue maintenance. The occasional/accidental budget surpluses soon disappear into other, more immediately and politically attractive, uses. As I write this, pleas for unemployment benefits during the Covid-19 crisis have been unaccompanied by requests for corresponding finance in the form of increased taxes, perhaps on those less injured by the lockdowns.

Nor are the debts redeemed. "When national debts have once been accumulated to a certain degree, there is scarce, I believe, a single instance of their having been fairly and completely paid," Smith ([1776] 1937, p. 882) wrote. "The liberation of the public revenue, if it has ever been brought about at all, has always been brought about by a bankruptcy; sometimes by an avowed one, but always by a real one, though frequently by a pretended payment," meaning inflation. For example, although the U.S. national debt more than tripled between 1950 and 1980, its real value fell 25 percent as prices almost quadrupled, and the debt/GDP ratio fell from 76 percent to 26 percent – before rising to 108 percent in 2010.

The long nineteenth century, 1815–1914, following closely upon Smith, was a partial exception to his pessimistic assessment in its monetary discipline that was enforced by the gold standard. Prices were stable over long periods and national debts were restrained. The U.K.'s debt was about the same in 1914 as in 1815, and American budgets were usually in surplus except during the Civil War. The U.S. debt increased from $64 million in 1860 to $2,755 million in 1866, but was paid down to $961 million by 1893, and was not much larger (despite the Spanish–American War and the Panama Canal) at $1,188 million in 1914.

Banks were less needed for government finance during that century than during the major wars before and after – European powers were almost continuously at war or on war footings in the eighteenth and twentieth centuries – although they were also called on to address financial crises, many of their own making. Banks have often been pushed into the finance of public activities and then bailed out of the consequent financial misfortunes, as we will see in the following chapters. The histories of banks and their governments are stories of alternating mutual support and collapse – in modern times as much as the Middle Ages and before.

Governments have always been borrowers and regulators. They have encouraged the formation of banks as sources of credit but have been jealous of them as rivals for power. The Bardi family bank lent England's Edward III (1327–77) 900,000 gold florins during the Hundred Years War with France, which he failed to repay, as well as 600,000 florins borrowed from the Peruzzi's, leading to the collapse of both families' banks. Edward's grandfather, Edward I (1272–1307), had executed or expelled moneylenders whose lending failed to meet his demands. Nevertheless, they and their replacements continued into the next century, financing some of the early voyages of discovery, including Christopher Columbus and John Cabot.

The Welsers were a German banking and merchant family prominent in international finance in the sixteenth century especially as financiers of the Holy Roman Emperor Charles V (1519–56). Along with the Fugger family, the Welsers controlled large sectors of the European economy, and accumulated enormous wealth through trade and finance. They received conquest and settlement rights to the Province of Venezuela from Spain in 1528. There is a Fugger–Welser–Medici trading game with a medieval background.

Venetian bank failures between 1496 and 1533 were not directly due to government defaults, although the consequences were just as grave. They arose from the system of war finance and the erosion of the values of government debt. Although wars were a recurring feature of Venetian life, they were treated as unusual emergencies – much as in the United States in the twenty-first century, as Smith predicted. They were financed by forced loans on the wealthy. In return for payments, citizens received government obligations, which might have been good investments if they had not been issued in excess. Lenders were forced to sell bonds at depreciated prices and withdraw funds from banks to meet the demands of forced loans (Lane 1937).

Although eventually surpassed by corporate enterprises, family merchant and investment banks continued to be important in the finance of large private and public enterprises into the twentieth century. The Duc de Richelieu, prime minister of France 1815–18 and 1820–21, who sorted out French finances following Napoleon's wars, with the help of Baring Brothers, called that banking firm Europe's "sixth great power," after Austria, England, France, Prussia, and Russia. They had financed the Louisiana Purchase for the United States, railways in Argentina in the late nineteenth century (which led to the Barings Crisis), and lasted until the speculations of a rogue trader in 1995 (Wechsberg 1966, pp. 90–93; Ziegler 1988; Fay 1997).

At the end of the nineteenth century, J.P. Morgan & Co. rescued the gold standard in the United States by borrowing in Europe, organized U.S. Steel in 1901, the world's largest firm at the time, and orchestrated the end of the panic of 1907. Kuhn Loeb, Rothschilds, and others affected power politics, for example, by large loans to Japan (partly because of Russia's treatment of its Jews) that were partially credited with its victory in the Russo-Japanese War of 1904–05 (Best 1972).

There is no better example of the game than banks' high-risk support of government housing policies and their bailouts during the Great Recession. Commercial banks – short-term lenders to business on the basis of demand deposits – had become the principal financial institutions before the mid-nineteeth century. Their government charters required lending to those governments, such as the purchases of state bonds by state-chartered banks and U.S. bonds by nationally chartered banks (Dewey 1922, pp. 206–11; Rolnick and Weber 1983). Banks have also been used to suppress private in favor of government spending even in peacetime (see Chapter 5). The current international Basel agreement for the regulation of bank risk requires preferences for government debt despite its interest-rate risk. Charles Calomiris et al.'s *Fragile by Design: The Political Origins of Banking Crises* (2014) is a useful account of this interdependence. Banking systems are always and everywhere political constructs, outcomes of "games of bargains," the players being governments, bankers, and their clients.

The demand liabilities of banks, essential to exchange and economic activity, are routinely assumed to make the institutions inherently fragile and therefore in need of regulation. There are many official restrictions on bank structures, portfolios, and actions intended to reduce their risk of failure, such as bank size, cash reserve and capital requirements, disclosure, and portfolio allocations. Banks are legally separated from commerce because of fears that some firms might gain financial advantages despite the loss of diversification.

In fact, there is a good deal of evidence raising doubt about commercial banks' inherent fragility. Even in the United States, the country with the most bank failures, their failure rates were about the same as business failure rates in general between the Civil War and the Great Depression (Benston and Kaufman 1986). Then from the mid-1930s to the 1970s, bank failures were almost non-existent. The previous major cause of the undiversified U.S. bank failures, volatile farm prices, was displaced by farm prosperity (Cottrell et al., 1995). Increases in bank failures after the 1970s were due to volatile monetary policy and interest rates, government pressures on bank portfolios, such as sub-prime real estate, and increases in financial-asset insurance and bailouts reducing the expected costs of failure to bank owners and increasing moral hazard.

Government regulations may have done as much or more to increase than reduce bank risk-taking. Efforts to reduce runs by limiting deposit withdrawals have been thwarted by the regulators. At the peak of the 1933 bank run, Federal Reserve banks refused assistance to banks not committed to pay deposits in full (Wicker 1996, p. 122). Governments have also encouraged, even forced, maturity mismatching by pushing banks into mortgage lending. Salvaging failed banks is part of the banker–government arrangement in which the former are reimbursed for the risks of financing the latter's programs. One of the costliest bailouts came during the Great Recession of 2007–09, after banks had financed the packages of subprime mortgages issued by government agencies under the impression that *This Time is Different* (Reinhart and Rogoff 2010), that the housing bubble would never burst.

We have not improved on ancient practices, and perhaps have made them worse by requiring taxpayers to pick up the pieces – although it's their (our) own fault because they (we) have not only failed to monitor our political representatives but have erected bureaucratic obstacles which interfere with effective monitoring, based on the assumption that deposit insurance, capital ratios, and regulators take the place of investor oversight (Redish 2001; Wood 2020).

The British pound sterling, worth a pound of silver in Charlemagne's (768–814) time, had lost 90 percent of its value by the end of Henry VIII's reign in 1547, most of it to inflationary war finance, after which it maintained its commodity value (except for wartime interruptions) until the 1930s (Feavearyear 1931, 346–7). The gold value of the U.S. dollar was also maintained (except for the Civil War interruption) from 1792 to 1933. The abandonment of the gold standard in favor of fiat money has since resulted in the erosions of both currencies by more than 95 percent.

INTERESTS AND POLICIES

There may be a lesson in the joint rise of stable currencies and representative governments with respect for property in the nineteenth century, and their reversal with the return of executive dominance the next century. The first examples below (Chapter 2) are the monetary policies of the Bank of England during the troubled years following the European Wars ending with Napoleon's defeat at Waterloo. The structures of government and finance affected monetary policies, and so did the people (interests) involved. The deflationary resumption policy after 1813 involved a contest between long-term property and short-term economic (especially employment) interests, with the central bank in the middle. In 1847, the Bank responded to threats to short-term stability (Chapter 3), as it did on other occasions before its government takeover during World War I. The reconstituted government Bank was less concerned with economic instability in its determination to restore long-term financial arrangements in the City's interests after the war (Chapter 4), when the Bank of England's governor was able to find the domestic costs of tight-money – unemployment – "greatly exaggerated." So whose monetary policy was it?

These discussions amount to examinations of hypotheses regarding the relations between monetary policies and politics, including choices between rules and discretion under crisis conditions. Their expanded uses for democratically doubtful fiscal purposes during the Great Recession (2007–09) increased doubts regarding the independence of central banks, but the issue is not new. The role of central banks, especially during crises, has always been a significant political issue (Alesina and Stella 2011). "[T]he Bank of England is now … remote from party politics," *Economist* editor Walter Bagehot (1873, p. 90) wrote during a quiet period, but it was founded as "a Whig finance company … by a Whig Government because it was in desperate want of money, and supported by the 'City' because the 'City' was Whig," willing to finance William III, who had overthrown the Tory-inclined James II.

The Bank was chartered in 1694, during the Nine Years' War between France and the Grand Alliance that included England. In 1696, King William wrote to his ministers in London from the battlefields of Europe, "… in the name of God determine quickly to find some credit for the troops here, [or] all is lost, and I must go to the Indies." The Bank's charter was extended the next year in return for another low-interest loan. "Here was the crisis of the war," David Ogg (1955, p. 433) wrote, "it was financial."

U.S. Treasury Secretary Alexander Hamilton persuaded Congress to charter the Bank of the United States in 1791 against the opposition of the mainly rural Jeffersonian/Republicans, who were able to deny its renewal in 1809. John Marshall wrote in his *Life of George Washington* that Hamilton's economic program, especially his plan for a national bank, "made a deep impression on many members of the legislature; and contributed, not inconsiderably, to the complete organization of those distinct and visible parties, which, in their long and dubious conflict for power, have since shaken the United States to their centre" (1807, vol. iv, p. 224). The War of 1812 brought the Bank's renewal, but President Andrew Jackson vetoed the bill that would have extended its life. He, like Jefferson, opposed the banks on the populist grounds that they were used by the elite to exploit the people. Their fiscal conservatism (budget surpluses) also reduced governments' need for banks (Olsen 2010; Larson 1981; Wood 2005, pp. 123–34).

Bank and public attitudes were affected by the catastrophic Great Depression and the intellectual Keynesian Revolution which followed (Chapter 5), but a lesson of all these discussions is that monetary institutions and policies in the U.S.A. and U.K. have been created and managed in the interests of the politically well-positioned. This was also demonstrated in the U.S.A. in the nineteenth century (Chapter 6), by the Federal Reserve's behavior during the Great Depression (Chapter 7), and the crisis of 2008, when officials assured the public that the $700 billion of their tax-money that was voted to bail out Wall Street was really for the benefit of Main Street (Chapter 8). An implication of these discussions is that studies of central banking should take structures, governance, and political interests into account at least as much as the more publicized official mandates.

Later chapters try to show that the self-interested determinants of monetary policies also operate in other areas, such as the famines which have resulted more from government policies than food shortages, and military engagements, including America's "endless wars" which depend on devices which enable the government's backdoor finance and lack of accountability (Chapters 9 and 10).

THE ELITE

Government policies – social and economic – are often assumed to be (or ought to be) decisions of the elite, of the best and brightest, as opposed to the passionate and uneducated majority. Political science professor Donald Brand (2016) wrote:

> We have entered a new and dangerous age of populism. Populists succeed when they appeal to the passions of voters, rousing them through fear and anger to reject the messy compromises that are intrinsic to a politics of moderation, and to look for scapegoat targets upon which they can vent their frustrations. Populists of the right have embraced nativism and populists of the left have targeted Wall Street and kindled class war. For more than a decade, populism has undermined Congress as an institution, leading to increased partisan polarization and representatives who find it difficult to seek compromises for fear of being challenged in primaries by partisan hardliners.

On the other hand, the record of the elite, when they have had their way, has not been impressive. David Halberstam's name for their performance during the Vietnam War, *The Best and the Brightest*, was sarcastic. More recently, *New York Times* columnist David Brooks (2018) asked "How has such amazing talent [the educated elite, who went to the right schools] produced such poor results … from Vietnam to Watergate to the financial crisis."

In contrast, Brooks wrote, "The older establishment won World War II and built the American Century." He ignores the possibilities that it also contributed to the origins of that war, the Great Depression and the Dust Bowl, and destroyed an efficient and stable monetary system. The rebelliousness of the disappointed middle-class or populists, call them what you will, recently and historically, may have been responses to the failures of the elite establishment.

In *Capitalism, Socialism, and Democracy*, Joseph Schumpeter (1942) described democracy as a system of government where elites compete through elections for the right to rule the populace, undertaking to enact their understanding of the will of the people (Elliott 1994). In the course of criticizing the extension of the franchise in his work on *The English Constitution*, Bagehot (1872, p. xxiii) expressed the fear that

> both our political parties will bid for the support of the working man; that both of them will promise to do as he likes if he will only tell them what it is .... I can conceive of nothing more corrupting or worse for a set of poor ignorant people than that two combinations of well-taught and rich men should constantly offer to defer to their decision, and compete for the office of executing it. *Vox populi* will be *vox diaboli.*

We will have "the supremacy of ignorance over instruction and of numbers over knowledge."

The attitudes of the elite/establishment/office-holders toward the population, their smug presumptions of superiority, are very old, and so have been their failings. The episodes discussed here consider the causes of this situation as stemming from the distributions of information and the costs of failure. The regulators/policymakers are distant from the effects of their policies. There was considerable distress leading to complaints about government policies during the Great Depression that went virtually unnoticed in official circles, and were not altered until emergencies forced them. Adam Smith's accounts of the benefits of free exchange relied on the distributions of information and consequences, ignored in economics texts, and undervalued by outsiders, including legislatures and regulators. The rejection of a failed model requires the effects of its failings to be palpable. "The uniform, constant, and uninterrupted efforts of" individuals to better their conditions, "[l]ike the unknown principle of animal life, ... frequently restores health and vigour to the constitution, in spite, not only to the disease, but of the absurd prescriptions of the doctor" (Smith [1776] 1937, p. 326).

This is a story not of changing central banks, but of their continuities. Their record as stabilizers has been mixed, with little or no improvement over time, as they have vacillated between rules and discretion, with large gaps in their learning, evidenced notably but not exclusively by their policies during the Great Depression and Great Recession. Their subordination to governments' fiscal conveniences has been unchanging. The so-called Federal Reserve declaration of independence in the 1951 Treasury-Fed Accord, for example, was followed by unprecedented peacetime inflation as governments ran continuous deficits.

2. Aristocratic government and the Bank of England during the Age of Reform

[Those objecting to the continuation of the government's relations with the Bank of England] knew not the solid advantages resulting to the public from its connections with the present company; they saw not the difficulty that must now attend the breaking up of the present company; ... the Bank, from long habit and the usage of many years, was a part of the constitution ...; all the money business of the Exchequer being done at the Bank ..., with much greater advantage to the public than when it had formerly been done at the Exchequer.

–Prime Minister Lord North, House of Commons, June 13, 1781

The national debt had grown 50 percent during the American War, and the Government needed finance. The proposed bargain that the Bank of England lend the Government £2 million at 3 percent interest in exchange for an extension of its charter from 1787 to 1812 passed the House of Commons 103 to 30. Some believed the price of the loan was too high, especially considering the privileges already given the Bank. On the other hand, governments had generally been satisfied by its services since the Bank's creation in 1694.

Its central bank is an important part of a nation's socio-political-economic environment. Monetary policies have always been social and political as well as economic. The first four sections of this chapter describe that environment and its participants in the early nineteenth century, and the last two concentrate on the political/economic relations and practices of the Bank of England.

GOVERNMENT

The British political system between the Glorious Revolution of 1689, when the Catholic James II was replaced by the Dutch Protestant Prince of Orange, William III, and the Great Reform Act of 1832, has been called the Age of Oligarchy. The head of government was the monarch, even though the seventeenth and eighteenth centuries saw a rise in the power of Parliament, especially the House of Commons, to the supreme position made inevitable by its power of the purse. Five percent of the adult population meeting the requisite property qualifications were eligible to vote, and the nobility and their relations occupied the most prominent political places. Several prime ministers were in the House of Lords. Only after the Marquess of Salisbury (1885–92, 1896–1902) did prime ministers in the House of Commons become the rule (Cook and Stevenson 2014, ch. 3).

Commoners in Parliament were still chosen much as in the thirteenth century, when sheriffs were directed to send two knights from each county, to which were added two citizens from each city, and two burgesses from each borough (a town or district, an administrative unit). They were asked to join the nobility in meeting the king's financial needs, and with the rising commercial and then manufacturing wealth and interests, the Commons developed as a representative body separate from the hereditary and mainly agricultural House of Lords. The Chancellor of the Exchequer, the government's chief financial minister, was (and is) always a member of the House of Commons. When the prime minister was in the Commons he also headed the Exchequer, but when he was in the Lords a member of the House of Commons was designated the government's chief spokesman in that body.

Representation of cities and boroughs increased over time, especially during the sixteenth century, when many "seats" were created by Royal Charter. "The practice of creating boroughs of insignificant voting strength to secure the election of members expected to support the policies of the Crown began during the reign of Edward VI" (1547–53), and was expanded under Elizabeth I (1558–1603), who was generous in creating "pocket" or "rotten" boroughs with a few voters controlled by patrons. Their reliability was furthered by absence of the secret ballot, which did not come until late in the nineteenth century. The borough of Old Sarum, for example, had seven voters who returned two members of Parliament. In 1793, 51 boroughs totaling less than 1,500 voters sent members to the House of Commons, while growing cities like Manchester, Birmingham, Leeds, and Sheffield were unrepresented. Seats were bought and sold, the average price in 1830 being estimated at £6,000. Proposals to bring order to the system were frequent but none succeeded until 1832 (Wilding and Laundy 1971, pp. 638–40). The *Great Reform Act* of that year ended rotten boroughs, the new cities were given representation, and the electorate was raised from 500,000 to 813,000 (one in five adult males) out of a population of 14 million. The Act was the first of a succession of measures that by 1885 encompassed a majority of adult males with secret ballots.

Although often titled themselves, or related to aristocrats, government officials were not usually dilettantes. Many, increasingly with time, were effectively professional politicians and/or civil servants. This may be a reason for the late development of a professional civil service in Britain. As an identifiable group with similar backgrounds and interests, they were able to form coherent policies even if sometimes disrupted by personal animosities and partisan contests.

Norman Gash (1977, p. 39) saw the foundations of modern Conservative policies in these aristocratic but politically sensitive governments:

> Though by training and circumstances Lord Liverpool [prime minister 1812–27] and his colleagues were defenders of the existing order, most were at the same time anxious to stand well with the 'respectable' as distinct from the popular or radical elements in the country. Given their social and political backgrounds, they could hardly have wished otherwise. Few of them belonged to the old aristocracy. Most, and nearly all their leading figures, were drawn from middle-class families [more precisely the upper-upper middle class]. Of the four peers who formed the more ornamental section of the Cabinet ..., only ... two had any claim to length of lineage.

One's grandfather was a barrister who became Lord Chief Justice, another was the son of the younger William Pitt's (1759-p. 83) close friend and advisor. "[Of] the rest, Liverpool's father was a commoner who ... earned his earldom by unflagging political service to George III"; Robert Stewart (Viscount Castlereagh, Foreign Secretary 1812–22) was the son of a newly ennobled Irish politician and landowner; George Canning (Foreign Secretary 1822–27) was the disinherited elder son of an Irish small landowner; Nicholas Vansittart (Chancellor of the Exchequer 1812–23, created Baron Bexley 1823) was from a merchant family; Henry Addington's (Viscount Sidmouth 1807, Home Secretary 1812–22) father was the elder William Pitt's (1708–1778) physician and he was a boyhood friend of the younger Pitt; John Scott (lawyer and Lord Chancellor, 1801–27, Lord Eldon) was the son of a coal fitter; William Huskisson (financial advisor and President of the Board of Trade, 1823–27) came from the Staffordshire small gentry. Robert Peel's (Chief Secretary for Ireland 1812–18, Home Secretary 1822–27) grandfather was a Lancashire yeoman and his father a textile manufacturer. In *The Age of Eloquence, 1812–22*, Arthur Bryant (1950, p. 369) called the group "of gentle rather than aristocratic origin."

> The fact that substantially the same set of men continued in office under the same Prime Minister for fifteen years at a time of social and economic difficulties not only permitted but virtually demanded the eventual formulation of some settled line of policy. The contemporary structure of politics, on the other hand, which was the essence of the old eighteenth-century system in its final weak but purified stage, effectively denied the possibility of controlling the legislature either through patronage or through party. (Gash 1977, p. 38).

Table 2.1 shows the fragile distributions of government supporters and opponents in Parliament during Liverpool's premiership.

Table 2.1   *Political leanings of Liverpool's Parliaments*

Parliament	Govt.	Govt. fringe	Waverers	Opposition fringe	Opposition
1812–18	253	78	102	83	143
1818–20	261	80	48	16	171
1820–26	250	99	114	66	154

Source: Cook and Stevenson, 2014, tab. 3.1.

Majorities were not assured. Effective government required the accommodations of ideas and interests without the tools possessed by modern parties.
These included inseparable local and national interests. Local government was
in the same aristocratic and upper-upper-middle-class hands as at the national
level, mostly the landed gentry – the "country gentlemen" – yielding over time
to commerce, finance, and industry. Competition existed between individuals,
families, and interests, but they shared a desire for the stability of their social
and economic positions.

"They were not fools," however. They wished to retain the authority and
privileges which tradition had given them, "but they were ready to use their
common sense and accept" the changes demanded by the population, which
though not formally represented, was recognized as the ultimate constraint on
the government's actions (Woodward 1938, p. 50). The ruling class accepted
"the direction in which society was moving ... to ensure that it did not move
too rapidly" (Hilton 2006, p. 393). The local oligarchies were as interested
in stability as the national government. "[I]f a well-established Member of
Parliament did not affront a sizeable section of his constituency, he could
have a safe seat for life." The system allowed MPs "to rise above the party
level and work in the general interest. This was called 'preserving the peace
of the country.'" The Government's repressions of protests during the years
after Waterloo made it unpopular in some circles but it was supported by the
majority, who favored stability (Johnson 1991, pp. 405, 450; Veitch 1913,
p. 80; Webb and Webb 1963, ch. 1).

James II's (1685–89) interferences with the traditions of local government –
its privileges and obligations – contributed to his downfall, as well as to their
continuation and even reinforcement until the reforms of the 1830s, made
necessary, according to the Webbs (1963), by the administrative problems
and possibilities of modern urban conditions. The stability of the Hanoverian
regime (the four Georges and William IV, 1707–1837) rested, in the last analysis, on the smooth and successful functioning of local deference structures,"
that is, *local* relationships involving *local* elites with *local* ambitions and
obligations" (O'Gorman 1989, p. 6).

Electoral control of these constituencies was "never straightforward," but nevertheless "accomplished through 'patronage', 'influence', and 'corruption'" (O'Gorman 1989, p. 27). Patronage was difficult in Liverpool's time. It had been eroding at least since Edmund Burke's 1780 speech on economical reform, with the winding up or transforming of offices and sinecures, many of which had been in existence since medieval times. Britain was being transformed from a medieval country ruled by corruption to a competent and responsible modern country in which the national government was fundamentally honest – "and it was because ministers knew it was happening that they had a confident belief that the British constitution was basically sound, that the system could be reformed from within, and that they ought to resist cries for radical change" (Johnson 1991, p. 395). Reform was understood to be possible without violent revolution.

GOVERNMENT FINANCE

Modern British government finance was developed during the seventeeth century, and national budgets chosen by legislatures and partly financed by central banks are still with us. The public represented by Parliament votes taxes on itself to pay for the services it wants from government. Taxes support but limit government, although the limits are stretched by government borrowing. The efficiency of such a system requires the responsibility and cooperation of its legislature and executive, the latter being the monarch during most of British history. The breakdown of British government finance in the seventeenth century – caused by disagreements between the spender (the king) and taxpayers (the public) – was replaced after 1689 by placing taxpayers' representatives (Parliament) in charge of spending as well as taxing. However, Parliament (like the king) also wanted to be able to borrow, and for that reason established the Bank of England. Some of the conflicts leading to the modern system of finance, the system with which Liverpool had to deal, and the Bank's place in it, are discussed below.

All three parliaments called by Charles I (1625–49) in the 1620s were stingy, and conditioned their finance on uncomfortable changes in the king's policies, especially his High-Church preferences. They were all speedily dissolved, and in 1629, Charles resolved to manage without Parliaments until "his people shall see more clearly into his intents and actions; when such as have bred this interruption shall receive their condign punishment" (HC [March 10, 1629] 1813).

Short of funds without Parliament's taxes, he resorted for revenue to "desperate measures." Military service was required under martial law and soldiers were billeted in private homes. He called on the counties and boroughs for voluntary payments of funds that Parliament had conditionally offered, "but from all parts of the country the answer came that money could not be granted 'save in a parliamentary way.'" Forced loans failed partly because judges found them illegal, although many who refused were imprisoned without *habeas corpus* (Tanner 1928, p. 59).

Over the next 11 years, Charles tightened the court's belt, ended his foreign adventures, borrowed as much as he could, sold crown lands and monopolies of doubtful legality, interpreted existing taxes more broadly, and collected them more aggressively. Small landowners eligible for knighthood were compelled to pay for the privilege, and Ship Money, normally paid by coastal towns to suppress piracy, was extended to the inland counties (Tanner 1928, pp. 75–6; Wedgwood 1955, pp. 155–61).

The crown's pressure on local officials to collect taxes of doubtful legality strained his relations with the "country" even among the tory gentry. Charles was overthrown by Civil War, and the victorious puritan general Oliver Cromwell attempted to rule the country as Lord Protector, without a king or a representative Parliament, during the 1650s. But his difficulties with the country and even a purged Parliament were not unlike Charles's. Unable to deal with the myriad of religious and other issues to the general satisfaction, and with the declining legitimacy of Parliaments, taxes became increasingly difficult to collect. An official in London responded to a general's complaint about arrears in pay: "We are so out at the heels here that I know not what we shall do for money. ... the Great Rebellion ... had collapsed from within." The public's unwillingness to pay taxes levied otherwise than by a legitimate Parliament brought Cromwell's Commonwealth down as it had the monarchy (Tanner 1928, p. 210; Woolrych 1958).

The monarchy was restored in Charles I's son, Charles II (1660–85), who resolved on better relations with Parliament, but was as resourceful as his father in finding financial expedients. In addition to his greater willingness to compromise, the son's pursuit of funds was assisted by the financial revolution. The Exchequer borrowed from the goldsmith bankers and anticipated tax receipts by interest-bearing paper issued for goods and services, redeemable for coin (gold and silver, that is, real money) in order of their issue as taxes were collected.

The position of the king was outwardly respected by the Cavalier (or Pensioner) Parliament of 1661–79, the longest in British history, but it had no intention of being governed by him. The landed gentry, although at least nominally monarchist, did not mean to part with the parliamentary rights gained during the Civil War. They were willing to provide defense by militia, but the militia had to be controlled by the Lord Lieutenants of the counties. They vocally asserted the supremacy of the crown over the armed forces but "took care that the only troops in the country should be under the local control of their own class" (Churchill 1956 ii, pp. 259–60).

Charles tried to secure parliamentary votes by the liberal payment of pensions, hence the Pensioner Parliament, which nevertheless lagged behind its promised payments to the crown, whose spending it regarded as extravagant. Financial relations became reminiscent of his father's time. In 1677, "the House of Commons presented an address to the King praying him to make such alliances as would secure the kingdom, quiet the people, and save the Spanish Netherlands, and it was intimated that as soon as the desired alliances had been entered into, plentiful supplies would be forthcoming." Charles expressed astonishment at the House's demand for an alliance with the Dutch against France, and was not above manufacturing history: "You have intrenched upon so undoubted a right of the Crown that I am confident it will appear in no age ... that the prerogative of making peace and war hath been so dangerously invaded." Those who control finance are in a position to determine whether war is fought, but the legislature's control of spending was not possible until post-1689 budgets, and incompletely even then (Tanner 1928, p. 237; (HC [May 28, 1667] 1813)).

Charles's credit was insufficient for the unpopular and unsuccessful war against the Dutch that he joined as a junior and subsidized ally with Louis XIV in 1672–74, and defaulted on his debt. Partial payment was eventually resumed but his credit never "really recovered." This was one of the "reasons why the City welcomed the Liberator [in 1689], under whom £1,300,000 was at last repaid to Charles II's creditors" (Feavearyear 1931, p. 104; Hill 1961, p. 221).

Financial control was also contested in the early United States. Congress at first voted appropriations in lump sums. The appropriations bill of 1789 was thirteen lines long and identified four items: civil and military expenses, the public debt, and pensions. Secretary of the Treasury Alexander Hamilton did not think more detail was necessary, but Congress was not satisfied and although an inquiry found no dishonesty in the Treasury accounts, "there had been an application of some specific appropriations to objects other than those directed." An act of 1800 directed the Treasury secretary to "digest, prepare, and lay before Congress, at the commencement of every session, a report on the subject of finance, containing estimates of the public revenue and public expenditures" (Dewey 1922, p. 116). Not until 1809 did Congress order expenditures to be limited to the objects for which they were appropriated, and that shifts of funds between departments required its approval (Bolles 1894 ii, pp. 189–90).

When Charles was succeeded by his brother, James II, people grumbled about the new king's Catholicism. They desired political stability, however, and gave him leeway. His goals turned out to include the removal of restrictions on Catholics in public offices and the practice of their religion, which required friendly Parliaments or, even better, financial independence of them. Two days after his accession he wrote to the French ambassador:

> I have resolved to call a Parliament immediately and to assemble it in the month of May. I shall publish at the same time a declaration that I am to maintain myself in the enjoyment of the same revenues the King my brother had .... It is a decisive stroke for me to enter into possession and enjoyment. For hereafter it will be much more easy for me either to put off the assembling of Parliament or to maintain myself by other means which may appear more convenient for me. (Speck 1988, p. 43)

James's attempts to get around the "country," or control it, backfired, although his affairs went smoothly for a while. He obtained what he hoped would be a malleable Parliament by means of active electioneering and liberal spending. Two hundred (of 513) members of the Parliament assembling in May 1685 "were directly dependent on the king for their livelihood and 400 had never sat in the House before. Bribery was rampant. A minister felt justified in publicly reprimanding a member who had voted against the crown: 'Sir! Have you not got a troop of horse in His Majesty's Service? Yes, my lord, but my brother died last night and has left me £700 a year'" (Hill 1961, pp. 230–34).

"Luck further strengthened James's hand" in the form of rebellions led by the Duke of Monmouth (an illegitimate son of Charles II) in the West Country and the Presbyterian Earl of Argyll in the Scottish highlands. The country rallied behind the king, and in June Parliament voted him the revenues for life that it had only granted his brother periodically. The customs and excise alone brought him more than Charles had received. So the government slipped from the financial yoke which Parliament had historically placed on it (Smith 1999, p. 162; Ogg 1955, pp. 144–8; Hill 1961, p. 220).

The king's independence could not be stretched indefinitely, however. Charles II had realized that his position rested on property, especially the Tory landed gentry that was committed to the Established Church. "I will stick by you and my old friends," Charles had told a Tory supporter in 1680, "for if I do not I should have nobody to stick to me." "Tory" referred to one of the two main political parties, or more appropriately, broad political views since party organizations were primitive. The other was "Whig." These names arose during the Exclusion Crisis of 1678–81 to distinguish those who wanted to exclude Catholics from the throne, the Whigs, from those who defended the lawful succession, the Tories. The Whigs favored the idea of a contract between the king "under the law" and his subjects, who were entitled to resist misgovernment. They were most often found in the rising professional and commercial classes (Macaulay 1855 i, p. 257; Hill 1961, p. 232).

Both sides were anxious to avoid another civil war:

> This is the essential if usually unspoken background to late seventeenth-century politics. The propertied classes could not forget the lesson [of military rule] they had learnt in 1646–60, just as kings did not forget the lesson [of Charles I's execution] of 1649. So political opposition was never pushed to extremes; ... The House of Commons might criticize, but did not fundamentally oppose government, so long as government did not attack the interests of those whom the members represented. (Smith 1999, p. 61)

James's religious fervor drew him across these lines. His fall, Bishop Gilbert Burnet (1724–34 i, p. 341) wrote, was

> ... one of the strangest catastrophes that is in any history. A great king, with strong armies and mighty fleets, a vast treasure, and powerful allies, fell all at once: and his whole strength, like a spider's web, was ... irrecoverably broken at a touch.

The explanation lay in James's assault on his twin pillars of support, beginning with the open practice of his religion, and the appointment of officials in defiance of the *Test Act*, requiring them to receive the Sacrament publicly according to the rites of the Church of England. Parliament refused James's requests to repeal the *Test* and *Habeas Corpus Acts*, and he prorogued (dismissed) it in November 1685, not to meet again during his reign.

Financially secure and with an army periodically concentrated near London to impress the populace, James felt free to pursue his religious and political objectives. He brought Catholics into the government, imposed them on the universities, and established an Ecclesiastical Commission to control the clergy. He also began to develop a party organization for support in the country. For this he needed the support of dissenters (non-Anglican protestants), in whose favor he dismissed uncooperative and often long-standing county and borough officials.

Having learned little from his father's experiences, James attacked the social as well as the economic fabric of England by assaulting the long-standing relationships on which local government depended. Leading gentry were dismissed from local offices "unless they would pledge their support for repeal of the Test Act. And who replaced them? Ordinary persons both as to quality and estates (most of them dissenters) .... It was too much even for Tory loyalty." Lord Keeper Guilford had warned in 1684 that if the gentry were discontented, "the whole use of the law is lost; for they are sheriffs, etc." (Hill 1961, pp. 236–7).

In 1688, leading interests joined in inviting the Dutch William of Orange (grandson of Charles I) and his wife and cousin, Mary (daughter of James II) to jointly take the English crown. Mary had been raised a Protestant and had been first in the line of succession to the English crown before the recent birth of James's son to his new Catholic wife. All parties of the convention which assembled after James's flight were determined to remedy the gaps in responsibility. In January 1689, the Whig William Sacheverell urged the Commons to "secure this House, that Parliaments be duly chosen and not kicked out at pleasure, which never could have been done without such an extravagant revenue that they might never stand in need of Parliaments" (Smith 1999, p. 61).

The new arrangements between private interests and government were credible, Douglas North and Barry Weingast (1989) wrote, because they provided for commitments by the parties. The Glorious Revolution sought a solution to one of history's central dilemmas: state control of coercive power for social ends. Promises and good intentions are not enough. What is required is a self-enforcing constitution. The problems were essentially fiscal and consisted primarily of two parts: Englishmen wanted the king to be free of incentives to seize property, force or renege on loans, sell monopolies, or impose illegal taxes. They also wanted to ensure that government revenues would be applied to the purposes taxpayers desired.

The solution also had two parts: satisfaction of the king's financial requirements as a matter of course instead of the uncertain outcomes of periodic battles with Parliament; and parliamentary legal supremacy, meaning supremacy of "the king in Parliament." The method was substitution of the national debt for the king's purse. Instead of voting money to the king and hoping for the best, Parliament would allocate funds to the appropriate civil departments and monitor them.

This was easier resolved than accomplished. Parliament had adopted the principle of supply – taxation for specific uses – in 1665, but was unhappy with the government's practice of borrowing against future taxes to avoid its control. The fault was partly Parliament's because of the undependability of its votes, the uncertainty of customs and excise revenues, and the slackness of local officials reluctant or unable to collect assessments on themselves and their friends (Douglas 1999, p. 10).

The Treasury was in the early stages of becoming the financial controller that we know today. Macaulay wrote that even under the Pension Parliament, "the great English revolution of the seventeenth century, that is, to say, the transfer of the supreme control of the executive administration from the crown to the House of Commons, was proceeding noiselessly, but rapidly and steadily" (Macaulay 1855 i, pp. 131–2).

> ... no English legislature, however loyal, would now consent to be merely what the legislature had been under the Tudors .... The gentlemen who, after the Restoration, filled the Lower House, though they abhorred the Puritan name, were well pleased

to inherit the fruit of the Puritan policy. They were indeed most willing to employ the power which they possessed in the state for the purpose of making their King mighty and honoured, both at home and abroad: but with the power itself they were resolved not to part.

Tax collections began to go to the Treasury instead of directly to the various departments, and William was voted an annual sum much less than Charles II or James II for the courts and civil government – the "civil list." A supporter complained that the king was kept "as it were at board wages." Even those were watched. In 1696, Parliament directed a commission to examine the government's accounts from November 5, 1688 (when William landed in England):

> … to the intent that their Majesties and this kingdom may be satisfied and truly informed whether all the same revenues, moneys, and provisions have been faithfully issued out, disposed, ordered, and expended for the ends and purposes aforesaid; and that their Majesties' loyal subjects may thereby be encouraged more chearfully to undergo the like burthens for the support of their Majesties government and the farther prosecution of the war. (Grellier 1810, pp. 22–4)

The weapon of finance had brought the king under the law but that still left Parliament. An exchange of despots might not be an improvement. The new arrangement depended on responsible Parliaments which it was thought might be achieved by frequent elections. The Triennial Act of 1694 required a new Parliament at least every three years, although this was extended to seven years in 1715, in order to reduce the electoral burden and/or assist stability. The lives of Parliaments had been limited only by the king's pleasure. The king continued to be important in his powers to dissolve Parliament and form ministries, that is, to take the lead in policy, which, however, to be effective required the support of the taxpayers' representatives.

The principal financial commitment of Parliament was adoption of the land tax as a permanent measure. Land taxes were very old, and the major local source of revenue. At the national level they had been reserved for war emergencies. They now became the main revenue nationally as well as locally, and because Parliament was made up of property owners, a large portion of the taxes they voted were on themselves (Grellier 1810, pp. 18–20, 53–4). The king was constrained but assured a living wage, while Parliament was supreme but paid for it.

Not everything was solved, of course, and a word on pensions and the difficulties they presented a century later is worth stating. George III (1760–1820) made liberal use of pensions (increasingly thought of as bribery) to secure his political ends, such as the continuation of war in America. Samuel Johnson's dictionary defined a *Pension* as "An allowance made to anyone without an equivalent. In England it is generally understood to mean pay given to a state hireling for treason to his country."

BOX 2.1   BOSWELL, *LIFE OF JOHNSON*, JULY 14, 1763

When Johnson was criticized for accepting £300 a year (£70,000 in today's value, from the King for literary merit), he said: "I wish my pension were twice as large, that they might make twice the noise."

In 1780, in the midst of an unpopular war and an escalating national debt, the House of Commons resolved "that the influence of the Crown has increased, is increasing, and ought to be diminished," and affirmed its right to inquire into all areas of public spending. The "economical reformers" led by Edmund Burke were strengthened by Cornwallis's surrender at Yorktown in October 1781. Parliament was petitioned by London, Bristol, and elsewhere, complaining of depressed trade, and asked for the "the abandonment of the war and relief to the burdened taxpayer." In February 1782, the House moved to address the King against a continuance of the war, and the prime minister resigned. Government contractors were excluded from the House of Commons, several superfluous offices and clerkships were abolished, and the Pensions List was reduced and ordered to be reported to Parliament. George Veitch wrote in his account of *The Genesis of Parliamentary Reform* that "Burke could have received no higher praise than a disgusted politician gave unwittingly when he complained that 'Burke's foolish Bill' had made it a very difficult task for any set of men either to form or maintain an administration" (Veitch [1913] 1965, pp. 66–80).

THE AGE OF REFORM

The *Age of Reform* was identified by E.L. Woodward (1938, pp. 37–8) as 1815 to 1870, so overlapping the *Age of Oligarchy*:

> [T]here was about the year 1815, an increase in the rate of change, a greater stir and movement in every sphere of activity [characterized by] "rational and purposive control," based upon measuring, counting, and observing, ... especially in the production and distribution of things, largely by individuals working for private gain, [s]omething like an anarchy of individual profit-seeking .... Thus one of the most important facts of the age is the emergence of a class of manufacturers and business men who ... knew nothing of the cult of tradition, custom, and inherited beliefs which Burke described as characteristic of the whig landed aristocracy ....

They had acquired through their own activities a very different mental outlook. They regarded the cult of tradition as bound up with the old regime of guilds, of government regulation, and an uninventive technique .... These industrial leaders were rationalists ... who had learned to weigh every act, to secure that these acts were mutually consistent and in harmony with a desired end. They made in this way a complete break with the modes of their predecessors who were content merely to imitate their fathers.

Boyd Hilton's (2006) New Oxford History of England, *A Mad, Bad, and Dangerous People*, chose 1783–1846 for the country's transformation from primarily an agricultural to a market economy, with its implications for finance, on the way to becoming the workshop of the world. Karl Polanyi (1944) called it *The Great Transformation*, during which England's social and political upheavals produced a market economy. A distinguishing characteristic of the "Market Society" was that humanity's economic mentalities were changed. Prior to the great transformation, people based their economies on reciprocity and redistribution, and were not rational utility maximizers. Afterwards, they were more economically rational, behaving as neoclassical economic theory would predict. The creation of capitalist institutions not only changed laws but also altered economic mentalities.

The population doubled between 1780 and 1840. More than three-fifths were under 24 years old during the first half of the nineteenth century. "As it is the power of exchanging that gives occasion to the division of labour," Adam Smith had written in 1776, "so the extent of this division must always be limited by the extent of that power, or, in other words, by the extent of the market." The period has been called variously the Coal, the Steam, and the Iron Age, but these were merely contemporary fuels and their outputs. Economic development was a consequence of the growing markets and scientific and industrial genius and innovative spirit unleashed by the new respect for human liberty (Hilton 2006, pp. 2–24; Smith [1776] 1937, p. 17; McCloskey 2010).

"Material progress had long outrun administrative order," Woodward wrote. "It is in this sense that a great deal of the talk about *laisser faire* must be discounted, or at least put into its proper context." The term often amounted to an admission that a condition must be endured because no solution was at hand, and that therefore responses must be left to individuals acting in their own interests. "The treatment of social and economic questions was more haphazard and empirical than Englishmen were ready to acknowledge. If a practical solution suggested itself, if a tentative experiment could be made, the doctrine of *laisser faire* would be thrust aside, only to be used again after another failure to discover the way out of a difficulty" (Woodward 1938, p. 15).

We might choose 1783 (end of the American Revolution) or 1776 (*Wealth of Nations*), when the pressures for change (in ideas and the economy, with implications for government) were clearly building, 1815, when they could be addressed, or 1820, when the postwar system had settled down, as the beginning of the Age of Reform. The French Revolution (1789) had retarded official accommodations of new ideas and methods, which were often rejected as Jacobin. They were ready to burst the dam at the war's end. It is remarkable that the Bank of England and the government, both committed to stability, survived, and even became stronger in these years. The unpopular repressive government of 1815–20, when discontent was greatest, and the respected reform government of 1820–27 were essentially the same, with the same prime minister, Lord Liverpool, from 1812 to 1827, whose term was ended only by a debilitating stroke.

Paul Johnson (1991) found *The Birth of the Modern* during 1815 to 1830. In 1815, on the eve of Napoleon's defeat at Waterloo, reactionaryism seemed triumphant everywhere, but by 1830 a decisive shift toward democracy had taken place. In the intervening 15 years, the matrix of the modern world was formed: the U.S.A. became a global power, Russia expanded rapidly, Britain penetrated Arabia and the Middle East, Latin America threw off Spain's yoke, and an international order that would endure for a century took shape. It was the age of Andrew Jackson, Wordsworth, Goya, Faraday, Beethoven, Bolivar, Lyell, and Ricardo, second to Smith in the rank of economists and author of the first rational economic system.

LORD LIVERPOOL

Monetary policies in this period, as in others, can only be understood in their relations to governments, especially government budgets. Lord Liverpool's governments survived elections in 1818 and 1820, called according to the Septennial Act (requiring parliamentary elections at least every seven years) and the death of George III, although not with majorities. Parties were not organized sufficiently to regularly command majorities in those days. The memberships of Parliaments indicated in Table 2.1 suggest that successful governments required the cooperation of independents, which had to come increasingly through reason as bribery, pensions, and patronage declined.

The Liverpool governments nevertheless reflected the prime minister's steadiness of purpose while balancing conflicting interests. Robert Banks Jenkinson, the second Earl of Liverpool (Figure 2.1), was a good fit into the politics of the day. He provided steady leadership in unsteady times. His accomplishments, although remarkable, tend to be overlooked. Histories of the nineteenth century that dwell on the celebrated deeds of prime ministers Sir Robert Peel, William Gladstone, and Benjamin Disraeli, pass quickly over Liverpool, who occupied that office more than any of them, and superintended as many or more accomplishments. Disraeli's (1844, p. 59) label of Liverpool as "the arch-mediocrity who presided rather than ruled over [a] cabinet of mediocrities," had more to do with style than achievements, compared with the flamboyant and often divisive Disraeli. As long-time leader of the Conservative Party and prime minister (1868, 1874–80), the outsider Disraeli employed conflict and drama to further his goals of "One Nation" (joining the working class with conservatives against the "liberal urban elite") and the empire, whether genuinely or opportunistically neither his allies nor his opponents were sure (Smith 1987).

There were fewer misunderstandings of the steady Liverpool, who compares favorably in achievement. He dealt smoothly with the Prince Regent when King George III was incapacitated, he steered the country through the period of radicalism and unrest, avoiding revolution in the revolutionary age which followed the Napoleonic Wars, he was sufficiently modern to support commercial and manufacturing interests as well as those of the land, and worked for compromise on the heated issue of Catholic emancipation. The revival of the economy strengthened his political position. He became, in the 1820s, leader of the reform faction of "Liberal

"He wished it to be … clearly understood that those persons who now engaged in Joint-Stock Companies, or other enterprises, entered on those speculations at their peril and risk. He thought it was his duty to declare that he never would advise the introduction of any bill for their relief; on the contrary, if such a measure were proposed, he would oppose it, and he hoped that parliament would resist any measure of that kind."

Source: https://commons.wikimedia.org/wiki/File: Earl_jenkinson_(cropped).jpg.

Figure 2.1   *Robert Banks Jenkinson, second Earl of Liverpool, Secretary of State for War and the Colonies, 1809–12, Prime Minister, 1812–27*

Tories" who lowered the tariff, abolished the death penalty for many offences, and reformed the criminal law. He did not try to force reform in the face of an opposition made stronger by fears of the Jacobins after the French Revolution, moving only as far and as fast as the public would peaceably accept.

The objective of Liverpool's government was the welfare of the nation as seen from the standpoint of the aristocracy, which, while not coincident with the nation at large, had much in common with it, particularly its desire for stability. The shift toward free trade "did not represent an 'intellectual' acceptance of free trade," but rather, Boyd Hilton (1977, p. 305) argued, the "pragmatic ... need to secure food supplies and stable employment for a rapidly growing population."

The middle classes were growing, but they as much as the aristocracy wanted security. They were not necessarily happy with aristocratic rule, but they shared the fear of the mob. A continuing question was to what extent the cabinet should notice the people, how far it should bend in favor of change. Unfortunately, the unenfranchised were short of ways other than violence to express their complaints. Much of Liverpool's success was due to his personal closeness to his constituency, despite his aristocracy, which every day confronted these problems (Cookson 1975, pp. 1–16).

Liverpool's professionalism was derived from his place in the world passed to him by his father. Charles Jenkinson (1729–1808) was born into a well-connected Oxfordshire gentry family, although as the son of a younger son, advancement required considerable exertions of his own. After public school and Oxford, he considered entering the Church, and was offered a living, but was attracted to politics. "He took a prominent part in the hotly contested Oxfordshire election of 1754, writing squibs and lampoons for the whigs," and became private secretary to a succession of well-placed government officials, eventually Prime Minister Lord Bute (1762–63). More than a secretary, the young man was "hard-working and assiduous. [H]e seems to rely very much on me in all his public concerns," Jenkinson said of a superior.

He kept his place when Bute fell, and, having been elected to Parliament, rose in the ranks of the Treasury until, in 1778, Lord North made him "secretary of war, an important post during the American conflict and one which brought him into close contact with the king," a relationship which he never lost. In spite of or perhaps because of his self-effacing manner, the opposition thought him an *éminence guise* (*Dictionary of National Biography*).

North continued as Chancellor of the Exchequer, as was usual, when he became prime minister, but depended on Jenkinson, whom he called "the fittest person to have the direction of the finances of this country," although not in the cabinet or spokesman for the Government in the House of Commons, "where his manner was uneasy." A fellow member of the House "commenting on an important speech ... against repealing the Stamp Act (1766), praised its content and argument, but added that 'from defect of voice, it was ill heard.'" Another member wrote that "No ray of wit, humour or levity pervaded his speeches. He neither introduced into them metaphors, digressions, nor citations. All was fact and business."

Jenkinson rose above the common height, although "his lank limbs and figure were destitute of elegance or grace, and his manner was reflective and cautious, while his eyes ... were usually, even in conversation, directed downwards toward the earth. Something impervious and inscrutable seemed to accompany and to characterize his demeanor, which awakened curiosity while it ... discouraged inquiry." His manners were polite, calm, and unassuming; grave, if not cold; but not distant, without any mixture of pride or affectation. "But in recompense for these deficiencies of an ornamental kind, he possessed more useful and solid attainments calculated to raise their possessor in life."

No man in an official situation was reputed "to understand better the principles of trade, navigation, manufactures, and revenue." His writing and speaking on these subjects were "Supple, patient, mild, laborious, persevering, ... and always cool, he never lost the ground that he had once gained .... As a speaker in the House of Commons, he rose seldom, unless called out by particular circumstances; nor, when on his legs, did he ever weary the patience of his auditors .... His language had nothing in it animated or elevated. Scarcely was it ... always correct or exempt from ... inelegancies. But it never was defective in the essentials of perspicuity, brevity, and thorough information" (Wraxall 1818, p. 187).

Jenkinson left office with North in 1783, but was "too useful" to be left out of Pitt's government for long, where he was involved in the negotiation of commercial treaties, although, "having begun his career before Smith's *Wealth of Nations* appeared in 1776, his approach to trade remained mercantilist and he was less taken with free-trade notions than Pitt." As became true of his son, Jenkinson moved with although slower than the times. Likewise his political career, which was slowed but solidified by his avoidance of factional conflicts for power. In 1786, he was made Baron Hawkesbury, the name of one of his Gloucestershire estates, and became president of the Board of Trade and chancellor of the duchy of Lancaster, posts that he held for seventeen and eighteen years, respectively – "one of the workhorses of the administration." He became the first earl of Liverpool in 1796.

He wrote extensively on finance and economics, the best known of his writings being *A Treatise of the Coins of the Realm*, published in 1805 in the form of a letter to the king. It was primarily a history of the damages done to trade by the many debasements of the English coinage, ending with a criticism of the excessive emissions of paper currency since the suspension of the gold convertibility of the pound in 1797. He pointed out the practical impossibility of bimetallism and argued that in view of the importance of money as the measure of the value of property, it ought "to be perfectly uniform and at all times the same" (Jenkinson 1805, p. 9). His ideas became law when the administration of his son made gold the sole standard in 1815.

When forced by age and illness to resign his government offices in 1803, he wrote that he had been "'solely and separately attached to his Majesty not only from duty but from affectionate inclination ..., during a period of almost fifty years'" (1805, p. 125). "He has been described as foreshadowing a modern civil servant, unattached to party, but there was much in Liverpool of his tory ancestry, a sense of personal loyalty to the monarch, and he was a man of the past as well as of the future." In fact he differed from a modern civil servant in his political responsibility. Continuation in his offices was conditional not only on his usefulness to his superiors and colleagues but on the electorate's acceptance of his governments (*Dictionary of National Biography*).

The education of Liverpool's eldest son, Robert (1770–1828), was "carefully monitored by his father, who ensured that in addition to the classics and mathematics he studied the more unconventional subjects of French, history, European politics, and political economy." His family's expectations of an eminent public career "was impressed on him from an early age." Educated like his father at Charterhouse and Oxford, "he was an industrious and sober student," and as a young man "struck observers as having an unusually wide knowledge, particularly of European history and politics .... He was also," his biographer said, "perhaps because of his father's constant supervision and the absence of a mother's affection [she had died shortly after his birth], emotionally immature and lacking in natural self-confidence, though conciliatory and good-natured."

"He always quotes his father," it was said of Robert, and the lives of father and son blended together in an experience of nearly three-quarters of a century in high politics. His early years were dominated by his father. "If Liverpool lacked imagination, he lost it following his father's precepts; if he compensated for this deficiency by perseverance and industry, it was his father who instilled in him these virtues." "You should not be satisfied in doing your [school] exercises just so as to pass without censure, but always aim at perfection; and be assured that in doing so you will by degrees approach to it," the father wrote the 14-year-old schoolboy. "I hope also you will avail yourself of every leisure moment to apply yourself to algebra and the mathematics: you will thereby attain not only a knowledge of those sciences, but by an early acquaintance with them you will acquire a habit of reasoning closely and correctly on every subject." Lest he be inclined to relax, "I would wish you for the present not to read any novels, as they will only waste your time, which you will find not more than sufficient for the pursuit of more useful and important studies" (Brock 1967, ch. 1; Yonge 1868 i, ch. 1).

The young Liverpool was seen as self-important, pushful, and disputatious, but later, especially as prime minister, he was praised for his kindness, amiability, fairness, and consideration. He had also become "convinced of the bad effects arising from that habit [of dispute]," a practice recommended by successful contemporaries. Thomas Jefferson advised his grandson to follow Benjamin Franklin's practice "never to contradict anybody," which will fail to persuade them and in fact produce an enmity which will strengthen their opposition to your views (Koch and Peden 1944, pp. 589–93).

Liverpool's authority stemmed from his character as much as from hard work and expertise. What some called his lack of imagination, many found a predictability on which they could rely. He had a cautious mind which combined with political astuteness and an understanding of people that accommodated reform, but not too novel or too fast. "Above all, the country trusted his pure and unquestioned integrity," a biographer wrote. He became virtually an institution, but was as impersonal as most institutions. His private life contained no scandal and there were no anecdotes or extravagant virtues or failings upon which the public mind could take hold. Other ministers with fewer accomplishments are remembered for some particular deed or failing; Liverpool with 15 years as prime minister, gives his name to a government and nothing more. His chief utterances, some of which are given below, are relegated to books on banking and finance.

Some of his apparent personal weaknesses were actually strengths. "The frankness and amiability of his character made him a man whom others forbore from hurting .... He was extremely sensitive to the opinions of others, and, when accused of harshness or injustice, he suffered the greatest anguish of mind," and his colleagues "refrained from harassing him unduly" (Brock 1967, pp. 27–8). His social awkwardness seemed to combine with his amiability to secure agreement in his presence.

"I have been long enough in life," he wrote to a friend, "to know the advantages of a straight course on the one hand, and all the inconveniences which arise out of contrivances on the other" (Brock 1967, pp. 33–4; Yonge 1868 iii, p. 147). This may be seen in Liverpool's approach to patronage. The numerous independent members of Parliament presented problems to governments which Liverpool's honesty did not make any easier, at least in the short run. He refrained from promising what he could not deliver. "I believe," he wrote to an applicant,

> that there is no individual in a public situation who has been more cautious on the subject of making promises than I have. In most cases in which I have made one either directly or implicated I have desired the individual to write to me in order that he might have an answer which should state beyond the power of future misconceptions what the nature of the promise was and what qualifications or exceptions were connected with it. (Brock 1967, p. 88)

He wrote in another letter:

> I do not see how it is possible for me to hold out the expectation suggested to Lord Charleville. I could have had *four seats* from Sir L. Holmes and *three* from Sir W. Manners [potential supporters of the Government in the House of Commons] if I could have promised them that they should have been made peers upon the first creation. I have lost them and I would rather lose them than make an engagement, and though it has been intimated to me that, without making an engagement, I might have held out the expectation. However, I have always felt that such a course of proceeding was either a virtual engagement or an act of deception. [Even beyond] my indifference to office unless I can hold it creditably, I am satisfied that a disposition to contract engagements of this description will in the end rather weaken than strengthen any government. (Parker 1899, p. 143; Brock 1967, p. 89)

The stability of the Government during the volatile period following Waterloo owes much to Liverpool's character:

> If there is a dark age in nineteenth-century England, it is the five years [after 1815]. It was a period dominated by the fears of the upper classes and the discontents of the working classes; it was a time in which national glory had grown stale, in which the propertied classes were conscious of fighting a rearguard action, and in which a bitter populace lacking education and understanding of political affairs was ready to follow any inspiring leader.

But a revolution did not happen, and with the return of prosperity in the twenties,

> there was also a change in the whole tone of Government; ... the very suspicion of revolution had vanished, and broad outlines of Victorian England had been sketched by a Government which has some claim to be called the first of the great improving ministries of the nineteenth century [although the discussion here is primarily about monetary policy]. (Brock 1967, p. 1)

His father's influence secured young Robert's place in Parliament in 1790, although he had to wait until his twenty-first birthday before he could take his seat. He actively supported the Government in Parliament, especially its military policy toward France, and was one of the first junior ministers to enlist in the militia. Hawkesbury (as he was known after his father became an earl until he became the second Lord Liverpool upon his father's death in 1808) became Foreign Secretary in 1801, and unlike his father was an effective speaker for the Government on the front bench before performing that function in the House of Lords.

Pitt's death in 1806 left the country without a secure government. Disagreements about the conduct of the war, together with personal enmities, interfered with cooperation until, finally, the conciliatory Liverpool joined a combination in which Spencer Perceval was prime minister from 1809 to 1812. He accepted the unattractive secretaryship for war, "which had an alarming record of failure and management." Despite the recent failures of the British army in Spain, on the basis of General Arthur Wellesley's (later the Duke of Wellington) assurance that with reasonable resources he could stand up to the French, Liverpool was able to persuade Parliament to provide support sufficient for an increasingly successful Peninsular War from 1808 to 1814. The British army with Spanish guerillas was at times the continent's only opposition to Napoleon. It contributed to his eventual defeat by showing that the French could be beaten and by siphoning his troops from other areas.

Liverpool's assurances to Wellesley in 1809 were a model of commitment to an agreed well-defined objective. After satisfying himself of the favorable prospects of Wellesley's plans, he wrote to the general that "when he accepted the seals of the War Department, he laid it down as a principle that, if the war was to be continued, we ought not to suffer any part of our efforts to be directed to other objects." He also gave assurances that the government had agreed to leave "him a large discretion for his operations," and of its perseverance "in the Peninsula as long as it could be maintained with a reasonable expectation of success" (Yonge 1868 i, p. 306). The general and the Secretary lived up to their agreement, supported by Napoleon's mistakes and the public's support of the enterprise – unlike some of the ill-defined and unbounded commitments and failures in the following chapters, such as America's endless wars.

After Perceval's assassination, Liverpool, despite his youth, was the logical choice most able to secure the cooperation of a competent and politically viable cabinet. Other candidates were more ambitious, but less compromising, and only the "unselfish and unifying," the "honest and dependable," Liverpool, almost by default, could form a government (Hilton 2006, p. 221). He still ranks as the youngest and longest-serving prime minister (assuming office in 1812 at age 42 and serving until 1827) next to the younger Pitt (24, 1783–1801 and 1804–06).

His first actions were to announce the neutrality of the ministry over the divisive issue of Catholic civil disabilities and the revocation of recent Orders in Council (including restrictions on trade and the right to seize British subjects from foreign ships) – just too late to prevent the American declaration of war. The peace with France after Napoleon's defeat also aimed at stability. The integrity of pre-war France was preserved, along with the independence of Spain, Portugal, and the Netherlands, and most British conquests were returned. The terms were unpopular in Britain, where the punishment of France was popular, but they demonstrated a vision and courage in officials lacking in 1919. Foreign Minister Castlereagh was vilified but he had the backing of the Government. Peace with the United States after the War of 1812 was also generous in view of the relative military positions of the two countries. The

Government calculated that the military and diplomatic costs of a continuation of the war outweighed the probable gains, and peace at long last on all fronts was appealing (Perkins 1964; Bew 2011, pp. 333–7, 447–8; Nicolson 1946). Public complaints of the high taxes required by the national debt also showed resistance to costly conflicts.

Liverpool's accomplishments were especially impressive given the fact that he never had an assured majority. Party discipline in the modern sense was non-existent, parliamentary reform had taken away most of the funds for votes that George III had used, conflicts were numerous, and Liverpool lacked both charisma and the reputation of a strong leader. He had an "untidy appearance," slouching and looking "As if he had been on the rack three times and saw the wheel prepare for a fourth." His health had never been robust and for many years suffered from a painful form of phlebitis in his left leg. Credibility, competence, and the ability to compromise nevertheless proved more important than charisma (*Dictionary of National Biography*).

Moreover, Liverpool was driven by a sense of duty to the state and was tolerant of the feelings and political positions of others. He showed a sensitive nature that his colleagues were reluctant to disturb. "His speeches were characterized by clarity, command of detail, and objectivity; and he had the rare quality of always doing justice to the argument of his opponents," one of whom called Liverpool "the honestest man that could be dealt with. You may always trust him … and though he may be going to answer you after a speech, you may go out and leave your words in his hands and he will never misrepresent you" (Brock 1967, p. 29).

An historian observed that

> during the long premiership of Liverpool an imperceptible change took place in one aspect of English manners: at the end of the 18th century, [when] the average Englishman endorsed Adam Smith's [opinion of] that 'insidious and crafty animal, vulgarly called a statesman or politician'; by the time of the great Reform Bill there is already found the alliance between politicians and the respectable middle class. Victorian governments would have been utterly different in character had not politics become the profession for honest men as well as the recreation of landed aristocracy. (Brock 1967, pp. 30–31)

The younger Liverpool's economics were more advanced than his father's in his adherence to the ideas of Adam Smith. He said in the House of Lords in 1812, that "It has been well said in a foreign country, when it was asked what should be done to make commerce prosper, the answer was laissez-faire; and it was undoubtedly true that the less commerce and manufacturers were meddled with the more they were likely to prosper." Smith was the most quoted author in Parliament during these years, but little could be done in wartime, and even afterwards the application of laissez-faire was subject to interests and special considerations. Liverpool supported the *Factory Act of 1819* to protect children in the cotton mills, assisted the movement for Church building during depression in manufacturing towns, and yielded to the powerful landed interest in the Corn Law tariffs. In supporting the bill to regulate the working hours of children, he said:

> Free labour ought not to be interfered with ...; but to have free labour there must be free agents; and ... children were not free agents. [I]t was therefore necessary to resort to some legislative enactments to prevent them from being exposed to the excessive labour to which they were at present exposed in cotton factories. (Brock 1967, p. 44)

Even during the troubled years following Waterloo, Liverpool's government tried to balance interests with the longer-term goal of stability. The clear and close connections between government and governed also help explain Liverpool's efforts to avoid or smooth crises instead of, like some of his successors, creating or worsening them for political ends – "Never let a crisis go to waste" – and also his government's defense of the Bank of England's financial support of the war, its cautious but determined restoration of the gold standard after the war, and its efforts to achieve a steady monetary policy thereafter.

THE BANK OF ENGLAND

The Bank of England was founded in 1694 as part of a bargain with the Government for cheap finance. There had been several proposals for a national bank as a source of profit and contributor to the general prosperity. William Petty had argued that a bank would "almost double the Effect of our coined Money" by means of notes and checkable deposits secured by fractional reserves of coin (Horsefield 1960; Petty 1682). But the Bank of England had to wait for the right conjunction of circumstances, such as a government with a low credit rating in need of money.

Great Britain and its allies were at war with Louis XIV's France, and their finances were desperate. King William wrote his ministers from the Continent: "... in the name of God determine quickly to find some credit for the troops here." He feared mutiny or desertion because he lacked the money "sufficient for their subsistence; so that if you cannot devise expedients to send contributions, or procure credit, all is lost and I must go to the Indies." "Here was the real crisis of the war," Ogg (1955, p. 433) wrote. "It was financial."

A corporate bank had been delayed by (i) public and government fears of concentrated finance and (ii) finance's fear of government depredations. In 1640, "being at his wits' end for money," Charles I ordered that nothing should be paid out of the mint. Those who had deposited silver to be coined received interest for their "loans," and were eventually repaid, but the financial community remembered the incident. Samuel Pepys wrote in his diary on August 17, 1666, after a reference to the 1640 episode, "The unsafe condition of a bank under a monarch, and the little safety to a Monarch to have any City or Corporacion alone … to have so great a wealth or credit makes it hard to have a bank here."

However, government finance had been reorganized and made more accountable. Revenues and spending were managed by the same people – Parliament – which improved the government's credit, although not sufficiently for the mercenaries on the continent who wanted coin. The government borrowed from "everyone who would lend," and resorted to tontines and lotteries. "Finally, and almost as a last resource, they founded the Bank of England" (Feavearyear 1931, pp. 114–15).

A corporate charter was offered to "the Governor and Company of the Bank of England" in 1694 on condition that they raised £1.2 million, to be lent to the government at 8 percent, secured by customs and excise taxes. The Bank would receive £4,000 for "management," and its charter would expire on payment of the principal, with a year's notice, but not before 1706. To prevent the Bank from becoming a vehicle by which governments circumvented the legislature, the Act limited government loans to those authorized by Parliament, and prohibited the Bank from buying crown lands, which had been an important part of royal finance since Henry VIII.

The required capital was quickly subscribed, and the Bank proved useful as a ready source and capable manager of finance for the government. The Bank's involvement with the government was illustrated by its handling of coin remittances to the armies on the continent, in connection with which the first deputy governor was killed by an enemy bullet in 1695 (*Dictionary of National Biography*, Michael Godfrey).

The Bank was a private, profit-seeking firm whose management was entrusted to a governor and a deputy-governor, normally serving two one-year terms (until World War I) before returning full-time to their normal employments, and 24 directors, most of whom in the early years "were substantial City merchants and members of the leading City companies" (Acres 1931 i, p. 21). Their backgrounds changed with the economy, and Bank historian John Clapham (1944 i, p. 116) wrote of the 1930s that "the London merchant or merchant banker of Victorian type was declining, [and] ships and railways, steel and chocolate, leather and beer, the trades of Canada and South Africa, and the China trade all were, or had been, represented."

The charter was extended in 1697, 1708 (during the War of the Spanish Succession), 1713, 1742 (War of Austrian Succession), 1764 (Seven Years War), 1781 (American War), and 1800 (to 1833, French Wars), always as part of a bargain for finance. Its monopoly privileges were expanded: in 1708 by the prohibition of note issues to any other association of more than six persons, and in 1710 by Parliament's promise to recognize no other "Corporation, Society, Fellowship, Company or Constitution in the nature of a Bank" during the life of the Bank of England. By 1781, in the opinion of the prime minister (see the epigraph to this chapter) its support of the government and finance in general had made the Bank a part of the national fabric.

There were costs, however. L.S. Pressnell (1956, pp. 5–6) suggested that the occasion of the market restrictions favoring the Bank of England "may well have been a rash of financial failures in the two or three years preceding. [But they] long outlasted any reasonableness ...; by the time [the limit on bank size was] abolished by the legislation of 1826 and 1833 it had done much harm by depriving the country of a banking system" needed during "a period of rapid economic growth."

The limit on bank size retarded specialization, and "credit remained largely a subsidiary or auxiliary occupation. Even when large numbers of country banks began to appear in the second half of the eighteenth century, many self-styled bankers were engaged extensively in non-banking enterprises. Equally, quasi-banking functions were performed by many who never called themselves bankers." The Bank of England, which could have been called the Bank of London, failed to use its ability to establish branches and promote its notes outside the metropolis (Pressnell 1956, pp. 6, 12; Ashton 1948, pp. 100–101).

The Bank weathered several financial crises during its first hundred years (Clapham 1944 i, ch. 7; Hoppit 1986). That of 1793 is worth looking into because of its similarities to later occurrences. The number of banks outside London (the "country" banks) had grown from a dozen in 1750 to over 300 in the 1790s, and were represented in every part of the island (Baring [1797] 2015). They were small because Parliament had limited note issues, except for the Bank of England, to small partnerships. (Not until the next century did the growth of payment by check make this constraint unimportant.) Furthermore, they had not yet become familiar with – or chose not to follow – sound banking principles such as the maintenance of adequate reserves. They relied on the Bank of England to discount their paper. As Vincent Stuckey testified in 1832:

"My customers give their money to me, and look to me for it; I do the same to the Bank" (House of Commons (hereafter HC) 1832, Q1145).

> Scores of banks failed and the Bank of England was blamed – or praised – for "putting them down" during the Crisis of 1793. Merchant banker Sir Francis Baring criticized the Bank's severity.
>
> The foreign market was either shut, or rendered more difficult of access to the merchant, [and] the country at large had no other resource but London; and, after having exhausted the bankers, that resource finally terminated in the Bank of England.
>
> … it might have been right for the Bank to lessen the amount of the accommodation which individuals had been accustomed to receive, but then it ought to have been gradual; their determination, and the extent to which it was carried, came like an electrical shock.
>
> In such cases the Bank are not an intermediate body, or power; there is no resource on their refusal, for they are the *dernier resort*. (Baring [1797] 2015, pp. 19–20)

The Bank needed help, and on April 23, 1793, Prime Minister and Chancellor Pitt met with eleven "City men," including the Lord Mayor, four Bank directors, and Baring. They agreed that the Government would assist the market by issuing up to £5 million of *Exchequer bills*, which were interest-bearing anticipations of receipts issued for goods and services in denominations as small as £1, exchangeable for coin as taxes were collected; called England's first paper money (Montagu, 1696; Feavearyear 1931, pp. 101–7; Shaw 1906). The plan did not pass Parliament and receive the royal assent until May 9, but its expectation, the "feeling that credit could be obtained, was enough to calm people's fears and to prevent many from actually asking for it" (Andreades 1924, p. 189). There were 338 requests for a total of £3.8 million; 238 of these were granted for a total of £2.2 million, with 49 refused and the rest withdrawn. Only two of the borrowers went bankrupt, some repaid their debts before they fell due, and the Government made a profit of £4,348.

The central role of the Bank in maintaining payments was stated shortly thereafter by the banker Henry Thornton:

> [I]n order to effect the vast and accustomed payments daily made in London, payments which are most of them promised beforehand, a circulating sum in bank notes, nearly equal to whatever may have been its customary amount is necessary
> ….
> There are in London between sixty and seventy bankers, and it is only through them that the larger payments of London are effected …. The amount of bank notes in the hands of each banker, of course, fluctuates considerably; but the amount in the hands of all probably varies very little; and this amount cannot be much diminished consistently with their ideas of what is necessary to the punctuality of their payments, and to the complete security of their houses. There is little room for reduction …: the notes which may chance to circulate …, if we suppose the usual punctuality of payments to be maintained, and the ordinary system of effecting them to proceed, can admit also of little diminution …. A large proportion of the London payments

are payments of bills accepted by considerable houses, and a failure in the punctuality of any one payment is deemed an act of insolvency in the party. The London payments are, moreover, carried on by a comparatively small quantity of notes; and they, perhaps, cannot easily be effected, with due regularity, by a much smaller number, so complete has been the system of economy in the use of them which time and experience have introduced among the bankers. There is, moreover, no substitute for them .... They serve ... both to sustain and regulate the whole paper credit of the country .... [A]ny very great and sudden diminution of Bank of England notes would be attended with the most serious effects both on the metropolis and on the whole kingdom. A reduction of them which may seem moderate to men who have not reflected on this subject – ... for instance, of one-third or two-fifths – might, perhaps, be sufficient to produce a very general insolvency in London, of which the effect would be the suspension of confidence, the derangement of commerce, and the stagnation of manufactures throughout the country. (Thornton 1802, pp. 114–15)

Thornton's warning was ignored by later legislation, particularly the Bank Act of 1844, which tied the Bank's notes to its gold reserve, with consequences that Thornton also predicted:

Gold, in such a case, would unquestionably be hoarded through the great consternation which would be excited; and it would, probably, not again appear until confidence should be restored by the *previous* introduction of some additional or some new paper circulation.

As occurred in 1847, 1857, and 1866. This is what central banking is, or ought to be, about: the maintenance of the payments system, the preservation of the highway over which business is conducted, as Adam Smith ([1776] 1937, bk. 2, ch. 2) said, which was the reason for the Federal Reserve Act but ignored during the Great Depression and reduced to secondary status more recently compared with other objectives. The Bank Act of 1844, which was designed to preserve gold convertibility, also ignored Thornton, but as we will see, was suspended when it interfered with payments.

Thornton's book was stimulated by the wartime shift to a fiat currency. Britain went to war with France in 1793, the Government pressed the Bank for finance, much of it in secret in violation of the Bank's charter. Its reserve was depleted, and in 1797, rumors of an invasion led to a run on the Bank, and Pitt's Government permitted it to suspend the gold convertibility of its notes. The suspension lasted the duration of the war, and beyond, and allowed an easy money policy which by 1813 had nearly doubled the price level. There was talk of resumption after markets settled down shortly after the suspension, but Baring objected:

My chief reason is that credit ought never to be subject to convulsions; a change even from good to better ought not to be made until there is almost a certainty of maintaining and preserving it in that position; for a retrograde motion in public credit is productive of consequences which are incalculable. With this principle in view, I am averse to the Bank re-assuming their payments generally during the war whilst there is a possibility of their being obliged to suspend them again. (Baring [1797] 2015, p. 69)

Governments resisted efforts to force convertibility during the war because of its potential for limiting war finance, but after the emergency wanted to return to the traditional standard (Cannan 1919; Wood, 2005, pp. 14–20). There was resistance from the public and business interests afraid of adding a deflationary influence to an already depressed postwar economy. Monetary policy alternatives included devaluation, that is, accepting the going price of gold permanently (in the vicinity of £5 per ounce, compared with the pre-war standard of £3.89), adopting a paper standard which might be regulated to provide greater price stability than under the gold standard, and David Ricardo's recommendations to restrict the convertibility of gold to 60-ounce ingots and eliminate gold coins. The Government hesitated, giving the impression of being, "generally speaking, in favour of a return to cash payments on the old basis some day," although the Bank was exhausting the Government's patience (Yonge 1868 ii, p. 360). Figure 2.2 shows the increases in money and prices, and decline in the value of the pound, during the war, and their reversal after 1814.

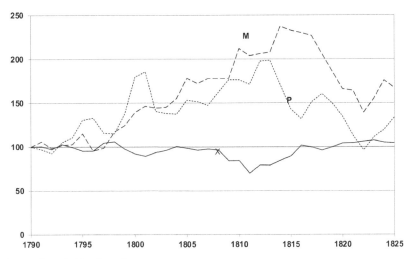

Source: Compiled by the author.

Figure 2.2   *Bank of England Notes and Deposits (M), Exchange Rate (X) and Price Level (P) (annual averages)*

By an Act of 1803, convertibility of the Bank's notes was to be resumed six months after the end of the war, but in 1814 this was moved back to July 5, 1815, then to July 5, 1816 (HC 1819, p. 3). Resumption would probably have been practicable on the latter date because the exchanges, having risen as money and prices fell, stood at par. But neither the Government nor the Bank had worked out the mechanics, and it was decided to wait. Return was moved to July 5, 1818, and Parliament ordered "that the Directors of the Bank ... make such preparations as to their discretion and experience may appear most expedient for enabling them to resume payments in cash without public inconvenience, and at the earliest period" (HC 1819, Preamble; Acworth 1925, pp. 72–3).

But in September 1817, when the Bank offered to redeem notes at par, an unconvinced public withdrew gold and bet on continued suspension. Parliament extended the Restriction Act to July 1819, and appointed committees of inquiry into the method of resumption. Recommendations were submitted in early May 1819, and the *Resumption Act*, called Peel's Act after the chairman of the Commons Committee, was passed before the end of the month. It laid out a schedule of increases in the gold value of the currency (a pound consisting of 20 shillings (*s.*) of 12 pence (*d.*) each) from £4 1*s.* from February 1, 1820, to £3 19*s.* 6*d.* from October 1, 1820 to £3 17*s.* 10½*d.* (par) from May 1, 1821, in amounts not less than 60 ounces. The Bank might at any time after February 1, 1820, fix any rate between £4 1*s.* and £3 17*s.* 10½*d.*, but such intermediate rate having once been fixed, that rate not to be subsequently increased. From May 1, 1823, the Bank was to pay its notes on demand in the legal coin of the realm.

The Bank directors registered a protest with Parliament against the burdens that would be imposed upon them by an Act which made a private establishment responsible for the national currency under a system that required it to anticipate the future:

> If the Directors of the Bank have a true comprehension of the views of the Committees in submitting this scheme to Parliament, they are obliged to infer that the object of the Committees is to secure, at every hazard, and under every possible variation of circumstances, the return of payments in Gold at mint price for Bank Notes at the expiration of two years; and that this measure is so to be managed that the mint price ... shall ever afterwards be preserved, leaving the market or exchange price of Gold to be controlled by the Bank solely by the amount of their issues of Notes.
>
> It further appears to the Directors, with regard to the final execution of this plan ..., that discretionary power is to be taken away from the Bank, and that it is merely to regulate its Issues and make purchases of Gold so as to be enabled to answer all

possible demands whenever its Treasury shall be again open for the payment of its Notes ....

The Directors ... cannot but feel a repugnance [toward] a System which, in their opinion, in all its great tendencies and operations, concerns the Country in general more than the immediate interests of the Bank alone ....

But when the Directors are now to be called upon, in the new situation in which they are placed by the Restriction Act, to procure a Fund for supporting the whole National Currency, either in Bullion or in Coin, and when it is proposed that they should effect this measure within a given period, by regulating the market price of Gold by a limitation of the Issue of Bank Notes, with whatever distress such limitation may be attended to individuals, or the community at large, they feel it their ... duty to state their sentiments thus explicitly ... to His Majesty's Ministers on this subject that a tacit ... concurrence at this juncture may not, at some future period, be construed into a previous implied sanction on their part of a System which they cannot but consider fraught with very great uncertainty and risk.

It is impossible for them to decide beforehand what shall be the course of events for the next two, much less for the next four years; they have no right to hazard a flattering conjecture, for which they have not real grounds, in which they may be disappointed, and for which they may be considered responsible. They cannot venture to advise an unrelenting continuance of pecuniary pressures upon the Commercial world of which it is impossible for them either to foresee or estimate the consequences. (*Representation by the Directors of the Bank of England to the Chancellor of the Exchequer*, May 20, 1819)

The Bank feared for itself and the community upon whose prosperity it depended. The politics of resumption in this case differed from the post-World War I era, when the Bank was more than willing to lead the way, no matter what.

Merchants and bankers, frightened of the planned deflation, sympathized with Governor George Dorrien's view that "It is very difficult to say when the Bank could with propriety resume its cash payments, it must always be judged of by experience." But the Government, "piqued by the Bank's intransigence," "abandoned" it (Hilton 1977, p. 41).

Lord Liverpool defended the plan by emphasizing its gradual and therefore "less injurious" operation. In any case, it was time to return to a fixed standard of value, as his father had stressed in *Coins of the Realm*. Those who opposed the plan, he said, in reality objected "to returning to cash payments at all." Unrestricted paper money had never been adopted "by any civilised country from the beginning of the world." Besides, how would it operate? Everyone "knew the disgraceful measures, reverted to, even in this country, in former times, to depreciate the standard of value; but even that alternative, bad as it was, presented advantages not to be found in the rejection of a standard altogether." He complimented the integrity and patriotism of the Bank of England, but pointed to the "inevitable effect" of releasing it from the obligation of redeeming its notes in the precious metals. "It would, in fact, be to invest them with the unrestrained power of making money" (Yonge 1868 ii, pp. 386–7):

> Would Parliament consent to commit to their hands what it would certainly refuse to the Sovereign on the throne, controlled by Parliament itself, the power of making money without any other check or influence to direct them than their own notions of profit and interest?

The plan had been drawn up by the respected Ricardo, who was also its most persuasive supporter in the House of Commons. "The decision to resume was, for Ricardo, a 'triumph of science and truth over prejudice and error; for the country gentlemen, an act of intuitive morality'; ... and for the government generally, a tactical blow against the City and Bank in a constitutional battle for power and responsibility" (Hilton 1977, p. 48).

Unfortunately, its application did not go smoothly. Knowledge that the notes would appreciate caused them to reach par quickly, and speculative gold holdings flowed into the Bank. Full resumption was achieved in two years rather than four, and money, prices, and employment fell (Feavearyear 1931, p. 208; Cannan 1919, p. xxxiii).

Thomas Attwood, banker, political reformer for extension of the ballot, and Birmingham's first Member of Parliament, expressed much of the public's view of resumption. He argued that "depreciation of the currency is beneficial to a country [except to] holders of monied obligations, who ought to be bought up, or compromised with, by the public, rather than suffer the national welfare to be arrested by a crippling of the circulation" (1817, p. 163). He later asserted that "More injustice had been done to, and more misery had been endured by, the productive classes" during each of the contractions 1819–22 and 1825–28 "than would have been done to or endured by the fund owners if the Government had abolished the whole national debt at once (1828, p. 94). But the primacy of property prevailed.

BOOM AND BUST, 1822–25

Depression turned to expansion, led by investment in the newly independent countries of South America, and the Bank joined the post-restriction credit expansion (Page 1919, pp. 69–72). Its gold reserve, which had reached £13.8 million in February 1824, fell to £3.6 million in August 1825. This was practically the country's entire reserve, for "there was but little gold in the provinces .... Add to this the fact that many of the country banks as well as their customers were heavily involved in the purchase of shares in bubble flotations, and it becomes clear that the situation was at least as full of danger as that of 1793 or 1797" (Feavearyear, 1931, p. 219).

Liverpool saw "the peril not only to individuals, but to the whole country, from the blind indulgence of this craving for sudden wealth" (Yonge 1868 iii, p. 342). On March 25, he took the occasion of a debate on a bill on joint-stock companies to comment on "that general spirit of speculation which was going beyond all bounds, and was likely to bring the greatest mischief on numerous individuals." He urged them

> ... to reflect what would be the situation of the public if (not to speak of actual war) ... any embarrassing event were to occur. Their lordships would recollect that when commercial embarrassment occurred during the late war, bankers and merchants came forward and applied to parliament for aid, which they obtained by issues of Exchequer bills. He wished it, however, to be clearly understood that those persons who now engaged in Joint-Stock Companies, or other enterprises, entered on those speculations at their peril and risk. He thought it was his duty to declare that he never would advise the introduction of any bill for their relief; on the contrary, if such a measure were proposed, he would oppose it, and he hoped that parliament would resist any measure of that kind ...

Bailouts with convertible currencies are more difficult than with fiat money. They risk suspension in the former but there is always more paper, which helps explain the official irresponsibilities of 2008 and other recent occasions.

The press sympathized with the Government, and when the crisis began, *The Times* (November 29, 1825) warned (Feavearyear 1931, p. 220):

> As for relief from the King's Government, we can tell the speculating people and their great foster-mother in Threadneedle Street, that they will meet with none – no, not a particle – of the species of relief which they look for. The King's ministers know very well the causes of the evil, and the extent of it, and its natural and appropriate remedy, and we may venture to forewarn the men of paper, that no such help as they are seeking will be contributed by the State.

The Bank's belated increase in interest in December made matters worse. News "that the Bank was returning a considerable portion of the bills sent for discount by even the largest houses" provoked runs on the country banks. "On Sunday, the 27th, partners of the London houses were fetched from church to supply gold to their desperate provincial customers .... In three weeks sixty-one country banks and six important London houses ceased payment" (Feavearyear 1931, p. 220; Johnson 1991, pp. 889–903). The Bank's own situation was desperate. On December 15, it turned to the Government for help either in the form of Exchequer Bills or authorization to stop payment. The Government refused. The Bank was told to "pay out to the last penny," and to lend freely on securities already in existence. Former governor Jeremiah Harman recollected the incident for the Committee of 1832:

> Did any communication take place between the Bank and the Government respecting an Order in Council to restrain payment in gold at that period? – Yes, it was suggested by the Bank.
>
> What answer did His Majesty's Government give to that? – They resisted it from first to last.
>
> It was stated by the late Mr. Huskisson … that he as a member of the Administration at that time suggested to the Bank that if their gold was exhausted, they should place a paper against their door stating that they had not gold to pay with, but might expect to have gold to recommence payment in a short period; do you recollect such a suggestion? – There was such a suggestion.
>
> What would, in your opinion, have been the consequences of that paper placed against the door of the Bank, without preparation to support commercial and financial credit? – I hardly know how to contemplate it.

Thrown on its own resources, Harman told the Committee, the Bank had lent assistance

> by every possible means, and in modes that we never had adopted before; we took in stock as security, we purchased Exchequer Bills, we made advances on Exchequer Bills, we not only discounted outright, but we made advances on deposit bills of exchange to an immense amount; in short by every possible means consistent with the safety of the Bank; and we were not upon some occasions over nice. (HC 1832)

The Bank worked overtime to produce notes, and sent agents into the country to lend them, raising its discounts in a few weeks from £5 million to £15 million. The panic ended, the drain of gold from the Bank became a trickle, and by spring had turned around.

There was sentiment for the relief of distressed firms, such as the issue of Exchequer Bills on the security of the goods of troubled merchants. Leader of the House of Commons George Canning had doubted "whether we should get through the crisis without an issue of exchequer bills, which, objectionable as it may be … in principle, appears to be the only remedy in which the moneyed world will look with confidence." Even though Liverpool had warned that the Government would give no relief to speculators, the general opinion was that since "the whole mercantile body, … Tierney at the head of the opposition, [and] every man of the old Pitt party expressed a unanimous concurrence in that measure, we all thought it would do us no great harm to adopt it as a special remedy in a special case (Croker 1884 i, p. 314; Brock 1967, p. 209).

They failed to take account of "their leader's adherence to the principles of *laissez-faire*. Throughout the year he had deprecated any proposals for Government interference, now he refused completely to concur in any measure which would teach men the habit of relying upon Government when their own efforts failed" (Brock 1967, p. 209).

The Government's response to the 1825 crisis differed significantly from that to which later generations have become accustomed. For example, Federal Reserve Board Chairman Ben Bernanke (2015) wrote a book about his role in the 2008 crisis entitled *The Courage to Act*, a euphemism for politically motivated bailouts and the prevention of market adjustments. In fact, Bernanke and his associates lacked Liverpool's courage *not to act*, which has not gone unnoticed (Kinsley 2015). Liverpool's success may be attributed to the greater economic sophistication of the British Parliament of his day than the modern American Congress.

Business and finance were well-represented in Parliament in the nineteenth century. Nor was systemic risk any less:

> I know [Liverpool said] that if I studied my own ease or popularity, I could not do so more effectively than by coming down to Parliament with such a proposi- tion. If I have not adopted that course, I trust the House will give me credit for abstaining from it from a thorough conviction that it was not likely to be attended with beneficial results. I have always thought that the precedent of 1793 ... was not a favourable one and therefore ought not to be followed. But there is a great difference between that period and the present; for it cannot now be pretended that the commercial distress which now existed has any connection with political events [war finance] .... What would be the effects of such a measure? Not to leave the people to rely upon themselves. What is that but the very evil I have deprecated; namely, looking to government for aid, to relieve them from the consequence of their own extravagance. It is now three or four years since the landed interest was suffering great distress: and not a month passed at that time that I was not beset with the most urgent applications for relief by the issue of Exchequer Bills, [which] were rejected. (HC 1803, xv, p. 450; Brock 1967, p. 210)

Accordingly, when a petition for the issue of Exchequer Bills was about to be presented in the House, Liverpool told Canning that he would resign if such a measure was forced upon the Administration, and authorized Canning to say this in the House. Canning felt he could not "leave Lord Liverpool in the lurch," and announced to the House "in a very bold and uncompromising tone that if the House chose to adopt the proposed measure they must also be pre- pared to find Ministers to execute it, for ... they *would not*; and this he repeated very steadily, and to the ears of some country gentlemen offensively" (Croker 1884 i, pp. 324–5; Brock 1967, p. 210).

Liverpool suggested that "the best mode of solving the difficulty was for him to retire from office, the rest of the members of the Government retaining theirs". Fearing the Government could not continue without Liverpool, his colleagues remonstrated with him and reached a compromise in which the Bank of England would be asked to use its power to issue notes on the deposit of goods, and also to purchase a limited quantity of Exchequer Bills to afford relief to the public. "The government would pay part of its debt to the Bank 'to prevent them from experiencing any inconvenience in so doing,'" Liverpool said. But this "was upon a different principle than that of direct relief by the government" (Brock 1967, p. 211).

Economist Thomas Tooke criticized even this concession. The characteristic of commercial distress was the lack of lenders and buyers, he wrote. "The issue of Exchequer bills would supply neither of these wants. Since they went straight to persons in distress, the number of buyers and lenders would not be increased .... The issue of Exchequer bills would benefit certain people, it would direct capital into certain channels, but it would not be a measure of general relief" (Tooke 1826, p. 213).

3. The commercial crisis of 1847

> My confidence is unshaken that we are taking all the precautions which legislation
> can prudently take against the recurrence of a monetary crisis. It may occur in spite of
> our precautions, and if it does, and *if it be necessary* to assume a grave responsibility
> for the purpose of meeting it, I dare say men will be found willing to assume such
> a responsibility. I would rather trust to this than impair the efficiency and probable
> success of those measures by which one hopes to control evil tendencies in their
> beginning, and to diminish the risk that extraordinary measures may be necessary.
> –Prime Minister Sir Robert Peel to the governor of the Bank of England,
> who had requested provisions allowing suspension of the Bank Act.
> (Parker 1899 iii, pp. 140–41)

The Bank of England narrowly survived the years following the resumption
of gold payments because of its lackluster performance as revealed especially
by its near failure in 1825. Other bankers wanted to be rid of a competitor
with legal advantages, anyway, and the Government was no longer financially
dependent on the Bank, which had owed its existence to the former's wartime
needs in 1694, and indeed much of the time until Waterloo – including the
Nine Years' War (1688–97), the War of the Spanish Succession (1701–14),
the Seven Years War (1756–63), the American Revolution (1775–83), and the
French Revolutionary Wars (1792–1815). The next century of Pax Britannica,
however, saw a balanced budget on average. The small deficits during the
Crimean and Boer Wars were offset at other times so that the national debt was
about the same in 1914 as in 1815 (Mitchell 1962, p. 403). Peace, a good credit
rating, and alternative sources of funds through Post Office Savings Banks and
the capital markets made the Exchequer "independent of the Bank and the City
power." The Chancellor "now never had to beg … when he [had] occasion for
sums in seven figures" (Morley 1903 i, p. 651; Clapham 1944 ii, pp. 272–4).

Survive it did, however, though with the loss of some of its monopolistic
privileges and subject to a legislated rule that tied its currency to its gold. But
what if the rule threatened a currency shortage through a loss of gold? Would
the Bank and Government suspend it to avoid a crisis? The Government
refused a commitment, as indicated by the prime minister's statement in the
epigraph to this chapter, but we will see that the answer turned out to be affirmative in practice as the nineteenth century progressed, when the prosperity of
the privately owned Bank depended on that of its customers and the economy.
We have already seen that the Bank hesitated to impose convertibility after
Waterloo. This was a different attitude than after 1914, when the Bank had

effectively become a government agency, was less concerned with the immediate needs of the domestic economy, and took the lead in forcing a return to
convertibility.

MONETARY RULES VS. DISCRETION

With the end of war finance, the Bank's primary public responsibility became
monetary stability, presumably requiring it to offset the speculative proclivi-
ties of the public. Regrettably, it preferred to join those activities. The Bank's
position was also threatened by potential competitors. It had become recognized that in opposing the establishment of other joint-stock banks the Bank of
England claimed a monopoly it did not possess. It had also benefitted from the
requirement that private incorporations required sometimes difficult to obtain
special acts of Parliament until the uniform procedures of the *Joint Stock
Companies Act 1844*, and limited liability did not come until 1855. The *Act
of 1708* had prohibited companies of more than six partners from issuing bills
or notes payable on demand, but said nothing about banks of deposit, and the
growth of payment by check made the monopoly of note issues less important
(Joplin 1822, p. 49; Feavearyear 1931, p. 223; Thomas 1934, pp. 72–3).

The Government had begun negotiations with the Bank in 1822 for an
extension of its charter (due to expire in 1833) in exchange for an act explicitly
recognizing joint-stock banks of issue as long as they did not maintain offices
within 65 miles of London. The Bank reluctantly agreed, but the Government
did not proceed, "mainly because of strong opposition in Parliament to the
renewal of the Bank's charter" (Thomas 1934, p. 49).

In 1826, after the failures of many small banks during the recent crisis and
without any offsetting concession to the Bank of England, legal sanction was
given to joint-stock banks of issue if they did not maintain offices within 65
miles of London. The now-solvent Government also waited until near the
end of the Bank's charter before considering an extension. A committee was
appointed "to inquire into and report upon the expediency of renewing the
Charter of the Bank of England; and also on the existing system of banking
by Banks of Issue in England and Wales," and it began to take evidence in
May 1832, some of which was of historic importance and will be discussed
below. The next April, Chancellor of the Exchequer and Leader of the
House of Commons, Lord Althorp (courtesy title as successor to the Earl of
Spencer), "began negotiations with the Bank on the subject of the renewal of
the Charter," and after some difficulties, terms were agreed in May (HC 1832,
Q559).

The Chancellor brought the subject before the House of Commons at the end of the month,

> proposing that the Bank privileges should be continued for a limited period; that its Notes should be made a legal tender; that one-fourth of the debt due from the public to the Bank should be repaid [to reduce the dependence of the government on the Bank]; that the allowances to the Bank for management of the National Debt and other public business should be reduced by £120,000 per annum; that the laws restricting interest to 5 per cent should be repealed, so far as concerned bills not having more than three months to run; that Joint Stock Banks should not be allowed within a certain distance from London. (HC 1832, Q559)

The usury ceiling on the Bank's lending rate was removed in the expectation that it would be used to restrain speculation, and Bank Rate became the foremost instrument of the Bank's monetary policy, documented in R.G. Hawtrey's (1962) *Century of Bank Rate* (1832–1932). The Bank's notes were made legal tender to mitigate runs on gold. The issues of other banks were limited to their existing amounts so that Bank of England notes became dominant – a monopolization of the currency that sowed the seeds of later crises.

There was considerable opposition in the House from those

> who thought the terms were 'extremely disadvantageous to the Public', but a Bill based on these resolutions was introduced in July. [I]t was immediately noticed by the Governors of the Bank that an important variation from the terms agreed upon had been made. [T]he clause for preventing the establishment of banks consisting of more than six partners in London, or within sixty-five miles thereof, had been omitted.

The Bank remonstrated with the Chancellor, claiming that the bill violated its Charter. "The law officers of the Crown, however, considered that banks of deposit were not prohibited by the existing Acts, and to prevent any doubt in the matter a clause was introduced into the Act of 1833 permitting the establishment of banks with any number of partners, 'in London and within 65 miles thereof', provided such banks did not issue notes payable on demand."

After Althorp refused the Bank's complaints, "and threatened to postpone [the Bill's] consideration" if they held out, "the Directors of the Bank consented to its provisions." Its Charter was extended to 1855, "but with a proviso that in 1844, if Parliament should think fit and the money owing by the Government was repaid [which had ceased to be difficult], the Charter could be suspended on one year's notice" (Acres 1931, pp. 458–61).

In its argument for renewal, the Bank had promised a new leaf in the form of the Palmer Rule (named after Governor Horsley Palmer, who had described it to the Committee of 1832) by which its notes would change one-for-one with its gold. Speculation and an over-issued, depreciated currency would lead to the cashing in of notes for gold to export, which would restrain money and have a stabilizing effect. This could take time, of course, and an adequate reserve was necessary.

In addition to defending the gold value of the currency, Governor Palmer told the committee, the Bank was prepared to preserve financial stability by standing ready to lend on good security at all times above the market rate. The Bank thus stands aloof from speculation, but "that public rate is always open to individuals if circumstances should arise to render such applications necessary …. The Bank *then* becomes the main support of the commerce of the country" (HC 1832, Q559). Palmer's concept of the Bank as lender of last resort put him with Francis Baring and others in anticipating the more famous expression by Walter Bagehot in *Lombard Street* in 1873.

Palmer told the Committee that the Bank was particularly qualified to perform this function because "as a commercial body [it] is at all times enabled to judge the character of the application so made, though they should be only occasional, yet they are at times of very considerable importance to the parties making such applications" (HC 1832, Q559). This close relation between the Bank and its customers, knowledge of each other being important to the profits of both, differed from the pro-forma examinations of modern banks by remote bureaucratic agencies. For example, in 2007, as on other occasions, the Federal Reserve, which is not a bank, was one of the last to know of the banking system's problems (White 2010; Wood 2015, ch. 7).

The Bank seemed always to have persuasive assurances of "we'll do better next time," but its performance in the 1830s failed to show improvement. There was little evidence of the Palmer rule. The Bank's credit exacerbated rather than moderated conditions. It joined the railway boom in the middle of the decade, and in 1839 had to turn to the Bank of France for a credit to offset the loss of gold. The country's price level rose from 84 to 113 between 1835 and 1839, and fell back to 84 in 1843 (Mitchell 1962, p. 470).

Another rule receiving more attention in Bank statements than in performance was the retention of a third of their assets in gold and silver ("treasure" or "reserves"). So Palmer told a parliamentary committee was ideal for a "full currency … in ordinary times," but at no time during the 1830s was it attained. Thomas Tooke (merchant and sometime director of the Bank, but best known as a historian of prices) pointed out that "whenever the Bank got into this position its own leaders favoured, it was apt to show signs of 'impatience … to reduce the [barren] stock of bullion.'" The prestigious Director George Warde Norman admitted in 1840, that the Bank's "duties to the currency and what it held to be its duties to the public [particularly its stockholders] clashed" (Clapham 1944 ii, pp. 162–3; Tooke 1840, p. 114; HC 1840, Q1892). "Years of controversy between the advocates of different methods for reforming the banking system of [England and Wales] had led to no practical results, and five parliamentary committees ... had not felt themselves competent to make any recommendations" (Acres 1931, p. 496).

Samson Ricardo carried on his brother's proposal to completely remove the currency from the conflicts of profit-seeking private interests to a public board of commissioners with a single task. At the opposite end, William Gilbart, chairman of the London and Westminster Bank, advised the elimination of the Bank of England's virtual monopoly of the currency and letting it be determined by competition among banks. The misbehavior (such as the speculation of which the Bank had been guilty) of a competitive bank would cause its notes to be returned to it by other banks, he said, whereas the monopoly Bank of England lacked outside as well as internal constraints (HC 1841, Q1362; Gregory 1929, p. 111).

On the other hand, a Bank director argued in a letter to the Chancellor: "A single issuer might be easy to deal with, but how are we to deal with five hundred?" (Feavearyear, 1931, p. 245). This argument has always carried considerable weight even with regulators professing an interest in competition. They are evidently attracted by the supposed ease of regulating a few large firms compared with many competitors whose behavior might be less manageable. Such an attitude might help explain the government's continuation of the Bank's monopoly despite its subpar performance historically.

A cost of this monopoly, however, had been the Bank's discretion resulting in excessive fluctuations of the currency. That "unlimited freedom of issue was a danger to a country exposed, by its exceptional position as the commercial center of the world, to the effect of crises occurring in all the other markets of production and consumption." Among the "various proposals ... put forward for establishing control over the circulation of the paper currency" were those of economist and journalist Colonel Robert Torrens and banker Samuel Jones Loyd (the first Lord Overstone from 1850), who proposed to give the Bank of England a monopoly of the issue and separate it into Banking and Issue Departments "so that the function of the Bank as 'manager of the circulation' might be kept quite distinct from its ordinary banking business, and that the issue of Notes by the Bank should be regulated by insistence on some proportion being maintained between the amount of bullion held and the amount of Notes in circulation." The avoidance of overissues caused by the Bank's inability to resist market and government pressures required the discipline of a legal currency rule, Loyd argued, specifically one which made the currency behave as it would under a pure (complete) gold standard (Acres 1931, p. 468; Torrens 1837, pp. 55–8; Loyd 1840, p. 15).

Banks of issue are confused with banks of discount, Loyd maintained, whereas the objects of the two are entirely different. "The sole duty of the former ... is to take efficient means for issuing its paper money upon good security and regulating the amount of it by one fixed rule. The principal object and business of the latter ... is to obtain the command of as large a proportion of the existing circulating medium and to distribute [lend] it in such a manner as shall combine security for repayment with the highest rate of profit. [W]hen prices are rising, profits increasing, and every merchant ... is desirous of extending his operations," and demands credit for this purpose, "is it not inevitable that" bankers should abuse their power of issuing paper, the effect of which would "give a further stimulus to the existing tendencies of the trading world, and ultimately to aggravate the convulsion to which they must lead." Woodward (1938, p. 107) noted that "The regulation of the note issue was a means of protecting property, upon which" the major parties were agreed.

Moreover, the persons who exercise the right of issue are "not a body of individuals qualified (by their total separation from all such interests) to exercise a dispassionate and disinterested judgment; but on the contrary, men the most largely engaged in mercantile and monied operations, and, therefore, more than any other class exposed in their private interests to the immediate effects of any action upon the currency" (Loyd 1840, pp. 13, 31–3; Andreades 1924, pp. 281–2).

There was considerable sentiment for currency reform of some kind, possibly the market discipline of competition as argued by Gilbert or tightening the legal regulation of monopoly as provided in previous Bank charters. The political leader in the achievement of the latter was Sir Robert Peel, prime minister, 1835–36 and 1841–46. Peel spent his life between the industrial North and London. He was born in Bury (Greater Manchester), and when he was 2 years old his family moved to Tamworth in the Black Country, just north of Birmingham. He was the eldest son of Sir Robert Peel, first baronet, a printed calico manufacturer, and referred to himself as the son of a cotton spinner. A brilliant student, he was educated at Harrow and Oxford, where he earned an unprecedented double first at Christ Church.

He did not go into the family business but in 1809 secured a seat in Parliament for an Irish rotten borough of a couple of dozen voters. He supported the Government and soon became under-secretary (to Lord Liverpool) of state for war and the colonies, and answered questions relating to the Department in the House of Commons. In 1812, when Liverpool became prime minister, Peel became chief secretary for Ireland for six years, the longest tenure of that office in the nineteenth century. He oversaw the passage of the Resumption Law in 1819. As Home Secretary (1822–29), he established the Metropolitan Police Force, popularly called "bobbies." His premiership was active, including the *Factory Act* and the *Bank Charter Act of 1844*. He made enemies through his support of the repeal of Catholic disabilities (1829) and the Corn Laws (tariffs, 1846) after initially defending them, on the grounds laid out in his *Tamworth Manifesto* (1834) that the conservative veneration of ancient rights and institutions did not prevent the "careful review of institutions, both civil and ecclesiastical," and "the correction of proved abuses and the redress of real grievances." The Manifesto was a statement of principle a well as an electioneering document. "No Government can stand," he said, speaking to a country in which less than 10 percent of its citizens had the vote, "unless it be supported by public opinion" (Prest 2009; Gash 1972, pp. 93–9).

Peel was persuaded by Jones's and Torrens's argument for the formal separation of the Bank's functions, including the responsibility for a stable currency that was later called central banking. He told the House of Commons:

> Our general rule is to draw a distinction between the privilege of issue and the conduct of the ordinary banking business. We think they stand on an entirely different footing. We think that the privilege of issue is one which may be fairly and justly controlled by the State, and that the banking business, as distinguished from issue, is a matter in respect to which there cannot be too unlimited and unrestricted a competition. (Sir Robert Peel, House of Commons, May 6, 1844)

As far as the persons chosen to manage the currency, that is, to apply the 1844 rule, Peel said that a special bank or board of issue could be specially established but

> the true policy in this country is to work, so far as it be possible, with the instruments you have ready to your hand – to avail yourselves of that advantage which they possess from having been in use, from being … a part of the habits and usages of society. They will probably work more smoothly than perfectly novel instruments of greater theoretical perfection …. We think it the wisest course to select the Bank of England as that controlling and central body. (Andreades 1924, p. 288)

THE BANK CHARTER ACT OF 1844

The Act endorsed the Bank's monopoly of the currency and divided it into two departments, the Issue Department, which exchanged currency and gold on a one-to-one basis as the public desired, and the Banking Department, which would behave like any other (profit-seeking) bank. The first balance sheets of the new arrangement are shown in Table 3.1. The notes of the Issue Department, as required by the Act, equaled the sum of its gold and silver (£12,657,208 + £1,694,087) and its constant fiduciary issue of £14 million.

A comparative history of central bank behavior

Table 3.1   *Bank of England Return, September 7, 1844*

Bank Department	£	£	
Issue Department			
Government securities	11,015,100	28,351,295	Notes
Other securities	2,984,900		
Gold coin and bullion	12,657,208		
Silver bullion	1,694,087		
Assets	28,351,295	28,351,295	Liabilities
Banking Department			
Government securities	14,554,834	3,630,809	Government deposits
Other securities	7,835,616	8,644,348	Other deposits
Notes	8,175,025		Other liabilities and capital
Gold and silver coin	857,765	19,148,083	
Assets	31,423,240	31,423,240	Liabilities and capital

Note: The Bank's return was required to be published weekly in the *London Gazette*, and was also published elsewhere, including *The Economist*. The items have been rearranged and some have been renamed in conformity with modern usage.
Source: Compiled by the author.

The revised Bank quickly ran into trouble. A railway boom was underway and the Banking Department had ample reserves (gold and silver of £857,765 plus holdings of the Issue Department's currency of £8,175,025, convertible into gold), amounting to three-quarters of its deposits, with which it joined the "mania" (Feavearyear 1931, p. 261; Wood 2005, ch. 5). It cut its lending rate (Bank Rate) from 4 percent to 2½ percent the day after the passage of the 1844 Act, which remained below market rates for the next three years.

The Bank's private loans had risen 60 percent by the summer of 1846, although the Banking Department's note reserve was maintained because there was little change in the public's demand for notes. The Issue Department actually gained gold. Gold began to leave the country, however, as the poor harvests of 1845 and 1846 meant increasing grain imports while "the rise of price produced a wave of speculation and an inordinate number of corn bills which the banks were called upon to discount …. The Bank of England, having supplied the market with from 7–10 millions of floating funds by discounts and by market loans, was in a bad position both for curbing speculation and for checking the drain. As soon as it attempted to do so there was bound to be a shrinkage of credit and a risk of panic" (Feavearyear 1931, p. 259; see also Ward-Perkins 1950 and Dornbusch and Frenkel 1984). Several witnesses before the parliamentary committees which investigated the commercial distress of 1847, including the governor and deputy-governor of the Bank, stated "that earlier steps in Autumn 1846 and Spring 1847 by the Bank of England might have obviated the necessity for more stringent measures later" (HC 1848, p. iv). In fact, the Bank raised its interest rate from 3 percent to 4 percent in January and to 5 percent in April. But its note reserve fell from £9.5 million in December to £2.6 million in April.

The Bank's (that is, the Banking Department's) reserve ratio was getting low, but it could not force the return of notes by calling in or not renewing loans without risking a crisis. It informed customers that its discounts would be cut in half, but debtors' weaknesses caused it to relax the pressure, and easy credit returned.

The problem shifted to low agricultural prices. The large imports of grain and prospects of a good harvest in 1847 brought down the price of wheat from 14s. to 8s. a bushel. The Bank's lending continued to grow, but in August grain merchants began to fail. By mid-September the crisis had spread to the bill-brokers and panic was beginning in all trades and industries. "Early in October, with the payment of dividends, [the note reserve] fell to £3,409,000, and Bank rate was raised again to 5½ percent. At the same time the Bank announced that no further advances would be made on public stocks (government bonds), which set those who had used the latter as collateral security selling frantically, and caused a panic on the Stock Exchange" (Feavearyear 1931, p. 263).

Country banks felt the pressure of the Bank's tight monetary policy, and asked for assistance. Gold in the Bank exceeded £8 million, a respectable amount by traditional standards, but it was not available. The relevant reserve was now Bank notes in the Banking Department, and on October 23 these were £1.5 million, 11 percent of deposits. Debtors wanted credit, and the assurance of credit, and promised the Bank that credit would not be converted to notes. A check written on a Bank deposit was ordinarily as good as its notes, but the Bank would not take the chance.

The public turned to the Government, and for "a fortnight the Chancellor of the Exchequer, Sir Charles Wood, was occupied continuously in meeting the arguments and pleadings of those who wanted the Act suspended. Again and again he refused" (Feavearyear 1931, p. 263). He later told the House (November 30): "Parties of every description made applications to us for assistance [saying] 'We do not want notes, but give us confidence.' … They said, 'We have notes enough, but we have not confidence to use them; say you will stand by us, and we shall have all that we want; do anything, in short, that will give us confidence. If we think that we can get bank notes, we shall not want them. Charge any rate of interest you please, ask what you like.'"

So the Government resisted the market's pleas, but what did the Bank think? By the "Bank," we mean its directors, who were its management. Who were these people, and what were their goals? The original 1694 Act provided for 24 directors, from whom its chief executives, the governor and deputy-governor, would be selected for one-year terms. Until World War I, they normally served two successive terms and the deputy succeeded the governor. The directors were for many years predominantly "substantial City merchants and members of the leading City companies." They changed over the years with the economy, and Bank historian John Clapham wrote of the twentieth century that "the London merchant or merchant banker of Victorian type was declining, [and] ships and railways, steel and chocolate, leather and beer, the trades of Canada and South Africa, and the China trade [were] represented" (Clapham 1944 ii, p. 419).

A one-third annual turnover of directors had been imposed by law to discourage the perpetuation of cliques, although the eight who stepped down were taken from among those who had not "passed the chair" (been governor), and usually returned the next year. (Required rotation was ended at the end of the nineteenth century.) The senior advisory body was the Committee of Treasury, consisting of the directors who had passed the chair, so-called because it had been formed to "attend the lords of the Treasury" (led by the prime minister and the Chancellor of the Exchequer), the Bank's main customer.

Palmer was aware of the Bank's (a private company's) responsibility for "the whole circulation of the country," and believed with Henry Thornton that this was the proper arrangement. Money should be in the hands of "a commercial company, independent of the Government." It would thus be "less liable to abuse" from political interests – quoting Lord Althorp, who had steered the 1833 Act through the House of Commons (HC 1832, Q551–5; Thornton 1802, p. 259).

The Bank's first governor, Sir John Houblon, was typical of his successors as a member of the merchant banking Grocers' Company and from a Huguenot family from Lille. The first deputy governor, Michael Godfrey, was also a merchant and financier (mainly in the wine trade) and son of a merchant. Things had not changed much two centuries later, when Bagehot (1873, p. 199) wrote that the typical new director was "a well-conducted young man who has begun to attend to business, and who seems likely to be fairly sensible and fairly efficient twenty years later." Four senior directors at the time of the 1847 crisis are illustrative:

Sir John Pelly (1777–1852), first baronet (1840), director (1822–52) and governor (1841–42) of the Bank, was the son and grandson of captains in the service of the East India Company. He became a director of the Hudson's Bay Company in 1806, and afterwards deputy governor and governor. He sent out exploring parties including for the Northwest Passage, and his contributions to his company's explorations are commemorated by Cape Pelly on the north coast of Alaska. In 1838, he traveled to St. Petersburg to help negotiate the Company's lease of a portion of the Alaskan peninsula from Russia. In 1840 he was created a baronet on the recommendation of Lord Melbourne (*ODNB* 2004).

William Cotton (1786–1866), director (1822–66) and governor of the Bank (1842–45, his term extended to provide continuity of work on the 1844 Act) was the son of a mariner and merchant, and his wife was daughter of a merchant and Bank director. He was educated until the age of 15 at Chigwell grammar. He considered the Church, but entered the firm of a friend of his father set up to exploit his invention of steam-driven rope-making machinery. Cotton, who became a partner in 1807, was also of an inventive bent, held several patents, and became a fellow of the Royal Society in 1821. His later years were devoted to church-building, schools and amenities for the working classes, and other philanthropic activities (*ODNB* 2004).

John Heath (1790–1879), director (1823–72) and governor (1845–47) of the Bank, was born into a nonconformist merchant family with Huguenot connections in Genoa, Italy. His father's family had been involved in the west-country wool trade in the 1720s. He was educated at Harrow School (1797–1806), after which he joined the London house of Heath & Co. He also served as chairman of both the London Life Association and the Society of Merchants Trading to the Continent and master of the Grocer's Company in the City of London, and was elected a fellow of the Royal Society in 1843 (*ODNB* 2004).

James Morris (1795–1882), head of Morris, Prevost & Co., merchants, Bank director 1827–80, was elected deputy-governor of the Bank in 1847, and soon became governor in place of *William Robinson*, the failure of whose corn-dealer firm had compelled his resignation (Bank of England 2013).

The Bank's directors were mostly merchants, dependent on credit markets and the state of trade, and involved in the country's social and political life. They were unlike twentieth-century central bankers in their personal dependence on prosperity.

In June 1844, while the Bank Charter Bill was before the House of Commons, former Governor Palmer and Henry Bosanquet, a director of the London and Westminster Bank, warned Peel that the limitation of the note issue might interfere with the Bank's assistance to the market. Bosanquet sympathized with the long-term objectives of the Bill. "But I feel confident that in the practical working of the system of currency acting (as it is proposed) as if it were exclusively composed of metal, there will be moments when sudden voids will be created in the circulation, …, which if not in some way provided for, may be the cause at times of a total suspension of business throughout the country." He proposed that "during the first five years of the new system, whenever the rate of interest at the Bank of England shall have risen to eight percent, it shall be lawful for the Issue Department to make advances at that rate of interest on the deposit of Exchequer Bills; the loans to be repaid and the bills sold whenever the rate of interest shall have fallen below eight percent." Thirty London bankers supported the request, but Peel dismissed their fears in his letter to the governor (see the epigraph to this chapter).

The Government's hand was forced by the failure of several large banks during the week beginning Monday, October 18, 1847. On Saturday the chancellor told the Bank to lend as freely as it wished, and if this involved an increase in the fiduciary issue beyond the legal maximum, Parliament would be asked for an act of indemnity. He suggested that a rate of interest of at least 8 percent be charged. The length of the letter confirming this direction is a consequence of the Government's attempt to reconcile the conflict between its refusal to admit the inadequacies of the 1844 Act and the necessity of dispensing with the Act under pressure.

Downing Street, 25 October 1847

To the Governor and Deputy Governor of the Bank of England. Gentlemen,

Her Majesty's Government have seen with the deepest Regret the Pressure which has existed for some Weeks upon the commercial Interests of the Country, and that this Pressure has been aggravated by a Want of that confidence which is necessary for carrying on the ordinary Dealings of Trade.

They have been in hopes that the Check given to Transactions of a speculative Character, the Transfer of Capital from other Countries, the Influx of Bullion, and the Feeling which a Knowledge of these Circumstances might have been expected to produce, would have removed the prevailing Distrust.

They were encouraged in this Expectation by the speedy Cessation of a similar State of Feeling in the Month of April last.

These Hopes have, however, been disappointed, and Her Majesty's Government have come to the Conclusion that the Time has arrived when they ought to attempt, by some extraordinary and temporary Measure, to restore Confidence to the mercantile and manufacturing community.

For this Purpose, they recommend to the Directors of the Bank of England, in the present Emergency, to enlarge the Amount of their Discounts and Advances upon approved Security; but that, in order to retain this Operation within reasonable Limits, a high Rate of Interest should be charged.

In present Circumstances, they would suggest that the Rate of Interest should not be less than Eight per Cent.

If this Course should lead to any Infringement of the existing Law, Her Majesty's Government will be prepared to propose to Parliament, on its Meeting, a Bill of

Indemnity. They will rely upon the Discretion of the Directors to reduce as soon as possible the Amount of their Notes, if any extraordinary Issue should take place ...

Her Majesty's Government are of opinion that any extra Profit derived from this Measure should be carried to the Account of the Public, but the precise Mode of doing so must be left to future Arrangement.

Her Majesty's Government are not insensible of the Evil of any Departure from the Law which has placed the Currency of the Country upon a sound Basis; but they feel confident, that, in the present Circumstances the Measure which they have proposed may be safely adopted, and at the same Time the main Provisions of that Law, and the vital Principle of preserving the Convertibility of the Bank Note, may be firmly maintained.

> We have the Honour to be, Gentlemen, Your obedient humble Servants,
> J. Russell (Prime Minister), Charles Wood. (Gregory 1929 ii, pp. 7–8)

News of the Act's suspension and renewed Bank lending restored confidence immediately, and notes, now that they could be had, were no longer wanted. The new notes hurriedly printed by the Bank were not taken and the fiduciary issue was not exceeded.

Critics' prophecies had been fulfilled, but Peel and Wood denied that the 1844 Act was to blame. Although it had not been as effective on all fronts as Peel had hoped, most of the Act's goals were secured. "Its first object was that in which I admit it has failed, namely, to prevent by early and gradual [steps] severe and sudden contraction and the panic and confusion inseparable from it." But in "two other objects of at least equal importance ... my belief is that the Bill has completely succeeded," namely the preservation of convertibility and the prevention of the aggravation of speculation by the abuse of paper money (House of Commons, December 3, 1847). The Act's defenders pleaded that the crisis would have occurred under any system:

> All legislation – every system – proceeds upon the supposition that men will be actuated by the ordinary motives of human action; and against the consequences of their conduct, when it is influenced by other motives, no system and no legislation can provide. It is no fault of the principle of the Act of 1844 that it was unable to provide against that state of things against which no other principle and no other system that has ever yet been advocated for the regulation of our currency could have protected us. (Sir Charles Wood, House of Commons, November 30, 1847)

The Act was as good as the wit of man allowed, and no one could tell the future. In simultaneously defending the Act and the Government's decision to break it, the chancellor said the Government had followed the course recommended by the best authorities, and quoted Loyd's (1844) *Thoughts on the Separation of the Departments of the Bank of England*:

> For all contingencies which can be reasonably anticipated, and which are suscep-
> tible of being previously defined by law, the firm application of the provisions of
> the Bill is essential, and against the occurrence of these contingencies which are not
> capable of being foreseen and defined by law, but which are not altogether impos-
> sible, the Bill itself affords the best protection than can be obtained. Should a crisis
> ever arrive "baffling all ordinary calculations" and not amenable to the application
> of any ordinary principle, the remedy must be sought not in the previous provisions
> of the law, but, quoting Mr. Huskisson's words, "in the discretion of those who may
> then be at the head of affairs, subject to their own responsibility and to the judgment
> of Parliament."

Anyway, the chancellor said, again quoting Loyd (1844, p. 388): "To guard against commercial convulsions is not the direct or real purpose of the Bill. To subject the paper issues to such regulation as shall secure their conformity in amount and value with and consequently their immediate convertibility at all times into metallic money, is the purpose to which the provisions of the measure are avowedly directed." "I should have little faith in any system of currency," he added, "which professed to accomplish more than to regulate the circulation."

Its alleged primary object – the convertibility of the note – had been violated, although the authorities had behaved in accordance with John Stuart
Mill's interpretation of the Act. Mill wrote for the 1857 edition of *Principles
of Political Economy* (bk. 3, ch. 24.3) that "I think myself justified in affirming
that the mitigation of commercial revulsions [rather than the convertibility
of the issue] is the real, and only serious, purpose of the Act of 1844. No
Government would hesitate a moment" to stop convertibility in order to assure
the continuity of the Bank of England's support of the financial system "if
suspension of the Act of 1844 proved insufficient."

The objective of the rule was admirable, but a responsible Bank and
Government were not prepared to allow its strict application to impoverish the
country by obstructing the currency. Breaking the law in desperate circumstances was good policy.

Before leaving these financial difficulties, it should be noted that they had
been self-imposed by the Government's adoption of a legally rigid portfolio
formula (Redish 2001). Abiding by the law in this case was bound, from time
to time, as had been predicted by some familiar with the money markets, to
force disastrous shortages in the currency. This was like bank reserve requirements in the United States. Legislatures and other regulators in that country
have not understood the nature of reserves, which in battle and finance are
meant to be available. "Required" reserves are by definition not reserves,

and have interfered with bank lending when desperately needed. The Federal Reserve's commitment to gold/money reserve requirements during the Great Depression, for example, overrode concern for the economy.

Frequently, in addition to the nineteenth-century Bank, regulators have forborne the strict application of requirements. Thomas Kane (1922, pp. 366–71), an official of the U.S. Comptroller of the Currency, wrote that in 1908 (shortly after the Panic of 1907) "probably 75% of the examiners' reports," and conditions reports of the banks themselves "disclosed violations of the law of one kind or another," calling for letters to the offending banks. However, the Comptroller did not think these letters were necessary and told a bankers' group that he had given "directions to the office force that no letters should be written to the banks which were calculated to annoy them. [H]e stated that the United States was the only country in the world that had such a foolish law, that the banks complained of its hardship, and that he did not propose to require them to observe it."

"Shortly after the panic or currency famine of 1893," large amounts of certified checks, certificates of deposit, cashier's checks, and due bills from employers arose (in convenient denominations such as $1, $5, ... $50) "to take the place of currency in the hands of the public." These served illegally to avoid reserve requirements as well as the 10 percent tax on state bank notes. "This temporary currency, however, performed so valuable a service in such a crucial period in moving the crops and keeping business machinery in motion, that the Government, after due deliberation, wisely forbore to prosecute. In other words, the want of elasticity in our currency system was thus partially supplied. It is worthy of note that no loss resulted from this makeshift currency" (Hepburn 1903, p. 374).

A. Barton Hepburn was comptroller in 1892–93, and afterward an executive of various New York banks. His successor, James Eckels (1893–97), also praised clearinghouse issues and officially denied they were currency. If they had been used as currency, he reasoned, the offending banks would have been fined. He became president of the Commerce Bank of Chicago upon leaving the Comptroller's office (U.S. Comptroller of the Currency 1907, p. 64; Timberlake 1993, p. 207).

NOTES ON ENGLISH POLITICS AND MONETARY POLICY

Governor Palmer testified before the 1832 Committee that the circulation should be in the hands of "a commercial company" such as the Bank, "independent of the Government" and therefore "less liable to abuse" from political interests. Adding in opposition to those favoring politically regulated money, he did not believe "that a bank formed of political individuals, or of commissioners, would have the same general knowledge of the commercial transactions of the country as a body formed of commercial persons" (Gregory 1929 i, pp. 1–8).

Bagehot (1873, p. 90) wrote of the origins of the Bank of England in *Lombard Street*:

> Of all institutions in the world the Bank of England is now [1873] probably the most remote from party politics and from "financing." But in its origin it was not only a finance company, but a Whig finance company [see Box 3.1]. It was founded by a Whig Government because it was in desperate want of money, and supported by the "City" because the "City" was Whig ....
>
> The Government of Charles II (1660–85) had brought the credit of the English State to the lowest possible point, ... and the Government created by the Revolution of 1688 could hardly expect to be more trusted with money than its predecessor. A Government created by a revolution hardly ever is.

BOX 3.1   PARTISAN POLITICS AND PUBLIC DEBT: THE IMPORTANCE OF THE WHIG SUPREMACY FOR BRITAIN'S FINANCIAL REVOLUTION

Political partisanship regarding the Bank developed from the cleavage in British politics after 1688 between the Tory and Whig parties, two coalitions for which members tended to vote cohesively in Parliament and which shared features akin to modern political parties. The Whig and Tory parties developed in a British social context that has been referred to as a "divided society" with individuals divided over both economic and non-economic issues. The Tory party was dominated by landowners and advocated policies like reducing taxes on agricultural income that suited Great Britain's "landed interest". Because the land tax was necessary to service the rapidly growing stock of government debt, many Tories also openly railed against Britain's "monied interest", at times calling for measures equivalent to a default on debt. In addition to their positions on financial issues, Tories also took common stands on non-economic issues involving monarchical prerogative, religious toleration, and involvement in foreign wars. In contrast to the Tories, the Whig party was a heterogeneous coalition made up of both members of "the monied interest" (in particular those who owned government debt) and those British landowners who shared similar preferences with the monied interest over issues like religious toleration, foreign policy, and constitutional reform. Credible commitment to service debt depended on the fact that members of the Whig party adhered to a party platform of continuing to service debt, favoring development of institutions like the Bank of England, and voting to maintain taxes necessary to repay debt.

Source: Stasavage 2006.

However, Bagehot (1873, ch. 8) believed the Bank's shortcomings, particularly its failure to comprehend its proper role in the monetary system, were due less to conflicts of interest than to the lack of knowledge – failures of training and experience. What was wanted, in place of temporary, essentially amateur, governors, was a permanent CEO, or at least a permanent deputy who was a banker.

Maybe. Maybe not. The dominance of an individual is not necessarily superior to the perpetuation of a culture rooted in the experience of an institution. In any case, Bagehot's advice was not adopted until by the force of circumstances, particularly the Great War, the Bank had become a public institution (although it was not officially nationalized until 1946). Walter Cunliffe, who had become governor in the usual way in 1913, was kept until the war's end in 1918, and Montagu Norman, after three years as deputy-governor, served as governor from 1920 to 1944. The performance of neither of these men lent much support to Bagehot's recommendation of long-serving governors.

The 1844 Act led to two more financial crises over the next 20 years, the first instigated by the American crisis of 1857, which had profound "repercussions on the British financial system," Hawtrey wrote. British "gold was withdrawn for export thither in considerable quantities [and] the credit of merchants and banks with American connections was shaken and big failures occurred. Distrust grew into panic, and the Bank of England had once again to meet a formidable demand for currency." Bank Rate was raised several times in October and November, but when the reserve kept falling, the Bank obtained, as in 1847, a letter from the Government "promising indemnifying legislation if the Bank should find it necessary to break the law limiting the fiduciary issue .... On this occasion the law was actually broken," although by a small amount (Hawtrey, 1962, pp. 25–6).

When the failure of Overend, Gurney and Co., the nation's largest discount house, was announced on May 10, 1866, there was an immediate rush for currency, and on May 11, the Bank received another indemnifying promise from the Government. The end of the limit on the supply of the currency ended, as before, its excess demand, but on this occasion, actually in September, after the next meeting of the Court of Bank Proprietors, the Governor explained the Bank's action. Bagehot considered this an historic action and described it in *The Economist* of September 22, 1866, as summarized in Box 3.2.

The Bank had behaved reasonably well on this occasion, Bagehot admitted, although uncertainty and panics would be reduced if it assured the market of its support from the beginning by continuously standing ready to be lender of last resort. Bank directors denied this responsibility, and pointed out that other banks held fewer reserves when the Bank of England increased theirs'. However, there were no financial crises after 1866 until 1931, for several possible reasons: because markets counted on the Bank's application of Bagehot's advice, consolidation improved the stability of banks, government budgets were in surplus after 1815, and/or lower tariffs reduced the problems of crop failures (Wood 2005, pp. 89–92, 112–13).

BOX 3.2   MEETING OF THE PROPRIETORS OF THE BANK OF ENGLAND (SEPTEMBER 13, 1866)

This meeting may [after much controversy and an unwillingness to admit its full responsibilities] be considered to admit and recognize the fact that the Bank of England keeps the sole banking reserve of the country.

"A great strain," the governor said "has within the last few months been put upon the resources of this house, and of the whole banking community of London; and I think I am entitled to say that not only this house, but the entire banking body, acquitted themselves most honorably and creditably throughout that very trying period. Banking is a very peculiar business, and it depends so much upon credit that the least blast of suspicion is sufficient to sweep away, as it were, the harvest of a whole year. But the manner in which the banking establishments generally of London met the demands made upon them … affords a most satisfactory proof of the soundness of the principles on which their business is conducted. This house exerted itself to the utmost – and exerted itself most successfully – to meet the crisis. When the storm came upon us, on the morning on which it became known that the house of Overend and Co. had failed, we were in as sound and healthy a position as any banking establishment could hold; and on that day and throughout the succeeding week we made advances which would hardly be credited. I do not believe than anyone would have thought of predicting … the greatness of those advances. It was not unnatural that in this state of things a certain degree of alarm should have taken possession of the public mind, and that those who required accommodation from the Bank should have gone to the Chancellor of the Exchequer and requested the Government to empower us to issue notes beyond the statutory amount, if we should think that such a measure was desirable. But we had to act before we could receive such power, and before the Chancellor of the Exchequer was perhaps out of his bed we had advanced one-half of our reserves, which were certainly thus reduced to an amount which we could not witness without regret. But we could not flinch from the duty which we conceived was imposed upon us of supporting the banking community, and I am not aware that any legitimate application for assistance made to this house was refused.

4. The Bank of England and the Great Depression

Chairman – Have you in view when you raise or lower the Bank Rate what are or may be the consequences to the industrial position of the country?
Norman – I should answer by saying that we have them in view, yes, but that the main consideration in connection with movements of the Bank Rate is the international consideration, and that especially over the last few years so far as the international position is concerned ... we have been continuously under the harrow.
–Chairman of the Macmillan Committee on Finance and Industry and the Governor of the Bank of England. (Montagu Norman, 1930)

This chapter is about the monetary policies of the Bank of England from the later nineteenth century through the heyday of the international gold standard to its downfall in the 1930s. The primary determinant of monetary policy was, as usual, the needs (or convenience) of governments. The stability of finance before 1914 was due not only to the gold standard but also, and perhaps as a consequence, balanced government budgets. The continuous, sometimes substantial, inflation since 1931 (prices had almost tripled by 1960), was due to the opposite.

Another influence was the changed structure of the Bank. Its private character before 1914, with its merchant-banker management, made it more sensitive to the public's economic problems than after its effective conversion to a government department during World War I, after which convertibility of the currency overtook economic stability as an objective.

CONTINGENCIES AND COMMITMENTS BEFORE 1914

We have seen that governments insisted on fixed money rules that might be relaxed if considered necessary by those in power. We also saw that some critics wanted contingencies recognized in law, a desire which gained strength from the events of 1847. An 1848 House of Lords Committee on the Commercial Distress asked

> ... whether the Restrictions of the Act of 1844 are not attended with grievous and unnecessary Evils. [An] Attempt to enforce by Law, under all Circumstances, one fixed and inflexible Rule for the Management of a national Bank of Issue seems inconsistent with the best written Authorities, with the general Principles of

Economic Science, as well as with the Testimony of many Witnesses of Practical Knowledge and Experience .... It has been shown that an Enlargement of the Issues of the Bank under a favourable Foreign Exchange, would frequently be expedient at Times, when, under the Provisions of the Act, no such Enlargement would be possible, and even in Cases where by the Act a compulsory Contraction would be enforced.

There was no better evidence of this, in the judgment of the Committee, than the Government's letter of October 25, 1847. However, although the necessity of abrogating the restrictions of the Act in the conditions prevailing at the time was unquestioned, the letter raised new problems.

> But even if those Restrictions were originally defensible when enacted, their Hold on Opinion, as well as their Authority in Practice, have been materially impaired by the Letter by which they were superseded – by its acknowledged Necessity and by its undeniable Success. The Precedent is established, and its Application will inevitably be called for on other Occasions; and it may so happen that the Principle of Relaxation will be applied under Circumstances less urgent and less justifiable than those which occurred in 1847. The Committee are therefore of the opinion that it is expedient for the Legislature to provide specifically for the Manner and the Responsibility of relaxing these Restrictions in Times when it can be done consistently with the perfect Convertibility of the Note – an Obligation which should never be forgotten.

The Committee cited the testimony of Samuel Jones Loyd: "You cannot build up in this Country an enormous and complicated System of Credit without being occasionally, under some very peculiar and extraordinary Combination of Circumstances, exposed to the Possibility of Panics seizing the Public Mind, which cannot be regulated by any systematic legislative Provisions, but which must be met, according to the Exigency of the Moment, by some extraordinary and exceptional Measure." Robert Peel and William Cotton, who had been the governor of the Bank when the act was passed, had also expressed their opinions that "such Contingencies will not be unfrequent."

The Committee wondered what had happened to the rule of law:

> To leave these Cases, when they do arise, to be dealt with by the irregular Exercise of the mere Authority of the Crown and its Advisers, setting aside 'once in Five or Six Years,' or even at Periods more remote, the express Provisions of a distinct Statute, appears wholly inconsistent with that Fixity and Order which it is, or ought to be, the Object of all Law to secure.

It understood the inconsistency of optimal plans, for which Finn Kydland and Edward Prescott (1977) became Nobel laureates: optimal short-term behavior may be inconsistent with long-term plans. For example, the discouragement of settlement in flood plains for reasons of safety is thwarted by short-term interests; and similarly for long-term prices and the short-term Phillips curve; and a long-term no-bailout policy and panics in the short term. Warnings of moral hazard may carry little weight in the short term. On the other hand, long-term plans may be approximately satisfied if there is a chance of discipline in the short term, called "constructive ambiguity" by Marvin Goodfriend and Jeffrey Lacker (1999).

> In conclusion, the Committee think it right to add, that, whilst they feel deeply the Necessity of a sound System of Legislation for the Bank of England, and for all other Establishments entrusted with the Privilege of issuing Notes as Substitutes and Representatives of the current Coin of the Realm, they are far from suggesting that it is upon Laws, however wisely framed they may be, that Reliance can or ought exclusively to be placed. The best Banking System may be defeated by imperfect Management; and, on the other hand, the Evils of an imperfect Banking System may be greatly mitigated, if not overcome, by Prudence, Caution and Resolution. In the Confidence universally and justly placed in the Bank of England the fullest Testimony is borne to the Integrity and good Faith with which its great Transactions have been conducted; and the Opinion of the Committee in this respect is best shown in their Desire to see vested in the Bank a wider Discretion than they possess under the Act of 1844 – a Discretion which the increased Knowledge produced by Experience and Discussion, and in which the Bank of England can hardly fail to participate, will enable them to exercise to the Advantage of their own Corporation, to their own Honour, and to the permanent Benefit of the Public, and more especially of the Commercial Classes of England. (House of Lords 1848)

Even so, the Committee thought some reorganization, "to obviate" criticisms of the Bank would not be amiss. It was glad to hear from Cotton that the Court of Directors had decided to abandon the principle of election by seniority and to select "as Governor and Deputy Governor the Directors they consider best qualified for the Situation." They also learned "that in order to secure the services in the Committee of Treasury of a Director [George Warde Norman], the ordinary preliminary conditions of having filled the Chair was dispensed with when the health of the party rendered his appointment as Governor inexpedient." Furthermore, Governors Cotton and Horseley Palmer had each been re-elected for another year because "continuity of action was required in consequence of the pending renewals of the charter." The committee was also attracted to a proposal of banker G.C. Glyn:

> I consider that it would be well that the Bank Court should have in it certain Persons not elected by the Proprietors, who should be appointed under Act of Parliament for a limited Time, or in any other Way which may be deemed advisable, not immediately by the Government or the Proprietors, and not removable by the Government, and that they should have, not an absolute Veto upon the proceedings of the Bank Court, but if they dissented from the Majority their Reasons for that Dissent should always be submitted in Writing, and that they should be laid before Parliament, if Parliament saw fit, from Time to Time. I think that the Introduction of these

Commissioners and their Protests and Influence would exercise a very wholesome Control upon the Body of Governors, and at the same Time would not deprive them of that Power of which as representing the Proprietors it would not be right that they should be deprived.

Public directors waited 80 years, however, and public disclosures of policy questions a century and a half.

In June 1873, the month in which Bagehot's *Lombard Street* appeared, Chancellor Robert Lowe introduced a bill "to provide for authorizing in certain contingencies a temporary increase of the amount of Bank of England Notes issued in exchange for securities" subject to the conditions that the chancellor and the prime minister were satisfied, *first*, that Bank Rate was not less than 12 percent, *second*, that the foreign exchanges were favorable, and *third*, that "a large portion" of outstanding notes was "rendered ineffective for its ordinary purpose by reason of internal panic" (Clapham 1944 ii, p. 289). But the bill got nowhere and was withdrawn, possibly because its terms were too "cumbrous and exacting" (Palgrave 1903, pp. 91–3). *Bankers Magazine* (July 1873) thought Lowe had put the trigger rate high to spare the Chancellor's responsibility.

Clapham (1944 ii, p. 290) thought "indifference to banking reform was no doubt a testimonial to the combined skill and good fortune of the Bank" in dealing with a variety of situations since 1866 – "from the quiet times of the late sixties through continental war, Parisian revolution, post-war trade boom and subsequent collapse, between 1869 and 1874." Not so after 1925. The Loyd–Peel–Wood aversion to explicit provisions for contingencies continued until the *Gold Standard Act of 1925*. Its declining confidence in the Bank's skill or luck finally led Parliament in the *Currency and Bank Notes Act of 1928* to adopt the recommendation of the Lords' committee 80 years earlier. The 1844 principle of a fiduciary limit was retained provided that "the Treasury may authorise the Bank to issue bank notes" beyond that limit if the Bank represents "to the Treasury that it is expedient" to do so, subject to the requirement that "Any minute of the Treasury authorising an increase of the fiduciary issue under this section shall be laid forthwith before both Houses of Parliament." The "exact significance" of this new contingency clause, T.E. Gregory (1929, pp. lix–lx) observed, "depends not only upon the terms of the legislation itself but also upon certain 'undertakings' given by the Governor of the Bank of England as to the manner in which the Bank intends to interpret the spirit of the Act." These undertakings were revealed to Parliament by Sir Laming Worthington-Evans, who moved and spoke for the Act on behalf of the Government.

Responding on May 14, 1928 to questions about the conditions under which the fiduciary issue might be increased, Worthington-Evans said: "I do not pretend to be able to forecast every contingency which may cause the Governor of the Bank to make the application and which may make the Chancellor of the Exchequer of the day agree to an increase in the fiduciary issue ...." But he indicated, in addition to events such as those of 1847, 1857, and 1866, "a new kind of emergency" had arisen because of the development of the sterling area. "Now that foreign banks have adopted the practice of accumulating a large reserve of sterling bills it is possible that owing to a change of policy on their part a large sum of gold might be withdrawn in a short time." On May 22, he reported to the House that "the Governor of the Bank has read what I said ... and he has authorised me to say that that does represent the general intention of the Bank." *The Economist* observed (May 12, 1928) that there are "many unknowns" in the new world of scarce gold and high and fluctuating prices. However, "We think the country may rely upon those to whom discretion is given to see to it that industrial recovery is not penalised for the sake of forcing our currency into a rigid mould." In fact, the country was already being subordinated to the currency in the overvaluation of the pound decided several years earlier, as we will see below.

In the event, the fiduciary issue was raised from £260 million to £275 million in the Bank return of August 5, 1931, to avoid a contraction of credit in the face of a loss of gold and a holiday increase in the note circulation (*The Economist*, August 8, 1931). This was a few weeks before the suspension of convertibility on September 21, by an Act of Parliament that also empowered the Treasury to regulate dealings in foreign exchange. The Bank's reserve was still substantial – notes of £56 million, 41 percent of deposits, in the Banking Department – and gold of £135 million. But the £200 million withdrawn from London since mid-July had been met largely by drawing on £130 million of foreign credits provided by France and the United States, which were exhausted. It was decided that continued convertibility would be short-lived and involve a needless waste of the remaining gold. Furthermore, the Government was unwilling to allow any further restrictions of credit in the face of 22 percent unemployment. "If, in the language of 1848, the price of convertibility of the note was to be a further disemployment of labour, the position had become untenable" (*The Economist*, September 26, 1931; Williams 1963).

CENTRAL BANKING AFTER BAGEHOT

> An opinion appears to have been entertained by some persons, though not by the Governor and Deputy-Governor of the Bank of England, that the Bank is released by the Act of 1844 from any obligation except that of consulting the pecuniary interests of its Proprietors.
>
> It is true that there are no restrictions imposed by law upon the discretion of the Bank in respect to the conduct of the Banking, as distinguished from the Issue Department. But the Bank is a public institution, possessed of special and exclusive

privileges, standing in a peculiar relation to the Government, and exercising, from the magnitude of its resources, great influence over the general mercantile and monetary transactions of the country. (HC, *First Report from the Secret Committee on Commercial Distress*, June 8, 1848)

This section is concerned with the two sides of monetary policy – its determinants and effects – from the appearance of Walter Bagehot's *Lombard Street* (and the adoption of the gold standard by the Western world) in the 1870s, to the outbreak of war in 1914. I begin with the effects of the Act of 1844 and *Lombard Street* on the attitude and behavior of the Bank of England, and find them small compared with other forces, old and new.

Monetary Policy and the Act of 1844

James Morris and Henry Prescott, respectively governor and deputy-governor of the Bank, testified before the *Committee on Commercial Distress*, of which Francis Thornhill Baring, grandson of the founder of Barings' and the chancellor of the exchequer who had called the Committee of 1841, was chairman:

Q2651. (*The Chairman*) Will you state to the Committee what you consider the effects of the Act of 1844 upon the responsibility of the Bank? – (*Mr. Morris*) The effect of the Act of 1844 was to create a separation between the two departments, the issue department and the banking department; over the issue department we have no control whatever, and the effect of the Act of 1844 is to oblige us in the banking department to look to the amount of our deposits, and the amount of reserve that we have for meeting our deposits.

Q2652. Do you consider that the Act of 1844 relieved you entirely from any responsibility as regarded the circulation? – Entirely.

Q2653. With regard to the banking department, in what condition did the Act place you? – It placed the Bank of England in the condition of any other bank, except that we were carrying on business on a much larger scale, and we had also Government deposits to deal with.

How might these answers be reconciled with the committee report quoted above and the answers that follow?

Q2654. It has been stated that the effect of the Act of 1844 was to relieve you from any other responsibility than that which you had to your own shareholders, with the view of making the dividend for them as large as it could be made; do you consider that the Bank was relieved from all responsibility as regards the banking department with reference to the public interest? – ... the issue department will naturally take care of itself; with respect to the banking department, we have a duty to the public to perform, and a duty to perform to the proprietors; our duty to the proprietors would lead us to make the best dividend we could for them; but in doing that we are bound to take care, considering the power that the Bank have, as a large body, not to interfere generally with the monetary affairs of the country. I have always considered that the two interests were united, the proprietors' interest and the public interest; I have always found that whenever a step has been taken to promote the interests of the proprietors at the cost of the public, it has invariably fallen back upon us, and instead of bettering ourselves we have put ourselves in a worse position. – (*Mr. Prescott*) I should say that in all the important measures of the Bank, such as in reducing or raising the rate of interest, the first thing that the directors look to is the public interest rather than the interest of the proprietors of the Bank.

Q2655. That is, you consider that the managers of the Bank are bound to look to the public interest more than to the particular interest of the proprietors? – They are bound to consider both.

Q2656. (*To Mr. Morris*) You consider that the two interests coincide? – Yes; I do not see how the two interests can very well clash.

This attitude of what was good for the Bank – or General Motors – was good for the country would in the next century be a source of amusement and alarm. But in 1848 the spirit of Thornton and Smith was abroad. And at least for the Bank of England that spirit and their attitude had considerable logical support. The Bank's disclaimer of responsibility for the quantity of money was not new. The directors had stated it to the *Bullion Committee* in 1810 and to the *Resumption Committee* in 1819. Macroeconomic outcomes such as the quantity of money and the price level were outside their control. On the other hand, they could not escape their involvement with the credit markets. Lenders have special responsibilities during payments crises; they must show forbearance or bring the structure down around them. Their survival is tied to the public interest. Attempts to impose these two distinct responsibilities – for the money supply and for financial stability – on the Bank thus generated distinct reactions by the directors – disavowals of the first and acceptance of the second. This was not changed by the 1844 Act.

Monetary Policy and Bagehot

The Bank of England had nearly always come to the aid of the market in crises, but belatedly and uncertainly, Bagehot complained, making matters worse before they got better. It would be better, he advised, if the Bank stood ready to act as lender of last resort from the beginning. In conclusion, he proposed three changes in the Bank's policies for the purposes of averting financial crises and reducing their severity when they occurred. First, "There should be a clear understanding between the Bank and the public that since the Bank hold our ultimate banking reserve, they will recognize and act on the obligations which this implies; that they will replenish it in times of foreign demand as fully, and lend it in times of internal panic as freely and readily as plain principles of banking require." The second proposal was necessary to the effectiveness of the first: since "the mind of the monetary world would become feverish and fearful if the reserve in the Banking Department ... went below £10,000,000," it "ought never to keep less than £11,000,000," and "must begin to take precautions when the reserve is between £14,000,000 and £15,000,000." Third, "We should diminish the 'amateur' element; we should augment the trained banking element; and we should insure more constancy in the administration" (Bagehot 1873, p. 12).

The Bank adopted none of these recommendations. Addressing them in reverse order, we have seen that notwithstanding the good intentions which had been expressed to the Lords Committee of 1848, there was no significant change in the appointment procedure or tenure of the Bank's managers until World War I, when the gold standard system assumed by Bagehot's recommendations had ceased to exist (Clapham 1944 ii, p. 418). A larger Bank reserve had been recommended by bankers/writers J.W. Gilbart and Thomas Tooke – their minimum was £10 million in gold – for the same reason as Bagehot's. They wanted the Bank to be in a position to neutralize the credit effects of gold drains. However, the Banking Department did not raise its reserve until the rise in the world's gold production and its own liabilities in the 1890s. R.H.I. Palgrave complained in 1903 (pp. 82–3) that the country's note and gold reserves were as inadequate as in 1844. The average note/deposit reserve ratio of the Banking Department was the same in the three decades after *Lombard Street* as from 1844 to 1873.

Criticisms of "the inadequacy of the nation's banking and gold reserves" increased after the Baring crisis of 1890. Governor William Lidderdale begged Chancellor of the Exchequer G.J. Goshen to say nothing in a forthcoming speech "that might imperil our 'very inadequate Banking Reserves.'" Goshen had been pressing for a larger reserve, but Lidderdale noted that "the larger the Bank's own reserves, the less the bankers like to keep *their* money unused." He had spoken plainly to the bankers within a few days of the crisis in a speech at the Guildhall; and now he "sometimes almost regretted having prevented the panic threatened" by his "assault" – "they are a stiffnecked and rebellious race, each caring only for his own corporation." He later observed that the banks seemed to sense danger when the Bank's reserve fell below £10 million. They then called in short loans from the market. Several times when the reserve had approached £9 million, "the demand on the Bank of England was *very* heavy." The governor asked the chancellor to press the banks to keep greater reserves. If the banks would not keep more, he would "look round for compensation in other ways, and these ways must produce the same result (less profit to the bankers, more to the Bank) as their leaving more money here" (Clapham 1944 ii, pp. 344–5; Sayers 1976, p. 33).

The Bank had gone in the opposite direction of the large reserves recommended by the Banking School (Tooke 1826) and Bagehot (1873). The discount rate of Britain's central bank was the most volatile in Europe. The Bank of England had apparently decided on a flexible rate as a means of economizing on its reserves in the interests of profit. Banker Palgrave (1903, p. viii) urged the opposite because "Great instability in the rate of discount is a very prejudicial thing to the interests of commerce and hence to those of banking."

So how good was the Bank's performance of its alleged responsibility as lender of last resort? Although it never followed Bagehot's recommendation of a public acknowledgment of that responsibility, it is possible, as is commonly believed, that the market came to rely on the Bank to behave as he had advised. Such confidence was hardly put to a test, however. The Bank had often come to the support of large firms, and under more difficult circumstances of speculation, external drains, and general economic and financial weakness. The Bank believed that Barings, despite having bet heavily on Argentine securities, was solvent (Clapham 1944 ii, p. 329), but that had not been true of Overend Gurney in 1866, when "there was so much unsound business ... that something like a crisis was probably in any case inevitable; the trouble could hardly have been got over with such smoothness as that of 1890" (Hawtrey 1962, p. 110). Another Bank historian, R.S. Sayers (1951), thought the development of central banking in the nineteenth century "hardly conscious," and Clapham (1944 ii, pp. 286–90) was skeptical.

So there was considerable uncertainty regarding the Bank's behavior under stress. Bagehot conceded, indeed emphasized, that it is not easy to know when to build the reserve and when to use it. "The practical difficulties of life often cannot be met by very simple rules: those dangers being complex and many, the rules for encountering them cannot well be single or simple" (Bagehot 1873, ch. 12). No simple rule being available to the Bank, we cannot expect to find a simple explanation of its behavior. Hankey, who remained a director until 1893, never abandoned the circumspect attitude that had been criticized by Bagehot. He thought Bagehot's advice too simple, insufficiently qualified. The offending passage in the first edition of his book in 1867 was still unchanged in the fourth edition of 1887. That he might, as Bagehot suspected, have been representative of the directors is suggested by Palgrave's complaint in 1903 of the apparent absence of a system in the determination of Bank lending rates: "A distinct statement of policy on the part of the Bank as to the course of action they would follow in any time of business pressure, as well as on many other points, is now greatly needed" (Palgrave 1903, p. 61). We have seen that Lidderdale almost regretted the Bank's assistance, and in the January 1875 *Bankers' Magazine* thought the Bank might reasonably refuse assistance to "a deputation from Lombard Street, which, after having turned their backs on the Bank for perhaps several years, might come on any day like the Black

Friday of 1866, with a message that 'our reserve is nearly exhausted, what can you do to help us?'" (Clapham 1944 ii, p. 343).

An unconditional commitment to provide liquidity must increase its demand. This had been understood by Loyd, Norman, and Peel, and was the basis of their dislike of guarantees. They anticipated Bagehot's argument and believed the possibility of refusal would render the need for assistance less likely. The moral hazard inherent in an easy lender of last resort has been termed "the Bagehot problem" (Hirsch 1977; Rockoff 1986; Wood 2003).

Financial Stability after Bagehot

The Bank was again authorized to break the law in 1857 and 1866, and in the former case, following exports of gold to meet a financial crisis in the United States, the fiduciary issue was actually exceeded. But there was no financial crisis between 1866 and 1914, the so-called "Baring crisis" of 1890 being known as the crisis that did not occur. Since every decade from the 1820s to the 1860s had experienced a serious crisis, it is natural to wonder why none occurred during the next half-century. We have seen that the improvement cannot be credited to monetary legislation or explicit policies of the central bank. Fortunately there are several reasonable explanations connected with the development of financial institutions and changes in the structure of production and Government finance.

The three main instigators of crises between the founding of the Bank and the middle of the nineteenth century were crop failures necessitating food imports, war finance, and fragile financial institutions. The first problem was solved by the repeal of the Corn Laws (tariffs and other restrictions on grain imports) in 1846, lower shipping costs, abundant North American wheat, and improvements in domestic agriculture. Crop failures became less common, and when they occurred were relatively less important. The proportion of wheat consumption supplied by imports rose from one-twelfth before the repeal of the Corn Laws to one-half in 1870, and four-fifths in 1914 (Ó Gráda 1981). The development of international finance and the credibility of the gold standard made it possible to finance trade deficits without resort to gold shipments or credit restrictions.

The pressures on London caused by the demands of the country banks in the 1790s, 1820s, and 1830s were a source of concern and eventually led to the elimination of legal obstacles to large banks beginning in the 1820s and limited liability in 1862. Bagehot (1873, ch. 9) remembered that when the joint-stock banks began to grow their critics had predicted that they "would fast ruin themselves, and then cause a collapse and panic in the country." Private-banker Loyd had testified to the 1832 Committee that "Joint-stock banks, being of course obliged to act through agents and not by a principal, and therefore under the restraint of general rules, cannot be guided by so nice a reference to degrees of difference in the character of responsibility of parties" (HC 1832, Q3306). Adam Smith had expressed similar views about joint-stock companies, but thought banking an exception because it "was capable of being reduced to a routine" of "strict rules." In fact: "To depart upon any occasion from those rules, in consequence of some flattering speculation of extraordinary gain, is almost always extremely dangerous, and frequently fatal, to the banking company which attempts it." Loyd, on the other hand, thought discretion especially important to banking (Smith [1776] 1937, p. 713; Bagehot 1873, ch. 9; Gregory 1929 ii, p. xliii).

Bagehot could write in 1873 that "The joint-stock banks of this country are a most remarkable success." They were just getting started. The years following the crisis of 1866 "witnessed a rapid change in the structure of the banking system." From the distribution of a relatively small volume of credit among a large number of banks, "by the growth of the joint-stock banks and by the process of amalgamation, a much larger volume of credit [was by 1914] concentrated in the hands of a very few banks" (Feavearyear 1931, p. 292). The number of banks fell from nearly 400 to 66, and the number of joint-stock banks from 121 to 43. Branches increased from one for every 13,000 to one for every 5,000 persons (Clapham 1926; Crouzet 1982; Ashworth 1960). The stability of the new banks contrasted sharply not only with the situation earlier in the century but also with the contemporary United States, where banks were still subject to severe branching and portfolio restrictions.

Fiscal conservatism and professional management in government finances also contributed to financial stability and the security of the Bank. Regular budgetary surpluses meant the Bank was not pressed to over-extend itself as in Pitt's time. Peace, a high credit rating, and alternative sources of funds through the Post Office Savings Banks opened in 1861, and the regular issue of Treasury bills beginning in 1877 all contributed to William Gladstone's objective of making the chancellor "independent of the Bank and the City power when he has occasion for sums in seven figures." The Government's independence of the central bank may be a condition of the central bank's independence of the Government.

Financial Stability and the Gold Standard

It is noteworthy that the post-1866 period of stability in Britain coincided with the classical gold standard, which is sometimes supposed to have been a source of economic fluctuations. Adherence to gold is commonly thought to have meant the subordination of domestic stability to the convertibility of the currency at a fixed rate of exchange. Specifically, economies were rendered vulnerable to the international spread of business cycles by the submission of national policies to the "rules of the game" that forced contractions of money and credit when an adverse balance of trade led to gold exports, and the reverse when the trade balance was positive (Keynes 1925; 1930, ch. 36). Certainly, the gold standard was responsible for the long deflation of 1873–96 that followed increases in the demand for gold (arising from the adoption of the gold standard by growing industrial economies) unaccompanied by significant increases in supply. The period also had its share of business fluctuations.

But the classical gold standard was more flexible than is sometimes appreciated (Panić 1993; Triffin 1968; Eichengreen 1985). The development of international finance made it possible for countries to incur trade deficits without being forced to undertake monetary or fiscal contractions. Some developing countries – notably Argentina, Australia, Canada, and the United States – ran deficits for long periods. Their ability to borrow was a function of their income (repayment) prospects, which in turn depended on the willingness of the advanced saving/creditor countries of Western Europe to buy their goods. It also depended on their commitments to gold convertibility, which guaranteed, for example, the sterling values of the currencies earned from British investments abroad. It no longer followed that a temporary shock such as a harvest failure would force a monetary contraction. Most financial adjustments were accomplished privately without systematic cooperation between central banks, although emergency credits occurred and governments sometimes borrowed abroad when money was tight at home (Bloomfield 1959, 1963). The gold standard may be seen as a commitment mechanism contributing to stability (Bordo and Rockoff 1996; McCloskey and Zecher 1976). Keynes's (1925) regrets of the costs of the gold standard arose from a situation in which the Bank was forcing a deflation to impose an overvalued pound on an unbelieving market.

BANKERS AND ECONOMISTS ON CENTRAL BANKING UNDER THE GOLD STANDARD

> There can be no doubt that under the Act of 1844 a sudden exportation of gold must cause a sudden contraction of the notes in circulation. This 'self-acting' machine acts by jerks, like a steam-engine without a fly-wheel; and its advocates look to the banking department to supply the fly-wheel, and to cause the machine to move smoothly and equably. It may be doubted whether the banking department has the power of doing this. But when this is not done, the advocates of the act throw the blame upon that department. They resemble the court preceptor, who, when the royal pupil did anything wrong, inflicted the beating on his fellow student. (Gilbart 1856 i, p. 141)

We have seen that the machine *was* made to run fairly smoothly, and the Banking Department deserves some of the credit. But its contributions arose more from doing what came naturally than to the conscious construction of an optimizing policy to fit the new legal environment. "Peel's Bank Act ... seemed [to Barrett Whale (1944)] exceptional in English legislation because it did not represent an attempt to deal piecemeal with the immediate practical problems, giving support in this direction, imposing restrictions in that, but gave effect to a clear-cut theory – that banking ought to be separated from the control of the currency." Nevertheless, the financial system continued on the course that had been developing. It could hardly have done otherwise. It is almost impossible that a whole new system can be imposed successfully on a complex social structure from outside, especially one in the process of adaptation to an environment that is itself in the process of change. The effects of such an attempt might in various respects be good or bad. But they will be unpredictable. In the case of the Act of 1844, it can reasonably be argued that the attempt had almost no effect. If inevitabilities in human behavior exist, they must include bankers' concerns for their reserves and the maintenance of their credit. The Bank Charter Act did little if anything to interrupt the Bank's development of a policy that, to the best of its ability in an uncertain world, balanced the competing goals of profits and safety – with attention, however imperfect, to the ramifications of the actions of a large reserve bank. Although Gilbart (who knew better but had his own axes to grind) and others blamed subsequent crises on the Act, they were neither more frequent nor substantially different than before. Bagehot opened *Lombard Street* with a pledge not to weary the reader by another book on the Act of 1844, the effects of which had been greatly exaggerated. The Act was "only a subordinate matter in the money market," which could be studied independently of the irrelevant principles and unrealized purposes of its promulgators. Modern readers are also able to determine whether the new central bank contracts and their focus on monetary rules are bypassed because of their lack of attention to markets and fundamental commitments.

Not only did the financial structure develop, to the admiration of Bagehot, independently of the Act of 1844, monetary policy also showed, as he deplored, substantial continuity with the past. And so it continued. The Bank's lending behavior at the end of the century would have been familiar to Governor Palmer. As in his time, the Bank had found that a Bank Rate equal to the market rate – or even below the market when its reserve was large – might in optimistic times invite unsustainable expansion. But a rate high enough for safety meant the loss of customers. So in 1878 the Bank "announced, in effect, that henceforth, however large the reserve might be, money would never be available *ab libitum* to all and sundry at market rate. To its own regular customers ... discounts would be granted at the competitive rate. But to the market generally, the other banks and bill-brokers, accommodation would be available only at Bank Rate, which, it was understood, would in future bear no definite relation to the competitive rate and would as a general rule be higher" (Feavearyear 1931, p. 283; *The Economist* 1878, June 15). Evaluated from the standpoint of a private institution, this enabled the Bank to maintain steady customer relationships while maintaining control of its reserve. From a larger perspective, it was also consistent with a lender of last resort.

But the Bank held a smaller reserve than Palmer would have liked – although he might have adjusted, as the Bank did, to the increasing effectiveness of Bank Rate. The main reason that Bagehot (1873, ch. 12) gave for a large reserve was that Bank Rate worked weakly and slowly; "for experience shows that between £2,000,000 and £3,000,000 may ... be withdrawn from the Bank store before the right rate of interest is found which will attract money from abroad, and before that rate has had time to attract it." The century saw skepticism toward an effective Bank Rate turn to wonder. The increasing sophistication of the financial markets might have been a source of its increased power. A related explanation is that "Probably this growing sensitiveness was partly due to traders having learnt what to expect. If, when Bank rate rose to 6 percent, they all expected one another to become reluctant buyers, they would respond as expected buyers, and business would decline without the rate being raised any higher" (Hawtrey 1962, p. 61). The Bank was accused of overconfidence, but it got away with a small reserve by means of an active Bank Rate. It had learned how to manage its reserve *and* earn a profit. The "ultimate answer to Bagehot's problem," according to Sayers (1951), was "a powerful Bank Rate weapon with a 'thin film of gold.'"

But there were costs. Banker Palgrave complained that Bank Rate was changed too often, economist Hawtrey that it was not changed often enough. An increase in Bank Rate tended to operate primarily by reducing aggregate demand, incomes, and the public's transactions demand for money, including gold. Changes required considerable time before taking effect, and the Bank was tardy in making them. Hawtrey (1962, p. 275) believed that "an incipient expansion can always be checked by a rise in Bank Rate [especially if assisted by open-market operations in government securities] (Sayers 1976, pp. 37–43). If the adjustments of Bank Rate are wisely and promptly applied, quite small changes will suffice."

The Bank was not unaware of the costs of changes in Bank Rate. A lender who withdraws support does not have to be told of the effects on the borrower and the borrower's dependents. When Governor Palmer was asked by Thomas Baring of the Committee of 1848 (HC 1848 Q2007, 2113; who knew the answer) how an increase in Bank Rate exerted its influence, he replied: "It presses upon all branches of commerce in a way that is most prejudicial to them; the raising of the rate of interest I am given to understand stopped very largely the mercantile transactions of the country – exports as well as imports." "It is by the interference with trade that it acts," Baring continued, "and not merely by the inconvenience that it occasions to holders of bills? ... It causes the stoppage of trade" (Hawtrey 1962, pp. 27–8).

The Cunliffe Report of 1918, in which the Government declared its intention to return to the prewar standard as soon as possible, acknowledged that an increase in Bank Rate restricted credit, demand, and employment. But Hawtrey, Keynes, and some other economists believed the postwar Bank and Treasury had forgotten the magnitudes of these effects. Hawtrey reminded them that nineteenth-century monetary policy had exerted its influence by acting on domestic demand, reporting the above exchange between Baring and Palmer. Keynes wrote in "The Economic Consequences of Mr. Churchill" (who had become Chancellor of the Exchequer upon the Conservative party's return to power in 1924) that "Deflation does not reduce wages 'automatically.' It reduces them by causing unemployment. The proper object of dear money is to check an incipient boom. Woe to those whose faith leads them to use it to aggravate a depression."

When Keynes wrote in 1930 (ii, pp. 273–4) that "it may be too much to expect that ... countries will voluntarily sacrifice what they believe to be their own interests in order to pursue ... the rules of the gold standard game," he was referring to a Bank and Government that – in direct opposition to the direction of social change – had reversed the order of priorities of convertibility and commercial well-being of which Mill had spoken, and in their haste produced a reaction against their long-term objectives that still dominates monetary policy.

CENTRAL BANKS WERE (STRUCTURALLY BUT NOT FUNDAMENTALLY) DIFFERENT AFTER 1914

Change was obvious in the United States, where the newly created Federal Reserve System assumed most of the monetary functions of the Independent Treasury and the New York Clearing House. But it was no less present in Britain, where without benefit of law, the rotating, part-time, amateur company of merchants which had managed the Bank of England since 1694 was replaced by a full-time bureaucracy. The next section tells the story of how the new institution, with an altered structure of information and incentives, approached an old problem in resuming the gold convertibility of the currency at the prewar par.

The new Bank faced severe problems from the beginning. The difficulties which had confronted the Bank at the end of the French wars, although severe enough, were less than after the world wars of the next century. A major objective in every case was the restoration of the currency, seen as essential to domestic stability and London's place in international finance. The big difference between the nineteenth- and twentieth-century situations was that, in the former, Britain had emerged from the war stronger than before. The industrial and financial revolutions were still underway in 1815. This lead had diminished in the years before 1914, and during the costliest war in its history, the nation had lost the most productive part of its population, major export markets had fallen to newly industrializing countries, London's primacy in international finance was threatened by New York, and much of its overseas investment had been consumed by the war. Its international position was severely weakened. Yet the post-World War I Bank was more determined than ever to restore the currency.

NORMAN'S BANK AND THE RETURN TO GOLD

The New Breed

No one could say after 1914 that the Bank of England was like any other bank. The Government had always been the Bank's most important customer, but after 1914 its business was dominant. The Bank in effect became a government department with a permanent professional staff, and governors who served at the pleasure of governments instead of shareholders. The change was most obvious in Montagu Norman's governorship from 1920 to 1944 in place of the traditional two-year limit (Figure 4.1). The Bank's nationalization in 1946 did no more than "bring the law into accord with the facts of the situation as they have developed," the Chancellor of the Exchequer told the House of Commons, nor did it, said the leader of the opposition, Winston Churchill, raise a matter of principle (Fforde 1992, p. 7).

Much has been made of Norman's professionalization of the Bank. He was not satisfied with its concentration of "City men," and wanted a "new breed" of full-time professionals without ties to their own businesses (Hennessy 1995; Fforde 1992, ch. 1; Clay 1957, p. 310; Sayers 1976, ch. 22). A grandson of George Warde Norman, Bank director from 1821 to 1872, and Sir Mark Collet, governor from 1887 to 1889, Norman began a merchant banking career in Collet's firm of Brown Shipley in 1894, and became a Bank director the traditional way in 1907. But he soon departed from tradition. Relations with his partners at Brown Shipley, never smooth, were severed before the war, allowing him full time for the Bank. After serving as an unpaid assistant to the deputy governor and then the governor, he succeeded Sir Brian Cokayne as deputy governor in 1918, and governor two years later.

Norman's position as the first long-serving governor enabled him to put his stamp on the Bank. Members of staff were made directors, eclipsing the outside directors. The collection and analysis of statistics was organized in a new section in 1921, and in 1925 the addition of an economist was considered. Should he be a follower of Keynes? "A man chosen from the Cambridge

School, if under the influence of Mr. Keynes, might perhaps have acquired this desirable aptitude [of applying economics to practice]; but if he had also followed this Economist in his progressive decline and fall, dating from his *Tract on Monetary Reform*, he would be worse than useless" (Hennessy 1995, p. 314). No permanent economist was hired until the Cambridge don Humphrey Mynors came to the renamed Economics and Statistical Section in 1933. However, some of the Governor's Advisors, posts initiated in 1926, were economists. These included Walter Stewart, on loan from the Federal Reserve Bank of New York, 1927–30 ("a kindred spirit" to Benjamin Strong as well as Norman, "a man of instinctive judgments, not given to writing lengthy memoranda but at his most effective in the Governor's parlour," Sayers (1976, pp. 621, 405, 462) wrote),

"I should think that the internal effect of the alteration of the Bank Rate is as a rule greatly exaggerated, that its actual ill effects are much more psychological than real."

Source: https://upload.wikimedia.org/wikipedia/commons/2/2f/Time-magazine-cover-montagu-norman.jpg.

Figure 4.1   *Montagu, later Lord, Norman; Governor of the Bank of England, 1920–44*

and Harvard's O.M.W. Sprague (1930–33), who in 1931 was foremost among those advising a high Bank Rate to defend and then to restore convertibility.

Executive Directors were introduced in 1932. Whatever the benefits of the Bank's vaunted "modernization," they did not make top management's life any easier. "The fact that Norman had undertaken an increasingly onerous and time-consuming burden of work," notes Elizabeth Hennessy (1995) in her history of the Bank's management, "had thrown a corresponding increase of work-load on the Deputy Governors, who continued to be elected on the old system of rotation," and "it was clear by the end of the 1920s that what was needed was a full-time deputy governor, without ties to his own business elsewhere." Ernest Harvey, who served in that capacity from 1929 to 1936, was promoted from the Bank's full-time staff, as was his successor, B.G. Catterns (1936–45). Gone were the days when the senior committee of the Bank consisted of part-timers linked to the City and trade who had become directors as young men to serve 20-year apprenticeships on their way to four years as deputy governor and governor.

Some of the "new breed" reflected the changing interests of the Bank as it turned from monetary policy to the "rationalization" of industry, which became an outlet for Norman's energies after losing the traditional functions of a central bank in the 1930s. The interests of the Bank had been growing away from those of the financial community, and of the private sector generally, since the war. Governments had always been disinclined to let the Bank fail, but any ambiguity regarding that position was ended by the war. It was unthinkable that the monetary authority would be altered except by Parliament. Finally – and here is where the Bank grasped the power that had been given to the Fed – through its prestige and single-minded purpose combined with divisions in government and the public, the Bank was able to secure and then maintain convertibility between 1918 and 1931 almost without regard to its domestic effects, including the profits of the private customers upon whom its own survival had once depended, and upon which Thornton had believed that satisfactory monetary policy depended.

Paul Einzig wrote in 1932 (pp. 32–3) that "more has been done to bring the Bank of England up to date during the twelve years of Mr. Norman's regime than during the hundred years between the Bullion Committee [1810] and the Cunliffe Committee [1918] .... Incredible as it may sound, a few years ago the Bank of England did not possess either a statistical department or even a foreign exchange department."

"[I]t would not be fantastic to argue," Clapham observed in 1944 (ii, pp. 416, 421), that the Bank was further "from 1914 than 1914 was from 1844; in some not unimportant ways further from 1914 than 1914 was from 1714." During and after the Great War, he wrote:

> Central Banking was everywhere developing into a thing distinct from banking; and the advice and authority of the Bank of England, in whose half-unconscious and sometimes rather unwilling hands the practices of central banking had originally been worked out, were respected, extended and sought.

Respect there may have been, for a while, but some of the benefits of these changes for monetary policy were unclear. Professionalism did not make up for the loss of information and the shift in incentives implicit in Bank management's remoteness from the economy. At the end of his examination of *British Monetary Policy, 1924–31*, Donald Moggridge (1972) wrote:

> To a considerable extent, the root of the policy problem in 1924–5 and thereafter lay in a lack of knowledge. Policy-making depended almost exclusively on the use of rules of thumb, often disguised as general principles, derived from an earlier, less complicated and more benign age. It rested on instinct rather than analysis.

"Reasons, Mr. Chairman? I don't have reasons. I have instincts," Norman responded to Lord Macmillan's interest in the establishment of the Bankers' Industrial Development Company (Boyle 1967, p. 327):

> We understand that, of course, Mr. Governor, nevertheless you must have had *some* reasons. – Well, if I had I have forgotten them.

Arthur Salter (1932, p. 13) wrote after the 1931 crisis:

> Instinct works with a subtlety, a precision, an exactness, an ease, a regularity, that reason cannot rival [nor can experience] – and with practical success, so long as the environment in which it works is unchanged. But our environment ... has changed.

Questioned by Keynes and trade union leader Ernest Bevin of the *Macmillan Committee on Finance and Industry* (Q3516 [Einzig 1932, p. 177]) Norman pleaded:

> May I say a word? Of course, you may complain of me, Mr. Bevin, or of those bankers you have seen, that the evidence they have given you comes through their nose and is not sufficiently technical or expert. Of course, that may in some measure be true; I plead guilty to it myself to some extent, and it is a curious thing, the extent to which many of those who inhabit the City of London find difficulty in stating the reasons for the faith that is in them. Mr. Keynes must know that very well.
> *Chairman:* Of course, I suppose even a trade union leader sometimes acts by faith.
> *Bevin:* And finds that it has been misplaced.

Financial events had led the new Labour Chancellor of the Exchequer Philip Snowden to set up a committee in November 1929 "to inquire into banking, finance and credit, paying regard to the factors both internal and international which govern their operation, and to make recommendations calculated to enable these agencies to promote the development of commerce and the employment of labour." It was chaired by the Law Lord H.P. Macmillan and included two academic economists, four bankers, three industrialists, three Labour representatives, and a former senior civil servant.

The correction of unemployment was the major economic problem in the view of Labour. On the other hand, financial stability, essential to the international position of the U.K., which depended on a stable pound convertible into gold at the traditional rate, was most important to bankers and Conservatives. They had dominated the decision to re-establish the gold standard in 1925, and even after 1929, despite the decelerating economy, gold had retained its hold on most financial and economic "experts," such as in Henry Clay's memo to the prime minister for the guidance of the National Government in August 1931 (Skidelsky 1967, p. 457):

> If the Gold Standard goes, the trade of the world would be plunged into a welter of depreciating currencies and fluctuating exchanges, in which traders will not know from week to week how they stand or whom they can trust.
>
> English currency means more to the world than any other currency. London is the chief centre of international banking, the agency through which a large part of Europe's transactions with the rest of the world are financed. If the pound goes the currencies of half the countries in Europe will also go …. Foreign countries that have trusted us will lose thereby – but no other country can immediately take our place and the whole of the world's financial relations will be thrown out of gear. Revolution will follow in Central Europe, leading possibly to the triumph of international communism.
>
> The industries of the world are depressed. Recovery can only come if confidence in the future is restored …. No blow to confidence could be more shattering than the departure of England from the Gold Standard ….
>
> Above all, the abandonment of the Gold Standard would remove the chief obstacle to inflation. The Government could incur expenditure without thought of covering it by taxation.

Bevin was unimpressed. For him, he wrote in his 1931 report to his trade union's Executive Committee, the financial crisis

> … has arisen as the result of the manipulation of finance by the City, borrowing money from abroad on … short-term … and lending it on long-term [as must be true of an international banker]. As is usual, the financiers have rushed to the Government … attributing the blame for the trouble to the social policy of the country and to the fact that the budget is not balanced. (Bullock 1960, p. 510)

Bevin (1881–1951) was born in a West Country village, orphaned at 8 years of age, lived with relatives, and left school aged 11 to become a laborer, carter, and lorry driver in Bristol, where he joined the Bristol Socialist Society. By 1910, he had become secretary of the Bristol branch of the Dock, Wharf, Riverside and General Labourers' Union, then, in 1914, a national organizer for the union, in 1922, a founding leader of the Transport and General Workers' Union, soon to be the country's largest trade union, and its General Secretary 1922–40. He was Minister of Labour and National Service in the wartime National Government and Foreign Secretary in the 1945–51 Labour Government (Figure 4.2).

Brilliant and tireless, confident, outspoken, and with an economic education derived from participation in several national study groups, Bevin possessed "an essential background for creative economic policy, and the necessary assurance to challenge [the financially orthodox] Snowden's recipe for economic recovery" (Skidelsky 1967, pp. 406–7). Beatrice Webb noted in her journal that, "Without being conscious of it, Philip Snowden has completely changed his attitude – from being a fervent apostle of Utopian Socialism, thirty years of parliamentary life and ten years of Front Bench politics have made him the upholder of the banker, the landed aristocrat and the Crown" (1985, p. 250).

"The most conservative man in the world is the British Trade Unionist when you want to change him" (Speech to the Trades Union Congress General Council, September 8, 1927).

Source: https://commons.wikimedia.org/wiki/File: Bevin_Attlee_H_42138.jpg.

Figure 4.2   *Ernest Bevin. Cofounder and General Secretary (1922–40) of the Transport and General Workers' Union, Minister of Labour and National Service in the World War II coalition government, Foreign Secretary (1945–51)*

Siding with Snowden was Ramsay MacDonald (1866–1937), who had been born into a laboring family in a fishing village in the north of Scotland, was a founder of the Labour Party in 1900, and its first prime minister (for Labour 1922 and 1929–31, and the National Government 1931–35). Economic conditions had worsened since Labour's victory in June 1929, the rate of unemployment rising from 7 percent to 11 percent a year later, on its way to 15 percent, but the Labour government had yet to find a policy. MacDonald unhelpfully told a Labour Party conference in October 1930:

> It is not the Labour Government that is on trial; it is Capitalism that is being tried. We told you ... that the time would come when finance would be more powerful than industry. That day has come .... We told you ... that the time would come

when the man who went into the workshop and into the factory, and his employer as well, would no longer be in the simple relationship of master and man, but that the master would become impersonal, and that powers that have nothing to do with industry would control industry – the powers of gambling with credit. That day has come. (*Manchester Guardian*, October 3, 1930)

Finance had indeed gotten its way, with policies uninformed by experience. The new Bank lacked knowledge even of an earlier age which had not really been so benign. In his attack on monetary policy in "The Economic Consequences of Mr. Churchill," referring to the Chancellor of the Exchequer during the 1924–29 Baldwin Government, Keynes (1925) declared that the decision to resume and then maintain the convertibility of sterling at prewar rates amounted to "*the deliberate intensification of unemployment.*" The object of the Bank's credit restriction was

> ... to withdraw from employers the financial means to employ labour at the existing level of prices and wages. The policy can only attain its end by intensifying unemployment without limit, until the workers are ready to accept the necessary reduction of money wages under the pressure of hard facts.

In the *Tract on Monetary Reform* published in 1923, from a series of newspaper articles, Keynes accused the Bank of a belief, unsupported by the facts, in the extreme form of the quantity theory in which the only effect of monetary change is on prices, without disturbing production or employment. While this may be true in the long run, adjustments in the interval are painful, but "in the long run we are all dead" (p. 65). Ricardo had condemned the Bank for its rejection of the quantity theory, but he would not have pushed that theory as far as the new management seemed willing to go. Keynes quoted Ricardo's 1822 speech in the House of Commons: "If in the year 1819 the value of the currency had stood at 14*s.* for the pound note [par 20 shillings], which was the case in the year 1813 ..., on the balance of all the advantages and disadvantages of the case, it would have been as well to fix the currency at the then value, according to which most of the existing contracts had been made." The pound – now customarily quoted in dollars – had a par of $4.86, and traded at about $4.40 when Keynes wrote, although it had averaged $3.75 in 1920–21.

When Norman told the Macmillan Committee that Bank Rate was "effective" in "preserving the stock of gold," the Chairman wondered about the side effects (Q3328–33 [Einzig 1932, p. 185]):

> One of the problems to which we have been addressing ourselves is whether the use of the instrument of Bank Rate, effective it may be in achieving the purpose you have indicated, may not be accompanied internally with unhappy consequences. You may be effecting an operation of great value from the financial point of view which has nevertheless unfortunate repercussions internally by restricting credit

and enterprise. Your instrument may be doing good in one direction and harm in another. I should like to have from you your conception of the internal effect of the alteration of the Bank Rate ....

Norman: Well I should think that its internal effect was as a rule greatly exaggerated – that its actual ill effects were greatly exaggerated and that they are much more psychological than real ....

Chairman: But even if it has psychological consequences they may be depressing consequences, and may be serious?

Norman: Yes, but not so serious as they are usually made out to be, and I think that the benefit on the whole of the maintenance of the international position is so great an advantage at home, for industry, for commerce, for [interrupted]

Chairman: You take the large view. In your opinion, I gather, the advantages of maintaining the international position outweigh in the public interest the internal disadvantages which may accrue from the use of the means at your disposal?

Norman: Yes, I think that the disadvantages of the internal position are relatively small compared with the advantages to the external position.

Chairman: What is the benefit to industry of the maintenance of the international position?

Norman: This is a very technical question which is not easy to explain, but the whole international position has preserved for us in this country the wonderful position which we have inherited, which was for a while thought perhaps to be in jeopardy, which to a large extent, though not to the full extent, has been re-established. We are still to a large extent international bankers. We have great international trade and commerce, out of which I believe considerable profit accrues to the country; ... a free gold market ... and all of those things, and the confidence and credit which go with them are in the long run greatly to the interest of finance and commerce.

The Return to Gold

The war effort had depended heavily on borrowing. The public debt increased from £620 million to £7,414 million between the fiscal years ending March 1914 and March 1919. Much of it was supported (monetized) by Bank lending, and money and prices had doubled. Monetary expansion continued for several months after the war, with the public debt rising to £7,810 million in March 1920. Prices rose 25 percent during the two years following the November 1918 Armistice (Capie and Webber 1985, tab. 1.1; Mitchell 1962, tab. XIV5). The exchange rate was maintained by controls during the war to assure American creditors of the dollar value of their British investments. American inflation was also high, but less than in Britain (Figure 4.3), and with the loss of overseas markets and much of the workforce, it was feared that the recovery of prewar conditions, including the financial system characterized by free exchange under the gold standard, would take some time.

Work in that direction began quickly. In January 1918, the Treasury and the Ministry of Reconstruction appointed the *Committee on Currency and Foreign Exchanges after the War* (called the *Cunliffe Committee* after the Chairman Walter, Lord, Cunliffe, Governor of the Bank of England, 1913–18)

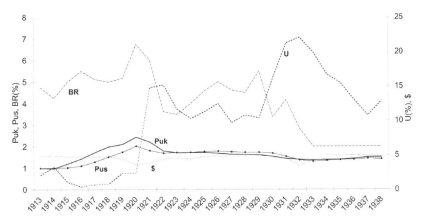

Source: Mitchell 1962; United States Census Bureau 1975.

Figure 4.3   *Bank Rate (BR), Unemployment (U), Dollar Value of Sterling ($), and UK (Puk) and US (Pus) consumer prices*

"to examine the problems of the transition from war to peace and to suggest appropriate policies," with members from the Treasury, the City, and academia (Moggridge 1969, p. 12). Its Interim Report, in August 1918, noted: "During the war the conditions necessary to the maintenance of [the gold] standard have ceased to exist. The main cause has been the growth of credit due to Government borrowing from the Bank of England and other banks for war needs." Its primary recommendation was (Gregory 1929 ii, pp. 334–70):

> In our opinion it is imperative that after the war the conditions necessary to the maintenance of an effective gold standard should be restored without delay. Unless the machinery which long experience has shown to be the only effective remedy for an adverse balance of trade and an undue growth of credit is once more brought into play, there will be grave danger of a progressive credit expansion which will result in a foreign drain of gold menacing the convertibility of our note issue and so jeopardizing the international trade position of the country.
>
> The pre-requisites for the restoration of an effective gold standard are:
>
> (a)   The cessation of Government borrowing as soon as possible ....
> (b)   The recognised machinery, namely, the raising and making effective of the Bank of England discount rate, which before the war operated to check a foreign drain of gold and the speculative expansion of credit in this country, must be kept in working order ....
> (c)   The issue of fiduciary notes should, as soon as practicable, once more be limited by law.

The last step meant a return to the currency rule of the Bank Act of 1844 – the "Cunliffe limit" – which had been suspended during the war. Resumption at a different par than before the war was rejected as firmly as a hundred years previously.

As after the French wars, the timing of the return to gold was much debated. This was partly because some were less committed to the gold standard, but many simply preferred to wait until the old system could be reinstated without deflation. They would have liked to see the pound rise to its old value freely, possibly because of an American inflation which ought to follow that country's accumulation of gold. The return to gold on prewar terms is a story of the triumph of a policy, with considerable reason and experience on its side, pursued by dedicated officials with a clear goal, over the more diffuse population that would actually bear the brunt of the policy but lacked an articulated, affirmative program.

The moderate stance of Cambridge Professor A.C. Pigou on the Cunliffe Committee was shared by several economists. However, his preference for a return at an unspecified opportune (relatively painless) time in the possibly distant future was too hesitant for the hawks. Sir John Bradbury, Joint-Permanent Secretary of the Treasury and a member of the Cunliffe and Chamberlain-Bradbury Committees wrote to an associate (Moggridge 1969, pp. 33–4):

> The general impression ... which [Pigou's written testimony to the latter Committee] leaves in my mind is rather flabby. "For the moment we propose to wait and see which way the cat jumps [American inflation and European exchange-rate policies]. If she jumps one way, and we can avoid jumping after her – and whether we can or not remains to be seen – everything will probably be all right. If it isn't, we shall be prepared to be a good deal braver than we are at the moment."
> I think that we ought to make it perfectly clear that we regard a return to a free gold market at the pre-war parity without long delay as of vital importance ....

By 1924, Bradbury was willing "to wait for a short time" for American prices to rise. But "we do not propose to wait indefinitely" (Moggridge 1969, p. 34).

Cunliffe's Final Report (December 1919) had waited for events before proposing a schedule for the return, as well as to consider changes suggested for the Bank of England. Regarding the latter, the Committee did not think that changes in the Bank's constitution and management beyond those made during the war (presumably the selection and service of the governor at the pleasure of the Government) were desirable. Regarding the former, the pound was turned loose in March 1919, and by November had fallen to $4.10. Its low of $3.38 would be reached in March 1920 (monthly averages). As in the United States, money and prices increased rapidly for several months after the war. The Committee could not recommend a date for resumption.

The inflation was followed by a sharp deflation and recession in 1920–21. Prices returned to approximate stability and the pound hovered near $4.50 for most of 1922–23. Unemployment stubbornly stayed above 10 percent, but officials were tired of waiting, and when the pound slipped in the first half of 1924, a Committee was appointed to plan resumption – chaired by the former Conservative Chancellor Austen Chamberlain, succeeded after he joined the new Government in October by Bradbury. There was some opposition to the gold standard among the witnesses and on the Committee, but most thought the return was a matter of timing. Norman wanted to go ahead, and asked for "a fixed and immutable date beyond all possibility of change and to leave me to work towards it." When it reported in October, however, the Committee recommended more "wait-and-see." It noted the deflationary "inconveniences" which would be involved in closing a 10–12 percent gap in the exchange rate, and suggested that the Government wait up to 12 months for American prices to rise. It proposed another look at the situation "not later than the early autumn of 1925" (Moggridge 1969, pp. 6–7; 1972, p. 50).

Table 4.1   *Parliamentary seats won in British general elections*

	Conservative	Labour	Liberal	Other
1922	344	142	115	14
1923	258	191	158	8
1924	412	151	40	12
1929	260	287	59	9
1931	522	52	32	9
1935	429	154	21	11

Source: Compiled by the author.

Table 4.2   *U.K. governments, 1922–39*

Beginning	Party	Prime minister	Chancellor of the Exchequer
10/22	Conservative	Bonar Law	Stanley Baldwin
5/23		Baldwin	Baldwin
1/24	Labour	Ramsay MacDonald	Philip Snowden
11/24	Conservative	Baldwin	Winston Churchill
6/29	Labour	MacDonald	Snowden
8/31	National	MacDonald	Snowden
11/31	National	MacDonald	Neville Chamberlain
6/35	National	Baldwin	Chamberlain

Source: Compiled by the author.

The pace was quickened by the results of the November 1924 general election (Tables 4.1 and 4.2). A shaky Labour/Liberal coalition was replaced by a large Conservative majority which set the political landscape for the next five years. Norman saw it as a green light, and visited the United States to negotiate a credit to support a fixed rate. Critics were still hesitant, and called attention to the already unusual combination of high unemployment and tight money. Midland Bank Chairman (and former Chancellor of the Exchequer, 1915–16) Reginald McKenna approved of the gold standard "on the whole," but in the short run, in present circumstances,

> You can only get back to a gold standard by a rise in prices in the United States relative to our price level. There is no other means of getting back. The notion that you can force prices down here until you get to the level of the United States if they remain constant [they actually fell slightly] is a dream .... The attempt to force prices down when you have a million unemployed is unthinkable .... You cannot get on the gold standard by any action of the Chancellor of the Exchequer .... He could cause infinite trouble, unlimited unemployment, immense losses and ruin, but he could not balance his budget while he was doing it, and he would have to begin again to borrow. (Moggridge 1969, p. 30)

The Bank and Treasury played down these effects and thought the undesirable consequences, if any, were worth the long-term benefits of the gold standard which should be secured as soon as possible. They were also willing to assume that American prices would begin to rise. When Churchill tried to allay fears by declaring that unemployment and falling wages had no more to do with the gold standard than the Gulf Stream, Keynes (1925) charged that he had been misled by his advisers, and was helpless because he had "no instinctive judgment":

> The Bank of England is *compelled* to curtail credit by all the rules of the gold standard game. It is acting conscientiously and "soundly" in doing so. But this does not alter the fact that to keep a tight hold on credit – and no one will deny that the bank is doing that – necessarily involves intensifying unemployment in the present circumstances of this country. What we need to restore prosperity today is an easy credit policy. We want to encourage business men to enter on new enterprises, not, as we are doing, to discourage them. Deflation does not reduce wages "automatically." It reduces them by causing unemployment. The proper object of dear money is to check an incipient boom. Woe to those whose faith leads them to use it to aggravate a depression!

Churchill lacked his customary self-confidence when it came to matters of finance. A quarter of a century later, debating another resumption and no doubt thinking of Norman and the Treasury civil service, he complained from the opposition front bench: "There is no sphere of human thought in which it is easier for a man to show superficial cleverness and the appearance of superior wisdom than in discussing questions of currency and exchange" (HC [September 28, 1949] 1803).

Moggridge found on examination of the records that Churchill deserved a better light. The decision was his responsibility, and he defended it publicly. But the records show that he was skeptical throughout, and resisted as much as was possible for a politician surrounded by experts all of one mind – and his instincts were sound. He asked questions and raised objections that could have been expected of an intelligent layman. His memorandum to his Treasury advisers and Norman in February 1925 appears in the Treasury files as "Mr. Churchill's Exercise." His questions/points – probably a combination of genuine doubts and solicitations of arguments to strengthen the case that he would have to make – may be summarized as follows (Moggridge 1972, app. 5):

1. Gold was a survival of rudimentary and transitional stages in the evolution of finance [Keynes and Ricardo had called it a "relic" of "a less-enlightened period"]. The nation was showing that stable money and credit could be managed without the gold standard.
2. Why is the United States so anxious that we return to gold? Is it in our interests that we share the costs of maintaining the value of gold?
3. What about the wider economic effects of the proposed return to gold? The high interest rates that seem to be required by resumption would administer "a very serious check" to industry, and leave the Government open to charges that it "favoured the special interests of finance at the expense of the special interests of production."
4. What's the hurry?

Churchill was sensitive to the go-slow preferences of economists and business-men who were reluctant to submit to the deflation that a quick return implied. Unemployment was 9 percent and rising. Would it not be better to let prices rise in the United States (with its surfeit of gold), and then resume converti-bility instead of resuming in the hope of American inflation? "Industrialists were perfectly well aware of the probable consequences of a return to the pre-war parity in 1925," Skidelsky (1967, p. 26) wrote, "but their warnings were brushed aside."

Churchill got little satisfaction. Otto Niemeyer and others in the Treasury focused on long-run benefits, and like Norman, minimized the short-run costs. Businessmen and labor leaders were dismissed as selfish and shortsighted inflationists. Norman declaimed from the moral high ground (Moggridge 1972, pp. 69–70, 271):

> In connection with a golden 1925, the merchant, manufacturer, workman, etc., should be considered (but not consulted any more than about the design of battle-ships) [even though, as we have seen, he admitted to being incapable of precise explanation. Only the experts, apparently were allowed to be guided by experts].
>
> Cheap money is important because 9 people out of 10 think so: more for psychological than for fundamental reasons .... The cry of 'cheap money' is the Industrialists' big stick and should be treated accordingly.
>
> The restoration of Free Gold *will* require a high Bank Rate: the Government cannot avoid a decision for or against Restoration: the Chancellor will surely be charged with a sin of omission or of commission. In the former case (Gold) he will be abused by the ignorant, the gamblers and the antiquated Industrialists; in the latter case (not Gold) he will be abused by the instructed and by posterity.

Still looking for a way out, Churchill referred Niemeyer to Keynes's criticism (in *The Nation*, February 21, 1925): "The Treasury have never, it seems to me, faced the profound significance of what Mr. Keynes calls 'the paradox of unemployment amidst dearth.' The Governor shows himself perfectly happy in the spectacle of Britain possessing the finest credit in the world simultaneously with a million and a quarter unemployed":

> It may be of course that you will argue that the unemployment would have been much greater but for the financial policy pursued; that there is no sufficient demand for commodities either internally or externally to require the services of this million and a quarter people; that there is nothing for them but to hang like a millstone round the neck of industry and on the public revenue until they become permanently demoralised. You may be right, but if so, it is one of the most sombre conclusions ever reached .... I would rather see Finance less proud and Industry more content.

Niemeyer replied that it was too late to reverse the engines. Since 1918, governments had declared for a return to gold as soon as conditions warranted, and the pound was trading at $4.80 on the foreign exchange markets, up from $4.30 the previous summer. A loss of nerve now would convince the world that Britain had never meant business, and no one could tell when another such opportunity would come.

A good part of the rise in sterling from November 1924 was speculative. Reinforced by the election, the Bank and Treasury reexamined the possibility of a quick return, and Norman visited New York to pursue the American offer of credits. Churchill wrote to the prime minister on December 12:

> The Governor of the Bank will, I hope, have told you this weekend about the imminence of our attempt to re-establish the gold standard, in connection with which he is now going to America. It will be easy to attain the gold standard, and indeed

almost impossible to avoid taking the decision, but to keep it will require a most strict policy of debt repayment and a high standard of credit. To reach it and have to abandon it would be disastrous.

Without any important change in the country's domestic or international situations, "imminent" resumption became a foregone conclusion. In its final report, submitted to the Government in early February, the Chamberlain–Bradbury Committee assumed convertibility in the near future. The timing of the decision had become a matter of circular reasoning: the price of the pound, which anticipated resumption at $4.86 (and the policies necessary to make it effective), was treated as evidence justifying resumption.

Chamberlain–Bradbury estimated that resumption would require an adjustment of about 6 percent in the price level, but expected the sacrifices involved to be "comparatively small." Keynes, on the other hand, thought that British prices and wages were more like 10 percent higher than in the United States. Figure 4.3 shows that the Ministry of Labour's Retail Price Index, after having risen one-third more than that of the U.S. Bureau of Labor Statistics' Consumer Price Index during the war, was brought to equality in 1924. Other indexes give other results, but none of them had much to do with Bank or Treasury thinking (Moggridge 1972, tab. 4). The final decision was made on March 20, 1925. Norman's diary records:

> Chancellor for lunch in Downing Street. Gold return to be announced April 6th or 8th. Cushion to be meanwhile arranged by Bank. I warn him of 6% Bank rate next month [it had been raised to 5 percent on March 5].

The announcement came as part of the Budget Speech on April 28, with the governor undertaking not to raise Bank Rate for at least a week. As it happened, the markets showed confidence in the Government's commitment. There was no immediate loss of gold, and the rate was not raised to 6 percent until October 1929, but money was still expensive compared with prewar periods of depressed trade, "another startling departure from earlier practice" (Hawtrey 1962, p. 134).

The rate was cut to 4½ percent and 4 percent in August and October, but when it returned to 5 percent in December, Churchill rang Norman in protest. The governor stuck by his guns, but the incident prompted a Treasury review of its relations with the Bank. A survey of former Treasury civil servants supported Norman's position that Bank Rate decisions belonged to the Bank. The Chancellor's wartime claim on the Bank's subservience (when Bonar Law declared that either he or the governor would have to go) had lapsed (Moggridge 1972, pp. 162–3; Clarke 1967, p. 102; Howson 1975, p. 35).

The pound and the Bank's gold reserve did well until 1929, the economy less so. The responsible politician and symbol of the increasingly unpopular decision was bitter. After another agonizing Budget Speech in April 1927, Churchill wrote to Niemeyer:

> We have assumed since the war, largely under the guidance of the Bank of England, a policy of deflation, debt repayment, high taxation, large sinking funds and Gold Standard. This has raised our credit, restored our exchange and lowered the cost of living. On the other hand it has produced bad trade, hard times, an immense increase in employment involving costly and unwise remedial measures, attempts to reduce wages in conformity with the cost of living and so increase the competitive power, fierce labour disputes arising therefrom, with expense to the State and community measured by hundreds of millions.

... the financial policy of Great Britain since the war has been directed by the Governor of the Bank of England and distinguished Treasury permanent officials who, amid the repeated changes of Government and of Chancellors, have pursued inflexibly a strict, rigid, highly particularist line of action, entirely satisfactory when judged from within the sphere in which they move and for which they are responsible, and almost entirely unsatisfactory in its reactions upon the wider social, industrial, and political spheres.

The hoped-for American inflation never came. Notwithstanding his pep-talks and promises of support for the pound, the New York Fed's Benjamin Strong led a policy that prevented America's gold from affecting its price level (see Figures 7.4–7.6). American consumer and wholesale prices fell 2 percent and 6 percent, respectively, between 1925 and 1929. British prices fell even more, and unemployment exceeded 10 percent. Churchill felt betrayed by the experts, and his Treasury private secretary remembered the venting of his anger on Norman:

> The events of 1925 and 1926 undoubtedly led to something very like an estrange-ment between the Chancellor and the Governor of the Bank of England. These two had some things in common – a profound sense of public duty, great vision, a pronounced obstinacy and desire to have their own way, jealous pride of posi-tion and so on. But they were totally unlike in others. Winston was a magnificent rhetorician. He also had a sense of mischief which kept creeping into his rhetoric. Norman was no talker. He found it difficult to assign reasons for the faith that was in him and he was not a believer in admitting anything in the nature of levity into the serious subject of public finance. Of course they met frequently – they had to – and this gave the Chancellor of the Exchequer abundant opportunity to make speeches about the evil effects of the gold standard – partly abusive, partly derisory and not entirely unmeant. The Governor retired more and more into his carapace, and the so necessary relations of confidence and candour ceased to exist. (Grigg 1948, p. 193)

The Tories were defeated in 1929 (MPs: Labour 287, Conservatives 260, Liberals 59), and McDonald's Labour Government promised to continue the defense of the pound. Its chief goal was the restoration of domestic economic activity, especially employment, but it accepted the bankers' argument that the traditional gold standard was necessary to that end even if it were attainable only in the (hopefully not so) long run. It had been assumed before the return to gold in April 1925, that the traditional instruments of central bank policy, such as Bank Rate, would deal effectively with the future as it had with the past. But the roles expected of governments and central banks had changed. Keynes's attitudes, Moggridge (1969, p. 90) wrote, were "symbolic of the changes occurring" when in his replies regarding depression remedies addressed to the Economic Advisory Council, he noted in July 1930 (Keynes' *Writings* xx, pp. 370–84):

> All the same I am afraid of "principle." Ever since 1918 we, alone amongst the nations of the world, have been the slaves of "sound" general principles regardless of particular circumstances. We have behaved as though the intermediate "short periods" of the economist between one position of equilibrium and another were short, whereas they can be long enough – and have been before now – to encompass the decline and downfall of nations. Nearly all our difficulties have been traceable to an unaltering service to the principles of "sound finance" which all our neighbours have neglected.
>
> This "long run" policy is a grand thing in its way – unless, like the operators of systems at Monte Carlo, one has not enough resources to last through the short run. Wasn't it Lord Melbourne who said that "No statesman ever does anything really foolish except on principle"?
>
> When we come to the question of remedies for the local situation as distinct from the international, the peculiarity of my position lies, perhaps, in the fact that I am in favour of practically all the remedies which have been suggested in any quarter. Some of them are better than others. But nearly all of them seem to me to tend in the right direction. The unforgivable attitude is, therefore for me the negative one – the repelling of each of these remedies in turn.
>
> Accordingly, I favour an eclectic programme, making use of suggestions from all quarters, not expecting too much from the application of any one of them, but hoping that they may do something in the aggregate.

ANOTHER SUSPENSION

During the election campaign of May 1929, Labour pledged both the defense of the pound and reduction of the large and increasing numbers of unemployment. Bank Rate was raised from 4½ percent to 5½ percent in February 1929, and 6½ percent in September along with the Wall Street boom and rising American interest rates. After the New York Bank's increase to 6 percent in August, Norman "urged on [Chancellor Snowden] the inevitability of a 6½%

Bank Rate" (Sayers 1976, p. 229). Then came the Wall Street crash in October, worsening economic activity, and a worldwide slide in interest rates, bottoming in May 1931 at 1½ percent for the discount rate of the Federal Reserve Bank of New York and 2½ percent for Bank Rate.

Instead of assisting economic expansion, however, the falling interest rates were a consequence of falling profits, economic activity, and borrowing. By early 1931, unemployment was more than double its value two years earlier. The Labour government faced difficult choices which Snowden tried to avoid, resulting in what has been called a Jekyll and Hyde performance (Skidelsky 1967, p. 320).

On January 14, 1931, while preparing his April budget, Snowden reported to the Cabinet on the financial situation. "The Budget prospect for 1931 is a grim one .... As each month passes with no sign of a lifting of the world economic crisis, the financial prospect constantly and steadily deteriorates." He stressed the need to take drastic measures to balance the budget. "There are disquieting indications that the national finances, and especially the continuously increasing load of debt upon the Unemployment Insurance Fund, are being watched and criticized abroad .... It is believed that there is a trickle of money being transferred from this country abroad. We cannot afford to let this movement increase .... Any flight from the pound would be fraught with the most disastrous consequences – not merely to the money market but to the whole economic organization of the country. It is imperative to take steps to combat this tendency, and to reassure the world as to our position." On the other hand, he would not advocate retrenchment because of his own convictions and possibly even more because he knew it would not be accepted by the parliamentary Labour Party or the unions.

Snowden and many others at home and abroad believed the credibility of the pound depended on the absence of a budget deficit, or "unsound finance." However, drastic measures were omitted from his budget. He "suggested that Members [of the House of Commons] neither should nor would expect him to provide for this by increased taxation. He expected [hoped?] that the recently appointed [bipartisan] May economy committee would find a solution to the political-economic conflicts."

Breaking with normal standards of ministerial and government responsibility, Snowden distanced himself from the statements and papers of Treasury civil servants. His assertion that a pessimistic "public Treasury statement merely expressed the private views of a Treasury official was a novel interpretation of the relationship between a Minister and his civil servants." McDonald commented that "This is not a document of Government policy ... it is one of those abominable things where really we will have to see whether we can put our foot down."

The first reports to reach the Bank of England "of distrust of sterling" started coming in after the middle of October 1930. Snowden had delivered a widely reported speech on October 15, in which he had said: "There is one item of national expenditure which is distressing me almost beyond measure, and that is the cost of unemployment [benefits]." He hoped to "be able to avoid any increase in taxation," however. "I think that the psychological effect of any increase in taxation will be very bad indeed .... I cannot say, but I shall do everything possible to avoid having to impose new taxation. Possibly I shall have to outrage my strict financial principles, and maybe do things that I could not justify in ordinary circumstances" (Skidelsky 1967, p. 321).

But borrowing for the unemployment fund was unbalancing his budget and would frighten foreign holders of sterling. He opposed on political and/ or economic grounds tax increases and tariffs, cuts in benefits, and budget deficits. Something had to give, and that was responsibility. No Labour government would raise taxes or cut benefits by the required amounts, and although Liberals and Conservatives were free with criticisms of Labour for their failure to act, they were unwilling to accept the electoral costs of doing it themselves. "Only a National Government would have sufficient authority to demand sacrifices from all classes. ... This is a question to be dealt with by no one party," Snowden told the House, "but in cooperation by all three parties in the House of Commons" (Skidelsky 1967, pp. 330–35).

The Government took the time-honored course of delay by committee. On March 17, 1931, the prime minister announced the appointment of Sir George May, retiring secretary of an insurance company, as chairman of the Economy Committee. Four of the other six members were also businessmen and two were trade union leaders, with terms of reference "to make recommendations to the Chancellor of the Exchequer for effecting forthwith all possible reductions in National Expenditure" (Skidelsky 1967, pp. 330–35).

Snowden presented his admittingly stop-gap budget on April 27. He accepted the prospective deficit, quoting Gladstone in saying that "it will be the duty of Parliament to deal with the matter when better times return." He rejected an increase in direct taxation because of its "depressing effect on industry," as well as a revenue tariff, which was simply a device for "relieving the well-to-do at the expense of the poor."

He put off hard decisions until August, hoping for better times, or if not, "national unity," suggesting that the parties might unite to push through harsh measures. In the meantime, the July 31 report of the May committee predicted a £120 million deficit, of which, the five business men on the committee advised, £24 million should be met by increased taxation and £96 million by economies, mostly at the expense of the unemployed, whose relief should be cut 20 percent. The two Labour men dissented, instead advocating more government spending, but they were ignored and Snowden and the Treasury had their ammunition for a stern budget (Taylor 1965, p. 288).

The cabinet set up an economy committee of its own, including MacDonald and Snowden, to study the May Report, and Parliament recessed until the autumn. The first meeting of the cabinet economy committee was scheduled for August 25, but on August 11, MacDonald was abruptly called to London to meet with an assembly of bankers who told him there was a run on the pound. Sir Ernest Harvey, Deputy Governor of the Bank of England, and Bank Director Edward Peacock informed the Government (1) that "we were on the edge of the precipice and unless the situation changed rapidly, we should be over it directly"; (2) that the cause of the trouble was not financial but political, and lay in the complete want of confidence in His Majesty's Government existing among foreigners; (3) that the remedy was in the hands of the Government alone.

This was hard analysis, but it had considerable support among "responsible" "experts." It was no good blaming the bankers and speculators, they said. The Government had to adopt measures that would end the "crisis of confidence" which threatened the pound. These by common responsible consent (particularly abroad) included a balanced budget. The *Le Temps* of August 12 said:

> It is truly disquieting, in view of the gravity of the financial situation in England, to see responsible organs of opinion insisting on throwing onto other countries the responsibility for a crisis, the fundamental cause of which, as the May Report has established, is the bad administration of the finances.

This view, which MacDonald and Snowden (at least implicitly) accepted, absolved the bankers of responsibility. Nothing (contrary to MacDonald's 1930 Labour conference speech) was wrong with the financial system, which therefore did not need to be changed (such as devaluation or going off gold), but rather the Labour government's social policies (such as unemployment benefits) which threatened a balanced budget.

"To accept this advice meant also to accept the orthodox financial system which Bevin and others in the Labour Party believed incompatible with socialist objectives, and which in any case they were convinced could no longer be made to work," Bevin's biographer wrote. Bevin's and the Trades Union Congress's view was that "the currency system based on the Gold Standard was breaking down." This was not a question of theory or ideology, but "a question of fact" (Bullock 1960, p. 478).

"I am not aware at the moment as to the actual line the Government proposes to take," Bevin wrote, "but our attitude to the problem must be perfectly clear. We must stand firm for the equitable distribution of the new burdens [if the Government's attempt to save gold continued] over the community as a whole, based upon the capacity to pay. The City must not be saved at the expense of the working class and the poorest of our people" (Bullock 1960, p. 480).

So the immediate problem for the Labour leadership was how to carry economies in the social services which would not only be deeply unpopular in the Labour Party, but also widely resented in the country (Skidelsky 1967, p. 389). The prime minister and the chancellor set out "to get the Oppositions to share with the Government the electioneering risks of cutting the social services." After meeting with the bankers, the Cabinet economy committee learned from a Treasury spokesman that the budget deficit was greater than they had been told, but – although it was generally believed the Labour Party would not accept a cut in workers' benefits sufficient for a balanced budget – MacDonald denied rumors of a split and said that "We are of one mind. We intend to balance the budget."

He could not count on his Party, however, and in any case did not want to be seen as traitor to the cause of protecting workers. So Labour leaders began to negotiate joint blame with the other parties, who finally agreed to the principles of equality of sacrifice and responsibility (Howson 1975, pp. 69–70).

On August 20, five members of the Cabinet attended a joint meeting of Labour's National Executive Committee and the General Council of the Trades Union Congress. Snowden's attendance was against his better judgment because he did not believe the TUC had any right to be consulted on Cabinet policy. Nevertheless, MacDonald led off the meeting with a review of the financial situation and drifted into the Cabinet's thinking in a speech that Bevin later characterized as "not worthy of an ordinary shop steward reporting the settlement of a local wage problem":

> There is no change of policy. If anything has to be suspended it will be restored as soon as the Government is in a position to restore it. There is no abandoning of principles, only bowing to necessities. Everyone responsible for a department is a Trade Unionist, or a Socialist, or both, and the meeting can trust us.

Union leaders, however, were unpersuaded of the necessity of a gold standard or the benefits of a balanced budget. They would not accept cuts in unemployment benefits, wages, or public works projects.

Snowden replied that in normal times the Government would agree with the General Council's position. But if sterling went, the whole international financial structure would collapse, and "there would be no comparison between the present depression and the chaos and ruin that would face us in that event. There would be millions more unemployed and complete industrial collapse." Bevin disputed this statement, and the meeting ended with the cabinet and union positions unchanged (Skidelsky 1967, pp. 409, 412; Weiler 1993, pp. 60–62).

Bevin contested finance in the best of times, and unsuccessfully stood for Parliament in the industrial constituency of Gateshead in the catastrophic 1931 election (when the number of Labour members fell from 287 to 52) on the major plank of the need "to socialize credit and impose control over the 'one man [Norman] who is exercising greater power than any autocratic king ever exercised in the history of Great Britain.'"

The Government, with considerable support, was determined:

> The refusal of the TUC to move one inch to ease [the prime minister's] difficulties, their overt attempt to dictate terms to an elected Government outraged his political conscience, aroused his personal vindictiveness, and steeled his resolve. (Nicolson 1952, p. 589)

The *Manchester Guardian* of August 22 found it

> ... a sad commentary on the machinery of democratic government that it should be possible for a body of thirty men, meeting with no preparation and discussing half-revealed proposals in a desultory fashion for several hours, to jeopardize the existence of a government.

Wasn't this in fact an exercise of democracy in which many groups, including bankers, apply their political influences as best they can? It is neither surprising nor illogical that strongly held positions were unmoved by half-revealed, obviously insincere, promises.

With the benefit of hindsight, moreover, a pretty good case can be made for the unions' position. Those countries leaving gold or devaluing in 1931, were in positions to suspend their deflationary policies and increase their spending, and as a group, including the U.K., recovered more quickly than those who did not (Eichengreen and Sachs 1985). In the longer term, however, as traditionalist monetary authorities had predicted, the loss of the gold constraint really did mean runaway inflation. British retail prices rose 14 times (at an annual rate of 5.3 percent) during the next 50 years.

The Treasury and the Bank of England tried again to "sound out" the possibility of more credits from the Federal Reserve Bank of New York. The response was "probably yes" conditional on sufficient budget economy, but this the Government could not promise. MacDonald was on the verge of resigning when it was arranged that the party leaders meet with the king, who requested him to lead a National Government "to deal with the national emergency that now exists." Baldwin was willing to serve under MacDonald, and share the ignominy of the unpopular policies.

The new cabinet was small, ten members: four Conservatives, four Labour (including Snowden at the Exchequer), and two Liberals. The Conservatives in Parliament unanimously endorsed the new Government, and all but one liberal, but only 12 from Labour (eight backbenchers in addition to the four in the Cabinet). The Labour majority's position soon hardened. They felt their leaders had succumbed to a bankers' conspiracy, "intrigued out of office by a ruthless and unscrupulous capitalist class" (Taylor 1965, p. 295). Branded as a traitor, MacDonald was expelled from the party, but Parliament passed Snowden's emergency budget on September 8.

The prospective deficit was eliminated by raising income taxes and cutting spending. Wages "paid by the state, from cabinet ministers and judges down to the armed services and the unemployed, were cut 10 percent"; except police 5 percent and teachers 15 percent. A bankers' credit of £80 million from Paris and New York bolstered the pound for a few days, but the final blow to confidence came on September 15 when sailors of the Atlantic Fleet at Invergordon mutinied against their pay cuts. On September 19, the Bank reported that its foreign credits were exhausted, and on September 21, Parliament suspended the gold standard.

The pound fell from $4.86 to $3.80, then $3.23, and fluctuated around $3.40 until the U.S. devaluation of mid-1933, then in the $4.90s until the beginning of war in 1939. None of the predicted financial disasters occurred. Deflation ceased, unemployment fell, and money and then output rose. The budget, helped by increased income taxes and reduced unemployment benefits, was balanced despite the substantial armaments program.

Notwithstanding the strenuous efforts they had made to maintain the gold standard, the City and the authorities received the news of the suspension calmly:

> The suspension of the gold standard caused no panic in London. Markets were confused and hesitant, and the Stock Exchange was closed for a couple of days; but there was no suggestion of a run on banks and no signs of any flight of capital …. By the end of the month, the Exchange with New York had settled down to a rate around 3.90. Opinion at home and abroad was reassured by a balancing of the Budget and by the return of a National Government at a general election on October 27 by a large majority. (Clay 1957, pp. 399–400)

Some at the Bank, especially Norman, saw the event as a disaster, but most there and at the Treasury, having tried their best, and failed, thought it was imperative that they settle on a policy that made the most of the situation. The gold standard might play a part in the policy, but it would not be an end in itself. The ends would lay in the domestic economy, especially price stability and employment.

Bank Rate had been raised from 4½ percent to 6 percent upon the announcement of the suspension, and some talked in terms of "temporary" and "early return," but on September 26, the Prime Minister's Committee on Financial Questions "was unanimous in holding that it would be a great mistake if the

Bank of England were to make it their aim to return to the gold standard at the old parity as soon as circumstances permit it," that is, to repeat its error of 1925.

On September 29, after pointing out that long-term financial policy was a matter for the Government rather than the Bank, the Committee told the prime minister that the Bank should be confined to keeping sterling within certain limits, about which it might be consulted. The pound remained strong, and Bank Rate was reduced in steps to 2 percent in June 1932, where it remained (except for two months at the outbreak of war in 1939) until in 1951 the new Conservative Chancellor, "after the most careful consultation with the governor of the Bank of England," raised it to 2½ percent (Sayers 1976, p. 573).

5. The Bank of England after the Great Depression

Whatever longer-term effects Suez [October 1956] may prove to have on the economy, it has certainly had the immediate effect of laying bare to the public eye, both at home and abroad, some of the weakness of which we have long been conscious.
You and I have, I think, both felt that the measures of the last few years, including the credit squeeze and various fiscal adjustments made by your predecessor and yourself, have helped to move the economy towards an uneasy equilibrium but have left some basic problems untouched. We have over the last five years been able to maintain our position on a see-saw, retaining just adequate confidence in the currency by a slender margin. After the events of the past few months I do not believe this is good enough.
–Governor Cameron Cobbold to
Chancellor Harold Macmillan. (Fforde 1992, p. 544)

The world's monetary history since World War II has to a large extent been the search for a system to replace the international stability of the idealized pre-1914 gold standard while accommodating domestic demands for growth, and as always, satisfaction of the government-of-the day's financial and political preferences. That history as it relates to the United Kingdom is the subject of the present chapter, and may be summarized with the help of Table 5.1 and Figures 5.1 and 5.3.

The 1945–51 period of the Labour government's "cheap money" policy, in which low interest rates were treated as virtually a moral obligation, and the resulting inflation are seen at the beginning, although the inflationary spike during the Korean War probably would have happened regardless of the monetary policy in view. The higher interest rates of 1951–70 reflected a rediscovery of interest as a price/rationing device but especially the upward drift of inflation. The problems arising from the Bank's (and Government's) attempt to have it both ways – economic growth without inflation – are alluded to in the opening epigraph to the chapter. The costs of neglecting the domestic prewar economy weighed heavily on the post-Keynesian Bank, but it still had (and was forced to have by the IMF) long-run price and exchange-rate goals. The end of a meaningful IMF (as an enforcer or coordinator of fixed exchange rates) in the early 1970s was followed by double-digit inflation until it was forcibly reduced by the public's reactions.

Table 5.1   Timeline of major U.K. monetary events, 1945–97

1945	Creation of the IMF
1945	The American loan
1947	Suspension of convertibility
1949	Devaluation of £ from $4.20 to $2.80
1956	Suez (run on reserves)
1957–66	Stop–go. Deflationary crisis measures of Thorneycroft (1957), Lloyd (1961), and Wilson (1966), and reflationary budgets of Amory (1959) and Maudling (1963)
1964–67	Callaghan's "bitter harvest," Jenkins's repression, and finally devaluation of the £ to $2.40
1971	Nixon closes gold window; end of IMF fixed rate system
1971–74	Heath–Barber inflation; attempted 5% growth brought stagnation and a rise in inflation from 6% in 1970 to 25% inflation in 1975
1976	Callaghan's "winter of discontent" and discovery that the "cosy world" in which "you could spend your way out of a recession … no longer exists"
1979–90	Prime Minister Margaret Thatcher, monetarism, and fall in inflation from double-digits to 4%
1997	After a resurgence (1988–90), inflation was reduced to 2%, and inflation targeting as agreed between the Chancellor and the governor was enacted by the new Labour Government

Source: Compiled by the author.

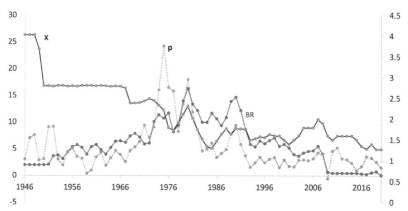

Source: Compiled by the author.

Figure 5.1   U.K. inflation (p, left), Bank Rate (BR, right), and U.S./U.K. exchange rate (X, right)

THE AMERICAN LOAN, BRETTON WOODS, AND THE 1947 RESUMPTION

Britain emerged from World War II as "the greatest debtor in the history of the world" (Sayers 1956, p. 486). Its overseas liabilities had increased five-fold between 1939 and 1945, to $14 billion compared with gold and dollar reserves of $2 billion. Most of its foreign assets had been liquidated. Even with "considerable austerity" enforced by "strict controls" on imports, a trade deficit of $3.2 billion was projected for 1946, according to Keynes's paper for the Cabinet in August 1945 (Keynes 1980, pp. 427–51).

Keynes's position as chief negotiator for Bretton Woods and the American loan might have owed as much to the Treasury's low stature as to his own talents. "Churchill had a fixed antipathy to the 'Treasury view,'" Skidelsky (2000, p. 158) wrote, "which he believed had misled him as chancellor in the 1920s and postponed rearmament in the 1930s .... On the other hand, Churchill had considerable respect for Keynes, whom he judged to have been right over the gold standard .... The Treasury's incorporation of Keynes can be seen as a shrewd move in its longer-term effort to gain control over economic policy."

Britain's war deficits had been financed by borrowing in the empire and American Lend-Lease, of which $2 billion per year was for non-munitions, the necessities of life. This was to continue for the duration of the war, and might provide "breathing space" to "allow some rebuilding of our export trade" since the war in the Pacific was expected to last for a year or two after Germany's surrender in April 1945 (Dow 1964, p. 17). However, Japan surrendered in less than four months and Lend-Lease was terminated immediately. The population faced lower living standards than in wartime. They had a debt "which no one else will be expected to carry," Keynes said, "not even the defeated enemy."

"There seemed no alternative but to seek a loan from the United States," recalled government economist, J.C.R. Dow (1964, p. 17). "But 'three months of very intricate discussions and some very hard bargaining' [quoting Chancellor Hugh Dalton's defense of the agreement in the House of Commons in December 1945], showed that a loan could only be had at a price; and the price aroused the deepest misgiving."

> Misgiving was due less to the financial terms of the loan than to the other conditions attached. It was a condition, first, that the United Kingdom should accept the Bretton Woods proposals for the International Monetary Fund and the International Bank. These would undoubtedly have been accepted in any case, though far less abruptly ....
>
> Even more onerous was the required undertaking to restore convertibility almost immediately. In the Bretton Woods negotiations the United Kingdom had insisted on remaining free to maintain exchange controls on current transactions for a transition period of five years ... But under the Loan Agreement, she had to agree to

restore the convertibility of sterling within one year of the agreement coming into operation.

Britain's was slated to become, within 18 months, the only convertible currency in the world except for the United States. "The debate in the House was therefore a scene of gloom and disillusion." Dalton had to confess that the commitment had been made "with very great reluctance." The former Chancellor Churchill, who had suffered a less precipitate resumption, told the House of Commons that the agreement was "so doubtful and perilous that the best hope is that in practice it will defeat itself, and that it is in fact too bad to be true" (Gardner 1956, p. 230). "We are sitting here today as the representatives of a victorious people, discussing the consequences of victory," said Tory MP Oliver Stanley. "If a visitor were to come ... from Mars ... he might well be pardoned for thinking that he was listening to the representatives of a vanquished people discussing the economic penalties of defeat" (Dow 1964, p. 18).

The Bank of England had opposed the arrangements with the United States, and indeed the entire line of thinking behind the British negotiations, but was left to carp from outside. Keynes had supported the arrangements as part of

> ... an ideal system which would solve the problem on multilateral lines by international agreement. This is an ambitious scheme. But the post-war world must not be content with patchwork. (Treasury memorandum, Dow 1964, p. 37)

The Bank "expressed support for Keynes' ultimate international objectives," Fforde (1992) records in his history of the Bank, but was "a consistent and determined critic of almost all his practical proposals for attaining them." It was skeptical of the early restoration of convertibility and free trade "that was passionately advocated by the U.S. Treasury and State Department." The Bank and Keynes's critics in the Treasury felt that he had succumbed to the Washington atmosphere of grand designs. Investment banker Robert (later Lord) Brand, the Treasury's representative in Washington, thought Keynes's approach "a great leap in the dark, ... a gamble, even if the world goes moderately well" (Dow 1964, pp. 33, 70).

Keynes realized that Britain had to conform to American wishes, and rejected these words of caution: "[T]his is not a case where we can muddle through without a drastic solution, grasping no nettles and just hoping it will be all right on the day" (Dow 1964, p. 93). "I favour an eclectic programme" rather than "principle" he had said in 1930 (see Chapter 4), but he and the Bank had exchanged positions. In a letter prepared for presentation by His Majesty's government to the U.S. government, the Bank argued as follows (in what amounted to a recant of its interwar policies):

> The discussions throughout have tended to assume two entirely different phases: (i) a transitional period and (ii) the final post-war period ("when things have settled down") when it may or may not be possible to introduce a completely new economic plan.
>
> This is, it seems to us, a somewhat misleading picture both for our own working and for presentation to others. The cardinal mistake and the greatest admission of defeat which we can make is to put up as a final objective something which we do not believe has a reasonable chance of coming about. We must set ourselves aims in which we believe and our policy must from the start be directed towards bringing them about. Progress can only be by trial and error but we must constantly strive to form and adapt our controls and our international economic relations with the ultimate goals always in view. We must never allow ourselves to contemplate a static transitional period and hope that on a given date one, two, two or three years after the war the heavens will open and our problems will be solved.
>
> It has come to be believed that exchange controls and trade controls are inevitably destructive and restrictive. On the contrary we believe that their intelligent use in co-operation with other countries is the only possible alternative to a regime of fluctuating exchange rates and speculative movements of funds, far more destructive of trade, and that if properly used they can be constructive and expansive: in fact, that without them the post-war world would inevitably fall back into the chaos of the Thirties. (Fforde 1992, p. 42)

So the Bank as well as the Treasury differed from before the war. The latter had become Keynesian in advocating budgets intended to stabilize demand rather than repeated annual balances, in place of the prewar "Treasury view" according to which government spending crowded out private investment. "There is probably no country in the world that has made a fuller use than the United Kingdom of budgetary policy as a means of stabilizing the economy," a Treasury official said. "Since 1941, almost all adjustments to the total level of taxation have been made with the object of reducing an excess in total demand or of repairing a deficiency" (Dow 1964, ch. 7; Peden 1983).

The Bank, on the other hand, was condemned to monetary policy according to the rigidity of the new fixed-rate monetary system as decreed by the United States on the basis of its optimistic determination to restore the pre-1914 world almost immediately. The Bank's primary pre- and postwar difference resembled the Treasury's in its new emphasis on the short run. It did not feel the country was ready to jump into a convertible fixed-rate currency, either immediately or as a fixed long-term plan. It wanted small movements as the country showed itself ready for them. The Bank and Keynes had changed sides about fixed plans.

The new system was kept going – sort of – by countries' refusal to take it seriously, especially considering their higher priority of full employment. In fact, after a quarter-century of half-hearted attempts to achieve the impossible gold standard, the world yielded to the dreaded flexible-rate system in 1971. In the meantime, it had to make do with the International Monetary Fund decided at Bretton Woods, New Hampshire, in 1944. Led by the U.S.A. and U.K., negotiations regarding the world's postwar monetary system had been underway since early in the war – actually since "the tripartite monetary agreement" of September 1936, in which the U.S.A. and U.K. announced that they would not react to the French devaluation, soon extended to Belgium, the Netherlands, and Switzerland.

The IMF was a system of agreed fixed exchange rates that theoretically could only be changed by consent of the members when they agreed that the existing rate was in "fundamental disequilibrium," and subject to conditions that would enable the troubled country to maintain its new rate. Unfortunately, the IMF contained fundamental inconsistencies that guaranteed its failure, primarily the full-employment goal which had been adopted by most countries following the Great Depression, and expressed in the U.K. in William Beveridge's *Full Employment in a Free Society* (1944), as well as Keynes's *General Theory of Employment, Interest and Money* (1936), and in the U.S.A. in the *Employment Act of 1946*, in which Congress declared "that it is the continuing policy and responsibility of the Federal Government ... to promote maximum employment, production, and purchasing power."

Under the pre-1914 gold standard, and even more so between 1918 and the 1930s, employment had taken a back seat to the exchange rate (the gold value of the currency). This was much less the case after the suspensions and devaluations of the 1930s. In the U.S.A., there was little chance after its 1933 devaluation that gold would again be allowed to interfere with domestic policies. Gold reserve requirements on Federal Reserve deposits and notes were eliminated when they threatened to become binding in 1965 and 1968, and the gold convertibility of the dollar that had been available to central banks was suspended in 1971 (Krooss 1969, pp. 3070–71, 3081).

World inflation had been significant between 1947 and 1970, and variable between countries, averaging about 2½ percent per annum for developed countries (76 percent for the period, much greater than before 1914), a little more in the U.K. – not a world conducive to fixed exchange rates.

There was also a shortage of gold in two senses: low production because of the rise in costs of exploration and extraction compared with the fixed gold price of $35 per ounce, and hoarding (especially by South Africa) in anticipation of an increase in the price of gold. The U.S.A. held 24 of 34 billion dollars of the world's gold reserves in 1948, which increased less than 1 percent annually. The system was called the dollar standard because international transactions were conducted primarily in dollars, backed by gold although conversions were discouraged (Federal Reserve Board 1975, pp. 913–18; Hirsch 1968).

However, in spite of exchange controls but in line with expanding economies, international transactions grew, and by 1970 had reached their 1929 role as a proportion of the world economy. Because of the near-stagnant gold stock, the required growth in international (gold and dollar) reserves depended on American trade deficits, which it dutifully supplied, although this necessary development was an increasing source of concern for the country's policymakers.

Finally, in 1971, with rising inflation, U.S. gold reserves of $11 billion, a threatened run on the dollar, and a looming election, President Nixon's government suspended convertibility and the new world of flexible exchange rates between fiat currencies began. One might reasonably have thought that with the loss of its *raison d'être* the IMF would have been terminated, but it continued with its actual primary mission of arranging bailouts of financially irresponsible countries. Turkey, for example, had "arrangements" with (and disbursements from) the IMF for 26 of the 57 years from 1948 to 2005, and more later (Arpac and Bird 2009).

BOX 5.1 RELATIVE INFLATIONS AND EXCHANGE RATES

If equivalent goods cost $10 in the U.S.A. and £2 in the U.K., then in the absence of tariffs and shipping costs, £1 is worth $5, and the dollar-per-pound exchange rate is $E = \$/\pounds$.

If British prices rise 50 percent to £3 and the exchange rate is fixed, U.S. prices will be
$\$15 = 5*\pounds3$.
If the exchange rate is flexible and the U.S. maintains a stable price level, the equation will be
$\$10 = 3.3*\pounds3$.

In fact, the IMF never really got started in the performance of its envisioned tasks. It had not been able to make "exchange rates a matter of international deliberation. Even the general realignment of exchange rates in September 1949 was undertaken with no more than token consultations with the" Fund. As before the war, changes were made unilaterally or after consultations among the major countries concerned. Chancellor Sir Stafford Cripps said the decision "had to do with matters that were entirely our own concern and upon which there was no question of consulting others, even our best friends." (Box 5.1 illustrates changes in relative prices and exchange rates.)

The transition period was taking longer than expected. Most members of the fund continued exchange and trade restrictions under the IMF's escape clause. The countries whose representatives had formulated the liberal trading policies underlying the Fund "were unable to accept the disciplines necessary to permit those policies to work" (Mikesell 1954, pp. 24, 29).

Britain had ended the war with an extensive payments network, and the Bank had plans "for a strengthened and integrated Sterling Area, a fixed sterling/dollar rate, the continued centralisation of foreign exchange and gold transactions through the Bank, control of outward capital movements, and the development of bilateral monetary agreements with non-sterling countries and currency areas" (Fforde 1992, pp. 40–41). It hoped that the recovery of exports, combined with import controls, would remedy the balance of trade and eventually permit the liberalization of trade and payments.

That seemed possible, at first. Exports grew rapidly and the Bank and Treasury made progress in getting sterling holders to agree to voluntary limits on conversions to gold and dollars. However, in 1947, the dollar shortage began to bite, a hard winter led to a fuel shortage, and other imports also grew faster than expected – because, according to the Chancellor's critics, the American loan was dissipated to put off the inevitable belt-tightening, or according to Dalton, a rise in U.S. prices worth $1 billion of the loan. "The Loan, upon which all other plans depended, negotiated with difficulty and intended to last three years or so, in fact lasted only one year and a half" (Dow 1964, p. 23). It had been hoped that the conversion of sterling to dollars could be controlled by a gradual lifting of controls, but with full convertibility at $4.03 on July 15 (although the Sterling Area had agreed to hold pounds), the drain quickened.

Officials considered trying to renegotiate the conditions of the loan or letting the pound float, but they felt bound to honor the agreement until a crisis made it impossible. The Marshall Plan had been announced June 5, but its funds would not be available until the following year. The Bank's Harry Siepmann described the situation on August 14 (Fforde 1992, p. 155):

> The pattern of our losses suggests a general acceleration due to an attempt by holders of transferable sterling to take cover without delay. Many reported instances confirm that sterling has already ceased to be a currency which commands international confidence and there is some evidence that many of our own nationals would transfer their holdings elsewhere if they could. The conclusion to be drawn is that the dollar drain must be expected to continue, not only undiminished but probably at an accelerating rate.

Convertibility was suspended on August 20. The crisis had followed the Loan Agreement "as night follows the day," Deputy Governor Cameron Cobbold (who had been with the Bank and close to Norman since 1933) recalled. This was more than hindsight. He had told a colleague at the time (Fforde 1992, pp. 162, 151):

> I have always personally believed that the whole pack of cards of Bretton Woods, Washington Loan, ITO etc., was unsoundly or at any rate prematurely built and that it would collapse under "transitional period" stresses. I agree therefore that convertibility in the Loan Agreement (by which our hands are tied and which precludes us from using our trade, etc., negotiating weapons) must be modified.

ONE CRISIS AFTER ANOTHER: CHEAP MONEY TO STOP–GO

Cheap Money

Britain shared America's desire for low interest rates to stimulate demand to prevent the renewal of deflation and depression. But for Chancellor Dalton, redistribution was paramount. "So long as the National Debt endures," he said in his April 1947 Budget Speech, invoking the authority of Keynes, who had died 12 months earlier, "the Chancellor of the Exchequer must be on the side of the borrowers of money as against the money lenders, on the side of the active producer as against the passive *rentier*." He liked to call on Keynes's argument that the rate of interest is a psychological phenomenon, "largely governed by the prevailing view as to what its value is expected to be." This meant, for Dalton, that it could be kept low by persuasion (and controls) in the face of demand-stimulating budgets (Keynes 1936, p. 203; Dow 1964, pp. 223–5).

He also believed that "There is no sense … in paying more than we must for the loan of money" (Dow 1964, p. 21). Quoting Keynes in support of his policy, "The active and working elements in no community, ancient or modern, will consent to hand over to the *rentier* or bond-holding class more than a certain proportion of the fruits of their work." When the piled-up debt demands more than a tolerable proportion, relief has usually been sought "either in straight-out Repudiation of the Debt or in devaluation of the Currency." Keynes's *Tract on Monetary Reform*, from which Dalton took this passage (1923, pp. 54–5), was in fact generally an argument for price stability, opposing inflation as strongly as deflation. "It is an overwhelming objection to the method of currency depreciation," he had pointed out, "that it falls entirely upon persons whose wealth is in the form of claims to legal-tender money, and that these are generally, amongst the capitalists, the poorer capitalists. It is entirely ungraduated; it falls on small savings just as hardly as on big ones." It is also true that consumers are among society's largest savers (Feinstein 1972, T28).

Dalton was upper-class (Figure 5.2). His father had been chaplain to Queen Victoria, and he had been educated at Eton and Cambridge, but intended his policies to alleviate the problems of the poor, who should not have to pay market-determined interest rates. The end of the war, sales of war materials, latter Lend-Lease payments, and the American loan also allowed cuts in taxes and internal debt. Bank Rate was kept at 2 percent, and the bond rate was brought down from 3 percent to 2½ percent between 1945 and 1947.

Trouble came in the latter year, which Dalton called *annus horrendus*, compared with the *annus mirabilis* of 1946, when he and the country discovered that the laws of economics as under- stood by the classics still held. Inflation burst through controls, a bond conversion failed to hold at 2½ percent, a fuel crisis led to power cuts, the balance of payments worsened, the Chancellor was unable to persuade his

Source: https://commons.wikimedia.org/wiki/File: Hugh_Dalton_HU_059487.jpg.

Figure 5.2   Chancellor Hugh Dalton, with his Dispatch Box

Cabinet colleagues to cooperate in budget cuts, and the resumption ended in a run on the pound.

Little changed under Dalton's Labour successors: Sir Stafford Cripps (1947–50), whose name is linked to austerity, and Hugh Gaitskill. There was still no monetary policy except cheap money, and chancellors continued to count on controls on wages, prices, and bank loans to hold back inflation. The Bank of England was relegated to a few technical tasks: operations in securities to enforce the Treasury's interest targets, supervision of an inconvertible cur- rency, and controls on bank advances (loans) – complicated, time-consuming, and in the end, impossible.

The Bank served as the Government's agent of credit control by suppressing private consumption and investment. But it was a reluctant agent. When the Treasury asked the Bank to look into ways of limiting bank loans (without raising their cost – another inconsistency), the Old Lady responded that quali- tative guidelines would not prevent loans from increasing in line with inflation.

"As long as the price-weapon, i.e. the rate of interest, is forsworn, there is no other criterion" (Fforde 1992, p. 362).

Was the Bank trying hard enough? Chancellor Gaitskell thought it would "be simpler merely to give [banks] direct instructions about the level of advances, with perhaps some guidance as to the particular borrowers who should be cut," always subject to the condition "that there should be no increase in the rate at which the Government borrows short-term." The Bank had continued to deflect the Government's pressures for quantitative controls, and Cobbold, governor since 1949, replied (Fforde 1992, p. 392):

> The main thought in our mind is that having gone a long distance, with considerable success, in keeping down advances by co-operation with the banking system, what is needed is something which will also influence the attitude of the potential borrower. It is true that no action will bite heavily and violently, short of a rise of a point or two in interest rates generally which would appear impolitic on general grounds at the moment. The effect of a smaller firming up of interest rates on the general mentality of the commercial community cannot be assessed by any rule of thumb and must be a matter of judgment. It is certainly possible that we are wrong but the consensus of opinion at the Bank is definitely that a small firming up on the lines proposed would have a material effect and would well justify the increased charge on the Exchequer. (Governor to Chancellor, June 21, 1951)

The head of the Economic Section and chief economic adviser to the Government from 1947 to 1961 had a low opinion of the Bank's intelligence and suspected its loyalty. After an angry meeting, Robert Hall wrote that "It is hard not to get the impression that the Bank, and the banks generally, do not think at all about credit control as economists do [more on this below], and indeed that they don't quite understand what it is all about." He later complained to his diary that "all we are asking is that the Bank should be neutral and not act against us in our struggle, as they must have been doing." Sometimes he thought that although the Bank had declared that nothing could be accomplished without raising interest rates, "they have told the offending banks all the same to go easy on their advances" (Hall 1991: *Diaries*, September 11 and November 18, 1948, and January 18 and February 2, 1949).

Norman's modernizations and expert advisers, notwithstanding, the Bank was still in the City, and if its personnel's fortunes were not as tightly linked to the community's as formerly, it still saw among its primary goals the health and stability of finance (Sampson 1961, pp. 356–67; Brittan 1969, p. 79). The Bank was even further from the Government's economists than its civil servants, and its fleeting contacts with the former were as unsatisfactory as in the United States. "In a meeting [the Bank] seem to agree and when it comes to the final draft they water it down so much that it is worthless," Hall wrote. They are "as obstructive as possible" (Hall 1991: *Diaries*, August 26 and September 4, 1949).

Hall was uncomfortable with economic theory in general, and skeptical of prices and markets as rationing devices. His research as an Oxford academic had involved a questionnaire circulated in the mid-1930s to which businesses responded that (a) interest rates played no role in their investment decisions and (b) did not set prices to clear markets or maximize profits, but rather charged "fair" mark-ups over costs (Meade and Andrews 1938; Hall and Hitch 1939).

The methods and conclusions of this research were suspect. Regarding (a), this was a period of significant inflation and very low and almost constant interest rates. Changes in interest could not have been an important factor affecting financial decisions. Regarding (b), it is not surprising that businesses do not articulate their decisions in the abstract "marginal" and "maximizing" language of economists. Furthermore, how many businessmen, even if they understand the question, will admit to maximizing profits – read: "gouge the public" – as opposed to asking "fair" prices? The market-insensitive mark-up pricing theory that Hall and his associates inferred from their questionnaire approximates routine, day-to-day, rule-of-thumb decision-making. But it does not explain across-the-board price changes. It does not touch the causes of the cost increases, which are themselves market prices. An outside, driving force therefore has to be invented, and in a jump of logic, a popular choice is wages. If we do not think too much about chicken-and-egg questions regarding wages, it is easy to conclude that forcibly stopping one terminates the other.

The cost-push formula was convenient for those who wanted cheap money without inflation. Unfortunately, the strategy which followed from this reasoning required the demonization of labor and a policy straitjacket that was to bring down governments of both parties. But that was in the future. The wage freeze of 1948–50 had been half-hearted, and Hall was unable to persuade his superiors to repeat the attempt. Not until near the end of his career did he get a Chancellor, Selwyn Lloyd, "who took inflation seriously." Previous Tory Chancellors had looked on wage and price controls as impolitic and impractical, encouraged, thought Hall's staff, by Treasury officials who were "market men" at heart (Jones 1994, p. 153).

There had been an exchange crisis in the summer of 1949, followed by sterling's devaluation from $4.03 to $2.80. The new exchange rate was to be supported by wage controls and tighter fiscal and monetary policies, but these intentions were derailed by an increase in spending for the Korean War. (The budget cuts announced in October 1949 were to take effect in the second half of the following year; North Korea invaded South Korea in June 1950.) A deteriorating balance of payments and a dollar drain in the summer of 1951 brought fears of another devaluation, and *The Economist* saw "the beginning of a new period of economic stringency." Labour had been returned with a slim majority in February 1950, to see its popularity fall with inflation, budget cuts, and the war, and was further weakened by the resignations of Health Minister Aneurin Bevan and Harold Wilson from the Board of Trade (over war spending and cutbacks in the health service) in April 1951. Gaitskell was forced to bring bad economic news and the necessity of cuts in imports just before the general election which had been called for October 25 (Dow 1964, pp. 41–5, 62).

Stop–Go

Cobbold had given Chancellors little respite from pleas for flexibility in interest rates, and he and his staff continued to search for new tactics. After another rebuff from Gaitskell, who nevertheless wanted banks to help restrict private investment, Humphrey Mynors (Executive Director and later Deputy Governor, 1954–64) wrote to a colleague (Howson 1993, p. 295):

> It is difficult to think of any novel arguments for dearer money. The familiar arguments must be mobilised, after studying where the opposition appears to be concentrated, and bearing in mind any change in the terrain since the last engagement.

They might try "pointing out that you could not control both quantity and price of any commodity, including money." Perhaps the "out of line and unreal" rate structure would "break down." The long rate had been allowed to rise to 4 percent (which Mynors saw as a "crack" in Gaitskell's armor), while the discount rate remained below 1 percent. The Government had been able to maintain low interest rates on Treasury bills since the 1930s by "recommended" bank demands for them as part of their "liquidity ratio," combined with short supplies sometimes approaching bill "famines." As in the United States, the Government could have low short rates if it did not take advantage of them (Sayers 1956, p. 148; Nevin 1955, p. 126).

Cobbold asked Otto Niemeyer if they could get around the Treasury's aversion to the budgetary effects of interest-rate hikes by segmenting the market for short-term debt so that Treasury bills would still bear interest of ½ percent while others paid more. The long-time Treasury and Bank adviser responded with the obvious (Fforde 1992, p. 384):

> The Treasury always lay too much stress on the purely Budgetary aspects of the question. (No doubt short-financing generates short views!) [exclaimed the man who with Norman had tried to impress the long view on Churchill] The importance (and effects) of the problem are far wider. Its neglect may easily produce economic results far more costly to the nation than any Budget cost of a remedy. People abroad mistrust Sterling. They know that we continue to inflate, and are well aware

where this will lead us, particularly when Marshall Aid ceases. We cannot counter this want of confidence by arguments about Budget cost – indeed that line only intensifies doubts about our resolution to secure sound finance; and these doubts are very expensive to us.

I see nothing to be gained by clever tricks to avoid the natural course. They will not carry conviction either at home or abroad. I believe they will even do us more harm than having to wait until we can carry the right policy.

On November 7, 1951, thirteen days after the election, the new Conservative Chancellor R.A. Butler announced, "After the most careful consultation with the Governor of the Bank of England," that it was "necessary to depart from the arrangements in force .... The Bank of England are today, with my approval, raising the Bank Rate by ½% to 2½%." Butler and Cobbold had had a long discussion on October 30, and arranged regular weekly meetings. For some time, Fforde wrote, relations between governors and chancellors had been "cordial, correct, but slightly distant. The Governor had been treated more like a senior Civil Servant than some special being who could be treated more like a colleague" (Fforde 1992, pp. 404–5).

The Bank was not back in charge, but it had gotten the ear of those who were. Hall resented this arrangement, which interfered with his efforts to coordinate economic policies. He complained to his diary (December 18, 1957) that the Bank wanted independence, which modern society would not permit. "The thing that I find most irritating ... is that the central fact is not being brought out and I do not suppose it can be brought out, which is that the Bank hardly collaborate with the Treasury at all in internal policy matters – the Chancellor talks to the Governor in private and the Bank neither give us their assessment of the situation, nor of the part they expect monetary policy to play in it."

The policies of the period, which became known as "stop–go," may be summarized as expansive government budgets and cheap money until a threatened or actual exchange crisis forced a fiscal retreat and/or tight money, after which the process would be repeated. Figure 5.1 shows the positive relation between Bank Rate and inflation, and after 1967, the covariation of unemployment and inflation.

Brittan's (1969, pp. 448–52) "stop–go" highlights included "the deflationary crisis measures of Thorneycroft in 1957, Selwyn Lloyd in 1961, Wilson in 1966 and the reflationary Budgets of Heathcoat Amory in 1959 and Reginald Maudling in 1963." We will look at the first episode in some detail because it tells us something of the Bank's thinking in the post-Keynesian era (not as changed as some had hoped) and its relations with Conservative governments (not as different from its relations with Labour as might have been expected from the first signals).

The fiscal expansion of 1953–54, including Housing Minister Harold Macmillan's "crusade," brought wage and price inflation and a negative trade balance. Bank Rate was raised from 3 percent to 3½ percent in January 1955, and 4½ percent in February. This was a high rate, the Bank pointed out in a letter to the Chancellor (Fforde 1992, pp. 631–2).

The Chancellor thanked the Bank and went in the opposite direction. An election was looming (and would be held on May 26, resulting in an increased Conservative majority), and in the April budget speech he announced a plan to boost the expansion with a cut in the income tax while relying on "the resources of a flexible monetary policy" to check inflation. Unfortunately, reported the Treasury's *Economic Survey*, "By the summer," it was evident "that the pressure of demand persisted and that monetary policy was not operating as rapidly as had been expected" (Dow 1964, pp. 78–9).

Policies over the next two years were deflationary, marked by Butler's take-backs in the October 1955 budget and the 7 percent Bank Rate in September 1957. The Tory acceptance of changes in Bank Rate had not carried with it a forswearing of controls. "Hire-purchase" restrictions on consumer credit were introduced in 1952, and Butler and his successors continued to press the Bank to "request" the banks to restrict their loans.

There was little evidence in spring 1955 of any effect of the recent increases in Bank Rate on advances, and the Treasury, "sharply on the lookout for such evidence," Fforde writes, suggested that the Bank ask banks to provide monthly instead of quarterly data; "not worth the extra work," responded the deputy-governor. Cobbold wanted to hold back advances to mollify the Chancellor, but disliked strong-arm tactics. He "was not keen to write letters," and avoided directives, preferring oblique signals in polite conversation. Bankers complained "that it was difficult to select the victims of restriction and they grumbled about the lack of restraint by nationalised industries" (Fforde 1992, pp. 632–3). Lord Aldenham, Chairman of Westminster Bank, showed little concern over his customers' and bank managers' lack of cooperation, but he was persuaded to write the appeal shown in Box 5.2.

BOX 5.2   RESTRICTIONS ON CREDIT: AN APPEAL TO BANK CUSTOMERS

TO THE EDITOR OF *THE TIMES*: Sir, – It is by now well known that it is the policy of her Majesty's Government to restrict the total volume of credit in order to curtail internal demand in the interests of the national balance of payments.

Such a policy makes it necessary for the banks to restrict their advances, and they have had to be, and must continue to be, more stringent in their attitude in regard to advances to customers, large and small alike, however reasonable those advances would be in normal times.

The banks therefore hope that their customers will understand that the present stringency is a matter of public policy and will cooperate with the banks by keeping their credit requirements as small as possible.

Yours faithfully,

Aldenham, Chairman, D.J. Roberts, Deputy Chairman,
Committee of London Clearing Bankers.

Post Office Court, 10, Lombard Street, E.C.3, June 28, 1955.

Such announcements and meetings had little effect, but in negotiations about just what the Government's directive should be, the Bank and banks resisted the official quantitative limit on advances. They escaped with a letter in which the Chancellor told the governor that "the necessary reduction in demand is unlikely to be achieved unless the total of bank advances is reduced below its present level." The governor told the banks that he expected to see a material reduction in advances by October and a further cut in December. They acted "decisively and without delay [and] agreed that the aim should be to cut advances by 10% by the end of the year (excluding repayments by Gas and Electricity)." They were, however, "Having obeyed the authorities with such alacrity, ... distinctly nettled to read that the Chancellor had assured [Shadow Chancellor] Gaitskell in the House that existing investment programmes would not be affected" (Dow 1964, pp. 639–40).

Advances remained below their mid-1955 level, Bank Rate was raised to 5½ percent and hire-purchase restrictions were tightened in 1956, and public spending was maintained – while total bank credit, money, wages, and prices continued to rise, leading to more meetings of chancellors and bankers (Dow 1964, p. 659). The Government's authority was weakened by the country's poor economic performance compared with the "miracles" elsewhere, "a weakening intensified by the Suez affair and the fall of Eden." (The British–French–Israeli attack on Egypt in October 1956 after its nationalization of the Suez Canal was aborted under American and Soviet pressure and led to the resignation of Prime Minister Anthony Eden.) The Bank stepped up its efforts to shift the focus of monetary policy from controls to interest rates. Cobbold's note to the Chancellor was partially reproduced in the epigraph to this chapter.

Macmillan, who was shortly to succeed Eden as prime minister, should have understood. The outflow of foreign exchange reserves had been a significant factor in the decision to halt the Suez adventure in November 1956, and might have explained his sudden switch from "the warmest cheerleader of the operation" to a strong supporter of those who wanted to abandon it, although he denied saying "we can't afford it" (Brittan 1969, p. 207). This does not mean, as we will see, that the experience would override existing beliefs.

Peter Thorneycroft, who succeeded Macmillan as Chancellor in January 1957, proved after an initial hard line toward the Bank to be more malleable. An increase in advances led him to write "a curt letter" to the governor in March expressing his concern that they might be losing control of the economy: "It is not so much that I think we ought to apply the brake any harder at the moment; but I do want to know that we have a brake that works" (Fforde 1992, pp. 670, 673).

After defending the banks and their judgments in accommodating "priority needs," Cobbold shifted to the attack. The banks had been made restless by the continued denial of competition. "A credit squeeze might be all right as a short-term instrument, but if it was necessary to prolong it for a long period something fundamental must have gone wrong elsewhere" (Fforde 1992, p. 673).

The issue was forced by an exchange crisis in August 1957, after the devaluation of the French franc. Pressure on the pound might have been increased by a signal from Thorneycroft that he was unlikely to do anything about inflation. In announcing a Council on Prices, Productivity and Incomes to "keep under review changes in prices, productivity and the level of incomes ... and to report thereon from time to time," he told the House: "There is clearly no simple act of policy which is a remedy for inflation. If there had been, it would have been discovered a very long time ago .... The Government, the private employers, the trade unions and the nationalized industries all have a part to play" (Dow 1964, p. 99).

The Bank, of course, knew very well how to stop inflation, and had done it many times. In any case, even the Treasury knew something had to be done, and a desperate Thorneycroft allowed the Bank to take the lead in their discussions. On August 22, just before going on holiday, Cobbold sent the Chancellor a letter outlining his proposals. The tune was unchanged. Credit restrictions were "played out," and other non-price measures were similarly ineffective. If signs of inflation were confirmed in September, measures would have to be taken: "They should be sharp and comprehensive," meaning especially "a drastic increase in Bank Rate either in one move or in quick stages" (Fforde 1992, p. 677).

The Bank's argument recalls Keynes's prescription for inflation: "a sharp dose of Dear Money." If you wish to stop an inflation embedded in people's expectations, you had better convince them you mean business (Howson 1973).

Thorneycroft also accepted the need for spending cuts, but would have to make the case to the prime minister. Macmillan had not been encouraging about the new direction of policy. His economic views were "coloured by his acquaintance with mass unemployment at his old constituency of Stockton-on-Tees in the interwar period," Brittan (1969, p. 203) observed. Whitehall officials "were said to keep a mental tally of the number of times he mentioned Stockton-on-Tees in any one week." "He always feared," added Richard Chapman in his study of the decision to raise Bank Rate, "that prosperity and full employment could be too easily sacrificed by a one-sided devotion to 'sound money' at the expense of other objectives" (Chapman 1968, p. 33)

It is interesting that the new money-control policy was some years before Milton Friedman and his collaborators had persuaded economists and policymakers of the importance of money to inflation. Whether because of events, arguments, or company – probably all three – the Chancellor's conversion was complete. "The speeches Thorneycroft made in his first six months in the Treasury were so different from those he made in his second six months," Brittan wrote, "that it is difficult to credit them with the same authorship." He said in the April Budget Speech:

> There are those who say that the answer lies in savage deflationary policies, resulting in high levels of unemployment. They say that we should depress demand to a point at which employers cannot afford to pay and workers are in no position to ask for higher wages. If this be the only way in which to contain the wage-price spiral it is indeed a sorry reflection upon our modern society.

By July, he was instructing the Treasury "to consider possibilities of checking inflation by taking firmer control of the money supply, and on August 7 directed that "a study should be made in the Treasury of the possibility of bringing about a measure of deflation in the economy." He had been quietly moving toward the Bank's position before the September negotiations without giving away his ability to bargain for a politically viable package. Announcement of his "September Measures" included, along with a commitment to hold Government spending in check, the following sentences:

> The Government are determined to maintain the internal and external value of the pound .... There can be no remedy for inflation ... which does not include, and indeed is not founded upon, a control of the money supply. So long as it is generally believed that the Government are prepared to see the necessary finance produced to match the upward spiral of costs, inflation will continue ....

Inflation slowed in 1958, although this was probably due as much to the international recession as to the new policy. In any case, the policymakers felt able to cut the Bank Rate to 6 percent in March, and by November it was 4 percent. In the meantime, advances and consumer credit were decontrolled.

What was learned from this episode? Probably nothing. At least, nothing changed. The institutions and ideas of the mid-1950s prevailed until they were shocked by similar but larger forces two decades later. Monetary policy would continue to be implemented by an institution (the Bank of England) at cross-purposes with the responsible body (Parliament). This point has been made more positively by describing central banks as sound-money consciences of the politicians, the Jiminy Crickets who remind them that they can't have everything but are attended to only when things have gone wrong. However the process is pictured, the stop–go policies implied by the inconsistent goals of continuous full employment and price stability continued.

Thorneycroft thought there had been a change. However, what he had intended to be a new policy, based on a new (or neglected) intellectual framework, rather than just a tactical move within an existing policy, was shortly rejected. Labour's criticism was to be expected. Patrick Gordon Walker said that one of the Chancellor's main objects "was really to declare war on the trade unions." "The whole trouble," said Harold Wilson, "is that the chancellor is trying to fight what is a cost-push inflation ... with the crude techniques which classical theory considers appropriate to a demand inflation. [M]erely to freeze the supply of money does not of itself freeze prices" (Dow 1964, p. 102).

Thorneycroft was more surprised by the lack of support from his own party, and resigned over the budget four months later when the Cabinet backed out of his pledge to hold down Government spending. His junior ministers, Enoch Powell and Nigel Birch, who had been "largely responsible for turning the anti-inflationary policies into a crusade," resigned with him. Their colleagues, who thought the £50 million involved a minor issue, were puzzled. The group apparently believed that there had been a genuine shift to a policy in which price stability had top priority. This was not an accurate reading of the minds of their colleagues, who regarded the September measures as a regrettably necessary tactical reaction to a crisis, to be reversed as soon as possible (Dow 1964, p. 102; Brittan 1969, p. 213; Shonfield 1958, pp. 248–9).

The revolving door of chancellors under Macmillan (four in less than seven years) reflected the unsettled policy. Amory, who succeeded Thorneycroft and lasted the longest, presented a pre-election "tax relief" budget in April 1959, and in the next 15 months brought back controls, raised Bank Rate, and resigned in favor of Lloyd, whose experience was similar. His successor, Maudling, was luckier in being able to pass the consequences of his "reflation" onto the Labour Government elected in October 1964.

THE BANK, PRIME MINISTERS, AND THE POUND: FROM ONE UNMENTIONABLE TO ANOTHER, 1951–67

Although the Bank had opposed immediate unrestricted convertibility after the war, it had not lost hope of the pound's return to its former primacy in international finance. This section relates three episodes in the history of the Bank's efforts to achieve or preserve the convertibility and stability of the pound – two of which, as in 1819 and 1925, were decided at the highest level after sharp battles within and between the Government and the Bank.

Robot

The sterling crisis in the winter of 1951–52 following the Korean War rearmament boom was another of a series of blows to sterling including the failure of the 1947 resumption and the 1949 devaluation, with little prospect of improvement. "It is not therefore surprising," wrote Fforde (1992, p. 169), "that the Bank then finally abandoned the whole evolutionary approach to convertibility that it had pursued since 1941." There seemed nothing left but "to make a virtue of necessity" and take a leap in the dark, as Keynes had done in 1946. The Bank joined the Overseas Finance Division of the Treasury in advocating a jump to convertibility, which would have to be done with a floating rate.

From a commitment to fixed rates, the governor had decided that "there was no advantage in sitting still and waiting for the deluge" in the form of another crisis suspension or devaluation. The proposal was given the code name Robot after its chief protagonists, Thomas ROwan, George BOlton, and OTto Clarke, the second from the Bank and the others from the Treasury (Seldon 1981, p. 171). The restoration of sterling required convertibility, but neither the level of reserves nor recent experience gave much confidence to its holders. The details were not filled in, but the basic idea was to allow the pound to float within wide limits, say, \$3.20 to \$2.40 instead of the current \$2.84 to \$2.76, and to unblock sterling balances in stages as conditions allowed.

The Chancellor was persuaded, and brought Robot to the Cabinet at the end of February 1952. Churchill liked the idea of "setting the pound free," but the proposal soon foundered on fundamental differences between just about everyone involved. The goals of the Treasury proponents differed from the Bank's. The former made the standard theoretical macro-stabilization case that a floating rate would take the pressure of the balance of payments off the domestic economy. A decline in exports, for example, would be allowed to affect the exchange rate without forcing internal adjustments.

This is not what the Bank had in mind. It had thought of the wider band as insurance, in place of a large stock of reserves that would permit greater convertibility. "I told the chancellor that I thought the argumentation good," Cobbold said of a paper by Clarke, "but that there was much too much 'floating.'" "So much for the benign equilibrating force that" some of Robot's proponents "had found so alluring," Fforde (1992, p. 438) commented. It had begun to look like another Bank scheme for tighter money, enforced by convertibility. Keynesianism had not completely divorced the Bank from its history.

Four months earlier, as he was putting together the new Government, Churchill told Oliver Lyttleman, later Viscount Chandos (1967, p. 343), Butler's rival for the Exchequer: "I have seen a Treasury Minute and already I know that the financial position is almost irretrievable: the country has lost its way. In the worst of the war I could always see how to do it. Today's problems are elusive and intangible, and it would be a bold man who could look forward to certain success." The difference was that the clear objective of the war – "Victory at all costs" – had been replaced by several complicated and sometimes conflicting economic goals. The prime minister's course with respect to Robot, however, was settled by his trusted adviser in matters of economics as well as the physical sciences. Lord Cherwell (F.A. Lindemann, "the Prof") favored the elimination of controls in general, including the restoration of convertibility – as conditions allowed. He argued that the freeing of the pound would have to wait for improved export performance. Convertibility without severe devaluation in the current situation of few reserves and an uncertain future of the balance of payments might force a policy of deflation leading to unemployment. The Government would not survive a departure from the postwar consensus in which full employment held first priority (Birkenhead 1961, ch. 10). Robot was dropped.

Convertibility, At Last

Robot was also damaged by the lack of consultation with other departments, especially the Foreign Office, about its effects on relations with the United States and Europe, and by its inconsistencies with existing commitments. It conflicted with the Bretton Woods agreement on fixed rates to be altered only by multilateral negotiation as well as with Britain's participation in the European Payments Union (EPU) that had begun in 1950.

The EPU arose from American efforts to liberalize trade and payments considering that the IMF's terms were too rigid. It was a clearing union which allowed members, helped by Marshall Plan aid, to run larger deficits than with the IMF. The negotiating machinery also enabled debtors to raise trade barriers. It was more like the Keynes Plan or the pre-1939 system than Bretton Woods, and Britain found it useful in 1951–52 (Milward 1992, pp. 348–51).

The Government and Bank also looked beyond Europe to their former glories across the seas. They wanted world status for the pound, which had been as good as gold and might be as good as the dollar. The Bank pushed a more ambitious version of Robot, called the Collectivist Approach, in which the Commonwealth and possibly continental Europe would join a managed float vis-à-vis the dollar. But it raised little enthusiasm in Europe or the United

States. Nevertheless, convertibility was made possible for Western Europe, including Britain, in 1958 by American payments deficits and the end of the dollar shortage, a shift in the terms of trade away from primary producers, and restrictive monetary policies begun the summer of 1955.

Even so, Britain's international position remained tenuous. Its reserves grew more slowly and erratically than those of its neighbors. In the 1960s, American, German, French, and Italian reserves would have covered half a year's imports, compared with two months' for Britain. And Bank Rate, now reserved for emergencies, and not always then, was not the powerful protector of the "thin film" of reserves it had been before 1914.

Defense and Devaluation, 1964–67

"Mr. Maudling's reflation" yielded "Mr. Callaghan's bitter harvest" when the latter succeeded to the Exchequer on Labour's narrow victory in the October 1964 election. Harold Macmillan had been succeeded the previous October by the lackluster Sir Alec Douglas Home in an arbitrary procedure much criticized in his own party. An election would have to be held within 12 months, and polls and by-elections were going against the Conservatives. This was the political backdrop of Maudling's decision, encouraged by political associates and academic economists, who believed that annual growth of 4 percent was attainable.

Employment was full and the Treasury thought the rate of increase in capacity was closer to 3 percent. But neither governments nor economists have liked the Treasury's gloomy arithmetic. The National Economic Development Council (NEDC, "Neddy") had been established in 1962 as an expert body, independent of the Treasury, to advise on policies for growth. Its purpose was to find a steady-growth path in place of the "stop–go" crises of the 1950s, preferably at the enviable rates across the Channel. It would give the Chancellor an alternative to the Treasury's somber notes. Neddy's members "in their off-guard moments," Brittan (1969, p. 249) noted, "jocularly referred to the Treasury as 'the other side.'"

What Neddy's creators got was the familiar demand–stimulus refrain. It was persuaded of a productivity speed-up that had been hidden by the 1961–62 recession. The high investment of 1960–61 "had not yet found expression in the output figures because demand had been held down" (Brittan 1969, p. 278). Taxes were cut and Government spending increased, and when prices rose and the balance of payments worsened, Maudling was praised for refusing to panic. His April 1964 budget took back only a small part of the benefits handed out the preceding two years. Professor E.A.G. Robinson wrote:

> It has been courageous (some critics would say foolhardy) in allowing the economy the chance of another year's expansion above the 4 percent rate without anything more than a delicate lightening of the pressure on the accelerator. (Robinson 1964; Hutchison 1968, pp. 224, 227)

The Spectator, edited by Iain Macleod (who would be Heath's first Chancellor until his death after a month), told Maudling that he

> ... must drive straight through fluctuations in the balance of payments .... If Mr. Maudling is really hoping to win the election he will have to show the public that he is up to date and "with it."

Anything else would have been "regarded as hopelessly stick-in-the-mud" (Day 1964). The goal of 4 percent, really a hope, had become a hostage to political fortune, brooking no qualification or reasoned discussion. In fact, the average rate of growth of output, 2.6 percent in the 1950s, never reached 3 percent in the 1960s or attained that average in any decade of the rest of the century. This is hindsight, but Maudling's reflation through deficits was no different from the policies of his postwar predecessors, and had the same effects: inflation, balance of payments difficulties, and exchange crises.

The possibility of devaluation had circulated in the months before the election, but the new Labour Government was surprised by the size of the problem, most strikingly an £800 million balance of payments deficit. The European Economic Community's Monetary Committee advised that sterling was in fundamental disequilibrium and should be devalued by 10–15 percent, a step also urged by the economic "left," including the new advisors brought to Whitehall from the universities. The Bank and the City opposed devaluation, but the decision not to devalue seems to have been taken independently of these views, on political grounds, immediately after taking office. Prime Minister Harold Wilson feared that another devaluation, after that of 1949 by the last Labour Government, would be an admission that Labour was unfit to manage the economy (Brittan 1969, pp. 291–92; Browning 1986, p. 4).

Devaluation would therefore have to be done quickly or not at all, Wilson told the Economic Club of New York on April 14, 1965:

> If an incoming Government were at any time likely to consider devaluing the nation's currency, political considerations would have dictated doing it on that first day, when the fault would clearly and unequivocally lie with those who had charge of the nation's affairs for 13 years. So that decision, once taken, was a decision for good. (*New York Times*, April 15, 1965)

Devaluation became "the great unmentionable" in the Government and Civil Service, and even, "to a large extent, by tacit and patriotic agreement, in the Press." Looking back, after the deed had been done, Professor Alan Day wrote in *The Observer* (November 26, 1967) that "open advocacy of devaluation was ... the next worse thing to publishing obscene literature" (Browning 1986, p. 5). The subject was hardly discussed by officials except in whispers behind closed doors. Deputy Prime Minister George Brown observed that the prime minister and Chancellor were "terrified lest talking, or even thinking, about devaluation should alert the world to what was going on," although Wilson's assistant remembered that "When he was alone the dreaded word 'devaluation' was sometimes mentioned" (Brown 1971, p. 104; Falkender 1975, p. 161).

The foreign exchange markets were not convinced, especially when, after the prime minister announced the severity of the problem and, "in Churchillian terms, his determination to take whatever measures were necessary for the defence of sterling," the Government failed to follow through (Browning 1986, p. 7). There were the usual gimmicks – import surcharges, tax rebates on exports, and talk of wage and price restraint – but the budget was not tightened significantly and the traditional call to quarters in these circumstances, a rise in Bank Rate, was not seen. The aspiration to 4 percent growth had survived the change of Government.

Wilson's statement on November 16 was followed by a run on sterling, which accelerated after Bank Rate was raised from 5 percent to 7 percent on the 23rd. This perverse reaction has been attributed to investors' interpretation of the unusual handling of the rise as a sign of panic, as well as to official statements that it was merely a technical adjustment that was not intended to deflate demand. On the 25th there was "a dramatic announcement from the Bank of England that 11 central banks, together with the Bank for International Settlements and the U.S. Export–Import Bank, had arranged a further $3,000m. of short-term credits which Britain could draw upon to protect the pound." This did no more than slow the outflow of funds, and further credits had to be arranged – and used – until devaluation from $2.80 to $2.40 in November 1967 (Brittan 1969, pp. 298–304).

Macroeconomic "policy" during these years – if such a word can be used – was ambiguous, vacillating, and inconsistent over time and between members of the Government. Budgets alternated between restrictive and expansionary, accompanied by verbal commitments to faster growth and the parity of the pound, apparently to be reconciled by price, wage, and credit controls. One of the sharpest inconsistencies was between the stated objectives of growth in total output, especially in exports, and the rising share of resources taken by public spending.

The ambiguity of government policy was institutionalized in a new Department of Economic Affairs (DEA), under George Brown, to plan macroeconomic policy, especially growth, while the Treasury looked after short-term finance. Its first task was to produce a National Plan for the economy that, in Brown's words, "would break the ancient Treasury tradition of making economic policy and industrial activity subject to all the inhibitions of orthodox monetary control" (Brown 1971, p. 104).

When Brown made his statement, unemployment was 1½ percent and his sums failed as completely for political institutions as for economics. No coherent policy could be gotten from accounts that were determined to conflict. As long as budgets and monetary policy were managed by the Treasury for the Chancellor and the Government, the DEA could only present alternative minority proposals that led to increased workloads, dissension, and finally arbitration by the prime minister. The DEA was terminated and economic management reverted wholly to the Treasury before the 1970 election, although Brown defended it to the end (Browning 1986, pp. 12–13; Brown 1971, pp. 87, 105, 113; Crossman 1975, pp. 58, 219).

Wilson was unlucky in his governor, George Rowland Stanley Baring, the Earl of Cromer, who had succeeded Cobbold in 1961. Relations between the Bank and the Government, never smooth, had deteriorated the last years of Cobbold's term. He was subjected to "a strong protest" from the new Chancellor, Lloyd, in July 1960 when bank advances showed a large rise in spite of his predecessor's calls to restrict credit in the face of an "overheating" economy. The protest was sent at Hall's instigation, who "was especially annoyed because only a month earlier the Governor had claimed that he had everything under control" (Jones 1994, p. 141). Hall (1991, p. 243) wrote in his *Diary*:

> It is one of the great disadvantages of monetary policy, compared to fiscal policy, that if you change taxes the revenue departments will go out and collect the money and be very unpleasant to the taxpayer if they do not get it. But if you try to tighten up on the money side, you get the Bank of England falling over themselves to soften the blow and to make all sorts of excuses for the bankers that they probably would be ashamed to make for themselves.

The prime minister was also dissatisfied, and sought the Chancellor's reassurance that Cobbold would leave at the end of the year as promised (Jones 1994, p. 142).

The desire for new and more compliant blood was heightened by the recent insinuations of the *Radcliffe Report*, no less damaging for their vagueness, touching on the Bank's competence and cooperation. It is not surprising that the call was to someone from outside the Bank. Cromer had not been a director, nor had he held any other position in the Bank, and was one of the few governors who had not been deputy-governor. At 43, he was the youngest governor in 200 years, and in some ways a throwback to the pre-Norman governors who had not (before their deputy governor service) been full-time in the Bank. Cromer was a merchant banker who would soon return to his firm (Barings, in 1966). Although governors of the "old Bank" had been long-serving directors, they were, like Cromer, typically brought up as merchant bankers in family firms to which they devoted their lives. Cromer had not been softened by the bureaucratic relationship between Bank and Government which had grown up since 1914, and did not see why he had to "get along." He did not see why he had to pretend that Maudling's or Brown's arithmetic added up. This might be why Peter Browning (1986, p. 27), sympathetic to the "third-way," through controls, between devaluation and deflation, thought "Cromer's grasp of macroeconomic policy had never been of the strongest."

Although the choice of a Baring for a new broom may seem odd, it was necessary to give assurance to the markets when someone from outside the Bank was selected to govern monetary affairs. But conflict was inevitable regardless of personalities when the Government wanted an accommodative a governor who would at the same time instill confidence in the currency. An important difference in the new governor was Cromer's confrontational and public style. For one reporter, he "emerged as the keeper of his country's financial conscience ... when he sounded solemn warnings against 'indulging ourselves' by 'an enlargement of governmental spending'" (Wechsberg 1966, p. 163). When in their "meeting of the minds" on November 24, 1964, Cromer demanded an about-face in the Government's economic and social programs to restore confidence in sterling, Wilson threatened to "go to the country" in defense of the Government's constitutional rights (Wilson 1971, pp. 37–8; Kynaston 1995).

Relations remained difficult, and "we had to listen night after night," Wilson recalled, "to demands that there should be immediate cuts in Government expenditure, and particularly in those parts of Government expenditure which related to the social services. It was not long before we were being asked, almost at pistol-point, to cut back on expenditure, even to the point of stopping the road-building programme, or schools which were only half-constructed" (Wilson 1971, p. 34).

> Indeed, in January, 1965, at a private lunch at No. 10, ... I told [Cromer] that Government expenditure was committed far ahead; schools which were being built, roads which were part-way to completion, had been programmed by our Conservative predecessors in 1962–63. Was it in his view, I asked him, that we should cut them off half-finished – roads left as an eyesore on the countryside, schools left without a roof, in order to satisfy foreign financial fetishism? This question was difficult for him, but he answered, "Yes."

A Wilson biographer observed that Cromer "found Wilson slippery and unsound and made little attempt to hide the low opinion he held of the prime minister; Wilson for his part found Cromer hectoring and bigoted, a wolf from the capitalist pack determined to thwart socialist policy if not actually destroy the administration" (Ziegler 1988, p. 194).

Cromer returned to Barings after a single term at the Bank, and relations improved with the accession of Leslie O'Brien in 1966. A career bank employee out of public school, Callaghan found O'Brien "Modest, quiet, considerate of the views of others but firm in his own beliefs, ... technically proficient" (Callaghan 1987, p. 195). Gordon Richardson, also an investment banker and governor from 1973 to 1983, had "generally good, constructive working relationships" with Labour Governments. Chancellor Denis Healey (1974–79) (1989, p. 375; Kynaston 1995) enjoyed the "creative tension." However, O'Brien and Richardson delivered even less financial stability than Cobbold or Cromer (see Figure 5.1). The annual rates of inflation during the tenures of the four governors (1949–61, 1961–66, 1966–73, and 1973–83) were 3.9 percent, 3.6 percent, 6.4 percent, and 13.6 percent, respectively.

COMPETITION AND CREDIT CONTROL

[T]he skepticism of the monetary authorities as to their power so to regulate credit as to maintain monetary stability ... has, I think, increased. At any rate they seem always unwilling to trust in Bank rate alone as a regulator. For example the resort to the "credit squeeze" in 1955, and to "special deposits" in 1961 to reduce the liquid resources of the banks. Yet the decisive effect of 7 percent in 1957 and 1961 is hardly to be denied. (Hawtrey 1962, pp. xi–xiv)

After falls in 1966 and 1967, inflation picked up again in 1968–71, even before the effective end of the IMF when President Nixon closed the U.S. gold window in August 1971. Labour had let up on its restrictions, and Edward Heath's Conservative Government that succeeded it in June 1970, terminated wage, price, and credit controls to promote competition and efficiency. In the monetary sphere it enacted a program called Competition and Credit Control (CCC) which was expected to restrain inflation.

Some years earlier, complaints of the ineffectiveness of monetary policy had led the Chancellor to appoint a *Committee on the Working of the Monetary System*, chaired by Lord Radcliffe. Its 1959 Report found the monetary system tremendously complicated, one which defied any sort of feasible monetary policy with predictable effects on money or interest rates. Inflation was something which just happened – was intrinsic in the modern economy – and increases in interest rates, if they could be achieved, were either ineffective, or if they could be raised sufficiently to slow inflation, might devastate the economy. Nor was money important. What mattered for demand was liquidity, of which money was only part. Anyway, money was undefined and therefore unmeasurable (Radcliffe 1959, paras. 504–28, 981).

The factually strong historic relation between money and inflation – which we have seen especially in the suspensions and resumptions of the gold standard in the eighteenth, nineteenth, and twentieth centuries – as well as the legendary effectiveness of Bank Rate (Hawtrey 1962) were dismissed. They had been replaced in many economists' thinking by ambitious Keynesian convictions that full employment might be achieved by increases in demand, especially government spending, the financing of which, it was alleged, had no effect on inflation. Rising prices and wages arose from market powers requiring administrative controls.

The Conservative Government's collapse may be said to have begun in March 1972 with Chancellor of the Exchequer Anthony Barber's expansionary budget which he expected "to ensure growth of output at an annual rate of five percent." Real public expenditures on such large items as the health service, the steel industry, local government, the Concorde, a third London airport, and the Channel tunnel, amounted to annual increases of 2.9 percent, 6.9 percent, 8.5 percent, and 12.4 percent, respectively, in 1971–74. The Upper Clyde Shipbuilders and Rolls-Royce were rescued. Taxes were cut so that the Public Sector Borrowing Requirement grew from 1.5 percent to 6 percent of GDP between 1970 and 1974.

But there was plenty of money. The 50 percent cut in bank reserve requirements proved to be important, and rates of increase in money rose from 2 percent in 1969 to 25.6 percent and 27.4 percent in 1972 and 1973, while inflation rose from 5.4 percent in 1969 to 16 percent, 24.2 percent, 16.5 percent, and 15.9 percent, respectively, in 1974–77.

The Government's determination to combat inflation by holding down, even freezing, wages, provoked industrial disputes – even the picketing of power stations which brought a restriction of electricity supplies and a three-day working week. For Heath, the contest had come down to the question of "who governs," the Government or the unions, and he turned to the electorate (Browning 1986, pp. 49, 50, 358). The election of February 1974 resulted in 301 seats for Labour and 297 for Conservatives (318 required for a majority), and Labour formed a minority government. In the election later that year, Labour won a bare majority (319 of 635), and Heath was deposed as Conservative leader in February 1975, in favor of Margaret Thatcher.

Conditions failed to improve. Inflation rose from about 10 percent annually during the four years of Tory (1970–74) rule to about 15 percent during four years of Labour, and unemployment doubled. The Labour Chancellor Denis Healey occasionally referred to money, but mostly followed Heath and Barber in focusing on taxes and subsidies as ways of influencing the price level. In his 1975 budget speech he said:

> We in the Government have honoured our side of the social contract by our pro-gramme of legislation on industrial relations, by fiscal legislation to secure a juster and more equitable distribution of wealth and incomes, by action on food subsidies and rents, and by generous provision for the pensioners and others among the under-privileged in our society ... the social wage now amounts to about £1,000 a year for every member of the working population.

Coming as close as he dared, Browning (1986, p. 66) wrote, "to saying that the trade unions ... had not kept their side of the bargain" by accepting the Government's pay guides. A few months' later, Wilson's successor as prime minister, James Callaghan, told a Labour Party conference:

> We used to think that you could spend your way out of a recession, and increase employment by cutting taxes and boosting Government spending. I tell you in all candour that that option no longer exists, and that in so far as it ever did exist, it only worked on each occasion since the war by injecting a bigger dose of inflation into the economy, followed by a higher level of unemployment as the next step. Higher inflation followed by higher unemployment. We have just escaped from the highest rate of inflation this country has known; we have not yet escaped from the consequences: high unemployment ... that is the history of the last 20 years. (Callaghan 1976)

Inflation fell from 22 percent in 1975 to 8 percent in 1978, but markets revolted against the wage and price restraints. In December 1978, "the Government was defeated in Parliament on its pay sanctions policy and announced that action would no longer be taken against firms in breach of the policy." Since the sanctions had never seriously been applied to workers, the Government was left with an unenforceable pay policy. The labor market was free, and pay demands considerably above 5 percent were made – enforced by strikes, stoppages, and massive picketing – and the country's "winter of discontent" had begun. The Conservatives led by Thatcher won the general election in May 1979.

  Controls, or rather attempted controls, were ended and the rates of change of money and prices came down, although not as rapidly as had been hoped, because, it was said, as in the previous administration, of underestimates of the Public Sector Borrowing Requirement (Browning 1986, p. 175). Even so, the annual rate of inflation (of the Retail Price Index, RPI) came down from 13.4 percent to 3.4 percent between 1979 and 1988, and then, after a brief rise, was steady in the vicinity of 2 percent to 2½ percent from 1992 to 2014, becoming more variable but still low over the next half-dozen years.

Table 5.2   *Annual per capita incomes, U.S. dollars, of large*
                    high-income countries

1960		1979		1999		2015	
U.S.A.	2,881	Sweden	13,834	Japan	36,357	U.S.A.	56,064
Canada	2,295	U.S.A.	11,302	U.S.A.	34,535	Australia	51,352
Australia	1,807	France	11,027	Sweden	30,557	Sweden	50,687
Sweden	1,983	Germany	10,920	**U.K.**	**28,168**	**U.K.**	**44,162**
U.K.	**1,381**	Canada	9,831	Germany	26,839	Canada	43,206
France	1,320	Australia	9,341	France	24,617	Germany	41,686
Germany	–	Japan	8,822	Australia	22,547	France	36,304
Italy	804	**U.K.**	**7,511**	Canada	22,224	Japan	34,629
Japan	479	Italy	6,735	Italy	21,890	Italy	30,642

Source: IMF, *World Economic Outlook,* April 2019.

Thatcher (1993, p. 706) believed the Bank and Treasury benefitted from the support of her monetarist backbone, although the country shared the world-wide reaction to the Great Inflation of the 1970s. More lessons were learned – or should have been learned – from the prosperity accompanying the reduction in inflation. Table 5.2 also shows the improvement in the U.K.'s relative-income position over the period, which might have had something to do with its improvement in price stability and reductions in regulation, although several countries had similar experiences.

INFLATION TARGETS

The first country with a formal agreement between the Government and the central bank for the containment of inflation was New Zealand. Its *Reserve Bank Act of 1989* required the Bank "to formulate and implement monetary policy directed to the economic objective of achieving and maintaining stability in the general level of prices." The precise objective was to be negotiated between the Minister of Finance and the governor of the Bank, and made public in a Policy Targets Agreement (PTA) which set forth "specific targets by which monetary policy performance, in relation to its statutory objective, can be assessed during the Governor's term" (Mishkin and Posen 1997).

The PTA was an attempt to add credibility to the Government's/Bank's monetary policy by imposing political costs on its failure. It was apparently successful as inflation fell from double digits in the mid-1980s to less than 2 percent from 1991. It replaced the New Zealand Reserve Bank Act of 1964, which had been typical of its time in aiming at "the highest degree of production, trade and of employment and of maintaining a stable internal price level," and getting none.

The U.K. (and several others) followed New Zealand in the *Bank of England Act of 1997*, illustrated in Figure 5.3, with the added twist that monetary policy was to be handled by a Monetary Policy Committee with a majority from outside the Bank, although chaired by the governor – after 66 years of being the responsibility of the Chancellor of the Exchequer, with the Bank as advisor. Labour had won control of Parliament in 1997 after 18 years of Conservative Government, and the Bank of England Act might have been a shrewd political move to take monetary stability as a campaign issue away from the Tories (Milesi-Ferrati 1995).

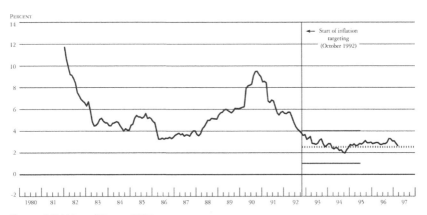

Source: Mishkin and Posen, 1997.

Figure 5.3   Actual and targeted inflation in the UK, 1981–97

As a final note to the development of the monetary standard, it should be realized that price or inflation targeting approximates the gold standard. If the central bank or treasury fixes its currency's (say dollar or pound) price of gold, the country's price level is a weighted average of other (market) prices relative to gold. Under modern price targeting, the monetary authority fixes the pound price of a basket of goods and arbitrage makes the market conform to the authority's target.

6. American monetary policy in the nineteenth century

> A sound currency is an essential and indispensable security for the fruits of industry and honest enterprise. Every man of property or industry, every man who desires to preserve what he honestly possesses, or to obtain what he can honestly earn, has a direst interest in maintaining a safe circulating medium, such a medium as shall be a real and substantial representative of property.
>
> –Speech by Senator Daniel Webster on rechartering the Bank of the United States, May 25, 1832

The American price level was about the same in 1900 as in 1830, although one cannot call the nineteenth century one of stable prices. Two-thirds of the century (1815–50 and 1864–96) saw falling prices – which by the way were mainly years of prosperity and famous economic advances associated with names such as Cyrus McCormick, Samuel F.B. Morse, Sir Henry Bessemer, Andrew Carnegie, John D. Rockefeller, Thomas Edison, Alexander Graham Bell, and Cornelius Vanderbilt – while two large inflations (1810–15, 50 percent) and (1861–64, 100 percent) were concentrated in wartime, all illustrated in Figure 6.1. Primary financial institutions included the controversial first and second Banks of the United States (1791–1811 and 1816–36), the first urged by Secretary of the Treasury Alexander Hamilton (1789–95) but whose recharter was rejected by Congress, and the second, whose recharter was vetoed by President Andrew Jackson. This left the country without a unique central bank until President Woodrow Wilson oversaw the creation of the Federal Reserve System in 1913. In the meantime, the principal influence on bank reserves and money was the U.S. Treasury's budget management, while the hundreds and then thousands of small and fragile State banks contributed to frequent financial crises. The monetary system – particularly State vs. federal banks, branch banking, and the monetary base (gold, silver, or fiat paper) – was a major source of political conflict. Among the issues were resumptions of the exchange rate (value of the currency) following the inflations.

Source: Compiled by the author.

Figure 6.1 *U.S. consumer price index 1800–1913*

THE PANIC OF 1819 AND THE FIRST AMERICAN DEPRESSION

Financing the War

Table 6.1 highlights the American economy from 1811 to 1825, against the backgrounds of a growing population moving west (increasing one-third every 10 years: 7.2 million, 9.6 million, and 12.9 million in 1810, 1820, and 1830, during and in the aftermath of wars in Europe and the Americas. The War of 1812 – called Mr. Madison's war in New England – occupies a complex place in American history. It was a reluctant and unpopular war in some sections while it was underway, and failed to achieve the hopes of its advocates, but entered the nation's memory as a great patriotic achievement – the second War of Independence because the country stood up to the mighty U.K.

The best-remembered American grievance leading to the war was the short-handed British navy's impressment of American sailors. The U.K. and France, with their allies, had been fighting for 20 years, France dominating on land and the U.K. at sea. The latter maintained a formidable blockade of Europe, wreaking hardship on American commerce and treating American and other seamen as a labor supply. After all, they might be British born.

President Thomas Jefferson tried to avoid war by persuading Congress to pass the *Embargo Act of 1807*, which forbade American ships from visiting foreign ports so as to avoid contact with the belligerents and show their dependence on American shipping. The Act was especially unpopular in maritime New England, which evaded the embargo as best it could.

Those agitating most strongly for war were the expansionist War Hawks from the South and West, led by Senators Henry Clay of Kentucky and John Calhoun of South Carolina, who complained of the British encouragement of Indian tribes, and wanted U.S. expansion into Canada. President James Madison's June 1812 call for a declaration of war with the U.K. passed the House 79 to 49 and the Senate 19 to 13 (no yeas from New England).

The U.S. experienced famous victories (including the Battle of Lake Erie, "We have met the enemy and they are ours," September 1813; Battle of New Orleans, January 1815, after but before knowledge of the peace treaty) and defeats (the burning of Washington, August 1814). Peace had been negotiated at Ghent, Netherlands (now Belgium) on December 24, 1814, unanimously ratified by the Senate in February. The Treaty confirmed the boundaries existing at the start of the war, and the maritime problems had disappeared with the fall of Napoleon. The biggest losers might have been the Indians, who lost British support, and the biggest winners the Canadians who did not wish to be absorbed by the U.S. Some historians have called the treaty "a victory for the West. No Eastern demand was satisfied by it; but once the British had withdrawn their claims to the sources of the Mississippi and control of the Northwest, the triumph of American expansionism was complete" (Dangerfield 1952, p. 105).

The possibility of the U.S. being dragged into the European wars had been recognized, but President Jefferson and Treasury Secretary Albert Gallatin were reluctant to bear the costs of preparing for an uncertain war. The bulk of the federal government's revenue was customs duties, much of which would be lost in wartime, and the Democrat–Republican (Jeffersonian) opposition to internal taxes was expected to continue in war, which Gallatin hoped to finance by borrowing. "To meet these loans in the future, we must depend on coming prosperity and the wisdom of successors; that is, favorable circumstances and rigid economy" (Dewey 1922, p. 129).

The first public loan (three months before the declaration of war) was placed without difficulty. However, the shortage of bank capital and the Government's dim prospects began to threaten public credit. "It was soon discovered that little financial support could be expected from the Eastern States – largely because of the bitterness of the commercial interests, whose prosperity had long been endangered by Jefferson's policy of embargo." Subscriptions were soon accepted at 12 percent discount; later at 20 percent; and portions were accepted in State bank notes worth but 65 percent of specie. "The total loss to the government in disposing of its loans during the war ... was enormous: [F]or loans of over $80,000,000 the Treasury received but $34,000,000 as measured in specie."

Table 6.1   *Money, prices, and the U.S. Treasury, 1811–25*

	Prices: Indexes 1821–25 = 100 and by weight				Money and banking: Nos. & $millions			U.S. Treasury			
	US WPI	Wheat $/bu.	Cotton $/lb.	UK WPI	Banks	Bank notes	Boston bank notes and deposits	Treasury notes	Revenue	Spending	Land sales
1811	135	1.846	.155	145	101	28	1.302		14.4	8.1	1.0
1812	142	1.774	.105	164	111		1.306	2.8	9.8	20.3	.7
1813	161	1.622	.125	169	127		1.712	4.9	14.3	31.7	.8
1814	190	1.482	.150	154	145		1.518	10.6	11.2	34.7	1.1
1815	173	1.565	.210	130	181	68	.773	15.5	15.7	32.7	1.3
1816	160	1.942	.295	119	205		.469	8.7	47.7	30.6	1.7
1817	133	2.406	.265	132	223		.670	.6	33.1	21.8	2.0
1818	131	1.981	.240	139	237		.493		21.6	19.8	2.6
1819	119	1.344	.240	128	261		.446		24.6	21.5	3.3
1820	107	.928	.170	115	263	50	.553		17.9	18.3	1.6
1821	102	.880	.143	100	254		.856		14.6	15.8	1.2
1822	104	1.248	.143	88	243		.380		20.2	15.0	1.8
1823	99	1.354	.114	98	248		.381		20.5	14.7	.9
1824	94	1.103	.148	102	253		.509		19.4	20.3	1.0
1825	98	.998	.186	113	257		.279		21.8	15.6	1.3

Sources: United States Census Bureau 1975, pp. 205, 209, 1104, 1106; Mitchell 1962, p. 470; Friedman and Schwartz 1970, pp. 218–21; Fenstermaker 1965, p. 41.

The president persuaded Congress to levy a few direct taxes in 1813 and 1814, but deficits mounted and reached their pre-Civil War peak in 1815 (Dewey 1922, pp. 131–9).

The number of banks in the U.S.A. more than doubled between 1811 and 1816, and their circulations tripled while their metallic-reserve ratio fell from 42 percent to 28 percent. The war was financed almost entirely by debt, mostly bonds purchased with State bank notes. Federal revenues actually fell between 1811 and 1814, unsurprisingly since they were mostly customs duties. The national debt, which had been reduced from $83 million to $45 million between 1800 and 1811, reached its pre-Civil War peak of $127 million in 1815.

Wholesale prices rose 40 percent between 1811 and 1814, alongside a land boom. Since 1800, the government had aggressively marketed its massive land-holdings through multiple land-offices offering credit payable over four years. There were many forfeitures and in 1819, land buyers owed the government $23 million. Petitions were regularly presented to Congress to relieve defaulting settlers (with considerable debate over the treatment of speculators), and in 1820, after the Panic of 1819, the public-land credit system was abolished and the government's asking price of land reduced (Gallatin 1831, pp. 286, 291, 296; Dewey 1922, p. 217; Rothbard 1962, pp. 39, 45). Money, prices, and budget data are presented in Table 6.1.

Restoring the Currency

End-of-war debts included the substantial obligations of State banks, whose specie reserves were small. Most banks outside New England had stopped the convertibility of their notes with the acquiescence of state regulators. The resulting variations in currency discounts from their face values hindered trade and attracted the attentions of the President and Congress. President Madison, who as a congressman in 1791 had opposed the creation of the first Bank of the United States, was now on the other side, and thought a U.S. bank might help restore a uniform national currency.

Senator Daniel Webster responded that a national bank was unnecessary, that the problem only needed compulsory redemption. A resolution was obtained, effective February 1817, that the Government would accept payment only in coin or redeemable bank notes, and would keep no deposits in "any bank which shall not pay its notes, when demanded, in the lawful money of the United States" (*Annals of Congress*, April 30, 1816, 1440, 1919). The charter of the second Bank of the U.S. (BUS) was also approved in April 1816.

The 1817 resumption was "neither universal nor genuine," however, and the BUS participated in the credit boom as fully as the state banks it was supposed to restrain. It expanded rapidly, establishing 18 branches by the end of 1817, which the head office failed to control. The notes of any branch were obligations of all, and some, especially Baltimore, vied to see who would be largest. There was also considerable corruption in both the state and U.S. banks. Three directors of the Baltimore branch (including Cashier James McCulloch of Supreme Court case fame) borrowed millions of dollars from their branch to speculate on BUS stock – unsuccessfully to their cost (Smith 1953, p. 104; Hammond 1957, pp. 260–62).

The BUS was also, for a while, encouraged by Treasury Secretary William Crawford's tolerance of State banks' tardiness in redeeming their notes. Some pressed for resumption but Maryland Congressman Samuel Smith deplored the pressures on state institutions. During the war, he said, "they had been the pillars of the nation, now they were the caterpillars." Virginia Congressman John Randolph feared the administration's power over the banks. On the other hand, "Every man present in the House, or out of it, with some rare exceptions, was either a stockholder, president, cashier, clerk, or doorkeeper, runner engraver, paper-maker, or mechanic in some way or other to a bank …. It was as much swindling to issue notes with the intent not to pay as it was burglary to break open a house …. But a man might as well go to Constantinople to preach Christianity as to get up here and preach against banks" (Dewey 1922, p. 149):

> Coupled with the expansion of bank-note circulation was the withdrawal of specie from the country; the dissolution of the United States Bank alone had caused the export of $7,000,000 which had been invested by Europeans in its stock. The drain of specie was greatest from the Middle and Southern States, so that when Washington was attacked by the British in 1814, all banking institutions except in New England, where more conservative methods had prevailed, were forced to suspend specie payments …. The direct loss to the government from poor or worthless bank-notes received during the four years 1814–17, amounted to over $5,000,000. (Dewey 1922, p. 145)

BUS branches in the South and West had loaned freely, and as the notes issued on such loans were redeemable at any branch East or West the capital of the Bank was unduly diverted to sections which did not enjoy commercial stability. The Bank finally, in August 1818, sent out orders to redeem no notes except at the office where issued, and reduced its credits – just when "commerce was struggling to recover from the inflation of the war period" (Dewey 1922, p. 152).

In July 1818, with demand liabilities above $22,360,000, the BUS had specie of $2,360,000, a ratio a little more than one-tenth, instead of the legally required one-fifth – and the Treasury would want specie of $2 million in October in payment of Louisiana Purchase debt. "The Bank was forced in self-preservation to do exactly the opposite of what a central bank should do, as 'lender of last resort and keeper of ultimate reserves,' which is to 'check expansion and ease contraction'. ... Instead, the Bank had stimulated the expansion and now must intensify the contraction. ... A popular hatred of it based on the grim efforts made to collect or secure what was receivable ... was never extinguished. ... 'The Bank was saved,' wrote the Jacksonian advisor, William Gouge, 'and the people were ruined'" (Hammond 1957, pp. 258–9; Gouge 1833 ii, p. 210).

Although the BUS got most of the blame, the "resumption ... was the Secretary's own." His power over the BUS derived from the Treasury's deposits and peacetime surplus. Secretary Crawford (1816–25) (Figure 6.2), former Georgia senator (1807–13), Secretary of War (1815–16), and a contender to succeed President Monroe, was in a strong position. He had the president's support and let it be known that acceptance of his plans for the Treasury was a condition for staying on the job

"The sufferings which have been produced by the efforts that have been made to resume, and to continue specie payments, have been great. They are not terminated, and must continue until the value of property and the price of labor shall assume that relation to the precious metals which our wealth and industry compared with those of other states, shall enable us to retain."

Source: https://upload.wikimedia.org/wikipedia/commons/9/90/WilliamHCrawford.png.

Figure 6.2   William Crawford, U.S. Senator from Georgia, 1807–13, U.S. Secretary of the Treasury, 1816–25

(Mooney 1974, p. 95). He also made an argument for the restoration of the currency that was at least as sophisticated as those given elsewhere in this book. Describing it in some detail will also help us understand those episodes. Crawford's 1820 *Report on the Currency* began with a discussion of the excess of undercapitalized bank notes with purchasing powers only fractions of their face values. Bank capital in 1817 had been reported as more than $125 million,

... but when it is recollected that, after the first payment required by the charters of the different banks they have generally gone into operation, it is probable that a considerable proportion of the remaining payments have added nothing to their active capital [and] a deduction being made of the permanent accommodation enjoyed by the stockholders in their respective banks, the active bank capital of the United States may be fairly estimated at a sum not exceeding $75,000,000. If a stockholder to the amount of $10,000 has a permanent accommodation in the bank of $8,000, he has, in fact, but $2,000 of capital in the bank. Such ... has been the process by which the capital of most of the banks has been formed ... since the commencement of the late war. [B]anks have been incorporated not because there was capital seeking investment, not because the places where they were established had commerce and manufactures which required their fostering aid, but because men without active capital wanted the means of obtaining loans which their standing in the community would not command from banks or individuals having real capital and established credit.

There was too much money, especially in the interior. The rapid increase of the currency,

... even if it had been wholly metallic, ... could not have failed to have produced a very great depreciation; but when it is considered that not only the increase, but the whole circulation, consisted of paper, not convertible into specie, some idea of its depreciation may be formed. The depreciation, however, was not uniform in every part of the Union. [T]he greatest depreciation of the currency existed in the interior States, where the issues were not only excessive, but where their relation to the commercial cities greatly aggravated the effects of that excess, [including] the suspension of specie payments by the banks.

Government surpluses and capital requirements reduced the currency, but the policy was

... not pursued with sufficient earnestness .... All intelligent writers upon currency agree that where it is decreasing in amount, poverty and misery must prevail .... As there is no recorded example in the history of nations of a reduction of the currency so rapid and so extensive, so but few examples have occurred of distress so general and so severe as that which has been exhibited in the United States. To the evils of a decreasing currency are superadded those of a deficient currency. But not withstanding it is deficient, it is still depreciated. In several of the States the great mass of the circulation is not even ostensibly convertible into specie at the will of the holder. During the greater part of the time that has elapsed since the resumption of specie payments, the convertibility of bank notes into specie has been rather nominal than real in the largest portion of the Union. On the part of the banks, mutual weakness had produced mutual forbearance.

Crawford began to take a hard line while understanding its consequences:

The extensive diffusion of bank stock among the great body of the citizens in most of the States had produced the same forbearance among individuals. To demand specie of the banks, when it was known that they were unable to pay; was to destroy their own interests by destroying the credit of the banks, in which the productive portion of their property was invested. In favor of forbearance was also added the influence of the great mass of bank debtors. Every dollar in specie drawn out of the banks, especially for exportation, induced the necessity of curtailments. To this portion of the community all other evils were light when compared with the iraperious demands of banks.

Yet he saw it as his duty to restore the value of the currency, and he understood the gold standard as well as any official discussed here:

As the currency is, at least in some parts of the Union, depreciated, it must, in those parts, suffer a further reduction before it becomes sound. The nation must continue to suffer until this is effected. After the currency shall be reduced to the amount which, when the present quantity of the precious metals is distributed among the various nations of the world in proportion to their respective exchangeable values, shall be assigned to the United States, when time shall have regulated the price of labor and of commodities according to that amount, and when pre-existing engagements shall have been adjusted, the sufferings from a depreciated, decreasing, and deficient currency will be terminated, individual and public prosperity will gradually revive, and the productive energies of the nation resume their accustomed activity.

As commerce is nothing more than the exchange of equivalents, the reduction in the price of the articles of such state, and the increased value of the currency will promptly produce a reaction; and gold and silver will return in the quantities required to redupe their value to that which they maintain in the adjacent states. With the return of specie, all other articles will return to the prices which they commanded before its exportation. Like fluids, the precious metals, so long as they are employed as the general measure of value, will constantly tend to preserve a level. Every variation from it will be promptly corrected, without the intervention of human laws.

Crawford responded to those who proposed to end deflation/depression by means of a national paper currency:

It may also be proper to observe that those sections of the Union where a discretionary national currency would be most likely be acceptable would probably derive from it the least benefit. In the west and south the complaints of a deficient currency have been most distinctly heard. [T]hey proceed in a greater degree from the disbursement of the public revenue than from any other cause. The great mass of public expenditure is made to the east. The revenue accruing from imports; though principally collected in the middle and eastern States, is paid by the great mass of consumers throughout the United States, That which is paid for the public lands, although in some degree drawn from every part of the Union, is principally paid, by the citizens of the west and of the south. The greatest part of the revenue accruing from the public lands, as well as that collected in the southern States, upon imports, has been transferred to the middle and eastern States to be expended. The necessity of making this transfer arises from the circumstance that the great mass of the public debt is held in those States or by foreigners whose agents reside in them; and from the establishment of dock-yards and naval stations in their principal ports. This transfer will continue to be necessary, until the public debt shall be extinguished,

and until the other expenditures of the Government can … be more equally distributed. If a national currency should be established, the demand for it in the southern
and western States, for the purpose of transmission, would be incessant; whilst its
return, by the ordinary course of trade, especially in the latter, would be slow and in
some degree uncertain.

The addition of a paper national currency would not avoid the necessary monetary and price adjustments:

The sufferings which have been produced by the efforts that have been made to
resume, and to continue specie payments, have been great. They are not terminated,
and must continue until the value of property and the price of labor shall assume
that relation to the precious metals which our wealth and industry compared with
those of other states, shall enable us to retain. Until this shall be effected, an abortive
attempt by the substitution of a paper currency to arrest the evils we are suffering
will produce the most distressing consequences. The sufferings that are past will, in
such an event, recur with additional violence, and the nation will again find itself
in the situation which it held at the moment when specie payments were resumed.
(Wm. H. Crawford, U.S. Treasury 1820, *Report on the Currency*)

Monetary tightening had come with the BUS's new administration of Langdon
Cheeves in spring 1819, shortly before the U.S. Supreme Court's *McCulloch
vs. Maryland* decision and the curtailment of business at the southern and
western offices and the prohibition of branches to draw on other branches
without supporting funds. Specie in the Bank's vaults was only $126,745,
Cheeves told a stockholders' meeting on April 1, 1819, while its net debt to the
eastern city banks was $79,126. "It is true that there were in the Mint $267, 978
and in transit from Kentucky and Ohio overland $250,000: but the Treasury
dividends were payable on that day to the amount of $500,000." "The wagons
full of specie from the West, however, arrived very seasonably the next day, or
a day or two thereafter" (Hammond 1957, pp. 263–5; Browning 2019, p. 167).
The East was relieved by the West.

"Feeling was especially bitter in Ohio, where the Bank's earlier extensions
of credit had been extensive …. Much Ohio real estate … was coming into the
Bank's hands on foreclosure." In February 1819, the Ohio legislature imposed
a $50,000 tax on each branch of the Bank (Chillicothe and Cincinnati) in the
State, and authorized the State Auditor in collecting the tax to enter every
room, vault, and other place in the branch office and open every chest and
receptacle. Concluding that he had no choice but to carry out the state law in
spite of *McCulloch vs. Maryland*, the Auditor directed an agent, John Harper,
of the Auditor's office to collect the amount due from the Chillicothe office.

The cashier of the office reported that Harper and two others, "without
any previous notice whatever suddenly entered the office, … jumped over
the counter, took … forcible possession of the vault [and] demanded to know

if I was prepared to pay the said tax; to which I answered in the negative and made an ineffectual exertion to obtain possession of the vault. Harper disregarded the reading of a court order protecting the Bank and proceeded to remove from the vault and a drawer specie and bank notes amounting to $120,425" (Hammond 1957, p. 267).

The BUS had issued little credit and circulation in New England and the Middle States. "In account of this sectionalism in its operations the BUS did not come into conflict with the strong local institutions of the East – but a great deal in the South and West, where it was greatly needed at the time but occasioned much ill-will in the long run" (Dewey 1922, p. 153).

"The conventional view of monetary policy, 1811–20," Richard Timberlake (1993, p. 13) wrote, begins with the termination of the first Bank of the United States, whose initial charter for 1791–1811 was not renewed, freeing the state banks of its restraining influence. Having no BUS to assist it, the Treasury financed the War of 1812 as best it could through the state banks. Without the restraining influence of a central bank, the number of state banks mushroomed [see Table 6.1], and most would neither pay specie nor accept each others' notes at par. [H]ence, the government was forced to receive its revenues in state-bank paper and treasury notes of all degrees of depreciation," and inflation developed from the proliferation of bank credit and notes (Catterall 1902, p. 4).

In fact, the history of inflation has had less to do with banking structures and the existence of central banks than with the needs of governments, especially in wartime. The American inflation corresponded with the government deficits arising from the War of 1812, just as the British inflation of 1797–1813 was associated with the suspension of the convertibility of the pound, which allowed the Bank of England to finance its war with France. The primary purpose of central banks has not been to restrain government borrowing, but to enable it, leading to monetary restrictions and depressions afterwards.

THE INDEPENDENT TREASURY, 1846–1914

> *Be it enacted* ..., Sec. 6. That the treasurer of the United States ... and all public officers of whatsoever character ... are hereby required to keep safely, without loaning, using, depositing in banks, or exchanging for other funds than as allowed by this act, all the public money collected by them ... till the same is ordered by the proper department or officer of the Government to be transferred or paid out ....
>
> Sec. 18. That on January 1, 1847, and thereafter, all duties, taxes, sales of public lands, debts, and sums of money accruing or becoming due to the United States ... shall be paid in gold and silver coin only, or in treasury notes ....
>
> Sec. 19. That on April 1, 1847, and thereafter, every officer or agent engaged in making disbursements on account of the United States ... shall make all payments in gold and silver coin, or in treasury notes if the creditor agree to receive said notes ... (*The Independent Treasury Act*, August 6, 1846)

The end of the BUS by Jackson's veto of Congress's bill to renew its charter required the federal Government to find other depositories. The *Act of June 1836 to Regulate the Deposits of Public Money* provided that the deposits of the federal Government be distributed among the states "in proportion to their respective representation in the Senate and House of Representatives of the United States" (Sec. 13, Krooss 1969, p. 972). Since most federal revenues were customs duties deposited in banks in the port cities, the Act in effect required a transfer of "specie from the place where it was most wanted, in order to sustain the general circulation of the country, to places where it was not wanted at all," Gallatin (1841, p. 391) wrote, and "the monetary affairs of the country were convulsed" (Bourne 1885, pp. 36–7). Others have argued that the Panic of 1837 and the subsequent depression owed more to the previous credit expansion and international gold flows than to the Government's choice of depositories (Hammond 1957, p. 457; Temin 1969, pp. 172–3; Timberlake 1993, ch. 5).

To avoid the problems raised by politically favored, "pet" banks as depositories, spurred by the losses caused by the many bank failures during the depression following the Panic of 1837, and to establish an independent organization to manage the Government's funds, Jackson's successor, President Van Buren (1837–41) proposed an "independent treasury" system by which the Treasury kept its money in its own, "sub-treasury," vaults. Webster attacked the system in the Senate:

> The use of money is in the exchange. It is designed to circulate, not to be hoarded. All the Government should have to do with it is to receive it today, that it may pay it away tomorrow. It should not receive it before it needs it, and it should part with it as soon as it owes it. To keep it – that is, to detain it, to hold it back from general use, to hoard it, is a conception belonging to barbarous times and barbarous Governments. (U.S. Congress, Congressional Globe 1838, app. p. 2)

The Independent Treasury bill was passed in 1840, but repealed the next year by the Whig Congress in anticipation of a new national bank, which, however, was vetoed by President John Tyler. Vice President Tyler, a Democrat, had succeeded William Henry Harrison, upon whose approval the bill had depended, after his death a month in office. The Independent Treasury was reestablished in 1846, and managed the Government's cash until the creation of the Federal Reserve in 1913.

The new system exposed the monetary base to shocks from federal budgets. Seasonal movements in net Treasury receipts often took reserves from circulation in active times such as the autumnal crop movements. The fiscal surpluses common to peace had longer-term deflationary effects. During the two decades of falling prices preceding 1896, for example, Treasury balances rose from $51 million to $258 million, which were significant compared with the average monetary base of $1 billion.

The country nevertheless did well under the new system. The period 1841–56 was the longest expansion in U.S. history, a recession-free period which has been called America's First Great Moderation. "The low volatility of industrial production and stock returns during the First Great Moderation, which occurred during a period without a U.S. central bank, is similar to that observed for the Second Great Moderation (1984–2007)" (Davis and Weidenmier 2017).

Treasury secretaries monitored by Congress moderated the most disruptive effects of the Independent Treasury Act as written. The Treasury sometimes supplied funds on occasions of stress by early payments of interest and debt redemptions, equivalent to modern open-market purchases. Secretary James Guthrie reported in the summer of 1853 that

> ... the amount still continuing to accumulate in the Treasury, apprehensions were entertained that a contraction of discounts by the city banks of New York would result, ... and ... might have an injurious influence on financial and commercial operations. With a view, therefore, to give public assurance that money would not be permitted to accumulate in the Treasury, a public offer was made on the 30th of July to redeem ... the sum of $5 million of the loans of 1847 and 1848. (U.S. Congress, Congressional Globe 1853, app. p. 250)

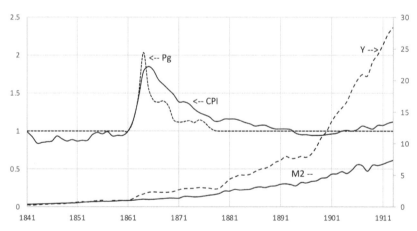

Source: Compiled by the author.

Figure 6.3   *Real GNP (Y), money (M2), price level (CPI), and gold price (Pg), 1841–1913 (1860 = 1)*

Resourceful applications of the System were made by both political parties throughout its life (U.S. *Treasury Reports*), the greatest demands on the Independent Treasury were made by the Civil War (Figure 6.3).

War, Suspension, and Resumption

The needs of the Civil War soon required the suspension of convertibility and its replacement by an inconvertible paper currency, the famous *greenbacks*. The dollar price of gold doubled between 1861 and 1864, and the prices of goods in general rose 75 percent. Resumption of dollar convertibility at its prewar value required substantial deflation.

Three approaches were considered. Some, including the Greenback Party's, opposed deflation, overlapping with the silver interests that later led resistance to the gold standard. Congress initially took the opposite view, and in December 1865, a House resolution stating "the necessity for a contraction of the currency with a view to as early a resumption of specie payment as the business interests of the country would permit" passed by a vote of 144 to 6. This suited Secretary of the Treasury Hugh McCulloch, whose "chief aim," was "to provide the means to discharge the claims upon the Treasury at the earliest date practicable, and to institute measures to bring the country gradually back to the specie basis, a departure from which ... is no less damaging and demoralizing to the people than expensive to the Government" (*Banker's Magazine*, April 1865, p. 783; Unger 1964, p. 41). However, the "resolution soon proved not to reflect the real sentiment of the people," historian Davis Dewey (1922, p. 335) observed. The Secretary had set about his task too energetically to suit most people. He was denounced as an impractical and dangerous theorist who expected to achieve specie payments by a "few legislative *whereases* and *be it enacteds*," while industry was paralyzed by his "species of experiment," charged letters to Congress (Unger 1959). In April 1866, Congress restricted purchases to $10 million a month for the next six months and $4 million a month thereafter. McCulloch protested. "How rapidly [the currency] may be retired must depend upon the effect which contraction may have upon business and industry, and can be better determined as the work progresses." He thought Congress's limit could be doubled "without injuriously affecting legitimate business .... There is a great adaptability in the business of the United States, and it will easily accommodate itself to any policy which the Government may adopt" (Secretary of the Treasury *Annual Report*, 1865; Krooss 1969, pp. 1467–8).

McCulloch proceeded as rapidly as he was allowed, and had cut the greenbacks almost in half when, in February 1868, Congress froze them at the amount then in circulation – \$347 million. Republican leader James G. Blaine of Maine summarized the pressures on Congress:

> Mr. McCulloch, in trying to enforce the policy of contraction represented an apparently consistent theory in finance; but the great host of debtors who did not wish their obligations to be made more onerous and the great host of creditors who did not desire that their debtors should be embarrassed and possibly rendered unable to liquidate united on the practical side of the question and aroused public opinion against the course of the Treasury Department. In the end, outside of banking and financial centers, there was a strong and persistent demand for repeal of the Contraction Act. [A]lthough it might be admitted that the entire nation would be benefited by the ultimate result, the people knew that the process would bring embarrassment to vast numbers and would reduce not a few to bankruptcy and ruin. (Blaine 1886, p. 328)

Georgia Senator John Gordon agreed:

> The people of the South and West are debtors; ... their obligations were formed ... when gold was at 110 to 150; and now to force them to pay in a currency equal to gold would be simply to increase their debts by the amount of 10 to 50 percent. (Cong. Rec., 43rd Cong., 1st sess., 13–15 (1872); Timberlake 1993, p. 108)

Direct representatives of the public, such as Blaine, Gordon and Sherman (Figure 6.4), were in the next century replaced by less knowledgeable or publicly attuned central bankers – as we will see in Chapter 7. The middle way to resumption as advocated by John Sherman from the hotly contested state of Ohio, and also Chairman of the Senate Finance Committee – that it should occur naturally by letting the country grow into the currency – became, with fits and starts, the official policy. Sound-money observers and historians complained that "procrastination became the norm; and after a few years many congressmen were paying only lip service to the resumption ideal" (Timberlake 1993, p. 91). So resumption was achieved between 1864 and 1879 without depression, not by retiring the greenbacks but through faster growth in incomes than money (3.8 percent per annum compared with 2.6 percent).

The monetary standard was one of the two principal political controversies of this period, the other being the tariff. The tariff was primarily combat between the high-tariff Republican and low-tariff Democratic parties, the latter position partly a consequence of pressure from the long-term anti-tariff Solid South. Monetary differences, on the other hand were distinctively geographic, between the financial sound-money East, and southern and western populists famously associated with frequent presidential candidate William Jennings Bryan. It has been argued that the New York sound-money Democrat Grover Cleveland (president of the U.S.A., 1885–89, 1893–97) was the model for the wicked witch of the East in the monetary allegory, *The Wonderful Wizard of Oz*; and Bryan, the foremost but sometimes compromising spokes-

"I have come home to look after my fences" (speech to his neighbors, Mansfield, Ohio).

Source: https://www.loc.gov/item/2017893118/.

Figure 6.4   *John Sherman, U.S. House of Representatives, 1855–61; Senate 1861–77, 1881–97; Secretary of the Treasury 1877–81*

man for silver money, for the cowardly lion (Baum 1900; Rockoff 1990).

President Grant's first Secretary of the Treasury, George Boutwell (1869–73), resumed its prewar stabilization policies, including early security redemptions, especially in the autumn, and in October 1872, stretched the law to reissue $5 million of retired greenbacks. Sherman protested, but his Committee sympathized with Boutwell's response that relief from panics had never been attained even in England "without the personal intervention of men possessing power." Furthermore, deflation ought to be avoided because "we have no right morally to alter debtor–creditor relations." His use of the greenback reserve was

… in its effect … substantially what is done by the Government of Great Britain through the Bank of England. The Secretary furnished temporary relief … by adding to the circulation of the country, diminishing its value … and changing the relations of debtor creditor …. Clothed with authority by law, … the Secretary of the Treasury could not sit silent and inactive while ruin was blasting the prospects of many and creating the most serious apprehensions in all parts of the country. It was a great responsibility; but it is a responsibility which must be taken by men who are clothed with the authority [in the Senate, to which he had been elected in 1872]. (U.S. Congress, Congressional Record 1874, app. 19)

Sherman chided his colleagues for their gestures to resumption while allowing money to increase and the premium on gold to continue (U.S. Congress, Congressional Record 1874, p. 700), but did not push for a more rigorous policy until after the 1874 elections, in which the Democrats won control of the House and gained several seats in the Senate. The Republican majority of the lame-duck Congress believed their loss had been caused by the conflicts between the Grand Old Party's (GOP) hard- and soft-money wings, and in the interest of party unity, looking toward the 1876 elections, accepted a compromise resumption plan worked out by Sherman: the limit on national banks (described in the next section) was removed; the Treasury was directed to redeem greenbacks at the rate of 80 percent of increases in national bank notes, with the proviso that greenbacks, which had risen to $382 million, would not be reduced below $300 million; and "on and after January 1, 1879, the Secretary of the Treasury shall redeem, in coin, the United States legal-tender notes then outstanding, on their presentation for redemption, at the office of the assistant treasurer of the United States in the city of New York, in sums of not less than fifty dollars" (U.S. Congress, Congressional Record 1875; Krooss 1969, pp. 1683–4).

The *Resumption Act* of January 1875 was received with a mixture of skepticism and indifference. Financial writers were unclear whether it was inflationary or deflationary, and thought its purposes purely political. A date had been set for resumption, but they saw nothing in the act to bring it about (Unger 1964, 260–62; Timberlake 1993, 110–12). Resumptionist Senator Carl Schurz asked whether some of the notes redeemed by the Treasury would be reissued, as in the past. Sherman answered that he would leave the interpretation of "redeem" to future Congresses, when greenbacks were down to the target of $300 million. "The case that is put … may never arise …. But if there is any doubt upon that question, I leave every Senator to construe the law for himself; and if there is a doubt about it, I say it is not wise as practical men dealing with practical affairs, seeking to accomplish a result, to introduce into this bill a controversy which will prevent that unity that is necessary to carry out the good that is contained in this bill" (U.S. Congress, Congressional Record 1874, p. 196). The hard-money Democratic Senator Allen Thurman complained that "it is very difficult to find what is in [the bill]. We know that there is a great deal of omission but the least possible amount of commission that ever I have seen in a great public measure" (Timberlake 1993, p. 197).

Anti-resumptionists were unable to command the two-thirds majority necessary to override the inevitable presidential veto, and the measure remained on the books until, to the surprise of nearly everyone, it was implemented as written. The plan was more restrictive than expected, especially in the hands of Sherman, who became President Rutherford Hayes's Secretary of the Treasury (1877–81) to apply the law that he had written. Although the $80 reduction in greenbacks for every $100 increase in national bank notes sounded inflationary, it had a restraining effect because the greenbacks were high-powered money – fractional reserves upon which an inverted pyramid of deposits rested.

Secretaries of the Treasury and Congress

Sherman exemplified the close working relations between Congress and the Treasury during the nineteenth century. He was a former congressman and senator. Only two of the ten secretaries serving full (four-year) presidential terms had not been a congressman: Richard Rush (1825–29), lawyer, advisor to presidents, and running mate to President John Quincy Adams in his bid for re-election in 1829, and Hugh McCulloch (1865–69, 1884–85), banker and the first Comptroller of the Currency.

Most secretaries had served on House or Senate appropriations or finance committees, and all, regardless of party, were sound money, pro-gold, advocates. Grover Cleveland and his Secretary during his second presidential term, John Carlisle (1893–97), had to deal with the Panic of 1993. They worked to end silver's threat to the gold standard and in so doing earned the enmity of agrarian, pro-silver, Bryan Democrats, which ended the political careers of both.

Carlisle was almost the last member of Congress to become Secretary of the Treasury, the exceptions being Lloyd Bentsen the first two years of Bill Clinton's presidency (1993–94) and Fred Vinson (1945–46) as President Truman replaced the New Dealers he inherited. President Woodrow Wilson's Secretary, William McAdoo (1913–18) later became a senator (1933–39). Secretaries thereafter were lawyers, bankers, and/or businessmen (until economist and former Fed executive Janet Yellen in 2021). From 1981 to 2021, almost half were investment bankers, three from Goldman Sachs.

The influences of these later secretaries on budgets and monetary policies have been mixed and often unclear. Their statements have appeared primarily to conform to their presidents' policies, although Franklin Roosevelt's Secretary, Henry Morgenthau, Jr. (1934–45), advocated a balanced budget. A bi-partisan, post-World War II, aspect of American fiscal policies has been the reduction of taxes as war spending increased. The large Kennedy tax cut (from 90 percent to 70 percent for the highest bracket) during an economic expansion received the support of both Keynesians and pro-growth conservatives, including investment-banker Secretary Douglas Dillon (1961–65). The top bracket was further reduced to 30 percent under President Reagan (see Figure 10.1). Taxes were a significant issue in the 1988 presidential campaign. Candidate George H.W. Bush took the lead in the polls with the promise, "Read my lips, no new taxes," and his later tax increase has been cited as a cause of his defeat in 1992 (Levy 1996).

Post-Civil War Congresses wanted resumption *sometime*, like post-World War I British businessmen and economists, but not at the price of immoderate present pain. Sherman and the country were fortunate in the favorable trade balance and gold inflow that coincided with the targeted resumption date

(United States Census Bureau 1975, U15, U24). But his record suggests that he would not (and could not) have forced resumption against an unfavorable tide. His political survival did not permit it. Ohio was a swing state, the geographical center of the nation's population most of the last half of the nineteenth century, and its politicians did not have the luxury of a reliable eastern hard-money or western easy-money position. Furthermore – and this may be most important – there was no third party, no central bank, whom the politicians could assign to administer the medicine.

This was the era of what Professor Woodrow Wilson (1885) called *Congressional Government*. "The checks and balances which once obtained," he wrote, "are no longer effective." The federal courts were under the appointive power of Congress, and the Supreme Court had declared its reluctance "to interfere with the *political discretion* of either Congress or the President." The president's cabinet had been made "humble servants" of Congress. In line with its British heritage, Congress in the course of exercising its power of the purse expected the Secretary of the Treasury to be its agent. While speaking for the Morrison resolution which prescribed the Treasury's cash management (see below), Senator James Beck reminded his colleagues that whereas the laws creating the other executive departments enjoined their secretaries to advise and act under the direction of the president, the Secretary of the Treasury was required "to make report and give information to either branch of the Legislature ... and generally to perform all such services relative to the finances as he shall be directed to perform .... We with the Secretary of the Treasury manage the purse; the president and the other secretaries control the sword" (U.S. Congress, Congressional Record 1886, p. 7675).

In the first American resumption a strong Secretary was able to use the national bank. "The Bank supplied the machinery, the secretary supplied the brains," Hammond wrote, and as we have seen, the Bank got the blame (Hammond 1957, p. 249). We will see that a strong Bank of England imposed an early and idealistic resumption over the protests of those affected in the 1920s. But in the United States during 1865 to 1879, the legislators were directly accountable for the currency. These are reasons – the political costs of imposing pain – that are given for divorcing the politicians from money. But devotion to the monetary theory of the day carries costs of its own.

Discretionary Monetary Management: Treasury Bank Deposits and Open-market Operations

Congress's monetary management was detailed as well as serious. The Treasury kept a large gold reserve to suit some members. There was no legal reserve or special resumption fund, although "by tradition public sentiment adopted $100,000,000 as the line of demarcation between safety and danger"

(Dewey 1922, p. 441). Some used a loophole supplied by an 1861 amendment "to allow the Secretary of the Treasury to deposit any of the moneys obtained on any of the loans now authorized by law ... in such solvent specie-paying banks as he may select" (Krooss 1969, p. 1174). Secretary Charles Fairchild (1887–89), who "always considered the needs of banks," used it to justify an expansion of Treasury bank deposits from $13 million to $54 million (Taus 1943, pp. 80–82, 269).

Some Congressmen still complained of the large sums in Treasury vaults, which might be applied to the debt to save interest expenses, and the Appropriation Act of 1881 gave the Treasury discretion to redeem Government debt. But balances remained high, and rose during Cleveland's administration (1885–89). His Secretary Daniel Manning (1885–87) wrote to Congressman Frank Hiscock that it would not be "prudent" to reduce the Treasury balance (Timberlake 1993, p. 154). In 1886, those wanting easier money secured House and Senate agreement to the Morrison resolution calling on the Treasury to apply its "surplus or balance ... over $100,000,000 ... to the payment of the interest-bearing indebtedness of the United States" at a maximum rate of $10 million a month. Ohio's A.J. Warner quoted Lord Overstone (Samuel Jones Loyd): "In adopting a paper circulation we must unavoidably depend for a maintenance of its due value upon the adoption of a strict and judicious rule for the regulation of its amount" – and asked why it was necessary to "hoard $228,000,000 in the Treasury of the United States? Is it to purchase the favor of Wall Street and the banks? If so it is altogether too dear a price" (U.S. Congress, Congressional Record 1886, pp. 6884–7).

Senator Beck argued that it was Congress's responsibility to direct the Secretary to relieve him of temptation and political embarrassment. Nelson Dingley of Maine, on the other hand, objected to Congress's interference "with a question which exclusively pertains to administration. This is the first attempt, I think, in the history of this Government to determine by a legislative resolution what should be the working balance of the Treasury .... No cast-iron rule can be laid down on a matter of this kind." Conservatives got a contingency balance of $20 million in the resolution, and authority for the Secretary to suspend debt purchases in emergencies. Benjamin Butterworth of Ohio believed the Secretary's discretion was "indispensable to the maintenance of the national credit," and called the Treasury reserve "the ballast which keeps our monetary ship steady as she moves through the sea of financial troubles which constantly threaten" (U.S. Congress, Congressional Record 1886, pp. 6937, 7675, 7998).

The Silver Question

The Treasury assisted the money markets during the panics of 1873, 1884, and 1890, but required assistance itself in 1893. We need to look at the American monetary system, which was in theory bimetallic but in practice a gold standard. A bimetallic monetary standard is one in which coins of two different metals are legal tender. They were commonplace in Western economies throughout most of recorded history. Under a typical bimetallic standard, gold and silver coins were produced by the official Mint and assigned exchange values which reflected their intrinsic metallic values. At its outset, the U.S.A. established a coinage system comprised of a silver Dollar containing 371.25 grains of silver, and a gold Eagle containing 247.5 grains of gold, reflecting the relative market value of gold to silver of 15:1. The legal tender value of the silver Dollar was $1 and of the Eagle was $10. The Mint typically bought gold and silver freely, that is, from anyone willing to sell at the Mint price, which usually was slightly lower that the value of the coins produced, the difference paying the costs of coining and sometimes profits (seigniorage).

There was, however, a difficulty with bimetallic standards. If coins were to be assigned values corresponding to the market values gold to silver, changes in the relative market value of the metals would disrupt the monetary system. Essentially, one of three things would happen. First, the coin whose relative market value had risen could be withdrawn from circulation making the monetary system either all gold or all silver. This phenomenon is predicted by Gresham's Law – bad money drives out good – named after Sir Thomas Gresham, the advisor to Elizabeth I of England, who noted the behavior in the sixteenth century. Another possibility was that both gold and silver coins would continue to circulate but not at par values: the coin whose value had risen would circulate at a premium. Finally, perhaps the coins would by custom both continue to circulate at par. The debate over which of these possibilities was in fact more prevalent, and in theory more likely, continues.

The nineteenth century saw dramatic reductions in transportation costs and a resulting integration of economies, raising the benefits of a common currency. In the 1860s, a world monetary conference endorsed a world money based on a gold coin. (The proposal was not ratified and fell victim to the 1870 Franco-Prussian War.) The choice of gold may have reflected its higher value – more prestige – and the desire to emulate the economic successes of Britain.

The major transition in fact occurred between 1850 (when only Britain and Portugal were on the gold standard) and 1880 by which time most of North America and Western Europe had adopted gold. Key factors in this timing were the Australian and California gold discoveries in the mid-nineteenth century. These caused a fall in the relative price of gold. As Gresham's law predicted, the result was a withdrawal of silver from circulation both in North

America and Europe. Gold became the de facto money as it became unprofitable to sell silver to the Mint.

Congress precluded the minting of the silver dollar in the 1873 *Coinage Act*. The silver dollar had not been minted for decades but the Act was subsequently criticized as the *Crime of '73* on the ground that it had led to the adoption of the gold standard. Germany had adopted that standard in 1870, financing the acquisition of gold (by the sale of existing silver coins) through the indemnity it imposed on France at the conclusion of the Franco-Prussian War. To avoid providing a sink for German silver, the French refused to buy silver, leading the Latin Monetary Union countries (France, Belgium, Italy, Switzerland, and Greece) to abandon bimetallism.

Although the gold standard was entrenched by 1880, during the last two decades of the nineteenth century there were attempts in the U.S.A. and Europe to return to bimetallism. The arguments were theoretical and political. A significant motivation was the rise in the price of gold after 1870 (in part due to the increased demands for gold), which generated deflation. Furthermore, silver discoveries reduced its value.

The period from the early 1870s to the mid-1890s has been called the Great Depression in the U.K. because of the nearly one-third fall in wholesale prices – a fall shared by other countries on the gold standard (Saul 1969). In the U.S.A., between 1880 (when it had resumed convertibility) and 1896, wholesale (including farm produce) and retail prices fell 30 percent and 9 percent, respectively.

The deflation became a *cause célèbre* among American debtors, especially Southern and Western farmers, who formed the Populist Party that championed indebted farmers against *elite* businesses, bankers, railroads, Democratic President Grover Cleveland, and the Democratic Party. William Jennings Bryan of Nebraska and Tom Watson of Georgia were the party's nominees for president and vice-president, respectively, in 1896. Bryan also secured the Democratic Party's presidential nomination that year.

Populist farmers joined with the silver interests to urge the revival of silver as an important part of the money supply and therefore end the deflation. They were joined by silver producers who hoped the government would buy the metal at above-market prices. The Comstock lode discovered in the Utah territory in 1859 had sparked silver explorations and a fall in the price of silver so that by 1890, the relative market values of gold and silver were 20:1, compared with the official rate of 16:1 at which the government exchanged the metals. Unfortunately for these vociferous but minority groups, a succession of conservative presidents from both major parties thwarted attempts to legislate the free coinage of silver (Timberlake 1993, p. 167).

Republican Benjamin Harrison narrowly defeated President Cleveland's bid for re-election in 1888, helped by a promise to "do something" for silver, and both parties submitted silver bills. Harrison's Secretary of the Treasury, William Windom, proposed the issue of treasury notes "against deposits of silver bullion at the market price of silver" as calculated by the Secretary. This, however, was not enough for westerners, even Republicans. Colorado Senator Edward Wolcott said they had given "handsome majorities for the Republican ticket." But, he said, "if the Windom recommendation, approved by the President, could have been announced before the election, it is my humble opinion that not a single state west of the Missouri River would have given a Republican majority" (Timberlake 1993, pp. 167–9).

The compromise measure called the *Sherman Silver Purchase Act of 1890*, continued the 16:1 official gold–silver price ratio, but limited purchases to 4.5 million ounces of silver a month, with Treasury notes issued for the purpose and redeemable in either gold or silver coin (Krooss 1969, pp. 1917–18, 1952–60). Its over-pricing led to the substitution of silver for gold in American money, and loss of the latter along with confidence in the American currency in a gold-standard world. The effects of the Silver Purchase Act were reinforced by falls in exports and Government receipts which contributed to gold exports, depressing investor confidence in the country's ability or desire to remain on the gold standard.

It also highlighted the rupture in the Democratic Party between the sound-money pro-gold easterners, including Cleveland, and the pro-silver westerners. The financial crisis led Cleveland to call a special session of Congress in the summer of 1893. (He had called attention to the "degradation" of the currency in his Inaugural Address in March.) He informed the special session that the Sherman Act "may be regarded as a truce, after a long struggle, between the advocates of free silver coinage and those intending to be more conservative" (Krooss 1969, p. 1915). The struggle had been tipped, he might have added, by a shift in power caused by the admission of six western states to the Union between 1886 and 1890. The price of silver had continued to fall despite the government's purchases. "This disappointing result has led to renewed and persistent effort in the direction of free silver coinage." But the "evil effects" of the Government's promotion of silver had already gone too far. The insistence of the United States, alone among the great trading nations, to commit to a constantly depreciating standard "has resulted in such a lack of confidence at home in the stability of currency values that capital refuses its aid to new enterprises .... Foreign investors, equally alert, not only decline to purchase American securities, but make haste to sacrifice those which they already have." A consequence had to be an end to the Treasury's ability to pay its notes in gold,

> ... and their discredit and depreciation as obligations payable only in silver ....
>
> I earnestly recommend the prompt repeal of the provisions of the act passed July 14, 1890, authorizing the purchase of silver bullion, and that other legislative action may put beyond all doubt or mistake the intention and the ability of the Government to fulfill its pecuniary obligations in money universally recognized by all civilized countries.

It is noteworthy that Cleveland's call for monetary restraint came during America's most severe depression between the 1830s and 1930s. He believed, like Herbert Hoover four decades later, that a condition of prosperity was confidence in the currency. Sherman defended both the Act and its repeal:

> Sir, "give the devil his due." The law of 1890 may have many faults, but I stand by it yet, and I will defend it, not as a permanent public policy, not a measure that I take any pride in, because I yielded to the necessity of granting relief, but I do say that the beneficial effects that flowed from the passage of the law were infinitely greater even in the percentage of money than the loss we have suffered in the fall in the price of silver. Without it, in 1891 and 1892 we would have met difficulties that would have staggered us much more than the passing breeze of the hour .... The immediate result of the measure was to increase our currency, and thus relieve our people from the panic then imminent, similar to that which we now suffer. The very men who now denounce from Wall Street this compromise were shouting "Hallelujah!" for their escape by it from free coinage. (Miller 1913, pp. xiv, 398)

The gold standard was still not assured. The Treasury attempted to maintain its reserve, but J.P. Morgan's sales of bonds on behalf of the Treasury for gold in Europe met with limited success because of hoarding and exports of gold "due to popular apprehension as to the success of the silver movement in the [1896] presidential election." The Treasury "finally recognized the futility of selling bonds for gold, most of which was shortly drawn out of the Treasury by the presentation of legal-tender notes for redemption" (Dewey 1922, p. 454).

"The victory for gold," declared A.J. Warner of the American Bimetallic Union, "is a victory of trusts and syndicated wealth, brought about by corruption and coercion, and not a victory of the people, or for the people, and it cannot last" (Merry 2017, p. 167). In his famous "cross of gold" speech that secured the Democratic nomination for president, William Jennings Bryan (1896, p. 226) declared that gold vs. silver "was a struggle between the idle holders of idle capital and the struggling masses who produce the wealth and pay the taxes of the country .... You come to us and tell us that the great cities are in favor of the gold standard. I tell you that the great cities rest upon these broad and fertile prairies. Burn down your cities and leave our farms, and your cities will spring up again as if by magic. But destroy our farms and the grass will grow in the streets of every city in the country."

The "populist" Bryan's "masses" were rather narrow in an industrializing society, and notwithstanding his imposing presence on the platform and in the history books, lost the 1896 election to the hard ("gold") money anti-inflationist William McKinley by the largest margin since war-hero Ulysses Grant's victory in 1872. The ratios of Democrat + Republican votes going to the former from 1876 to 1892 were 1.06, 0.99, 0.99, 1.02, and 1.07, and from 1896 to 1908 were 0.90, 0.88, 0.67, and 0.84.

The battle was essentially ended by increases in gold production and prices beginning in the mid-1890s, and gold was officially adopted as the sole standard in the Gold Standard Act of 1900. Bryan continued to gain the Democratic nomination (1900, 1908), and lose by large margins. The presidency and both houses of Congress were Republican from 1897 to 1911 (United States Census Bureau 1975, E40–42, Y83, Y204–7).

7. The Federal Reserve and the Great Depression

> An act to provide for the establishment of Federal reserve banks, to furnish an elastic currency, to afford means of rediscounting commercial paper, to establish a more effective supervision of banking in the United States and for other purposes.
> –*Federal Reserve Act*, December 23, 1913

Central banks affect money and prices through their dealings with commercial banks, whose structure, therefore, may be important to monetary policy. The first section below discusses the American banking system, which is at the center of money and credit, and has been used, often at the cost of stability, to achieve various political ends. The following section considers the various interests, especially the money center banks, behind the creation of the Fed, which helps us understand its responses to subsequent financial crises.

Note: From left to right: William McAdoo, Secretary of the Treasury; John Skelton Williams, Comptroller of the Currency; Adolph Miller, academic economist; Frederic Delano, railroad executive; H. Parker Willis, secretary; Charles Hamlin, lawyer; W.P.G. Harding, banker; Paul Warburg, investment banker.
Source: https://commons.wikimedia.org/wiki/File:United_States_Federal_Reserve_Board,_1917 .jpg.

Figure 7.1   Federal Reserve Board, 1914

Later sections consider the Fed's efforts to construct and apply a model of monetary policy, as well as differences within the system, especially between the Federal Reserve Board and Banks (Figure 7.1), arising from their different proximities to markets. Unfortunately, by most criteria, the Fed's response was inadequate in its first major test, the Great Depression, and has shown little improvement because the causes of its initial inadequacies, particularly its remoteness from the effects of its actions, still prevail.

THE AMERICAN BANKING SYSTEM

Background

Commercial banks in the United States have always required government (State or federal) charters and the regulations that went with them. They borrowed originally in the form of (mostly demand) deposits and lent mostly in the form of commercial loans. Until 1863, all American commercial banks (about 1,400) were State chartered (except for the short-lived first and second U.S. banks), but the *National Bank Act* of that year provided for nationally chartered banks. The Act was a war-finance measure by which the new national banks held reserves in the form of federal currency (greenbacks) and issued currency backed by U.S. bonds. The federal government hoped to drive the State banks out of existence by taxing their currencies, but checking accounts were found to do as well, and by 1913, nearly three-quarters of banks had chosen State charters, a ratio not very different from today's.

The heavy regulations on American banks (including cash and capital reserves, limits on charters, deposit insurance, and sometimes interest controls) have been rationalized on the dual grounds of protecting depositors' savings and the economic importance of money. Those regulations have often been counterproductive, however. The most damaging might have been the limits on bank branches. Until the 1980s, banks were confined to single States, and often even to limited areas within States, for example, to contiguous counties in some States and even unit banking (no branches) in most Midwestern and Western States. A cost of such limits was the lack of diversification, so that, because they were most restrictive in agricultural areas, the best predictors of American bank failures have been farm prices.

For example, after the expansion in the number of banks from about 27,000 to 30,000 between 1915 and 1920, accompanying the doubling of farm prices during World War I, they fell to 25,000 in the 1920s as farm prices fell back to their prewar levels. This decline in the number of banks was due mainly to suspensions rather than to mergers such as those which have dominated changes in the number of banks since the 1980s. Unfortunately, the recent increases in bank sizes have brought problems of their own (Cottrell et al. 1995; Federal Reserve 1943, tabs. 66–7).

The Fed is part of what a best-selling textbook has called "a crazy quilt of multiple regulatory agencies with overlapping jurisdictions. The office of Comptroller of the Currency has the primary supervisory responsibility for the 3,191 national banks …. The Federal Reserve and the state banking authorities have joint primary responsibility for the 976 state banks that are members of the Federal Reserve System. The Fed also has regulatory responsibility over companies that own one or more banks (called bank holding companies) and secondary responsibility for the national banks. The FDIC [Federal Deposit Insurance Corporation] and the state banking authorities jointly supervise the 6,548 state banks that have FDIC insurance but are not members of the Federal Reserve System. The state banking authorities have sole jurisdiction over the fewer than 500 state banks without FDIC insurance" (Mishkin 2006, pp. 231–2). There have been many proposals for simpler regulations, but existing interests are difficult to move.

The 10,715 banks referred to above applied to 2005, a one-third fall from the 1980s. A good part of the subsequent fall to about 4,700 in 2020 has been

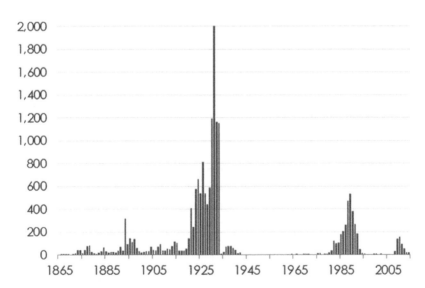

Note: "More than 17,000 banks have failed since the National Banking Acts of 1863 and 1864 created the modern American bank industry."
Source: Federal Deposit Insurance Corporation 1998.

Figure 7.2   Bank failures since the U.S. Civil War

attributed to the increased costs of regulation arising from the 2010 Dodd–Frank *Wall Street Reform and Consumer Protection Act*, and the proportion consisting of State banks has continued to grow, due, it is said, to their lower regulatory expenses and better access to the regulators (Reichert and Sheriff 2017).

The period of least failure of American banks was from the mid-1930s to the mid-1970s (Figure 7.2), which was perhaps the most prosperous period for farms in the nation's history (Gardner 2002, pp. 6, 341). However, the 1970s brought rising and fluctuating inflation, which meant rising and fluctuating interest rates, and uncertainty for banks and their borrowers – to which were added incentives and political pressures of Government programs to take on more risks.

Table 7.1   *Assets and liabilities of commercial banks in the United States (billions $)*

	1900	1929	1955	1970	2000	2019
Assets	*9.1*	*62.4*	*199*	*530*	*5,149*	*17,322*
Cash	2.3	9.0	41	85	223	1,689
Loans & leases in bank credit	5.1	36.1	75	297	3,329	9,807
Real estate	.5	6.3	19	71	1,562	4,499
Commercial			33	120	852	2,354
Consumer			16	64	523	1,537
Financial			4	24	68	539
Other	4.6	29.8	2	18	324	879
Investments	1.4	13.7	80	126	1,091	3,651
U.S.	.5	4.9	63	51	734	2,820
Other	.9	8.8	17	75	357	831
Interbank loans					214	811
Other	.3	3.6	3	22	353	1,476
Liabilities & capital	*9.1*	*62.4*	*199*	*530*	*5,149*	
Demand dep.	4.3	25.2	113	193	604	1,879
Time dep.	1.1	19.9	48	206	2,655	10,885
Other dep.	1.3	4.4	21	35		
Borrowings	...	1.7	...	18	996	1,997
Due to related foreign offices					233	...
Other	.4	2.6	3	36	233	
Capital & surplus (residual)	1.9	8.8	15	41	428	

Note: Cash = Cash assets = Cash items in the process of collection + Currency and coin + Bankers' balances (including reserves); Commercial = commercial, industrial, and agricultural; Financial = Including to brokers and dealers; Other deposits = U.S. government and interbank.
Sources: Federal Reserve Board, 1959 (*All-Bank Statistics, U.S. 1896–1955*); 1975 (*Banking and Monetary Statistics, 1941–70*); 2020 (*Federal Reserve Bulletin*).

Government and Growing Bank Risks

We know that governments have always actively intervened in finance, and President Franklin Roosevelt's New Deal beginning in 1933 accelerated those interventions (Figure 7.3). One of the best-known is *federal deposit insurance*. National and most State-chartered banks had been subject to *double liability*, by which bank stockholders were liable for depositors' losses of failed banks up to the amounts of their stock holdings. This provided an incentive to suspend the operations of nearly insolvent banks to limit assessments on owners. "Between 1865 to 1933, losses to depositors as a percent of total deposits at all banks averaged only 0.21 percent per year and less than 1 percent per year even in crisis years." However, because bank stockholders' losses had been substantial during the Great Depression, double liability was eliminated because, critics said, it harmed innocent stockholders with no share in bank management, it had not prevented the massive bank failures of the depression, and the new federally supervised deposit insurance would take its place (Kaufman 1992, p. 24; Macey and Miller 1992).

Bank failures almost vanished over the next 40 years, and deposit insurance became a popular success story. That period of stability, however, owed much to farm prosperity, low inflation, stable interest rates, and low-risk portfolios. Loans (L) as a proportion of bank earning assets (L + I, where I is mainly U.S. bonds) was 72 percent in 1929, fell during the Great Depression and World War II to less than 50 percent, and only recovered with business to 1920s levels in the 1970s (Table 7.1).

When bank failures rose (from annual numbers of about four in the 1960s to eight in the 1970s to 120 in the 1980s), it became common to blame the rising

Source: https://upload.wikimedia.org/wikipedia/commons/2/24/FDR_Inauguration_1933.jpg.

Figure 7.3   *Franklin D. Roosevelt and Herbert Hoover, March 4, 1933*

adverse incentives of deposit insurance, with some justification because deposits up to $5,000 were insured from 1934 to 1949, $10,000 to 1965, $20,000 to 1973, $40,000 to 1979, $100,000 to 2007, and then $250,000. The proportions of bank deposits insured rose from one-half during the 1950s to 1970s to three-quarters after 1980.

Banks pay premia for deposit insurance: 8.3¢ per $100 until 1991, then 19.5¢, risk-adjusted since 1993. The Federal Deposit Insurance Corporation's (FDIC) fund became dangerously low in the 1990s, but it was widely understood that Congress would bail out the fund if necessary to pay the promised insurance, a position that was made official by the formal extension of the FDIC's ability to borrow from the U.S. Treasury. The adverse incentives of deposit insurance induced reductions in bank capital and increases in risk through more loans to less-developed countries, real estate, and heavily indebted corporations (Peltzman 1970).

An inherent fragility of commercial banks is often assumed, but experience suggests that many of their risks and failures have instead been consequences of bank regulations and volatile monetary policies. We have seen some of the effects of laws against branching (and therefore diversification) and the inflation followed by deflation during and after World War I.

Moving forward in time, price fluctuations made the 1970s and 1980s difficult for banks and just about everyone else. The price of oil was sensitive to Western inflation (Wood 2005, p. 370), and the second oil price shock, which saw the price of a barrel of crude rise from $28 in 1975 to $54 in 1980, was followed by a fall to $20 in 1985. Bank loans had financed much of the oil exploration and development, and hundreds failed when the price fell (see Figure 7.2), to which was added the farm depression following the U.S. grain embargo on the Soviet Union. Successfully resisted by the States for nearly 200 years, even after the Great Depression, interstate banking was finally adopted, and mergers and takeovers reduced the number of banks in the country from over 10,000 in the 1980s to about 8,500 in 2000 and 4,700 in 2020 (Kaufman 2007; Federal Deposit Insurance Corporation 1998, "Quarterly Statistics at a Glance").

This period also marked the beginning of the Fed's policy of TBTF (too big to fail), that is, bailouts of large banks – such as Franklin National in 1974 and Continental Bank in 1984 – whose failures were assumed, without evidence or argument, to bring down the financial system. Federal Reserve officials referred to this practice as acting as "lender of last resort" but that is a misuse of the Baring–Thornton–Bagehot term and recommended practice of insuring means of payment to the financial system. They did not confuse the salvation of particular misbehaving but politically favored firms with that of the system. The moral hazard in this practice, which to this date reached its peak in the

2008 Bear Sterns bailout, is obvious, but was endorsed by the *Dodd–Frank Act*.

The growing risk of commercial banks has also been partly due to their growing maturity mismatch. Their main liabilities used to be demand deposits, whose threat of immediate withdrawals required, it used to be thought, short-term (even money-market) assets. National banks were originally forbidden to make real estate loans in order "to improve their safety and liquidity," and State banks had similar restrictions. Over time, however, because of political interests in agricultural credit and home ownership, real estate rose from 10 percent of bank loans in 1900, to one-sixth in 1929, 25 percent in 1955, and nearly 50 percent in 2000 (see Table 7.1), leading Alex Pollack (2016) to write in *The American Banker*, "'Commercial' Bank is a misnomer. 'Real Estate' Bank is More Apt" (see also Glock 2021, introduction). Political pressure on banks to finance low-income housing by means of subprime mortgages was an important contributor to the Great Recession.

Commercial banking is not inherently unstable, as the experiences of several countries have demonstrated. Compared with the nearly 50 percent failure rate of American banks during the Great Depression, failures were virtually absent in Canada and several European countries (U.K., Czechoslovakia, Denmark, Lithuania, Netherlands, Sweden) – due, apparently, to large bank size and diversification reinforced by macroeconomic policy, specifically the early suspension of the gold standard (more on this below) (Grossman 1994).

Michael Bordo, Angela Redish, and Hugh Rockoff (2015) asked "Why didn't Canada have a banking crisis in 2008 (or 1930, or 1907, or …)?" answering that its banking system was created as a set of "institutions whose size and diversification enhanced their robustness. Moreover it evolved into an oligopoly which was tightly regulated [by a single regulator] in a grand bargain whereby the chartered banks would provide financial stability in exchange for the Canadian government limiting entry to the industry" – not unlike the European systems of similarly large banks.

Firms, like people, avoid risks only if it is in their perceived interests to do so. Bank risk, perhaps measured by the probability of failure, might be reduced by required increases in capital, which, however, may be offset by increases in loans riskier than regulators comprehend. Even with open balance sheets, bankers understand their risks better than outsiders. Low-risk behavior is best achieved by substantial and long-lived expected returns, which might be helped by less costly regulations and examinations, as well as (hardly worth mentioning) fewer political pressures to take on risky projects. Of course volatile monetary policy is costly to everyone almost regardless how well they have behaved.

WHO WANTED A CENTRAL BANK?

The United States had no *central* or *national* bank between 1836, when the charter of the second Bank of the United States expired, and 1913, when the Federal Reserve System was created. The primary official monetary manager during this period – the largest holder of the nation's gold reserve – was the U.S. Treasury. Although called a *central bank* (but not by its founders, who deplored the suggestion of *centralization*) the Fed was not a bank, or a collection of banks. It dealt with foreign public banks but neither took deposits from nor made loans to American individuals or firms. Existing banks had made it clear they did not want competition from a national bank which enjoyed a special relationship with the Government. The banking interests which had supported Andrew Jackson's veto of the second Bank were still formidable. On the other hand, they saw the benefits of a public institution that would lend to them and bear the costs of the nation's reserve.

The Bank of England was a true central bank. It was a commercial bank at the center of the financial system, a bankers' bank, which had taken on the additional functions of issuing the nation's legal-tender currency and supplying liquidity in time of crisis, a lender of last resort. Since the British monetary authority – regulator of money – was also a central bank, other monetary authorities were called central banks.

The new central bank, as it was nevertheless called, was unlike any previous American institution. It was not adapted from the Independent Treasury or private clearinghouses, although it took on some of their functions. Existing institutions that could have been adapted to monetary control were bypassed – except for the gold standard (temporarily, as we will see), which remained the basis of the monetary system.

The Federal Reserve Act of 1913 was made possible by the combination of the traditional Federalist/Whig/Republican broad interpretation of the national Government's constitutional powers – which had seen limited successes in the Banks of the United States and the National Bank Act – and the capture of the Democratic Party by Woodrow Wilson's *New Freedom*. The populist fear of a monster central bank was relegated to the fringes, and banks and progressives got most of what they wanted.

The primary monetary problem at the end of the nineteenth century was considered by many to be the "inelasticity" of the currency, with a major culprit being the National Banking System's requirement that bank notes be backed by U.S. bonds. Banks were said to be unable or unwilling to extend credit in times of stress because of the insufficient supply or attractiveness of these securities. Professor Laurence Laughlin of the University of Chicago wrote: "an elastic banknote circulation, slowly rising, but expanding and contracting sharply with seasonal demand is imperative. Our present national bank circulation does not provide for this elasticity" (Kolko 1963; Livingston 1986; West 1977, p. 61).

The problem was exacerbated by the dispersion of gold reserves. "In a modern system constructed on credit," argued investment banker Paul Warburg (1930, p. 44), "cash must be centralized as far as possible into one big reservoir from which everyone legitimately entitled to it may withdraw it at will and into which it must automatically return whenever it is not actually used." Warburg was not alone in ascribing European financial stability to their central banks, an impression which contributed to the neglect of a greater defect of American finance – the thousands of small banks that failed at rates similar to the English country banks at the beginning of the nineteenth century. The latter had been absorbed into nationwide systems, but anti-branching laws prevented a similar evolution in the United States.

Warburg, who had been an investment banker with his family firm in Germany before coming to the United States in 1902, proposed a remedy for American monetary instability which presumed money markets along European lines. Some reformers wanted bank notes secured by assets arising in the ordinary course of commercial banking. These would provide sufficient security for noteholders if banks made sound loans, and would allow a more elastic issue. Warburg was skeptical of the quality of American bank loans, however. Many were long-term and illiquid, and subject to interest-rate risk, and bank short-term paper consisted mainly of unsecured "single-name" promissory notes that were effectively long-term because they were routinely rolled over. It was "not unusual for [business call] loans ... to run for 6 months or a year or even longer," a contemporary text informs us. "There is usually a mutual understanding ... between the bank and its customer that demand for payment of the note will not be made until some time which is convenient to the borrower .... A large commercial bank in Boston states that during its fifty years of existence it has not served a single notice on a borrower for payment of a demand loan and this case is probably by no means exceptional" (Dewey and Shugrue 1922, pp. 177–8; see also Mitchell 1925). Warburg wanted the two-name, self-liquidating real bills (that is, drawn against real goods) discountable at central banks that he had known in Europe. They would allow the "fluidity of credit .... A sound financial system must mobilize its commercial paper and make it a quick asset instead of a lock-up." The central reservoir by which this would be accomplished, his proposed United Reserve Bank, would be filled by the "power to request banks to keep with it cash balances proportionate to the amount of their deposits" (Warburg 1930, p. 47).

Although the architects of the Federal Reserve Act found it politically useful to fictionalize an opposition from the "money trust," the strongest advocates of a central bank were the large New York banks, who wanted to break loose from the restrictions of the *National Bank Act*. The United States was the world's largest economy and greatest trading nation, but most of its trade was financed in Europe or through private bankers instead of through the domestic deposit-taking commercial banking corporations. The 1863 Act had been interpreted by the comptroller to prohibit national banks from "accepting" bills of exchange, that is, from commissions for "guaranteeing" bills. The big banks wanted into this line of international finance with a central bank supporting the market. A central bank would also "free them, as holders of the nation's ultimate bank reserves, from responsibility for the stability of the U.S. banking system" (Carosso and Sylla 1991). The New York banks envied the profits accruing to the other London banks by letting the Bank of England keep the gold reserve.

Banks outside the money centers were cool to the idea of a central bank. They saw many disadvantages and little benefit in federal regulation. Small-town bankers' suspicions of proposals from New York were shared by their fellow citizens. The Baltimore and Indianapolis plans of 1894 and 1900 for increasing the elasticity of the currency by letting bank assets be the basis for notes had significant input from New York, but were marketed as proposals from middle-America. *The National Citizens League for the Promotion of a Sound Banking System* was formed in 1911 to promote the Aldrich plan, which was named after Senate Finance Committee chairman Nelson Aldrich but was essentially Warburg's proposal for a *United Reserve Bank*. "The reform should not take the shape of a dominant central bank," said Professor Laughlin, the Citizens League's spokesman, "nor should it be a creature of politics. For this reason the Government of the United States should not enter the discount and deposit business of banking; but … should supervise and regulate a cooperative means of assistance, like an enlarged clearing house association, in the common interest …. Moreover, in any legislation, care should be taken that control of our credit system should not pass into the hands of any sinister political or financial interests" (West 1977, pp. iii–iv). Laughlin and the League backed away from Aldrich and New York in 1912 when the Republican Party's problems (the Taft–Roosevelt split) made it apparent that any plan associated with them would fail (Livingston 1986, pp. 208–12).

Few would have predicted that a central bank would owe its establishment to a Democratic president, leader of the party traditionally most jealous of federal encroachments on the rights of individuals and states. A central bank was far from inevitable in the early years of the century. It is true that there was considerable support for such an institution and for monetary reform generally. But that had always been the case, and the reformers had seemed no stronger than on other occasions since Jackson's veto of the second Bank. A national bank had less support from Republicans in the early 1900s than from Whigs in the 1830s and 1840s. Main Street Republicans were almost as wary of Wall

Street as their Democratic neighbors. "Banking reform at the beginning of 1912 seemed a dead issue, of interest only to a few bankers and a seriously divided National Citizens' League for Sound Banking" (Kolko 1963, p. 217).

Looking back, however, after witnessing the rise of government intervention and the part played by Woodrow Wilson, subsequent generations have seen in the Federal Reserve a natural consequence of the post-Civil War crises which finally spurred Congress to action. There is something to be said for this view because the *Panic of 1907* heightened awareness of currency problems and made the monetary system a logical object of attention for the reform administration coming to office in 1913.

The Panic of 1907, the Aldrich Plan for a National Reserve Association, and the Federal Reserve Act

The panic of 1907, which saw call money rates above 100 percent, was accompanied by the usual palliatives, including clearinghouse loan certificates, increased Treasury bank deposits, and an emergency financial pool arranged by J.P. Morgan (Friedman and Schwartz 1963, pp. 156–68; Krooss 1969, pp. 164–5; Sprague 1910, ch. 5; Andrew 1908). However, 1907 differed from previous crises in the rapid response of Congress.

Aldrich proposed a plan for temporary currency expansions during emergencies in which banks would form voluntary *National Currency Associations* empowered – "if, in the judgment of the Secretary of the Treasury, business conditions in the locality demand additional circulation, and if he be satisfied with the character and value of the securities proposed" – to issue currency secured by United States, State and local Government, and railroad bonds. The bill was attacked by Western bankers as primarily a scheme to make a market for the securities held by New York banks and other members of the "Money Trust." An alternative version, with commercial paper as security, was proposed in the House. The *Aldrich–Vreeland Act of 1908* was a compromise in which bonds (but not railroad bonds) and short-term "notes representing actual commercial transactions [bearing] the names of at least two responsible parties" were eligible bases for emergency currency (Krooss 1969, pp. 2090–92).

The Act came into play only once before its expiration in 1915 – to counteract the currency withdrawals by Europeans in 1914. In addition to clearinghouse loan certificates of $212 million, $400 million of Aldrich–Vreeland currency were issued. "The maximum amount outstanding on any one date was $364 million," Friedman and Schwartz (1963, p. 172) report, "which was nearly one-quarter of the total amount of currency in the hands of the public before the outbreak of war, and nearly one-eighth of total high-powered money. The availability of the emergency issue probably prevented a monetary panic and the restriction of payments by the banking system."

Except for the composition of the central board and its authority over the branches, and the voluntary participation of commercial banks, Aldrich's longer-term plan resembled the 1913 Federal Reserve Act (Warburg 1930 i, pp. 178–369). It was unfortunate in its timing, however. The Republicans had lost control of the House in the election of 1910, and would also lose the Senate and presidency in 1912. Democrats associated Aldrich with the "money trust," and took a stand against his bill in the 1912 campaign. The banking community continued to push for reform and found an ally in Carter Glass of the House Banking and Currency Committee. Festus Wade, St. Louis banker and member of the Currency Committee of the American Bankers Association (ABA), promised Glass the ABA's cooperation "in devising a financial system for this country." He personally favored the Aldrich bill, but "any bill you submit will be a vast improvement on our present system." Chicago banker and President of the ABA, George Reynolds, said he was opposed to a true central bank (that is, a bankers' bank with branches throughout the country competing with existing banks). But Glass could "count on at least good treatment and a reasonable measure of cooperation by the ABA [for an] organization with branches located in various sections of the country dealing only with banks and the Government" (Kolko 1963, p. 226; Glass 1927, p. 86).

Glass's cooperation was conditional, however. He objected to the centralization in the Aldrich bill, and with the assistance of Laughlin's former student, Parker Willis, imposed on the basic Aldrich plan an organization of privately controlled independent regional banks. He hoped to break Wall Street's dominance through rival concentrations of power (Willis 1923; Morawetz 1909). The president-elect was favorably disposed to Glass's plan when it was explained to him in December 1912, but thought it needed a "capstone" – a central board – to control and coordinate the system. Glass was privately aghast at this backward step toward the centralization of the Aldrich plan (Link 1956, p. 212). But he accommodated Wilson with a Federal Reserve Board of six public members appointed by the president and three bankers chosen by the regional banks, although the bankers had to be dropped to placate William Jennings Bryan and his populist following. Bryan also prevailed over the protestations of Wilson and Glass to make Federal Reserve currency a liability of the United States instead of the regional Fed banks. His biographer Arthur Link noted the weakness of Wilson's resistance, who was evidently swayed by the argument of his confidant Louis Brandeis that "The power to issue currency should be vested exclusively in Government officials, even when the currency is issued against commercial paper. The American people will not be content to have the discretion necessarily involved vested in a Board composed wholly or in part of bankers; for their judgment may be biased by private interest or affiliation .... The conflict between the policies of the Administration and the desires of the financiers and of big business is an irreconcilable one" (Wilson 1966–94, *Papers*, v. 27, June 14, 1913).

The Federal Reserve Act did not require that the central board in charge of monetary policy be experienced in banking or the financial markets or that they should carry out their work in the proximity of those markets. It was enough to want to do the right thing – assumed automatic in public servants. Experience was a disqualification because it meant "bias" and "interest." "Let bankers explain the technical features of the new system," the president wrote to the Chairman of the Ways and Means Committee. "Suffice it here to say" that

> ... it provides a currency which expands as it is needed and contracts when it is not needed: a currency which comes into existence in response to the call of every man who can show a going business and a concrete basis for extending credit to him. More than that, the power to direct this system of credits is put into the hands of a public board of disinterested officers of the Government itself .... I think we are justified in speaking of this as a democracy of credit. (Wilson 1966–94, *Papers*, v. 31, October 17, 1914)

The Federal Reserve Act had something for everyone. The burden of the nation's reserve was shifted to a public institution that did not compete with privately owned banks, legal impediments to bank participation in international finance were lessened – Aldrich ([1910] 2009) had seen his promise of a plan "to make the United States the financial center of the world" made good – and although national banks were compelled to join the Federal Reserve System, the pain was softened by lower reserve requirements. In fact, membership was not compulsory because national banks could switch to State charters, and opposition from State banks had been circumvented by letting their membership be voluntary. Finally, the populists and progressives were persuaded to accept the bankers' organization by involving the government in the capital's "capstone" and substituting Government currency for bank notes.

The opposition in Congress focused on the dangers of political and big-bank control of the monetary system exercised through the central board. Although he had been less than thrilled with Wilson's "capstone," Glass warmly defended it in the House:

> The Federal reserve board, technically speaking, has no banking function. It is strictly a board of control, properly constituted of high Government officials, doing justice to the banks, but fairly and courageously representing the interests of the people. (U.S. Congress, Congressional Record, 63rd Congress, 1st session, September 10, 1913, p. 4645)

It would be "an altruistic institution."

It is an ongoing question whether the Fed – or any central bank – has improved general economic performance (Selgin et al. 2012), but strong evidence for a negative answer is offered by the 96 percent erosion of the dollar's worth since the Fed's creation. Table 7.2 indicates the Fed's power to produce such a massive result. Its capacities to extend credit and add to the monetary base are unlimited. It buys securities with costless debits of Federal Reserve liabilities (convertible into Federal Reserve notes), so that its income is substantial and its costs negligible, the latter less than one-tenth of the former in 1970. The Fed needs no congressional appropriation and pays (returns) most of its net revenue to the Treasury. Its constraint at first was gold reserve requirements, but those were loosened by large gold imports during World War I, and ended by the post-1933 understanding they would not be invoked.

Table 7.2   Federal Reserve system income statements

	1929 ($ millions)	1970 ($ millions)	2019 ($ billions)
Interest income	71	3877	103
Private discounts	60	56	...
U.S. securities	8	3,772	59
Private troubled securities			43
Other	3	50	1
Net operating expenses	35	309	12
Interest expenses			33
Dividends	10	41	1
U.S. Treasury and surplus	27	3,526	57

Note: Sums may not equal because of rounding. Differences between the three statements are due mainly to (1) most Federal Reserve income was from private bills through the discount window until the growth of federal debt in the 1930s and 1940s; (2) interest expenses began with the payment of interest on reserves in 2008; and (3) troubled securities arose from the TARP and AIG bailouts in 2008.
Source: Federal Reserve Board, *Annual Reports.*

GETTING STARTED

Handicaps: Inexperience Reinforced by the Lack of Clarity of Objectives, Incentives, and Information

The Federal Reserve began with disadvantages that were fatal for the monetary system that it was supposed to cure. Its founders differed over the purposes of the institution they were creating. It had been advanced initially as a support mechanism for clearinghouses during financial panics – "a clearinghouse for the clearinghouses," Warburg said in 1907. Republican Congressman

Everis Hayes of California noted that if the objective was in fact an elastic currency, simple adjustments to existing clearinghouse arrangements would be sufficient. "I believe that it would be safer to make efforts at the reform of our system more strictly along the lines of our own financial evolution than by borrowing from some foreign system." But by the fall of 1913 Congress was being asked to consider a radical departure, "the most powerful banking institution in all the world," with "the control and management of the banking and the credits of this country," lamented Republican Frank Mondell of Wyoming (U.S. Congress, Congressional Record, 63rd Congress 31st session, September 10, 1913, pp. 4652, 4691–2).

No one knew how the radically new institution would operate, or could be made to operate. The supervision of monetary institutions "so far as is necessary for the benefit and protection of all the people" is generally accepted, Mondell conceded. However, "the people pretty clearly understand nowadays that control through a Government bureau, by political appointees, is not synonymous with control by the people and for the people. Neither do people of ordinary intelligence confuse regulation and management. We regulate the railroads, we do not manage them. We regulate the package of meats, we do not appoint the men who run the business (U.S. Congress, Congressional Record, 63rd Congress 31st session, September 10, 1913, pp. 4652, 4691–2).

Some of its proponents expected the Fed's powers to be scientifically limited by the discipline of commercial paper. Oklahoma's Robert Owen, manager of the bill in the Senate, made statements along these lines, but he also looked to the Federal Reserve "to fix the rate of interest" so that "the business men of the country can hope to ascertain and know reasonably in advance what money will cost them in their enterprises …." In place of the high and fluctuating interest rates experienced by the United States, "we are going to have, in the future, the same stability of interest rates that prevails in Europe. I call your attention, for example, to the fact that for 75 per cent of the time the rate of the Bank of France has not exceeded 3 percent, … that the bank of Belgium has not exceeded 6 percent in 50 years, [and] the interest rates in Germany and in England have been of wonderful stability" (Krooss 1969, pp. 2419–35). A generous interpretation of Owen's position is that he hoped to prevent the high interest rates associated with liquidity crises, and he referred particularly to 1907. But his letters to the Federal Reserve Board in 1920 protesting an increase in the discount rate to 6 percent at a time when Fed credit and commodity prices were rising more than 20 percent per annum and call money rates had reached 11 percent suggested that what he really wanted was permanent easy money. In 1921, he informed the Board that "the Reserve Banks can well afford to make [loans] to whatever extent required by the country." He did not see why they should not set interest rates by the same criteria as commercial banks, which were "justified in charging six and seven percent because they pay two and three percent for deposits .... If the Reserve Banks would be content with the same margin of profit, ... they would be charging a rate of between three and four percent" (Harding 1925, pp. 195–200).

Except for the few that with Owen paid homage to the real bills doctrine, little attention was given to guidelines for the Federal Reserve's managers. Few wanted bankers to run the system, and Indiana Democrat Finley Gray believed they should be excluded on grounds of ignorance. Bankers "know no more about public currency than any other citizen of the country," he said.

> Banking is one thing and public currency is another thing.
>   History shows that wherever general public duty comes in conflict with private selfish gain in the same person, selfish gain always prevails over public duty. (U.S. Congress, Congressional Record, 63rd Congress, 1st session, September 17, 1913, p. 5109)

Others feared Treasury abuse of the System's powers. But if neither bankers nor the Government could be trusted with the currency, how were decisions to be made? Some looked for a "scientific" determination of money, and found it in the real bills doctrine. Section 13 of the Federal Reserve Act provided that

> Upon the indorsement of any of its member banks, any Federal reserve bank may discount notes, drafts, and bills of exchange arising out of commercial transactions; ... with a maturity ... of not more than ninety days.

However, neither this statement, nor the real bills doctrine, in general, is a useful guide to monetary policy because the rate of interest is still to be determined (Thornton 1802, p. 254). The gold standard might have guided central bank credit, although it had been found insufficient in Britain. In the United States the Fed's credit was soon determined by Government war spending, and during the Great Depression was immobilized by its fear of insufficient gold, which as with the Bank of England might have stemmed from a fundamental fear of inflation.

Five members of the Federal Reserve Board were appointed by the president, subject to the approval of the Senate, for ten years, a term expiring every two years, and also included the Secretary of the Treasury and the Comptroller of the Currency, *ex officio*. Presidents (called governors until 1936) of the twelve Federal Reserve Banks were chosen by their mainly banker and business directors. Policy disagreements between the Board and the Reserve Banks might have been (and still may be) due to diverse motives and knowledge arising from different backgrounds and environments. The greater political sensitivity of the Board is explained by its physical proximity to the president and Congress as well as to the considerable Washington seasoning of most of its members. Many Reserve Bank presidents, on the other hand, have been bankers, and they function in a bankers' milieu, in daily contact with the financial markets. Their greater reliance on market forces, particularly interest rates, compared with the frequent preference of the Board either for inaction or for quantitative controls, may be traced to the presidents' more direct experiences with market forces and their greater distances from political influences (Wood 2005, pp. 174, 189–91).

The first Federal Reserve Board was created in 1914 (see Figure 7.1). The Chairman (Secretary of the Treasury William McAdoo) and Comptroller of the Currency (John Skelton Williams) were southerners, bankers, and businessmen. Williams was formerly assistant secretary of the Treasury. Of the five appointees, Adolph Miller was an academic economist (the only one on the Board until the 1960s, when they became common) and recently Assistant to the Secretary of the Interior; Frederic Delano was a railroad executive who had served as an advisor to the War Department regarding the Philippine railroads; Charles Hamlin was a Boston lawyer and sometime Assistant Secretary of the Treasury; W.P.G. Harding was a Birmingham, Alabama banker; and Paul Warburg was an investment banker. The mixture of bankers and businessmen, many with previous government service, has continued, with the main change being the growing number of economists, many formerly of the Federal Reserve's staff.

Government Money Machine

Problems of goals, knowledge, and incentives in the Federal Reserve were soon placed in abeyance by the Treasury's seizure of the System to finance the war. Only a quarter of Government spending was paid for by taxes during World War I, and it continued at a high rate for several months after the November 1918 armistice. Sixty percent of Federal Reserve credit during 1917–19 consisted of purchases of U.S. securities or discounts of bills secured by those securities. These bills were made eligible for Fed discounting by an amendment to the Federal Reserve Act in September 1916 (Krooss 1969, pp. 2479–85). A later Director of Research for the Board described wartime monetary policy:

> … the Federal reserve banks were guided in their rate policy chiefly by the necessity for supporting the Treasury. The level of discount rates was kept low and preferential rates were granted on loans secured by Government obligations … and the discount rate was thus not used as a means of credit control – but as a method of helping the Government to raise the funds necessary for the prosecution of the war. It was not until the summer of 1919 that the use of the discount rate as a means of credit control received serious consideration. (Goldenweiser 1925, p. 40)

The Board considered rate increases as early as January 1919. But the Treasury was in the midst of a conversion of short-term to long-term debt, and "There was considerable sympathy within the Board for the problems facing the Treasury" (Wicker 1966, p. 30). Board Chairman W.P.G. Harding wrote regarding Reserve Bank requests for rate increases in April that the Secretary of the Treasury had communicated to him that the "failure" of the Government's loans "would be disastrous for the country. The Board, therefore, did not approve any advance in rates" (1925, p. 148). Similar requests were denied in July. Carter Glass, initially, as we have seen, an opponent of central control of the System, had become Secretary of the Treasury in December 1918, and continued the Government's desire for low interest rates. Both preferred to resist inflation by credit controls that distinguished between essential (productive) and non-essential (speculative) credit. Assistant Secretary of the Treasury Russell Leffingwell (1921) said the Treasury was "honor bound" to avoid the infliction of capital losses on the patriotic citizens that had financed the war effort.

Fed officials, including Governor Benjamin Strong of the New York Reserve Bank, had to consider the "strong outcry in Congress for the protection of the interests of holders of the previous loans, Liberty loans, which had suffered a decline in the market," although Strong had "a feeling – possibly because I do not live in the atmosphere of Washington – that it could have been resisted" (U.S. Congress 1922, pp. 503–4; Wicker 1966, p. 34; Strong 1930, p. 87).

The Board's attitude toward direct controls wavered between sympathy and weak resistance, but stronger opposition began to come from the Reserve Banks. The Board was caught in the middle of an acrimonious debate between Strong and the Treasury in October 1919, but sided with the latter despite Strong's threat of a public protest unless an increase in the discount rate was approved. Strong believed that attempts to ration credit were futile whereas Leffingwell was convinced that speculative credit expansion should be attacked by "a firm discrimination in making loans." He was "weary of the copybook texts" which claimed that credit was reduced by making it more expensive. Glass was angered by Strong's attempt "to dominate" the Treasury and the Federal Reserve, and threatened to seek his removal (Wicker 1966, pp. 37–8; Chandler 1958, pp. 135–9; Friedman and Schwartz 1963, pp. 222–39).

Increases in the discount rate – from 4 percent to 4¾ percent in November 1919 and 6 percent two months later – came after the Treasury informed the Fed that its support of the Government bond market was no longer required (Chandler 1958, p. 162). The increases were apparently dictated by the Fed's concern for its gold reserve: "the margin [free gold, Figure 7.4] was quite narrow," Goldenweiser (1925, p. 90) noted. (Federal Reserve Banks were taxed if their gold reserves fell below 40 percent of Federal Reserve notes,

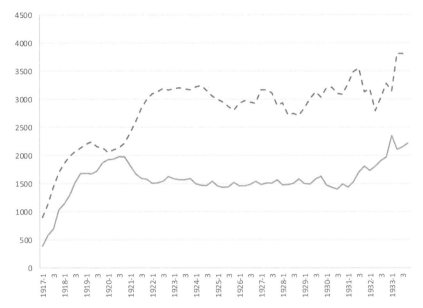

Source: Compiled by the author.

Figure 7.4   Federal Reserve free gold = total − required reserves

according to Section 11c of the Federal Reserve Act.) The January 1920 increase in the discount rate coincided with the peak in business activity, but the rate was raised again in June, to 7 percent, where it remained until it was reduced to 6 percent in April 1921, and then in steps to 4½ percent at the end of the year.

The 60 percent restriction of Federal Reserve credit in 1920–21 was matched by that in prices, and the contraction of output was one of the sharpest in American history. Chairman Harding later defended the Fed against "the contention that … rates should have been substantially lowered in April or May, 1920." The drastic falls abroad required a "corresponding fall of prices in this country," he said. Furthermore:

> The United States was a free gold market, and had it remained at the same time the cheapest money market in the world, our financial structure would have been subject to the severest strain. The Board in that event would have been forced to suspend the reserve requirements, which would probably have resulted in the presentation of large amounts of Federal Reserve notes for redemption in gold for hoarding, which would have reduced reserves still further. In such circumstances prices would have been sustained only in terms of irredeemable paper money. (Harding 1925, pp. 165–6)

And that, Harding feared, would have led to progressive inflations of credit and the currency. The reserve problem was soon resolved, as we see in Figure 7.4.

THE FED'S APPROACHES TO MONETARY AND CREDIT POLICIES

So what were the Federal Reserve's guides, or in modern terms, its models of monetary policy? The official answer was broadly, in ordinary times, conditioned by the gold standard and the Federal Reserve Act. The Gold Standard Act of 1900 had confirmed that U.S. currency was convertible at the rate of $20.67 per ounce of gold, for which the Federal Reserve Act made the Fed responsible. That Act also required Federal Reserve Banks to hold gold reserves of at least 35 percent against their deposit liabilities and 40 percent against their Federal Reserve notes in circulation.

So the price level was determined by the relative costs of gold and other goods. Gold discoveries, such as in California and South Australia in the 1840s, and technological developments in the extraction of deep deposits, such as in South Africa in the 1880s, meant cheaper gold, that is, higher gold-and-dollar prices of other goods. Countries on gold experienced inflation in the 1850s, deflation when gold production fell during what was called the Great Deflation between 1873 and 1893, and then inflation during the next 20

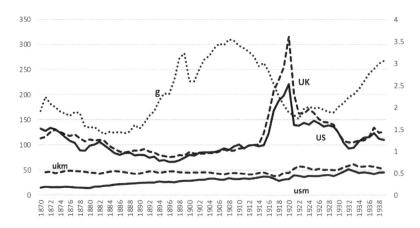

Source: Compiled by the author.

Figure 7.5   World annual rate of gold production (%) g; U.K. and U.S. price levels, 1914=100, UKP and USP; and U.K. and U.S. M/GDP, ukm and usm

years, after which most countries suspended their ties to gold during World War I. Figure 7.5 shows the similar movements in British and American prices between 1879 and 1914, during which both currencies were linked to gold and therefore to each other after the United States had resumed the dollar's convertibility following its Civil War suspension.

That still left the short-term discretionary task envisioned by the founders of the Fed, that is, the supply of liquidity and an elastic currency by performing as lender of last resort – at which it failed its first test in the 1930s. Combatants and others suspended the gold convertibilities of their currencies in order to be able to print enormous quantities of fiat money during the war. Their price levels typically tripled between 1914 and 1919. The U.S. price level also rose although it was not forced to suspend convertibility because of the inflows of gold and foreign currencies in payment for goods and for safekeeping.

Its large gold reserves gave the Fed leeway in its monetary policy. Unlike many countries after World War I, the U.S.A. was not compelled to pursue deflationary policies to conserve or build its gold reserves, even though its prices in the 1920s were double those before the war. Its Consumer Price Indexes in 1914, 1922, 1926, and 1929 were 100, 167, 176, and 171, respectively. Instead of using its gold to raise prices, as other countries had hoped, the Fed chose monetary stability. It chose not to play by the rules of the gold standard game, according to which gold inflows were allowed to raise money and prices and therefore reverse the gold movement to maintain an equilibrium distribution of gold. On the other hand, Americans lent dollars liberally to foreigners during the 1920s.

The Fed's approach to "Credit Policy" in these circumstances was outlined in the Board's *Annual Report* for 1923, which began with the realization that the traditional (gold restraint) guidelines for monetary policy had become inoperative. This was particularly true of "the [gold] reserve ratio," which "can not be expected to regain its former position of authority until the extraordinary international gold movements which, in part, have occasioned and in part have resulted from the breakdown of the gold standard, have ceased and the flow of gold from country to country is again governed by those forces which in more normal and stable conditions determine the balance of international payments."

If the gold reserve is an inadequate guide – and the Federal Reserve Act only specified minimum reserve ratios – by what criteria is the central bank to act? The *Report* first considered the goal of price stability, which had figured prominently in public discussions. But "price fluctuations proceed from a great variety of causes, most of which lie outside the range of influence of [Federal Reserve] credit …. No credit system could undertake to perform the function of regulating credit by reference to prices without failing in the endeavor." The Fed thus rejected the *Quantity Theory of Money* – according to which prices respond equiproportionally to money, which is controlled by the central bank (Fisher 1911).

Perhaps it is better to focus on a quantity – its credit – over which the Fed has greater control. Even there, however,

> No statistical mechanism alone, however carefully contrived, can furnish an adequate guide to credit administration. Credit is an intensely human institution and as such reflects the moods and impulses of the community – its hopes, its fears, its expectations.

Fortunately, there were "among these factors a sufficient number which are determinable in their character, and also measurable, to relieve the problem of credit administration of much of its indefiniteness, and therefore give to it a substantial foundation of ascertainable fact." Those factors were "in large part recognized in the Federal reserve act" as those "accommodating commerce and business." But how do we know when commerce and business, as opposed to the "speculation" deplored by the Board, are accommodated? The Act suggested a further guide to Fed credit by limiting its discounts to real bills. But as Harding had indicated in 1920, that was insufficient. Paper offered by a member bank when it rediscounts with a Federal reserve bank "may disclose the purpose for which the loan evidenced by that paper was made, but it does not disclose what use is to be made of the proceeds of the rediscount." Therefore "the technical administrative problem presented to each reserve bank is that of finding the ways and means best suited to … informing itself of … the extension of credit for speculative purposes." The end of the *Report* considered the "economic information [necessary] to measure changes in the volume of production and trade in relation to changes in the volume of credit."

We are interested in the determination of when credit is excessive or deficient relative to production and trade. Although "the interrelationship of prices and credit is too complex to admit of any simple statement, [t]he same conditions which predispose to a rise of prices also predispose to an increased demand for credit." The *Report*'s concern for "nonproductive credit" and the "undue accumulation or exhaustion of stocks" brings us to the price speculation that worried the Board in 1920. We come back to prices in the end, although there were suggestions of a lack of symmetry in that analysis. Speculative accumulations were unreservedly bad, but liquidations might be beneficial.

The Fed's work for the stability of credit is suggested by Figure 7.6, which shows that in the 1920s, Fed credit was managed so as to sterilize gold flows. British hopes that the United States would allow its large gold holdings to raise American prices and the exchange value of sterling were disappointed.

Some economists and legislators believed that price stability was the proper goal of monetary policy. That was Keynes's position in *The Tract on Monetary*

Reform, and Irving Fisher's in *Stabilizing the Dollar*. In 1922, Maryland Congressman Alan Goldsborough introduced a bill based on Fisher's proposal for a "compensated dollar" – derided by critics as the "rubber dollar" – in which the price of gold would be linked to a price index. If the index rose, the price of gold would be reduced in the same proportion, and the lower value of gold reserves would force an anti-inflationary monetary contraction. (This is the short-run effect. A longer-run effect would be a lower production of gold.) The bill did not attract much support at the time, but another effort by Goldsborough passed the House in 1932 by a vote of 289 to 60 before its suppression by the Senate (Studenski and Krooss 1952, p. 369).

A 1926 bill would have required the discount rate to be set "with a view to accommodating commerce and promoting a stable price level for commodities in general. All of the powers of the Federal reserve system shall be used for promoting stability in the price level" (Krooss 1969, p. 2667). Governor Strong and other Fed officials admitted the desirability of stable prices and the Fed's considerable effects. However, they resisted full responsibility, believing that an unqualified, price-level goal would interfere with other vital

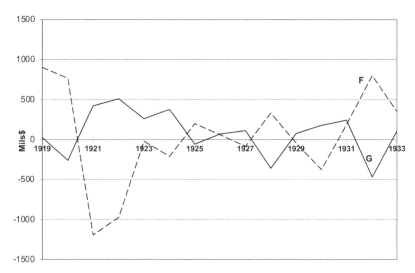

Source: Compiled by the author.

Figure 7.6   Changes in Federal Reserve credit (F) and gold (G), 1919–33

goals, financial stability in particular. Strong had written to Carl Snyder of his economics research staff in 1923:

> Now I don't like to talk about stabilizing gold, the purchasing power of money, or prices being stabilized by the Federal Reserve System, at all. It is bound to lead to confusion, heartburn and headache ....
>
> *Our job is credit.* It makes no difference if it's a deposit or a bank note. If we regulate and keep fairly constant the volume of this credit, – always with due regard to gold imports and exports, which is a part of the credit problem – we are doing our whole duty. Other price influences may then be dealt with by [Secretary of Commerce] Hoover, et al. They are not our job. Of course we should watch prices – and production and consumption and speculation, and lots of things – to insure that our "play" is correct in regulating volume. To come boldly forward, and volunteer to take the price problem onto our backs, and then *fail*, as we would surely do – is just criminal suicide. (Chandler 1958, pp. 202–3)

Strong elaborated on this point in congressional hearings. He said that "the amount of gold produced in the world has an effect upon prices" (ignoring other statements that its large holdings had severed gold from American policy) and reminded congressmen of the informational and incentive problems of central banking. The "assumption that the Federal reserve system has powers of great magnitude in the control of prices ought to be considered not alone from the standpoint of economics, but from the standpoint of human nature to some extent." Even if it is assumed, he said, possibly thinking of the "quantity theory extremists" of whom he sometimes complained, that the Fed "has the power to raise or lower the price level by some automatic method, by some magic mathematical formula, what safeguards are we going to introduce in regard to ignorance, stupidity, and bad judgment in the exercise of this power? How are we to deal with the problem of divided counsels in the system, where no action is possible because of differences of opinion?"

He also feared that such power would be the object of irresistible political pressures. What is the appropriate price index? The obligation to fix prices will be interpreted by each group as an obligation to "fix their prices" (U.S. Congress 1927). Under "such a mandate," he had written to Harvard Professor Charles Bullock (who had proposed to a meeting of Fed governors that they name the factors affecting discount rate changes), "within the past six months or so we would first have gone to jail for high sugar prices, and as soon as out on bail, been rearrested for low wheat prices (not to mention gasoline, building costs, wages, freight rates, professors' salaries and such like)" (Chandler 1958, p. 203; Meltzer 2003, p. 183).

His fears seem justified when we examine the attitude of the proposer of the 1926 stable-price bill, Kansas Congressman James Strong, who seemed more interested in validating the war-time commodity inflation for his indebted constituents than in price stability. "Our yardstick has a stable number of inches and our money should be stabilized in its purchasing power," he told the House. "The price level now stands at 160, a drop from 251," referring to the wholesale price index at its peak in 1920 rather than the 160 of mid-1916 or 100 in 1913 (U.S. Congress, Congressional Record, 69th Congress, 1st session, January 18, 1926, pp. 4301–3).

Sixty years later, during another agricultural depression, another Kansan urged that monetary policy be directed at the stabilization of a basket of commodity prices. At his "confirmation hearing before the Senate Banking Committee," Wayne Angell's "voice rose in indignation – nearly cracking at one point – when he described how sagging farm prices were affecting agricultural lenders. (He shared the ownership of two banks before joining the Fed.)" Angel had been a state legislator, and after failing in a bid for the Republican nomination to the United States Senate, Senate Majority Leader Robert Dole, also of Kansas, "vigorously lobbied the White House" for him as "a perfect candidate to represent agriculture on the Board" (*Wall Street Journal*, April 24, 1986).

The Fed's conviction of its impotence regarding the economy at large, compared with the financial markets, continued into the Great Depression. The *Strong rule* of monetary policy was found in the financial markets:

> As a guide to the timing and extent of any purchases which might appear desirable, one of the best guides would be the amount of borrowing by member banks in principal centers, and particularly in New York and Chicago. Our experience has shown that when New York City banks are borrowing in the neighborhood of $100 million or more, then there is some real pressure for reducing [Fed] loans, and money rates tend to be higher than the discount rate .... In the event of business liquidation now [April 1926] appearing it would seem advisable to keep the New York City banks out of debt beyond something in the neighborhood of $50 million. It would probably be well if some similar rule could be applied to the Chicago banks, although the amount would, of course, be smaller and the difficulties greater because of the influence of the New York market. (Federal Reserve 1926)

Which turned out to be a false guide during the Great Depression. For example, net borrowed reserves of Federal Reserve member banks were about $800 million in February 1932, all but $23 million outside New York and Chicago. "The degree of ease in the New York and Chicago money markets was no reflection, therefore, of conditions prevailing outside the area," later critics noted. The Fed failed to appreciate the level of fear in the economy. Its interest rate of 2 percent, which was raised to 3½ percent after the U.K. left gold in September 1931, was high in real terms, and its open-market purchases in 1932 went into bank excess reserves without affecting bank loans (Wicker 1965; Brunner and Meltzer 1964).

THE CRASH

The Dow Jones Industrial Average of the stocks of 30 large companies traded on American exchanges rose from 64 to 191 between August 1921 and February 1928, and doubled to its peak of 381 in September 1929. It declined in an orderly fashion to 299 on Saturday, October 26, but panic broke out on Monday, and in the greatest two-day crash in its history, the Dow plummeted to 212 at its low on Tuesday.

"The situation was greatly eased," Friedman and Schwartz wrote (1963, pp. 335, 339), by the New York banks, which "in the first week after the crash, ... increased their loans to brokers and dealers by $1 billion and the rest of their loans by $300 million. They were greatly assisted by the Federal Reserve Bank of New York, which in Governor Harrison's words, kept its 'discount window wide open.'"

After a 3 a.m. meeting with his directors, Harrison informed the Stock Exchange Clearing Committee before it met to announce the call loan rate Tuesday morning that the New York Fed was prepared to buy $100 million of government securities. In the event, it bought $132 million, more than had been authorized by the Open Market Investment Committee. Because of these "timely and effective" actions, according to Friedman and Schwartz, "there were no panic increases in money market rates such as those in past market crises, and no indirect effects on confidence in banks which might have arisen if there had been any sizable defaults on security loans. The market rallied to 230 at Tuesday's close and 274 on Thursday. Some of the Board criticized New York's actions, but in defense Harrison said that "it is not at all unlikely that had we not bought Governments so freely, thus supplementing the reserves built up by large additional discounts, the stock exchange might have had to yield to the tremendous pressure brought to bear upon it to close."

The Fed was later criticized for not resisting the great fall in money during the Great Depression (from about $48 billion in October 1929 to $30 billion in April 1933, seasonally adjusted). However, that concerned the economy as a whole, whereas the Fed was primarily concerned with the big banks and the central money markets. Harrison continued, without success, to push for easy money until September 1930, when, with the stabilization of New York banks, whose borrowing from the Fed had practically ceased, he joined the majority of the Fed in voting for the status quo (Federal Reserve Board 1943, p. 400).

The downturn was increasingly recognized as more than usually severe, and Board member Adolph Miller said "we ought to consider whether the System could not be helpful." However, the majority of his colleagues, Board members and Fed Bank presidents, opposed greater ease because (1) interest rates were already low and there was no reason to believe that further reductions would revive business, (2) it might bring more speculative activity, and (3) the U.S. gold position vis-à-vis Europe seemed to be in balance.

THE GREAT DEPRESSION

U.S. output, income and prices fell 25–35 percent between 1929 and 1933, the rate of unemployment hit 25 percent, net investment was negative in 1933, and the Dow Jones stock index bottomed at 40 in 1933, compared with 381 at its peak in 1929. We are interested in (1) whether there was an identifiable set of causes of this catastrophe and (2) the role of the Federal Reserve in its occurrence and scale.

The most popular explanations of the Great Depression are Keynesian and Monetarist, that is, exogenous shifts in the demand for goods (consumption and/or investment) or the supply of money; perhaps both, initiated by the former and made worse by the latter. Neither explanation, however, upon close examination, is very convincing. Robert Lucas (1987, p. 71) observed that the arguments for a "causal" role of money are weak because the claimed effects of money have been too large to be induced by the shocks observed and the propagation mechanisms assumed. The initial demand–shock explanations are also weak. Consumption as a proportion of GNP actually rose throughout the period, and the initial decline in investment was less than at the beginnings of other downturns. Money and demand seem more effects than causes.

These difficulties led many writers, including Paul Samuelson (in Parker 2002, p. 25), to conclude that "the origins of the Depression lie in a series of historical accidents," and that its explanation is "beyond the grasp of economic theory" (DeVroey and Pensieroso 2006). "I do not have a theory," Thomas Sargent told an interviewer, "nor do I know anybody else's theory that constitutes a satisfactory explanation of the Great Depression (Klamer 1984, p. 69).

Increasingly, however, students have accepted the gold standard as an integral part of the Great Depression, especially with the realizations of pressures on countries to apply tight money policies to protect their gold reserves, and that suspensions of gold convertibilities in the 1930s enabled economies to recover (Eichengreen 1992; Mundell 1993; Johnson 1997; Irwin 2012; Sumner 2015). In fact, it can be shown that a logically complete explanation of the outlines of the Great Depression – its cause, continuance, and severity – followed from countries' strict adherence to the gold standard in the form of their determinations to resume that system after the suspensions of World War I.

British prices slightly more than tripled between 1914 and 1919, and American prices slightly more than doubled. The British suspended the paper pound's convertibility into gold, enabling them to finance the war by fiat money. The U.S.A. also relied on paper money (via the Federal Reserve) for a good part of its finance, but the dollar's gold convertibility was preserved by gold inflows from American sales and for safekeeping. The dollar had become the dominant international currency, compared with which other currencies were measured, and in late 1920, the pound was valued at $3.50 on the international exchanges.

We have seen (Chapter 4) that the British government wanted the pound restored to $4.86, which, if productive relations had not changed since 1914, required British prices to fall nearly 30 percent relative to U.S. prices. That deflation underestimated the problem because American prices themselves had to fall significantly to re-establish the 1914 relative prices of gold and other goods. Figure 7.5 shows the 1930s re-establishment, at great social and economic costs, of 1914 prices. Several countries officially resumed convertibility at prewar rates in the mid-1920s, too soon because their prices had not fallen sufficiently to justify these currency values. So although the U.S.A. was prosperous in the 1920s, it was in a world of countries with overvalued currencies dedicated to deflationary monetary and fiscal policies. The U.S.A. with its large gold reserves helped support those currencies for a few years until a rise in American interest rates reversed the direction of capital flows.

In February 1929, worries about stock market speculation led the Federal Reserve Bank of New York to request the Federal Reserve Board's permission for an increase in its discount rate, despite weaknesses in retail and wholesale prices. That request and ten more requests were denied while the Board recommended that the Bank instead prescribe that its lending be directed away from speculative uses. The Board was told – again – that the uses of credit could not be controlled, and finally, in August, succumbed to the unanimous requests of the Banks to approve increases in their discount rates from 5 percent to 6 percent – just as the economic downturn was getting underway. Industrial production fell 11 percent by the end of the year, one-third by mid-1931, and another third by mid-1932, before beginning to rise in April 1933 (Federal Reserve Board 1977, S-27).

Fed discount rates had risen from 3½ percent to 6 percent between January 1928 and August 1929, the commercial paper rate from 4 percent to 6¼ percent, and U.S. bonds from 3.18 percent to 3.71 percent, with substantial effects on international capital flows (Federal Reserve Board 1943, pp. 441, 450, 469). American net investments abroad turned around, and foreign countries found it difficult to repay American loans, leading to devaluations and suspensions of gold conversion in 1931.

Officials had expected several years of deflation before the restoration of the prewar monetary system. They feared a shortage of gold, as well they might, given the wartime inflation and the resulting fall in gold production (Figure 7.5). They hoped to overcome the gold shortage through cooperative arrangements by which central banks would refrain from competing for gold, particularly by means of high interest rates, along with a willingness to hold each other's currencies (Clarke 1967, pp. 40–44; Eichengreen 1992, pp. 207–9; Kindleberger 1973, pp. 296–300). Some blamed the difficulties of gold resumptions on inadequate cooperation, although serious cooperation could hardly have been expected under the prevailing conditions of overvalued and therefore speculative exchange rates.

Kindleberger blamed the peculiar severity of the Great Depression on the absence of a world hegemon, on the hesitancy of the U.S.A. to take over the leadership of the world economy when Britain was no longer up to the role: "for the world economy to be stabilized, there has to be a stabilizer – one stabilizer." On the other hand, Lord Norman's understanding of the costs of resumption was far from enlightened. The Swedish economist Gustav Cassel (1922, pp. 254–7) wrote:

> If the War and all it brought in its train turned the world's monetary system upside down, that is no reason for trying to restore the monetary conditions prevailing before the War. They have nothing of an essential character in them. The essential factor was the high degree of stability attained at that time [1880–1914], and it is this stability we should now endeavor to restore …. The level at which the value of money is then fixed is … a matter of secondary importance.

On the other hand, Strong testified to a congressional committee on price stabilization (U.S. Congress 1927, pp. 306, 378–9) that:

> In the course of time, when the return to the Gold Standard by former gold standard countries begins to be felt upon prices throughout the world, and there is the readjustment of bank reserves resulting from that, then I think a very important step towards stabilization of prices will have been taken …. I have great confidence that when the time comes to conduct these things as they were in former years, a lot of the need for the type of [forcible exchange rate] management which has to be applied in the present situation will be eliminated. It will be more automatic.

He thought, like Norman, that once prices had fallen so that exchange rates were no longer overvalued, things would be okay.

Competitive deflations and the scramble for gold forced several suspensions in 1931, and allowed countries freed of the gold constraint to engage in expansionary or at least less restrictive fiscal and monetary policies. Those stubbornly remaining on gold, such as the United States, in so doing signaled their determinations to continue deflation, and their falls in prices and outputs accelerated.

The most common criticism of the Great Depression behavior of the Fed has been its failure to ease monetary policy, to allow the money stock to fall from $48 billion in October 1929 to $41 billion in September 1931 to $30 billion in March 1933. Easy money was unlikely, however, probably impossible given the acceptance of the gold standard on prewar terms, according to which prices had to fall to their 1914 level. Occasional increases in Fed credit had little effect on economic activity given these expectations, and the U.S. decline accelerated when it reaffirmed its determination to remain on gold in the fall of 1931 (Friedman and Schwartz 1963, pp. 712–14).

The economy did not turn around until the coming of President Franklin Roosevelt's inflationary regime, including devaluation, in March 1933. What ended the depression in the United States, Gauti Eggertsson (2008) wrote, was a change in the monetary policy regime, "leading to a dramatic change in inflation expectations … from contractionary [specifically to achieve 1914 prices] to expansionary." Stock prices rose 66 percent in FDR's first 100 days, commodity prices "skyrocketed," and investment doubled in 1933.

The Bank of England had been forced into the pound's severance from gold in 1931, but the Federal Reserve showed no response. The later (1933) decision by the United States was due to the Fed's greater independence, especially after Congress's hands-off resolution following the 1920–21 boom and bust, until the administration took control of monetary policy in 1933, and kept it until 1951. Monetary policy was changed by a new reform administration which had been given a mandate by a landslide election.

The Federal Reserve's record might be defended, or at least understood, on the ground that its defense of the gold standard was required by the Federal Reserve Act. On the other hand, it failed to push for a relaxation of that standard and, as in the U.K., the policy reversal was forced by the political reactions of the suffering populace.

There has been much talk of the Fed's independence, except in wartime, but its record has been uneven. By central bank "independence" is really meant "of the Treasury," that is, "of government financing requirements." The Fed was clearly under the Treasury's/administration's thumb 1915–20, 1933–51, and 1970–79, the last being the period of the Great Inflation beginning with President Richard Nixon's appointment of Arthur Burns to head the Fed, and partially other times as the Fed resisted, with varying degrees of success, presidential pressures for easy money.

The period of greatest Fed independence lasted from early 1920, when the Treasury released the Fed from its obligation to support government bond prices, to the beginning of the New Deal in March 1933. The 1920s were a decade of government surpluses; presidents Warren Harding and Calvin

Coolidge, possibly for that reason, were not inclined to interfere with monetary policy, Treasury Secretary Andrew Mellon was an advocate of stable prices, and the war and postwar experiences of inflation had left a strong impression on policymakers, including the depression president Herbert Hoover.

Deficits were large in World War I (as in World War II), and the Treasury sought to borrow at low (inflationary) interest rates, which it wanted to continue after the war ended. The resulting boom and bust attracted the attention of Congress, whose Joint Commission of Agricultural Inquiry issued a Credit Report on the boom and bust of 1918–21, when wholesale prices had risen from 200 in November 1918 (100 in 1914) to 244 in June 1920, before falling to 137 in June 1921. "In the early part of 1919," the Report (1922, pp. 12, 44) stated, the "discount policy of the Federal reserve banks was again subordinated to the" Treasury's "credit requirements, although at this time the tendency toward expansion, speculation, and extravagance was beginning to be apparent …. The commission is of the opinion that the difficulties anticipated by the Treasury Department [from rising interest rates] should not have controlled in this period and that the discount policy of the Federal Reserve … should not have yielded to the apprehension of the Treasury."

> The commission believes that had discount rates been raised … promptly and progressively beginning with the spring of 1919, much of the inflation, expansion, speculation, and extravagance which characterized the following 12 months or more might have been greatly retarded, if not wholly prevented.

Property's fears of inflation had been accentuated by the hyper-inflations occurring throughout the world during and after the war.

So, who opposed and eventually overcame the official willingness to suffer deflation and unemployment in the short run (hopefully) for the (hopefully) long-run benefits of the less-than-faultless gold standard? Many groups pressed for monetary expansion, to no avail. More than 50 bills to increase money and prices were introduced in the U.S. House of Representatives during the Great Depression, to no avail (Krooss 1969, pp. 2661–2), but neither Federal Reserve officials nor their institution were inconvenienced as they found safety in the rules they had been assigned.

In April 1932, Congressman Thomas Jefferson Busby of Mississippi urged the Fed "to cooperate with Congress, and launch out and shake off some of its fears about what might happen" if it tried to stop the deflation:

> I do not know whether you know it or not, but about one-fourth of the homes in my state have been sold for taxes during the present month …. Sixty thousand homes, 7,000,000 acres of land, one-fourth of all the property, because the people can not pay taxes; and when people get in that kind of condition, they can not … listen to fine-spun theories of fears that might arise in the event you took some step forward.

This was not the sort of problem that occupied the Fed.

> Governor Harrison – But you have got to remember one other thing, Mr. Congressman, There is always difficulty about the mechanics and the speed with which we operate. First of all, it is not always easy, over a certain number of days to buy as many Government securities as you might want. They are most popular investments and they are sometimes hard to get, and without completely disorganizing the market you sometimes can not purchase them as rapidly as you want them.
>
> [Y]ou run the risk, if you go too fast, of flooding the market or the banks with excess reserves faster than they can use them, or faster than it is wise that they should use them. The proper and orderly operation of the open market, I think, is to create a volume of excess reserves gradually, gradually increasing them, and keeping it up constantly, and not have periods when you have got excess reserves one week and none another week. (U.S. Congress 1932, pp. 492–5)

Busby's and Harrison's interests – individual well-being vs. orderly financial markets – were clearly different and sometimes opposed.

As an endnote, after having begun the chapter with the structure of American banking, it should be noted that banking structures apparently had little to do with the Great Depression. Friedman and Schwartz (1963, p. 351) attributed the severity of the depression in the United States to the aftermath of the so-called banking crisis of late 1930 which induced a collapse in money as people withdrew their deposits from banks. In fact, those failures were more an effect than a cause of the price declines. American prices had fallen steadily from 1925 to 1930, shrinking home values and other bank investments, and causing the failures of known-to-be-weak institutions. Other so-called bank runs were also local, limited, and understood, unlikely to have spurred general losses of confidence and runs (Wicker 1996, p. 24). In fact, the increase in the U.S. demand for money during the Great Depression was consistent with a gold standard explanation in which the price level is determined by the relative costs of gold and other goods, and money is demand-determined.

MORE OF THE SAME

The Fed's support of government finance has been more generous in the new century than at any time since World War II, from the Greenspan Fed's continuation of easy money into the recovery from the 2001 recession, to the great increase in Fed credit by the Bernanke Fed (over four times, 20 percent per annum, during 2006 to 2014), and the more than doubling by the Powell Fed during the 2020–21 Covid-19 crisis. Even before that crisis, from 2000 to 2019, Fed credit had risen more than seven times (10.3 percent per annum), compared with a quadrupling of the national debt (7.3 percent per annum), meaning a rise in the Debt/GDP ratio from 58 percent to 108 percent – much of which may be interpreted as a substitute for taxes in payment of the nation's endless wars (see Chapter 10).

8.   The Great Recession

> We heard from the chairman of the Federal Reserve that unless we act the financial system of this country and perhaps the world will melt down .... There was complete silence for twenty seconds. The oxygen left the room. Chairman Bernanke said, "If we don't do this tomorrow, there won't be an economy on Monday."
> –Senate Banking Committee Chairman Christopher Dodd on a meeting of congressional leaders with Ben Bernanke and Treasury Secretary Henry Paulson in Speaker Nancy Pelosi's office on September 17, 2008
> –Interview with Charlie Rose, November 26, 2008

Six days later, Paulson told the Senate Banking Committee that "bad loans have created a chain reaction and last week our credit markets froze – even some Main Street non-financial companies had trouble financing their normal business operations. If that situation were to persist, it would threaten all parts of our economy. ... Decisive action" is required "to fundamentally and comprehensively address the root cause of this turmoil," which is how he analyzed the housing slowdown that "has resulted in illiquid mortgage-related assets that are choking off the flow of credit which is so vitally important to our economy." We must "restore confidence in our financial markets and financial institutions so they can perform their mission of

"Our system of free enterprise rests on the conviction that the federal government should interfere in the marketplace only when necessary. Given the precarious state of today's financial markets – and their vital importance to the daily lives of the American people – government intervention is not only warranted, it is essential."

Source: https://georgewbush-whitehouse.archives
.gov/news/releases/2008/09/images/20080919
-2_p091908jb-0025-1-515h.html.

Figure 8.1   *President George W. Bush with Federal Reserve Chairman Ben Bernanke, SEC Chairman Chris Cox, and Treasury Secretary Hank Paulson, September 19, 2008*

supporting future prosperity and growth." The "decisive action" proposed by Bernanke and Paulson was Congress's allocation of hundreds of billions of dollars to buy banks' defaulted mortgages (Figure 8.1).

The problem in less inflammatory language had begun with "two shocks: market correction of an excess in the housing stock and a sharp increase in energy prices, which initiated a recession beginning the end of 2007. By themselves these shocks would probably have led to only a moderate recession." GDP had fallen less than 2 percent on an annual basis, and the rate of unemployment had risen from 4.9 percent to 6.1 percent between the first and third quarters of 2008, not out of line with other post-World War II recessions.

However, "A moderate recession became a major recession in summer 2008 when the FOMC [Federal Open Market Committee] ceased lowering the funds rate while the economy deteriorated. Concerned that persistent high headline inflation would raise expected inflation above its implicit 2 percent target, the FOMC imparted the kind of inertia to reductions in the funds rate characteristic of the stop phases in [the Fed's historic] stop-go monetary policy." Figure 8.2 shows the Fed funds rate and the rise in headline inflation as a consequence of energy prices, illustrated by oil in Table 8.1 (Hetzel 2012, p. 204; Miron 2009a; 2009b).

The rest of this chapter describes how the Federal Reserve and U.S. Treasury converted an ordinary recession into *the Great Recession*, tried to restore the speculative losses of favored financial institutions, and laid, or rather entrenched, the groundwork for more of the same. We focus on the United States, although bailouts and the lack of concern for moral hazard were also common in the United Kingdom and elsewhere (Darling 2012; King 2017; Fallon 2015).

Table 8.1   Headline (CPI) and core (CPI less food and energy) inflation and oil price

	Headline inflation	Core inflation	Oil
7/07	207.6	210.8	76.93
7/08	219.0	216.0	132.72
	5.5%	2.5%	

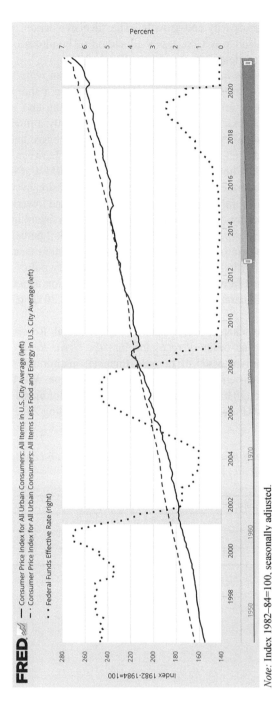

Note: Index 1982–84=100, seasonally adjusted.
Source: U.S. Bureau of Labor Statistics (https://www.bls.gov/).

Figure 8.2   Consumer prices and the Fed funds rate, 1996–2021

MAKING THE GREAT RECESSION

The 2008–09 recession started as the old-fashioned kind, with weaknesses in consumption and inventories like earlier postwar inventory cycles (Table 8.2 time-line). Trend growth in consumption had fallen across the last three business cycles, from 4.1 percent to 3.8 percent to 2.9 percent. This does not suggest excessive consumption made possible by the excessive accumulation of debt, as suggested by Fed Chairmen Alan Greenspan and Ben Bernanke (Angelides 2011). The shortfall of consumption from trend actually widened from May 207 until summer 2008, leading to unwanted inventories.

Table 8.2   *Timeline of the Great Recession in the U.S.A.*

2000–07	Easy to tight monetary policy
III/2005	Beginning of decline in residential investment
I/07	Peak of house prices
5/07	Beginning of shortfall in consumption
3/08	Bailout of Bear Stearns
4–8/08	Contractionary monetary policy
Mid-08	Intensification of recession
9/15/08	Lehman Brothers bankruptcy
9/17/08	Paulson and Bernanke cry fire
10/08	TARP bill passes
IV/08	Large fall in real GDP
I/09	Large fall in employment
2010	Peak in bank failures (157) compared with 25 in 2008

Source: Compiled by the author.

The fall in residential investment began in 2005Q3 (somewhat before the fall in house prices shown in Figure 8.3), but because housing is about 6 percent of GDP, even negative growth rates are not enough by themselves to cause a recession. For example, in 2007Q4, residential investment fell at an annualized rate of 29.3 percent but subtracted only 1.4 percentage points from GDP growth. The decline in residential investment was symptomatic of the excess stock of housing, and had to fall, as usual after rapid building periods. The same was true of inventories. On the other hand, the rapid recovery of house prices seen in Figure 8.3 raises questions about the existence of a bubble (although a good part of the later rise may be attributed to very low interest rates).

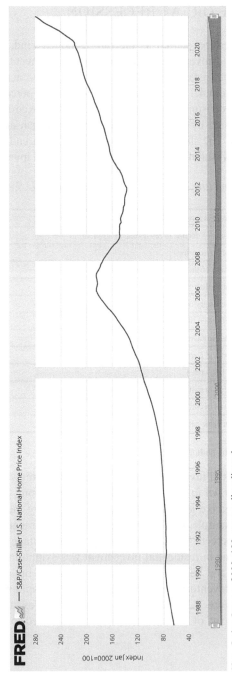

Note: Index January 2000=100, seasonally adjusted.
Source: S&P Dow Jones Indices LLC (https://www.spglobal.com/spdji/en/).

Figure 8.3   U.S. house prices

By summer 2008, financial intermediation – except for a few firms – had moved significantly away from securitization markets back to the banking system, and there is no evidence of disruption to financial intermediation significant enough to have prevented businesses and consumers from obtaining credit. As with other recessions, it is difficult to find evidence of a credit channel propagating an initial shock. Financial activities tend to be disrupted by declines in real activity more than the other way around (Gorton 1988; Calomiris and Gorton 1991; Ashcraft 2006; Konishi et al. 1993; Berrospide and Edge 2010).

Bernanke and Paulson had down-played the importance of housing (Wood 2015; McKinley 2008, pp. 9–12, 120–21), and there was no reason to want to turn off the housing correction, anyway. The economy was dealing with it as with other excesses. A slowing of the rate of increase in the housing stock was due, and so was the fall in house prices. Delaying adjustments by forcing/subsidizing housing might have increased future losses.

The fall in house prices could not be erased by fiat, nor could its wealth effects. Someone had to take the loss, presumably those lending to low-income house-buyers. Government turned out to be most solicitous of the former and its response was to transfer wealth from taxpayers to the banks. Bernanke and Paulson proposed a Troubled Asset Recovery Program (TARP) to enable the purchase of banks' failed mortgages – securing passage of the bill by raising hopes for bailouts of households, only to shift the funds to direct investments in troubled banks, such as purchases of their preferred stock. This approach was bound to be ineffective as a means of restoring the economy or housing market. Banks had little intention of throwing bad money after good by more investments in the falling housing market.

There was no good reason to save failed firms by restoring their losses, but Bernanke and Paulson were persuaded that saving an industry or a market depended on saving individual firms. Anna Schwartz (1992) had warned that "shifting from trying to save the banking system to trying to save bankers ... is not the same thing." The accounting failure of a firm – meaning its insolvency or inability to pay its debts – does not mean the disappearance of its productivity, but rather the transfer of ownership to its creditors. If a manufacturing business fails, its equipment, workers, and productive skills are not lost. They, particularly their profitable parts, may continue under new management, which is good news for the economy. The elimination of inefficient firms, or parts of firms, improves productivity. Government interventions obstructed these adjustments by discouraging private purchasers. It is difficult, even impossible, to compete financially with the Government, and a functioning market for troubled financial firms was destroyed by Government interventions.

Monetary policy in 2008 before the September 15 bankruptcy of Lehman Brothers departed in at least two ways from the 1980s and 1990s procedures of the Volcker–Greenspan era. First, the FOMC went back to the stop–go practice of associating the level of the funds rate with the stance of monetary policy rather than following a rule for the funds rate. In particular, perhaps because of the lack of recent experience with operating in an environment of near-price stability, FOMC members assumed that the 2 percent funds rate set at their April 30, 2008, meeting represented expansionary monetary policy. One might have thought central bankers had learned something from the Great Depression, recent Japanese experience, and other occasions during which historically low interest rates did not necessarily mean easy monetary policy. Second, it was driven by high headline inflation instead of allowing the energy price shock pass through to core inflation (Hetzel 2012, pp. 204–5).

Support for the argument that a moderate recession was turned into a major recession by Government interventions was the timing of the intensification (in rates of increase of unemployment and decline in consumption) before the financial turmoil associated with Lehman's bankruptcy. In spring 2008, the Fed worried about inflation, but when recession became apparent, focused on financial intermediaries and lowered interest rates slowly, so that Macroeconomic Advisors (2008) observed that "financial conditions have tightened more severely," contributing "importantly to the severe weakening of the economic outlook in our forecast." Paulson also told the *Financial Times* (February 1, 2010) that he had feared a run on the dollar, the collapse of which would be "catastrophic."

The recession, combined with the tight monetary policies of the world's central banks, painted a discouraging view of the future, similar to the Federal Reserve's influence during the Great Depression. "The story of the financial turmoil that began in August 2007 and revived in September 2008 is the story of the retreat of the cash investors who provided the short-term financing used by banks to leverage portfolios of long-term illiquid assets, especially" securitized subprime mortgages. "After August 2007, financial intermediation shifted away from securitization and back toward traditional bank lending. The cash investors who had provided the short-term financing for the securitized markets did not disappear. They put their funds into the insured deposits of banks and into government money-market funds." Credit-worthy borrowers continued to obtain credit, and banks "continued to have access to funding ... through the issuance of financial commercial paper, ... Federal Home Loan Bank funding, or ... traditional deposit taking" (Hetzel 2012, pp. 224–5).

The TARP bill failed in the House of Representatives, but was sweetened the second time around by adding help for homeowners facing foreclosure, specifically requiring the Treasury to guarantee home loans and assist homeowners in adjusting mortgage terms. It passed in early October.

The Fed's "focus on disruption to financial markets rather than on [its own] contractionary monetary policy as the source of the intensifying recession appeared in the failure of the FOMC to lower the funds rate" in September 2008. After all, said President Richard Fisher of the Dallas Fed, "rates held too low, too long during the previous Fed regime were an accomplice to that reckless behavior." The data suggest, however, that the real short-term interest rates maintained by the Fed were high relative to the natural rate of interest consistent with full employment, and the gloom spread by Bernanke et al. must have lowered the natural rate and increased the deflationary spread still further (Hetzel 2012, p. 234; Taylor 2009).

The Bernanke–Paulson Henny-Penny-like screams in September 2008, just preceded the acceleration of the downturn and might deserve much of the blame for adding "great" to an ordinary recession by undermining confidence in the financial system: "We didn't know things were this bad," to which were added the Fed's and Treasury's panic-stricken shifts in policy, including "save Bear, let Lehman fail, save Citi, let Wachovia fail, …" (Allison 2013, p. 167; Macey 2008)

A REVIEW OF FEDERAL RESERVE BEHAVIOR

The Fed's behavior was hard to make sense of. Spokespersons talked of a nonexistent liquidity shortage but in practice simply substituted failing mortgages for U.S. securities in its virtually unchanged credit during the two years preceding August 2008. (Officials often use *illiquid* in place of *insolvent*, possibly in an effort to sell their bailouts to the public.) Beginning in early 2007, banks and hedge funds reported increasing losses on subprime mortgages and mortgage-backed securities, especially adjustable-rate mortgages as interest rates rose through July 2006, and did not begin to fall until a year later. The crisis appeared in interbank lending markets in August 2007, when the London Interbank Offered Rate (Libor) and other funding rates spiked (Wheelock 2010). The Fed began to auction funds to banks against a "wide variety of collateral" in December.

The Fed's *Term Auction Facility* (TAF) was addressed to "elevated pressures in short-term funding markets" (Armantier et al. 2008). It was a response to what was already being called the subprime mortgage crisis and the widening spread between rates on overnight and term interbank lending that indicated a retreat from risk-taking. The Fed began to shift its credit from governments to mortgages, as shown in Table 8.3. U.S. securities were reduced from 91 percent to 23 percent of Fed credit between November 2007 and November 2008. Surprisingly in view of the announced purpose to enhance liquidity, the monetary base was held virtually constant until October 2008, and even afterwards the Fed's effect on money was slight because the increase in its credit went mainly into bank excess reserves and Treasury balances at the Fed.

TAF was revised in March 2008 to *Term Securities Lending Facility* (TSLF), "to relieve liquidity pressure in the credit markets, specifically the mortgage-backed securities market, by which primary dealers (including banks and the Government-sponsored enterprises Fannie Mae and Freddie Mac) can access highly liquid and secure Treasury securities in exchange for the far less liquid and less safe eligible securities. This helps to increase the liquidity in the credit market for these securities" (Federal Reserve Board announcement, March 8, 2008).

The Fed's terminology was careless. "Liquidity" means the ready accessibility of cash on terms approximating normal market values. In times of panic – shortages of cash often caused by hoarding – nothing short of cash is liquid, and even high-grade securities cannot be sold. This was true of some nineteenth-century panics/crises, but not 2007 and 2008, when there was plenty of cash. The spreads seen by the Fed were risk premia.

Table 8.3   Factors affecting the reserves of depository institutions, 2007–09 (Federal Reserve Board release H1. $ billions)

Weekly average ending	11/28/07	02/28/08	11/5/08	11/04/09
Reserve bank credit	*866*	*867*	*2,056*	*2,147*
U.S. securities	780	713	490	777
Repurchase agreements	46	43	80	0
Federal agency securities	0	0	0	147
Mortgage-backed securities [a]				774
Term auction credit [b]	0	60	301	139
Discount loans	...	...	80	22
Broker/dealer credit			77	0
Term asset-backed securities [c]				43
Credit to AIG				45
Asset-backed commercial paper; money-market mutual fund liquidity facility			92	0
Other credit extensions [d]			80	0
Commercial paper funding facility			226	14
Maiden Lane holdings [e]			27	66
Float	−1	−1	−1	-2
Central bank liquidity swaps [f]				32
Other Federal Reserve assets [g]	41	51	574	90
Gold and special drawing rights	13	13	13	16
Treasury currency outstanding	39	39	39	43

Weekly average ending	11/28/07	02/28/08	11/5/08	11/04/09
Total reserve funds	*919*	*919*	*2,108*	*2,206*
Currency in circulation	821	815	861	918
Reverse repurchase agreements	34	40	95	61
Deposits with FR banks other than reserves	12	12		
U.S. Treasury	5	5	590	97
Depository institutions clearing balances	6	7	6	3
Other liabilities and capital	42	44	61	64
Reserve balances with FR banks	8	8	494	1,062
(Excess)			(453)	(1,002)

Notes: [a] Guaranteed by Fannie Mae, Freddie Mac, and Ginnie Mae.
[b] Reserves auctioned by the Fed to depository institutions (see text).
[c] Loans to investors in asset and mortgage backed securities. "Citigroup, Ford, and JPMorgan Chase are among companies that have sold auto and credit-card debt through the TALF."
[d] Emergency loans to institutions including AIG.
[e] "To facilitate a prompt acquisition of Bear Stearns by JPMorgan Chase, the FRBank of NY created a limited liability company, Maiden Lane LLC, to acquire and manage them." AIG was added. [Maiden Lane is a street in New York's financial district; the original name in New Amsterdam meant "footpath used by lovers."]
[f] Dollar values of foreign currency.
[g] Accrued interest and accounts receivable; Reserve Bank premises and operating equipment; Term Asset-Backed Securities Loan Facility.
Source: Compiled by the author.

Walter Bagehot's (1873) advice to the Bank of England in times of panic had been to lend liberally at high interest rates on good security. The Fed violated both conditions. The confusion of liquidity and solvency, along with the incredible assumption that markets are less informed than regulators, led to another episode of too-big-to-fail bailouts. George Kaufman had explained them to a congressional committee (U.S. Congress 1991, p. 53):

> … systemic risk is … a phantom issue. It is a scare tactic…. The runs on Continental Bank in 1984, the large Texas banks in 1987–89, and the Bank of New England in 1990–91 were rational runs on economically insolvent institutions that moved funds not into currency to start systemic risk, but to safer banks. The delayed resolutions by the regulators did little more than increase FDIC [Federal Deposit Insurance Corporation] losses substantially. The small depositors are the only ones you need to worry about because they are the only ones who could run into currency. The big depositors can't. The only way that systemic risk, if there is such a thing, can occur is if there is a run on all banks into currency.

So-called runs have historically in fact been rational withdrawals from institutions known to be in trouble (Temzelides 1997; Walter 2005; Wicker 1996). Continental Illinois was the first rescue (1984) to be defended on the grounds that some financial enterprises are "too big to fail." The FDIC claimed during congressional hearings that Continental's failure would have exposed 179 small banks to high risks of failure. This figure was revised downward after investigation by the House Banking Committee and the Government Accounting Office to 28. Kaufman found that only two banks would have lost more than half their capital. The 1990 failure of Drexel Burnham Lambert had no systemic consequences, nor did Long Term Capital Management in 1998 (Kaufman 1990, 2000).

In fact, bank deposits were rising in 2007–08. Despite loose talk of the credit markets "freezing up" (or "melting down"), bank credit continued and mortgages were available to the credit-worthy at historically attractive interest rates. Figure 8.4 indicates that the abrupt increase in the three-month Libor rate relative to the overnight federal funds rate in August 2007, after the failures of banks heavily involved in mortgage-backed securities, as well as the jump in September 2008, after the failure of Lehman Brothers, were due to risk rather than illiquidity. Certificates of deposit (CDs) were in the same risk category as Libor, while overnight Fed funds were low risk (Taylor and Williams 2009). TAF probably "increased the risk premium ... because market participants interpreted the announcement by the Fed and other central banks as a sign that the financial crisis was worse than previously thought" (Thornton 2011).

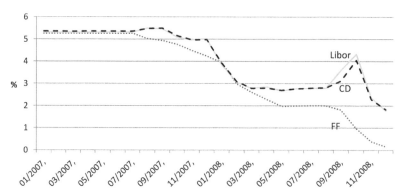

Note: Index January 2000=100, seasonally adjusted.
Source: Taylor and Williams (2009).

Figure 8.4   *Federal Funds and three-month Libor and CD rates, monthly averages 2007–08*

Also in March 2008, the Treasury decided to bail out the investment banking firm Bear Stearns, which was heavily exposed to mortgages. "Conventional wisdom holds that the housing industry collapsed because lenders of sub-prime mortgages had perverse incentives to bundle and pass off risky mortgage-backed securities to other investors in order to profit from high origination fees. The logic follows that banks did not care if they lent to borrowers who were likely to default since the banks did not intend to hold onto the mortgage or the financial products they created for very long." In fact, a few "financial institutions actually sought out risky mortgage loans in pursuit of profits from high-yielding securities), and ... held onto high-risk investments ... including Bear Stearns, Lehman Brothers, Merrill Lynch, and Morgan Stanley" (Fligstein and Goldstein 2014; Coghlan 2018).

Instead of seeking congressional appropriation, it was arranged that the Federal Reserve Bank of New York lend $30 billion to JPMorgan Chase (collateralized by Bear Stearns' mortgages rather than Morgan assets) to enable a merger with Bear Stearns while guaranteeing a selection of its obligations. Bernanke, chairman of the Fed since February 1, 2006, made the unsubstantiated claim that a Bear Stearns' bankruptcy would have affected the real economy and cause a "chaotic unwinding" of investments across the nation's markets (Bloomberg news service, April 2, 2008). Intervention was necessary, he said, because "market participants would not be adequate to deal in an orderly way with the collapse of a major counterparty," even though risk spreads indicated that orderly market adjustments had been underway (Bernanke 2008).

New York Fed President Timothy Geithner testified to the Senate Banking Committee that widening credit spreads were evidence that markets were not working; he called insolvency illiquidity, likened the situation to the currency crises of the nineteenth century, and called "the extensions of credit to Bear Stearns ... in keeping with the traditional role of lender of last resort" (U.S. Congress 2008: April 3; McKinley 2008, pp. 138–9, 310–12).

There was no basis for any of these claims. Nor was there any logic behind the idea that taxpayer credit directed to failing firms would reverse the falling course of house prices and make mortgages whole. The bailouts' principal effect was to retard market adjustments. The blow to wealth had occurred. The government's policy was to transfer that blow from those who stood to profit if things had gone well to the taxpayers (Carney 2008). "We've told the world we're not going to let any of our major institutions fail," Geithner reminded his colleagues. "We're going to have to make it really clear we're standing behind Citigroup," which was insolvent despite its receipt of $25 billion in TARP funds (Paulson 2010, p. 407).

The *Housing and Economic Recovery Act* of July 30, 2008 authorized the Federal Housing Administration to guarantee up to $300 billion of new 30-year fixed-rate mortgages for subprime borrowers if lenders wrote down loans to 90 percent of current appraisal value. It was intended to restore confidence in Fannie Mae and Freddie Mac, and encourage the flow of funds into the housing market. However, as of February 2009, only 451 applications had been received and 25 loans finalized, instead of the 400,000 homeowners that had been expected to participate. The shortfall demonstrated the emptiness of the government's promise to help Main Street borrowers, and followed from the program's high fees and interest rates, the required reduction in principal on the part of the lender, and the requirement that the federal Government receive half of any appreciation in value of the house. Fannie Mae and Freddie Mac were placed in government conservatorship on September 7, 2008.

TO BAIL OR NOT TO BAIL

In mid-2007, Bear Stearns, America's seventh largest securities firm and one of *Fortune*'s "most admired" companies, revealed that two of its investment funds, heavily invested in collateralized debt obligations (CDOs, commercial paper backed by often subprime mortgages), had lost nearly all their values, leading to several criminal and civil lawsuits by investors claiming they had been misled. Barclay's Bank, for example, claimed that Bear Stearns knew that certain assets in the Bear Stearns *High-Grade Structured Credit Strategies Enhanced Leverage Master Fund* were worth much less than their professed values. The suit claimed that Bear Stearns managers devised "a plan to make more money for themselves and further to use the Enhanced Fund as a repository for risky, poor-quality investments." The lawsuit said Bear Stearns told Barclays that the enhanced fund was up almost 6 percent through June 2007 – when "in reality, the portfolio's asset values were plummeting" (Hays 2008).

In March 2008, the Federal Reserve Bank of New York (FRBNY) provided a $25 billion loan to Bear Stearns collateralized by unencumbered Bear Stearns assets to provide the firm the liquidity for up to 28 days which the market was refusing to provide. Shortly thereafter, FRBNY had a change of heart and told Bear Stearns that the 28-day loan was unavailable to them. The deal was then changed to one in which the FRBNY would create a company (Maiden Lane LLC) to buy $30 billion worth of Bear Stearns' assets, and Bear Stearns would be purchased by JPMorgan Chase at $2 a share – a staggering loss as its stock had traded at $172 in January 2007, and $93 a share in February 2008 – although raised to $10 after shareholder complaints (Frontline 2009; Seeking Alpha 2008; Hussman Funds 2008; CBS News 2008).

Securities and Exchange Commission Chairman Christopher Cox said the collapse of Bear Stearns was due to a lack of confidence, not a lack of capital. He noted that Bear Stearns' problems escalated when rumors spread about its liquidity crisis. "Notwithstanding that Bear Stearns continued to have high quality collateral to provide as security for borrowings, market counterparties became less willing to enter into collateralized funding arrangements with Bear Stearns," Cox said. Bear Stearns' liquidity pool started at $18.1 billion on March 10 and plummeted to $2 billion on March 13. Ultimately, market rumors about Bear Stearns' difficulties became self-fulfilling, Cox (2008) claimed. Such statements were typical of spokesmen for insolvent companies even when, as in Bear Stearns' case, losses of confidence were justified by knowledge of their balance sheets. Neither Cox nor Geithner, Paulson, or Bernanke, in all their bailout rationalizations, tried to explain the probable consequences of government forbearance. The Bear Stearns bailout was viewed as an extreme-case scenario, and continues to raise significant questions about Fed intervention. Paul Volcker stated that the Fed has taken "actions that extend to the very edge of its lawful and implied powers" (*Wall Street Journal*, April 8, 2008).

Lehman Brothers was begun by German emigrants as a dry-goods store in Montgomery, Alabama, in the 1840s. They were often paid in cotton, became involved in the cotton market, and in the 1850s opened an office in New York, the center of commodities trading. They expanded into other commodities and securities, with worldwide involvement, and at the beginning of 2008, was the fourth largest investment bank in New York, and also one of *Fortune*'s "most admired." It, too, became involved in subprime mortgages, and on September 15, 2008, filed for Chapter 8 bankruptcy protection following the exodus of most of its clients, drastic losses in its stock, and devaluations of assets by credit rating agencies.

Lehman's had been one of the first Wall Street firms to move into the business of mortgage origination. In 1997, it bought Colorado-based lender Aurora Loan Services, and in 2000, acquired West Coast subprime mortgage lender BNC Mortgage. By 2003, it had $18.2 billion in loans and ranked third in lending. By 2004, this number topped $40 billion. By 2006, Aurora and BNC were lending almost $50 billion per month.

Lehman had morphed into a real estate hedge fund disguised as an investment bank. By 2008, it had assets of $680 billion supported by only $22.5 billion of capital. Its risky commercial real estate holdings were 30 times greater than capital. In such a highly leveraged structure, a 3–5 percent decline in real estate values would wipe out all capital.

Lehman could hardly be blamed for expecting to be bailed out and was unprepared for bankruptcy. It was larger than Bear Stearns which had been treated as too big to fail, it had repurchased shares at the beginning of 2008, and its actions generally were not those of a company husbanding resources. Reinforced by a meeting with Paulson, it took on more risk and rejected an offer of $18 per share as late as August 2008 (Fleming and Sarkar 2014; McDonald and Robinson 2009).

The day after Lehman Brothers filed for bankruptcy, Barclays announced its agreement to purchase, subject to regulatory approval, Lehman's North American investment-banking and trading divisions along with its New York headquarters building. On September 20, 2008, a revised version of that agreement was approved by U.S. Bankruptcy Judge James M. Peck. The next week, Nomura Holdings announced that it would acquire Lehman Brothers' franchise in the Asia-Pacific region, as well as Lehman Brothers' investment banking and equities businesses in Europe and the Middle East.

On September 12, Geithner had called a meeting on the future of Lehman, which included the possibility of an emergency liquidation of its assets. Bankers representing the major Wall Street firms were in attendance. The meeting goal was to find a private solution in rescuing Lehman and extinguish the flame of the global financial crisis. Lehman reported that it had been in talks with Bank of America and Barclays for the company's possible sale. However, the deal was vetoed by the Bank of England (Figure 8.5). Leaders of major Wall Street banks continued to meet late that day to prevent the bank's rapid failure. Bank of America's rumored involvement also appeared to end as federal regulators resisted its request for government assistance in Lehman's sale.

Lehman Brothers filed for Chapter 8 bankruptcy protection on Monday, September 15, 2008. JPMorgan Chase provided Lehman Brothers with $138 billion in "Federal Reserve-backed advances." Much of the firm was quickly purchased. On September 16, 2008, Barclays announced that they would acquire a "stripped clean" portion of Lehman for $1.75 billion, including most of Lehman's North America operations, revised on September 20 to a $1.35 billion plan to acquire the core business of Lehman (mainly its $960 million headquarters, a 38-story office building in midtown Manhattan with responsibility for 9,000 former employees).

Nomura Holdings, Japan's top brokerage firm, agreed to buy the Asian division of

"For centuries alchemy has been the basis of our system of money and banking. Governments pretended that paper money could be turned into gold even when there was more of the former than the latter. Banks pretended that short term riskless deposits could be used to finance long term risky investments. In both, cases the alchemy is the apparent transformation of risk into safety."

Source: https://members-api.parliament.uk/api/ Members/4280/Portrait?cropType=ThreeFour.

Figure 8.5   *Mervyn King, Governor of the Bank of England, 2003–13*

Lehman Brothers for $225 million and parts of the European division for a nominal fee of $2. It would not take on any trading assets or liabilities in the European units.

On September 29, 2008, Lehman agreed to sell Neuberger Berman, part of its investment management business, to a pair of private-equity firms, Bain Capital Partners and Hellman & Friedman, for $2.15 billion. The transaction was expected to close in early 2009, subject to approval by the U.S. Bankruptcy Court, but a competing bid was entered by the firm's management, who ultimately prevailed in a bankruptcy auction on December 3, 2008. Creditors of Lehman Brothers Holdings Inc. retain a 49 percent common equity interest in the firm, now known as Neuberger Berman Group LLC. In Europe, the Quantitative Asset Management Business was acquired by its employees on November 13, 2008 and has been renamed TOBAM.

There seemed no shortage of bids for failing company assets and the probable continuation of their profitable activities. But the day after Lehman's bankruptcy, the Federal Reserve Board authorized the New York Fed to lend $85 billion to American International Group (AIG), rising to more than $180 billion in May 2009. AIG had sold hundreds of billions of dollars' worth of credit default swaps (CDSs, contracts between buyers who make periodic payments and receive payoffs if underlying financial instruments default), and the Fed's loan allowed AIG to pay $53.5 billion to CDS counterparties, the largest being Société Générale, Deutsche Bank, and Goldman Sachs. Regulators had encouraged the CDS market by raising the credit ratings of bank loans insured by them.

On September 21, the Fed granted requests by the last two major investment banks, Goldman Sachs and Morgan Stanley, to change their status to bank holding companies, which gave them greater access to Fed funding in return for the fictitious tighter regulation of banks. Of the five largest investment banks existing before the crisis, Bear Stearns was acquired by JPMorgan, Merrill Lynch by the Bank of America, and Lehman was allowed to fail (Saunders and Cornett 2012, p. 414).

Summarizing the Fed's activities during the subprime crisis, former Fed economist and monetary historian David Humphrey (2010) wrote that it "deviated from the classical model in so many ways as to make a mockery of the notion that it is a lender of last resort," specifically by accepting "toxic assets" (mortgage-backed securities) above their market values as collateral for loans or buying them outright and supplying funds directly to firms understood to be insolvent. Until September 2008, the Fed also sterilized its direct lending operations through offsetting Fed sales of Treasury securities, in effect transferring some $250 billion in liquid funds from presumably solvent firms to potentially insolvent ones – a strategy opposite to Bagehot's, and which tended to spread rather than contain financial stress.

In September 2008, the Fed at last turned from sterilized to unsterilized lending, on a scale that doubled the monetary base in eight months (see Table 8.3). "At the same time, however, it began paying interest on excess reserves, thereby increasing the demand for [them], while also arranging to have the Treasury sell supplemental bills and deposit the proceeds in a special account. Thanks in part to these special measures, bank lending, nominal GDP, and the CPI [consumer price index], instead of responding positively to the doubling of the monetary base, plummeted" (Selgin et al. 2012).

Everything about the monetary policies of the 2000s – including the return to the stop–go policies of the 1960s and 1970s at the beginning, the bailouts of selected firms, credit reallocations, and gratuitous assaults on confidence – suggests that financial and economic problems would have been less serious if the Fed had stayed with what Hetzel (2012, pp. 128–48) called the "leaning-against-the-wind with credibility" rule of the Volcker and most of the Greenspan eras and their trust in market adjustments. The Fed possessed the powers to deal with the problems at hand, particularly to supply liquidity by open-market purchases of government securities. The recession in home-building, with its effects on the wider economy, would have occurred, along with the problems of over-zealous lenders. Failing activities would have been allowed to disappear, potentially profitable activities would have continued.

The Treasury had developed a "Break the Glass Capitalization (BTG) Plan," typically named after an emergency metaphor, in which the U.S. government would "recapitalize the banking sector by purchasing illiquid mortgage-related assets." The program was "designed to help banks resume lending and help stabilize the housing and mortgage markets" (Sorkin 2009, pp. 83, 90–93; Wessel 2010, pp. 176–7; McKinley 2008, pp. 257–8). The author of the program admitted to the secretary that there are no decision criteria that I can point to. "Ultimately, it's the combined judgment of Treasury and the Fed." Vincent Reinhart, former director of Monetary Affairs at the Federal Reserve Board, summarized the situation in early October:

> Until now, the responses of government officials have been inconsistent and improvisational. The first impulse was to extend the federal safety net to investment banks. Thus, in March, the Federal Reserve rescued Bear Stearns, breaking a 60-year-old precedent by lending to a non-depository. That set in motion an uneven process of failure and intervention. The private sector lost its incentive to pump capital into troubled firms and gained an incentive to pick among the winners and losers of the government intervention lottery. Lehman Brothers or AIG? Washington Mutual or Wachovia? Rather than forecasting underlying values, financial markets were predicting government intentions. We should not be here, but we are. (McKinley 2008, p. 259)

This was a candid admission by a Fed official that the crisis, if there was one, was of the Fed's own making by its market interferences. The CEO of one of the majority of healthy banks tells the story from their viewpoint. The bailout of Bear Stearns "was a terrible message to the capital market. Since Bear Stearns was the smallest of the top six investment banks, the implication was that the larger investment banks had an implicit" Government guarantee – making it less necessary to reduce their risks. However, one of those, Lehman, was allowed to fail on September 15. On September 25, after losing deposits of $16.7 billion in ten days, Washington Mutual was seized by the Office of Thrift Supervision, which sold most of its assets, including its branch network, for what was discovered to be a low price to JPMorgan Chase.

The disappearance of these institutions, both larger than Lehman, was political (see below), but had no effect on the system except to complete the demolition of the private market for bank capital. The greater-than-necessary losses to WaMu's bondholders and stockholders "destroyed the capital markets for banks," and prevented the troubled Wachovia Bank from finding a buyer at a market-relevant price. Most large institutions were healthy, and there were several potential buyers for those in trouble until the government interfered, when it became a game to see who could get the biggest subsidy. Private investors could not hope to compete with the Government, particularly when it lacked recognizable criteria for action (Allison 2013, pp. 162–3).

John Allison, CEO of BB&T (1989–2008), describes his own experiences with TARP, which he called "a blatantly obvious effort to bail out the giant money-center banks and the investment banks … designed by Paulson, a lifetime investment banker." Large healthy banks, which were the majority, were forced to accept TARP funds to provide cover for the few in actual need. Allison complained, but the healthy banks were denied meetings with Paulson or Bernanke, and all became subject to costly new regulations and "stress tests." He also argued that TARP violated constitutional limits on the uncontrolled use of taxpayers' money (Allison 2013, pp. 168–70).

BAILOUTS VS. BANKRUPTCIES

The Great Recession was largely an outcome of unexplained and erratic Fed and Treasury interventions, some of them involving choices between bailouts and bankruptcies. "The onset of the current financial crisis brought with it an unprecedented intervention in the financial markets by the Federal Reserve and the United States Treasury … on an ad hoc basis, with varying degrees of taxpayer support," wrote Kenneth Ayotte and David Skeel (2010). "In the Bear Stearns case, taxpayer funds facilitated a merger. In the AIG case, the Federal Reserve made a substantial direct loan to the company. With Lehman Brothers … the government declined to offer any money, and the company ultimately filed for Chapter 8 bankruptcy" [usually a plan of reorganization to keep a business alive and pay creditors over time]. Although it was hard to distil a consistent policy rule from the Government's rescue efforts, one guiding principle was the avoidance of bankruptcy filings because of "the supposedly severe consequences that would follow." Bernanke said on *60 Minutes* (March 15, 2009):

> There were many people who said, "Let 'em fail." You know, "It's not a problem. The markets will take care of it." And I think I knew better than that. And Lehman proved that you cannot let a large internationally active firm fail in the middle of a financial crisis.

Treasury Secretary Geithner similarly defended AIG's rescue loan on *This Week with George Stephanopoulos* (ABC, March 30, 2009):

> We were caught between these terrible choices of letting Lehman fail – and you saw the catastrophic damage that caused the financial system – or coming in and putting huge amounts of taxpayer dollars at risk, like we did at AIG, to keep the thing going, unwind it slowly at less damage to the ultimate economy and taxpayer.

These statements had no basis in law or experience. Bankruptcy may enable a firm or its parts to play a constructive role in markets going forward. "Bankruptcy of a large corporation does not leave a crater behind. Bankruptcy is reorganization and protection, not liquidation," John Cochrane reminded us in his *Grumpy Economist* blog (2020). "The point of bankruptcy is precisely to keep the business going. When a corporation files for bankruptcy, the stockholders are wiped out, bondholders lose a lot and become the new stockholders. The company rewrites a lot of contracts – union contracts requiring a plane to fly even with empty seats, contracts to buy fuel at high prices, gate leases, and so forth. Bailouts are bailouts to stockholders, bondholders, creditors, unions ... not to 'the corporation' which isn't a thing."

"[O]ne of the key arguments often advanced in favor of bailouts," Stephanie Ben-Ishai and Stephen Lubben (2011) stated, "is the ability to sidestep supposedly severe consequences that follow from a bankruptcy. Proponents of this approach focus on two particular 'shortcomings' of bankruptcy. First, critics emphasize the impact of bankruptcy 'on the value of the distressed firm itself.' Bankruptcy, the reasoning goes would severely dissipate the value of the firm's assets." These concerns are characterized as "firm-specific risks." Second, critics of bankruptcy cite the negative consequences of a bankruptcy filing outside the firm, as it "directly affects the firm's contractual counterparties, some of whom, such as lenders and derivatives counterparties, have direct claims on the firms, while others hold contracts whose value is tied to the distressed firm." The premise of this argument is that a bankruptcy filing has "spillover effects," such that on the bankruptcy of one firm, several others and possibly the economy are adversely affected.

On the other hand, there are significant drawbacks to bailouts. Ayotte and Skeel characterized them as "ad hoc" and "last minute rescue efforts." They argue that the rescue loan approach favored in the financial crisis increased uncertainty and moral hazard, and dampened the incentives of private actors to resolve distress before a desperate "day of reckoning" arose. These forces created substantial costs to the taxpayers.

Ayotte and Skeel tackle the two-pronged argument of bailout enthusiasts. With respect to the issue of firm-specific risks, they state that the "firm specific risks of Chapter 8 [bankruptcy] are overstated," adding that "the law gives distressed firms several advantages in bankruptcy that are unavailable outside of bankruptcy. These advantages help preserve firm value, allocate control rights to residual claimants, and do a more effective job of handling moral hazard concerns than taxpayer-funded rescue loans on the eve of bankruptcy." Ayotte and Skeel acknowledge that there is no perfect solution – when a firm is failing, someone always loses. They contend that the distress of financial firms thus poses an inescapable choice: regulators must either allow counterparties to take losses, and thus confront the possibility of systemic effects, or they must use taxpayer money to prevent the losses from being realized. Bankruptcy has proven to be an adequate mechanism for handling the former choice, and it is flexible enough to accommodate the latter.

With respect to the alleged systemic risks of bankruptcy, it is questionable whether they are restricted to bankruptcy proceedings alone. Indeed, "[s]ome of these systemic costs … would arise in any procedure that forces counterparties to bear losses when there are not enough assets to satisfy all counterparty claims." Jeffrey Miron (2009b) concurs, arguing that "U.S. policymakers should have allowed the standard process of bankruptcy to operate." Although bankruptcy "would not have avoided all the costs of the crisis … it would plausibly have moderated those costs relative to a bailout. Even more, the bankruptcy approach would have reduced rather than enhanced the likelihood of future crises."

Additionally, with respect to systemic risks, it is difficult to determine whether the "crisis of confidence" that occurs when a large firm goes bankrupt is a result of the actual bankruptcy, or the fact that a major business is in financial distress. Accordingly, the contention that filing for bankruptcy, in and of itself, initiates some kind economic domino effect remains to be proven. Moreover, for some, bankruptcy is not merely the "lesser of two evils"; rather, it is a beneficial choice. For example, Miron notes that "[f]ailure is an essential aspect of capitalism. It provides information about good and bad investments, and it releases resources from bad projects to more productive ones."

Two-thirds of large bankruptcy outcomes involve a sale of the firm rather than reorganization, but in any case, whatever the relative merits of bailouts and bankruptcies, the Fed and other authorities have had decades to develop a strategy of responses to financial problems upon which the markets might rely. Their behavior, however, has added to instead of moderating the uncertainties of markets and existing regulations. "Bernanke says that the financial system and the world would have ended without his dramatic intervention. If one is doing counterfactuals," Hetzel (2012) asked, "why start with Sunday evening September 14 and ask what would have happened if the Fed had allowed Citi to fail catastrophically? Why not start in the early 1970s and ask what the world would look like if the Fed and the regulators had not mindlessly bailed out any and every financial institution?" The Fed has failed to learn, and been forced to rely on the unaccountable language of discretion because of its refusal to be guided – and to be seen to be guided – by rules.

A REPORT CARD AND LESSONS FOR THE FUTURE

"[W]e need to protect the American people from financial disaster," Secretary Paulson testified. "You keep asserting that, but I don't hear persuasive reasons," Senate Finance Committee Chairman Max Baucus replied, but only got a repeat of the assertion. Congress passed the *Emergency Economic Stabilization Act of 2008*, on October 3, signed into law by President George W. Bush the same day. The Act authorized the Secretary of the Treasury to buy up to $700 billion of unspecified troubled assets from unspecified financial institutions.

No reasoned case for TARP was made by the Fed or the Treasury. The original BTG plan had called for $500 billion, but just as arbitrarily became $700 billion. "It's not based on any particular data point," a Treasury spokesman said, "We just wanted to choose a really large number" (McKinley 2008, p. 262). Congress was not told what might happen if banks did not receive the cash, beyond more unreasoned predictions of doom, or what banks would be required to do with the cash. "Make a case," Congress should have said. On the other hand, maybe they knew a case could not be made – at least by the Fed or the Treasury, which had previously shown their unawareness of economic conditions and relations.

Paulson exalting know-nothingness refused the possibility of learning when he said: "There is no playbook for responding to turmoil we have never faced" (*New York Times*, November 17, 2008). In fact, the failure of speculative loans based on the expectation of ever-rising prices has been, next to government excesses, the most common source of financial crises. A recent account, *This Time is Different* (2010) by Carmen Reinhart and Kenneth Rogoff, gives eight centuries of examples. Official responses have also been repeated. Particularly since the 1970s, failures and threatened failures have inspired bailouts, followed by complaints and admissions that they were unnecessary, only to be repeated.

"No one disputes that a few large banks were in danger of failing, but this does not justify a bailout," Jeffrey Miron (2009b) wrote. "Failure is an essential aspect of capitalism. It provides information about good and bad investments, and it releases resources from bad projects to more productive ones. [H]ousing prices and housing construction were too high at the end of 2005. This condition implied a deterioration in bank balance sheets and a retrenchment in the banking sector, so some amount of failure was both inevitable and appropriate. Thus, an economic case for the bailout needed to show that failure by some banks would harm the economy beyond what was unavoidable due to the fall in housing prices."

Belated realizations such as these and the large costs of bailouts found their way into law as Congress, in the *FDIC Improvement Act of 1991*, required the FDIC to intervene earlier and more vigorously when a bank gets into trouble, and to close failed banks by the least costly methods, raising the probable losses to bank stockholders and bond holders (Mishkin 2006, p. 279). Similar promises were made in Dodd–Frank.

Washington Mutual was five times larger than Continental Illinois in real terms. Yet the FDIC was able, after wiping out its shareholders and most of its secured bondholders, to sell it to JPMorgan Chase without inconveniencing its customers or disrupting the financial markets. Although Lehman Brothers was one of the largest dealers in credit default swaps, investigators found "no indication that any financial institution became troubled or failed" because of its failure. Nor did Lehman's inability to meet its obligations lead to the "contagion" which is the hallmark of systemic risk (Tarr 2010).

AIG's exposure was also easily settled (*Wall Street Journal*, November 27, 2009). A greater danger to banks than size has been their rate of growth. WaMu's 2005 strategic plan called for "increasing our Credit Risk tolerance," and an examiner of Lehman's bankruptcy wrote that it "made the deliberate decision to embark upon an aggressive growth strategy, to take on significantly greater risk, and to substantially increase leverage on its capital." When loans began to turn bad, "Lehman made the conscious decision to 'double-down,' hoping to profit from a counter-cyclical strategy" (Stanton 2012, pp. 33–4). Furthermore, the Bear Stearns example might have encouraged Lehman's expectations of a similar bailout, if needed.

This behavior had been seen before. Continental, WaMu, Lehman, Fannie Mae and Freddie Mac had grown too fast not to fail. Short of making them (and the regulators) learn from history that *This Time is [Not] Different*, the best public policy would have been to persuade them (managers, directors, stockholders, and creditors) that they would not be bailed out. That would have been difficult, however. They knew better, and their political, if not their economic, expectations were validated.

Official attitudes were unaffected by experience, and continued to reflect the attitudes expressed by Fed Governor John LaWare's testimony to Congress:

> It is systematic risk that fails to be controlled and stopped at the inception that is a nightmare condition that is unfair to everybody. The only analogy that I can think of for the failure of a major international institution of great size is a meltdown of a nuclear generating plant like Chernobyl.
>
> The ramifications of that kind of a failure are so broad and happen with such lightening-speed that you cannot after the fact control them. It runs the risk of bringing down other banks, corporations, disrupting markets, bringing down investment banks along with it …. We are talking about the failure that could disrupt the whole system. (U.S. Congress 1991, p. 34)

Talk about scare tactics! However, even systemic risk would not have made bailout the right policy. "To see why, note first that allowing banks to fail does not mean the government plays no role," Miron noted. Federal deposit insurance prevents losses by insured depositors, and was expanded, Federal courts and regulatory agencies (such as the FDIC) supervise bankruptcy proceedings. The activities of bankrupt firms do not necessarily disappear. The personnel and facilities remain. Shareholders and bondholders take the losses required to make mergers and sales of potentially productive firms attractive. Taxpayer funds go only to insured depositors. Banking continues. The payments system and financial intermediation survive. Typical arguments for the bailouts of Boeing, Chrysler, General Motors and other manufacturing firms sound as if their facilities are in danger of disappearing. Not so, of course. What might be changed, in fact, are their ownership and direction. The same is true of banking and financial intermediation (Miron 2009b).

There would have been takers for operations and assets at market prices because problems were limited to a few badly managed and/or unlucky firms. The governance of firms withstanding the crisis possessed certain features in common: "(1) discipline and long-term perspective, (2) robust communications and information systems, (3) the capacity to respond effectively to early warning signs, and (4) a process of constructive dialogue between business units and risk managers" (Stanton 2012, p. 14). These imply collegial/open rather than dictatorial/overbearing management. "Jamie [Dimon] and I like to get the bad news out to where everybody can see it … to get the dead cat on the table," a JPMorgan Chase executive said. The Fed–Treasury policy was to perpetuate the practices of those firms behaving oppositely, which lacked communication, suppressed news of risk, and were surprised by the bad news when it came, as the Treasury and Fed were surprised.

Lehman Brothers had many assets for which investors were willing to bid. "Some creditors didn't want to wait for their money, or take a chance that they wouldn't get paid at all." They sold to investment firms who had sent "teams to study Lehman's balance sheet to identify potentially valuable assets they could buy at discounts." In 2013, Paulson & Co. (after John Paulson, son of Ecuadorian–Lithuanian–Romanian parents, who had bet against the housing bubble) was more than a billion dollars up on these investments, and Elliott Management $700 million (*Wall Street Journal*, September 13, 2013).

Other institutions were saved with taxpayers' money under the mistaken (to be generous) notion that redistributing losses would make them disappear. In reality, in its purpose and effects, the "stimulus was not about improving economic efficiency but about distributing funds to favored interest groups" (Miron 2009a).

Official decisions were derived from politics rather than economics. The looming bankruptcy of Lehman Brothers at the end of summer 2008 was as threatening (or not) to the economy as Bear Stearns, Fannie Mae, and Freddie Mac a few months earlier. However, the political backlash against bailouts caused a rethinking of strategy. "I'm being called Mr. Bailout. I can't do it again," Paulson said. His chief of staff e-mailed him that "bailing out Lehman [w]ill be horrible in the press." Federal Reserve statements showed the same attitude (Wessel 2010, pp. 14–15; McKinley 2008, pp. 159–61).

Lehman was allowed to file bankruptcy on September 15, but on September 23, Bernanke and Paulson came to Congress with their $700 billion scare. The need was so urgent, they said, that Congress should act without hearings or debates (Isaac 2010, p 148). A few in Congress continued to resist, but President Bush urged the measure's necessity in a broadcast to the nation, and presidential candidates Barack Obama and John McCain issued a joint statement that "The effort to protect the American economy must not fail." The House's initial rejection catered to the popular opposition, then accepted the second time around more in response to the determination of the congressional leadership than to changes in the bill. Or perhaps the rejection was a token signal to the voters back home. "Monday I cast a blue-collar vote for the American people," Tennessee Republican Congressman Zach Wamp said. "Today I am going to cast a red, white and blue-collar vote with my hand over my heart for this country, because things are really bad and we don't have any choice."

TARP's purpose of jump-starting the system was not only bound to fail, it was counterproductive. The purchase of "$700 billion of toxic assets would have been a colossal waste of taxpayers' money," former FDIC chairman William Isaac (2010, p. 149) wrote. It looked like a "plan concocted by Wall Street for the exclusive benefit of Wall Street." Banks would not sell the assets to the government unless it offered more than they were valued by the market, investors would not buy them from the government unless they could get them cheap, the difference to be made up by taxpayers.

These events contributed to the 2008 *Occupy Wall Street* protests against corporate greed and income inequality, and perhaps Bernanke's efforts to identify himself with Main Street. He told *60 Minutes*:

> You know I came from Main Street. That's my background. And I've never been on Wall Street. And I care about Wall Street for one reason and one reason only because what happens on Wall Street matters to Main Street. And if we don't have stabilization in the financial markets, if we don't take the steps necessary to make sure that credit is flowing again, then my father couldn't get a loan to build his new store. (December 5, 2010).

The image is of Bernanke in front of his boyhood home in Dillon, South Carolina, where his father ran a drug store on Main Street.

The interviewer said "You're supposed to keep them [banks] out of trouble. So how did all this [financial crises] happen?" "Well, a lot of mistakes got made," Bernanke replied. "No question about it. But, you know, this was a much bigger thing than any single firm or any single individual. Over the last dozen years or so enormous amounts of savings have flowed into the United States and some other industrial countries. That savings has come from China and East Asia [and] oil producers. [H]undreds of billions of dollars ... have come into our financial system. And, you know, that would be great if we took that money and invested it wisely and got a high return. But instead our financial system didn't do a good job":

> We had a regulatory system that was like a sandcastle on the beach. When you had little small waves just lapping up against the sandcastle everything looked good. But when you had a big breaker come in, suddenly the system wasn't strong enough to deal with it.

Bernanke prided himself on his transparency, but this was not an encouraging example either of the problems or how the Federal Reserve saw and planned to deal with them. When asked about the Fed's responsibilities, Bernanke said:

> Well umm ... like other regulators we probably could have done more. [W]e've already put a lot of effort into reviewing our practices .... We are trying to strengthen our regulation [such as] the tougher regulation of large firms, [which] includes having a set of laws that allows us to wind [them] down .... It includes possibly having a systemic regulator ... that has some responsibility to look at the system as a whole.

In other words, it's all up to the regulators, who should have told the banks what to do.

In fact, Bernanke's "savings glut" explanation must be rejected. Negative saving in the United States more than offset positive saving elsewhere (Taylor 2009). But his statements reveal even more damaging beliefs affecting Federal Reserve policies, among the most important being the dismissal of markets and the importance of predictable policies in place of vacillations as during the previous four decades. Promises to provide them have been unfulfilled or disregarded.

DODD–FRANK

The purposes of the *Wall Street Reform and Consumer Protection (Dodd–Frank) Act* of 2010 were:

> To promote the financial stability of the United States by improving accountability and transparency in the financial system, to end "too big to fail," to protect the American taxpayer by ending bailouts, to protect consumers from abusive financial services practices, and for other purposes.

The Act required the identification of systemically important banks (SIB) (and other financial institutions) which would be subject to stricter capital ratios and required to submit updated emergency Resolution Plans to the Federal Reserve. These *stress tests* constitute evaluations of whether banks have sufficient capital to absorb losses as a result of adverse economic conditions.

Naming particular banks as "systemically important" (too big to fail) is an invitation to increase risks, perhaps in ways unseen or beyond the reach of regulators. Ben Bernanke told the Financial Crisis Inquiry Commission (Angelides 2011) that: "A too-big-to-fail firm is one whose size, complexity, interconnectedness, and critical functions are such that, should the firm go unexpectedly into liquidation, the rest of the financial system and the economy would face severe adverse consequences .... Governments provide support to these firms in a crisis not out of favoritism or particular concern for the management, owners, or creditors of the firm," he was anxious to assure the public, "but because they recognize that the consequences for the broader economy of allowing a disorderly failure greatly outweigh the costs of avoiding the failure in some way." Common means of avoiding failure include facilitating a merger, providing credit, or injecting government capital, all of which protect at least some creditors who otherwise would have suffered losses.

The potential advantages of more government involvement in dealing with potential crises are not supported by the frequent historical observations that central banks, and banks generally, have been poor forecasters of the future, the pre-2008 period being an example. Further tendencies that ought to inform public policies are that financial crises have tended to be caused by real forces

A comparative history of central bank behavior

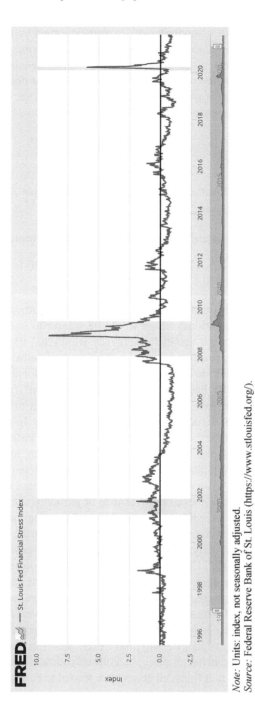

Note: Units: index, not seasonally adjusted.
Source: Federal Reserve Bank of St. Louis (https://www.stlouisfed.org/).

Figure 8.6   St. Louis Fed financial stress index

(such as the ends of housing bubbles in 1931 and 2007), and the occurrence of low-information runs on banks (just because of the failures of other banks) has been greatly exaggerated.

The stress depicted in Figure 8.6, which often turns from low to high on short notice, is based on interest-rate levels and differences, that is, on market predictions. So the regulators' views of the future are derived from those of the regulated, who in turn try to predict the former – chasing each other's tails. For example, the spread between corporate Aaa and Baa rates lay between 1 percent and 1.25 percent during the last half of the 1920s, 1.25 percent at the cyclical peak of August 1929, before rising to 4.34 percent at the trough of March 1933 (Federal Reserve Board 1943, p. 469).

Similarly, the spread was about 1 percent during the years before 2008, 1.15 percent in December 2007, compared with 3 percent in October 2010. The banks which failed during the Great Recession were those which had gone most deeply into subprime mortgages, became insolvent, and lost their investors.

"The primary driver of commercial bank failures during the Great Recession was exposure to the real estate sector, not aggregate funding strains" (Antoniades 2015, pp. 3–4). "The majority of commercial bank failures took place after 2008, that is, during a period by which funding pressures in the banking sector had completely abated. The timing of these failures suggests that the primary cause of failure for commercial banks cannot have been illiquidity due to aggregate shocks in the markets for wholesale funds, [but] by the deterioration of conditions in the real estate sector" to which banks had exposed themselves.

The tightening of regulations that has occurred since the crisis, while increasing loss absorbency, has also reduced the profitability of banks. The return-on-equity at large banks remains well below levels observed prior to the crisis (Nelson et al. 2021).

Regulatory capital was substantially increased after the crisis, Natasha Sarin and Lawrence Summers (2016) observed. Leverage ratios were reduced; and stress testing sought to further assure safety by raising levels of capital and reducing risk-taking. Standard financial theories predict that such changes would lead to substantial declines in financial market measures of risk, they said.

> For major institutions in the United States and around the world and midsized insti-
> tutions in the United States, we test this proposition using information on stock price
> volatility, option-based estimates of future volatility, beta, credit default swaps,
> earnings-price ratios, and preferred stock yields. To our surprise, we find that finan-
> cial market information provides little support for the view that major institutions
> are significantly safer than they were before the crisis and some support for the
> notion that risks have actually increased. … [W]e believe that the main reason for

our findings is that regulatory measures that have increased safety have been offset by a dramatic decline in the franchise value of major financial institutions, caused at least in part by these new regulations. This decline in franchise value makes financial institutions more vulnerable to adverse shocks. (Sarin and Summers 2016)

These findings support the view that the health of banks depends on the incentives of bankers to make them so. Bankers can always get around point-specific regulations, such as capital ratios, at a cost. Freely chosen reductions in risk, on the other hand, ought to raise franchise value.

These observations are supported by several statistical studies which have found "that franchise value helps offset the incentive for firms to increase risk because firms with the ability to generate profits will act to protect their valuable franchise .... Our empirical results support the theory that banks that are more efficient, are located in less competitive markets, or have valuable lending relationships operate more safely. We find that high-franchise-value banks hold more capital and take on less portfolio risk, leading to lower levels of overall risk. We also observe a negative relationship between franchise value and systematic risk (the risk related to factors that affect the banking industry as a whole) and between franchise value and firm-specific risk (the risk unique to individual institutions) .... When franchise value is high, banks are less inclined to take excessive risk .... As the thrift crisis of the 1980s demonstrated, institutions with low capital and low franchise value may have a strong incentive to increase risk and "go for broke" (Demsetz et al. 1996; Keeley 1990). On the other hand, it has been pointed out that franchise value reduces the cost of borrowing (Martynova et al. 2014).

Legislation and agency responses have ignored long-standing relations between the real (production and consumption) economy and finance, specifically the tendency of financial panics to follow and be consequences of the business cycle rather than the reverse. This has been recorded by Gary Gorton (1988), and we saw it in the U.K. in 1825, 1847, and the Great Depression.

Gorton found a set of stylized facts about banking panics, which, while extremely important since their reoccurrence has motivated bank regulation, are not well understood. The main stylized fact is that panics are systematic events linked to the business cycle. They turn out not be mysterious events, but manifestations of consumption smoothing on the part of cash-in-advance constrained agents reacting to changes in perceived risk predictable on the basis of prior information, specifically business failures. Banks hold claims on firms and when firms begin to fail, depositors reassess the riskiness of deposits. Depositors panic when the liabilities signal is strong enough, and when the information measure of the liabilities of failed businesses reaches a "critical" level, so do perceptions of risk and there is a banking panic. The cyclical behavior of the liabilities variable makes panics an integral part of the business cycle.

The tendency of banks, like other investors, to follow the business cycle – and often to be persuaded that "this time is different" – does not fundamentally alter optimal regulation. It may even reinforce it, which is to allow (even require) its subjection to market risks (but not regulatory costs) in the course of maximizing franchise value.

TOO BIG TO JAIL

Appearing before the Senate Judiciary Committee in March 2013, Attorney General Eric Holder acknowledged under questioning by Republican Chuck Grassley of Iowa, the ranking member, that the megabanks are too big to jail. "I am concerned that the size of some of these institutions becomes so large that it does become difficult for us to prosecute them," Holder said. "When we are hit with indications that if you do prosecute – if you do bring a criminal charge – it will have a negative impact on the national economy, perhaps even the world economy. I think that is a function of the fact that some of these institutions have become too large." Before becoming President Obama's Attorney General (2009–15) he worked at a Washington, D.C., law firm representing its multinational corporate clients, to which he returned after his service as Attorney General.

Several members of Congress from both sides of the aisle criticized Holder's position, but Congress has done nothing about it. A shortcoming of Holder's position, shared with other regulators, was his failure to distinguish between people and firms, which has meant the punishment of shareholders for the sins of executives, including their violations of ethical guidelines adopted by the former. This is not a good way to improve the behavior of (the managers of) firms.

Regulators' focus on firms at the expense of markets is another carryover from the Great Depression. Congress established various credit agencies in 1932, including the Reconstruction Finance Corporation, to lend directly to banks in need, although they had virtually no effect on bank lending, and the upturns in prices and the economy must be attributed to the shift in the monetary regime adopted by the New Deal. Bank loans did not begin to rise until 1943, and were not restored to pre-depression levels until the 1950s, as bank credit was directed to U.S. government securities (Figure 8.7) (Wood 2015, pp. 166–8).

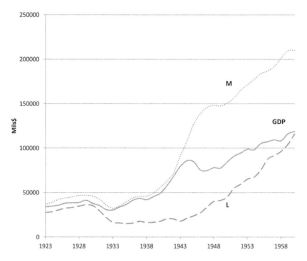

Source: Federal Reserve Bank of St. Louis (https://www.stlouisfed.org/).

Figure 8.7   M2, bank loans, and real GDP ($ millions, annual)

In a speech at the University of Chicago on Milton Friedman's 90th birthday (November 8, 2002), Federal Reserve Board Governor Bernanke said:

> Let me end my talk by abusing slightly my status as an official representative of the Federal Reserve. I would like to say to Milton and Anna [Schwartz]: Regarding the Great Depression. You're right, we did it. We're very sorry. But thanks to you, we won't do it again.

On the contrary, Bernanke's commitment to bank credit instead of monetary policy was already evident in his writings about the Great Recession. His reputation as an economist rests mainly on his 1983 paper on the "Nonmonetary effects of the financial crisis in the propagation of the Great Depression." The Great Depression has continued to be a significant object of enquiry partly because of its unexplained severity. Changes in money captured no more than half the change in output, the remainder, Bernanke argued, being due to the loss in intermediary services as measured by bank loans.

Unfortunately, Bernanke's study suffered several statistical flaws. His impressive correlation was the result of a single observation – the month of bank closings upon Franklin Roosevelt's inauguration on March 4, 1933 – followed by the beginning of the recoveries of money and output as seen in Figure 8.7 along with the stability of bank loans until the mid-1940s (Hori 1996; Romer 1992; Eggertsson 2008; Mazumder and Wood 2021).

Financial crises have often been attributed to insufficient regulation, particularly of bankers' greed, which has led to detailed and costly restrictions and requirements on individuals and institutions, such as reporting and capital, cash, and loan requirements. Government spending on bank regulations increased from $725 million in 1980 to $2.07 billion in 2007. To the multitude of existing agencies and oversights at the turn of the millennium were added several more, such as the Patriot Act, for protection against terrorism, and Sarbanes–Oxley, following fraudulent accounting scandals, which added to the already numerous banks' internal auditors, state bank examiners, the FDIC, and the Federal Reserve (Allison 2013, pp. 133–47; Henderson 2008).

The 1999 (Gramm–Leach–Bliley) repeal of the 1933 (Glass–Steagall) separation of commercial and investment banking had little, if any, effect on the financial sector. The 1933 Act had intended to restore investment bankers' domination of securities issues, into which commercial bankers had intruded during the expanding 1920s, but the latter had already dropped out during the Great Depression. Commercial banks returned to investment banking during the financial and inflationary developments of the last third of the century – often with the forbearance and even assistance of the regulators, which is a lesson in itself of the impotence of regulation in the face of market forces (Wood and Wood 1985, pp. 28–42, 61–3; Wood 2020, pp. 1–13).

CONCLUSION

It is hoped that this chapter will help weaken a couple of myths regarding the Great Recession: that because the Federal Reserve had learned from its mistakes during the Great Depression, it was able to prevent a repeat of that catastrophe. In fact, the opposite is nearer the truth. The Fed had failed to learn that saving specific failed institutions had not helped the system – the Fed *did* do it again – and its failure to supply cash to the system in a timely manner, along with its forecasts of catastrophe, were self-fulfilling.

The Fed's concern for the well-being of large, politically influential investors, as in the past, influenced its actions. Bailouts, which have been standard operating procedure at least since the 1980s, may be preferred to bankruptcies by stockholders and often executives.

Congress and the Fed also continued their failure to learn the ineffectiveness of point regulations. Capital requirements as a means of limiting risk are easily bypassed by a risk-preferring bank making risky loans, which are the greatest cause of bank failures. The only reliable way to induce banks to behave conservatively is to make them want to do so, that is, by aligning their incentives on the side of survival by encouraging franchise values by stable monetary policy and relaxing costly regulations.

9.   The politics of famine

In an extensive corn [grain] country, between all the different parts of which there is a free commerce and communication, the scarcity occasioned by the most unfavourable seasons can never be so great as to cause a famine .... [A]s corn grows equally upon high and low lands, upon grounds that are disposed to be too wet, and upon those that are disposed to be too dry, either the drought or the rain which is hurtful to one part of the country is favourable to another ....
When the government, in order to remedy the inconveniences of dearth, orders all the dealers to sell their corn at what it supposes a reasonable price, it either hinders them from bringing it to market, which may sometimes produce a famine even in the beginning of the season; or if they bring it thither, [it encourages the people] to consume it so fast, as must necessarily produce a famine before the end of the season.
The popular fear of [those who buy corn cheaply in low-price (high output) areas in order to sell in high-price (low output) areas] may be compared to the popular terrors and suspicions of witchcraft. The unfortunate wretches accused of this latter crime were not more innocent of the misfortunes imputed to them, that those who have been accused of the former.
–Adam Smith [1776] 1937, pp. 493, 500

There has been a good deal of discussion recently about the prospect of the food supply falling significantly behind the world population. There is, however, little empirical support for such a diagnosis of trends. Indeed, for most areas of the world – with the exception of parts of Africa – the increase in food has been comparable to, or faster than, the expansion of population. But this does not indicate that starvation is being systematically eliminated, since starvation ... is a function of entitlements [which depend on ownership and income] and not of food availability as such. Indeed some of the worst famines have taken place with no significant decline in food availability per head.
–Amartya Sen 1981, p. 7

MARKETS AND GOVERNMENTS

Markets, if left alone, without government interventions, operate to eliminate or at least alleviate famines. Production shortages in one area bring high prices in that area and therefore increased shipments from other areas. Smith argued that famines have resulted less from the general lack of food than from interferences with its distribution. A problem with this story is that those in need may not be able to afford the imported food because of rising prices and falling incomes in the diminished production areas. Famines have occurred more often, Sen wrote, because of the lack of income, ownership, or transfer entitlements than from food shortages.

Transfers, or rather the lack of them, are an important part of the explanation, of all, or nearly all, modern famines. Sen argues that the absence of famine in modern democracies, particularly Western Europe and North America, has been due less to their high average incomes than to their social security systems. "Democracy and an uncensored press can spread the penalties of famine from the destitute to those in authority. There is no surer way of making the government responsible to the suffering of famine victims" (Sen 1990, p. 12). In short, protection from famines requires political power, which for the poor requires democracy. Benevolence is not sufficiently reliable.

This chapter gives three examples of the tendency of government responses to food crises to share aspects of their responses to financial crises, although we are still be left with the question why, even in democracies, the poor get less than their fair share of government assistance during crises of all kinds.

THE IRISH POTATO FAMINE, 1845–49

A million Irish died during the Great Hunger, and another million emigrated, reducing the Irish population by 20–25 percent (Figure 9.1). The proximate cause of the disaster was a potato blight throughout Europe, also causing some 100,000 deaths outside Ireland and influencing the unrest underlying the European Revolutions of 1848 (Vanhaute et al. 2006). The greater severity of the Irish experience might have been due to the greater dependence of the Irish peasantry on potatoes, their initial poverty/bodily-weakness, and the British government's laissez-faire reluctance to intervene, leading to popular charges, continuing to the present day, of genocide. Young Ireland leader John Mitchel said that "God sent the potato blight but the English created the Famine." Tony Blair deserves great credit, Irish historian Tim Pat Coogan (2012) wrote, for having the political courage in his first month as British prime minister to apologize for the Famine and publicly acknowledge that "those who governed in London at the time failed their people."

Genocide is a controversial accusation, rejected by most historians (Ó Gráda 1999), but any serious judgment of the effects of the blight requires an appreciation of the Irish land tenure system, which was characterized by absentee landlords and dependence of much of the population on a single crop. Most productive land was owned by the English and managed by middlemen who rented it to the highest bidders. Rent was maximized by subdividing the land into plots as small as five acres. Most peasant families lived in one-room hovels.

There was little of the personal relationships between landlord and peasant which were common in England, and little incentive for land development in

Ireland because of the lack of peasant stakes in the land. Improvements were discouraged because of the lack of tenure and consequent rent increases. "It would be difficult to conceive a system more opposed to the progress of an agricultural community" (Ó Gráda 1999).

Source: https://commons.wikimedia.org/wiki/File: Famine_memorial_dublin.jpg.

Peasants produced the cash crops of grains and beef, much for export, to pay their rent, and the cheaper potatoes for food because of the latter's high calorie content even though they were sus-

Figure 9.1   Famine memorial, Dublin

ceptible to blight. The low incomes of peasants and high rents might have been due to their large population and poor bargaining positions, although that is undecided. The Irish population doubled between 1780 and 1845 (4 million to 8 million), before falling 20–25 percent during the famine, and another third (6.5 million to 4.4 million, close to that of 1780) between 1851 and 1911.

Before the famine, "the intensification of arable farming in Ireland during the last quarter of the 18th century and the increasing inclination of landlords to allow subdivisions" seemed to have meant "an Ireland of carefree peasant labourers who married as a rule in their late teens and lived on a diet consisting almost exclusively of potatoes, practices which changed radically after the Great Hunger" (Ó Gráda 1979; Connell 1965). The famine might own something to overpopulation in Ireland. Thomas Malthus (1808) wrote that "Among the subjects peculiar to the state of Ireland … is the extraordinary phenomenon of the very rapid increase of its population." But some others were growing as fast, England and Wales, for example, whose population more than doubled (from 7.5 million to 17 million) between 1780 and 1845, meaning that we must look elsewhere for explanations of the countries' different incomes, possibly discriminatory policies regarding land ownership and tenure. These differences before and during the famine were consistent with England's treatment of Ireland as a conquered country whose purposes were, first, security, to prevent its use by England's enemies, and second, revenue as a market for English goods, demonstrated by protective tariffs.

Sen argued with a good deal of empirical support that democracy is inconsistent with the occurrence of famines – because of its twin principal features: information (e.g., free press) and the distribution of political power. But these are relative terms. The alleviation of famine for some is costly, at least in the short run, so that it may be limited by the relative political powers of the helpers and the helped – just as for financial bailouts, between taxpayers and the banks.

During the Irish famine, as in many other famines, there were substantial exports of food from the country, as well as imports. But these were primarily the cash crops of grain and beef while the small tenant farmers lived primarily on the cheaper potatoes. They paid their rent in labor, while they grew potatoes, their most economical source of calories, on the small plots they were allotted. Holdings were so small that no other crop would suffice to feed a family (Litton 2006, pp. 9–10).

In 1843, understanding the "land question" to be the root cause of disaffection in the country, a Royal Commission had been established "to enquire into the laws regarding the occupation of land in Ireland." Even though the Irish radical repealer (of the Union), Daniel O'Connell, described the commission as "perfectly one-sided," being composed mainly of landlords, with no tenant representation, its 1845 report was sympathetic:

> It would be impossible adequately to describe the privations which [the Irish labourer and his family] habitually and silently endure … in many districts their only food is the potato, their only beverage water … their cabins are seldom a protection against the weather … a bed or a blanket is a rare luxury [and] their pig and a manure heap constitute their only property. (Woodham-Smith 1962, pp. 20–24)

The Commission stated that the bad relations between landlord and tenant were responsible for the deplorable conditions. There was no heritable loyalty, feudal tie, or mitigating tradition of paternalism as existed in England. According to Cecil Woodham-Smith, "landlords regarded the land as a source of income, from which as much as possible was to be extracted. With the Irish 'brooding over their discontent in sullen indignation' (in the words of the Earl of Clare), the landlords largely viewed the countryside as a hostile place to live." For good reason, as murders of landlords and middlemen were not uncommon. Ireland was a conquered country, the Catholic majority were subject to legal restrictions between the 1534 Act of Supremacy (Henry VIII) and 1829, and Catholics were subject to Anglican Church of Ireland tithes.

In 1851, a government commission reported 24 failures of varying severity of the potato crop in substantial parts of Ireland since 1728, including a third of the years between 1800 and 1844. "The unreliability of the potato was an accepted fact in Ireland," although never as bad as in the late 1840s, for which the country was unprepared. The 1845–46 blight has been traced from Mexico to the United States and then to Europe. It was reported in Ireland in September 1845, although the scale of destruction was not realized until after the harvest.

Prime Minister Sir Robert Peel (who had been Chief Secretary for Ireland, 1812–18) found the reports "very alarming," although there was 'always a tendency to exaggeration in Irish news'" (Woodham-Smith 1962, pp. 38–42).

Crop loss in 1845 has been estimated as one-third to one-half, and three-quarters was lost to blight in 1846, when the first deaths from starvations were recorded. The harvest was normal in 1847, but less had been planted so the yield was small. Yields were two-thirds of normal in 1848. "Since over three million Irish people were totally dependent on potatoes for food, hunger and famine were inevitable" (Kennedy et al. 1999, p. 69).

Peel acted quickly and against the feelings of much of his Conservative party. In November 1845, he arranged for the government's purchase of £100,000 of corn in the United States and its shipment to Cork to keep down the price of food. Then, "between September 1846 and March 1847, the government's principal famine policy was a program of public works which at its peak employed nearly 715,000 men and thus supported some 3.5 million people, nearly half the population of Ireland" (Bernstein 1995, p. 513).

In the meantime, Peel had broken with his party, and the Whigs led by Lord John Russell formed a government. There was a limit to the Government's help. "It must be thoroughly understood," Russell wrote in October 1846, "that we cannot feed the people" (Beckett, 1969, pp. 337–9). He and his colleagues hoped the Irish would take care of their own. The Poor Law, which had existed in England since Queen Elizabeth, had been extended to Ireland in 1838, by which assistance for the poor was financed by the rates (land taxes). However, Irish landowners were themselves too impoverished to support the system, and tried to save themselves by evicting their tenants, sometimes assisting their emigration.

Make-work projects, workhouses, and direct payments were insufficient for the starving Irish population, but the government in London was unwilling to endanger its balanced budget by increasing or even maintaining relief, partly, perhaps, because of the recession, including the 1847 financial crisis. The Irish nationalist, John Mitchel ([1873] 2005, pp. 94–6), charged

> … that, if Ireland was indeed an Integral part of the realm, the common exchequer of both islands should be used – to give alms, but to provide employment on public works of general utility. [I]f Yorkshire and Lancashire had sustained a like calamity in England, there is no doubt such measures as these would have been taken, promptly and liberally.

Since 1801, after the Acts of Union by the parliaments of Great Britain (England, Wales, and Scotland) and Ireland, the latter's parliament ceased to exist and Ireland sent 105 members (of 658) to the House of Commons of the United Kingdom and 28 (of 220) members to the House of Lords. The primary purpose of the Acts was to strengthen the Irish tie to Great Britain following the Irish rebellion of 1798.

The issue of Irish relief did not arise in the Parliament elected in 1847, however, even for the Irish members. It should be noted that the bulk of Irish MPs were landowners or the sons of landowners. That election saw candidates calling themselves Conservatives win the most seats, although they were split between Protectionists (the majority) and the minority of free traders, known as Peelites, led by the former prime minister, which left the Whigs, led by Prime Minister Lord John Russell, in a position to continue in government (Table 9.1). Peel lost control of the Conservative Party after the potato blight induced him to lead the repeal of the Corn Laws (tariffs on grain) by means of a coalition of Whigs and Conservative free traders, for which he lost the support of the protectionist majority of his party.

Table 9.1   The 1847 general election

Party	Seats	Irish members	Seats
Whig	292	Whig	25
Conservative	325	Irish Repeal	36
Chartist	1	Peelite	11
		Irish Conservative	29
		Irish Confederate	2
Total	618	Total	103

Source: Compiled by the author.

The Whigs' tenuous hold on the Government, made possible by the UltraTories, opposed to change, especially of the position of landowners, also acted against vigorous measures. What is best remembered, however, is less the lack of relief than its laissez-faire justifications. In March 1849, Peel told the House of Commons (Bernstein 1995, p. 519):

> I am quite willing to admit … that the true lesson to teach a man who is able to work, and particularly an Irishman who is able to work, is that it is much better for him to rely upon his own exertions for his support than to be dependent upon charity for the means of subsistence.

Public works had been the principal means of famine relief for 30 years, greatly reducing the extent of unimproved roads available for the purpose. Sir

Thomas Fremantle, Chief Secretary for Ireland, wrote to the prime minister in 1845:

> I regret to find that the apathy which exists among the [Irish] poor is very great & they seem to be impressed with the notion that … exertion is quite superfluous, as when their potatoes fail, the Gov. must feed them. (Bernstein 1995)

This attitude was general in Parliament and the civil service, and the public works program was dismantled at the end of 1846, primarily because of its cost to the English taxpayer, one suspects, but justified by the moral reasons discussed above, and its ineffectiveness on economic grounds, such as because many agriculturists left the land when most needed for the cash payments of public works.

The Whig government which took office in July 1846 was confronted with a worsening famine, and blanched at the prospects. They decided against further government purchases of food. It was obvious, Prime Minister Lord John Russell told the House of Commons,

> … that trade would be disturbed; that the supplies which are brought to us by the natural operations of commerce would be suspended; that the intermediate traders who dealt in provisions in local districts would have their business entirely deranged; and that Government would find themselves charged with that which it is impossible they can perform adequately – I mean, the duty of feeding the people. (Bernstein 1995)

The ill feelings between the two peoples grew with time and demands. The liberal Whig commitment to laissez-faire and therefore non-intervention was supported by the rebelliousness and ingratitude of the Irish. "The English people, both through their government and through private charity, had given generously to assist the Irish people in their hour of need, but the Irish were ungrateful" (Bernstein 1995). After the results of the 1847 general election, Russell's ministerial colleague, Lord Palmerston, wrote to him:

> I see that almost all the Irish Elections have gone in Favour of Repeal [separatist] candidates, and this just after Two or Three millions of Irish have been saved from Famine & Pestilence by Money which if the Union had not existed their own Parliament would never have been able to raise. This is not natural. (Bernstein 1995)

"Finally," Bernstein wrote, "the French Revolution of 1848, with the associated policy of national workshops … raised the spectre of socialism. Government intervention for social purposes now became associated with revolution and the destruction of private property."

In 1996, the U.S. State of New Jersey included the famine in the "Holocaust and Genocide Curriculum" for its secondary schools, as advocated by various

Irish-American groups and supported by legal advisors (Kennedy 2016, pp. 100–101). It concluded that the British government deliberately pursued an ethnicity-based policy aimed at destroying the Irish people and that the policy of mass starvation amounted to genocide. Box 9.1 contains the beginning of a report in the *Irish Times* of April 4, 2020, repeated from 1996, and the *Times* of London in 1846.

BOX 9.1   FOOD DEPOTS CLOSE TO TEACH IRISH A LESSON

Irish Times, Saturday, August 24, 1996
BRENDAN Ó CATHAOIR
London Times, August 24th, 1846: The new Whig government believes the Irish people need to be taught a lessen in self reliance. "There are times when something like harshness is the greatest humanity," echoes the *London Times*. In Ireland many relief committees deplore the decision to close the food depots at a time of unprecedented distress.

But the Whig ideologues consider a dangerous precedent was set last year: Sir Robert Peel's relief measures created an expectation that the government would again supply food. Lord John Russell has no intention of allowing his government to repeat the experiment.

He states: "It must be thoroughly understood that we cannot feed the people. It was a cruel delusion to pretend to do so." Repeated state intervention would not only paralyse private enterprise, but increase Irish dependence on Britain.

There is certainly support for such positions. Charles Trevelyan (1848), the civil servant most responsible for the Government's handling of the famine, described it as "a direct stroke of an all-wise and all-merciful Providence," which laid bare "the deep and inveterate root of social evil." The famine was "the sharp but effectual remedy by which the cure is likely to be effected. God grant that the generation to which this opportunity has been offered may rightly perform its part."

However, "virtually all historians of Ireland" reject the genocide allegations (Kennedy 2016, p. 111). Ó Gráda (1999, p. 10) argued that such claims overlook "the enormous challenge facing relief agencies, both central and local, public and private." A case of neglect is easier to sustain. Ó Gráda stated what was probably the most important explanation in his statement that the largest possible Government action may not have brought satisfactory immediate relief, which was probably beyond either their ability or their will, although the long-term neglect of property rights discouraged income growth and the diversity of crops, reducing the population's resistance to health and economic failures. The magnitude of the disaster was a consequence of short- and long-term political decisions, especially the latter.

THE GREAT BENGAL FAMINE

The autumn 1942 Bengal rice crop was a little less than normal (97 percent of the average of the preceding four years) and the winter crop (the largest) was 83 percent of normal – largely the result of a cyclone, followed by torrential rain and a subsequent fungus disease. Further, the Japanese occupation of Burma in 1942 had cut off rice imports from that region. The official *Famine Inquiry Commission* attributed the Bengal famine of 1942 to "the serious shortage in the total supply of rice available for consumption in Bengal" (Sen 1981, pp. 52–3).

British governments had been preparing India for self-government, pro-viding for increased local government and popularly elected legislatures, but retained control of its foreign and defense policies, as well as internal security and economic allocations during the war against Germany and Japan. The chief official was still the British Viceroy representing the crown. Significant policies were ultimately decided by the British Parliament. Bengal was a large eastern province including the Ganges River and its many mouths, Calcutta, and the modern Bangladesh.

The wholesale price of rice more than tripled between December 1942 and August 1943. The government had fixed a maximum price but unofficial reports suggest that the price doubled again before the end of the year. The famine revealed itself in rural districts away from Calcutta from late 1942 in hunger marches and deaths in the streets, and peaked in late 1943. The Commission originally put the death toll at 1.3 million, which was later admit-ted to be a serious underestimate.

"The experience was quite different in Calcutta," which was the center of British Asia's war production of materials, including those with which to fight the rapidly advancing Japanese threat. The official policy was based on the conviction that "the maintenance of essential food supplies to the industrial area of Calcutta must be … a very high priority among [the government's] war time obligations." The Government's Foodstuffs Scheme guaranteed food to the grain shops of industrial concerns. More than a million industrial and Government employees and their dependents were guaranteed food at prices they could afford. "Calcutta saw the famine mainly in the form of rural desti-tutes, who trekked from the [outlying] districts into the city; by July 1943 the streets were full" (Sen 1981, pp. 51–2).

The Famine Inquiry Commission's view that the primary cause of the famine was "a serious shortage in the total supply of rice available for consumption in Bengal" was the standard but seriously mistaken explanation. The supply of rice for 1943 was only about 5 percent less than the average of the preceding five years, 13 percent higher than in 1941, when there was no famine. Imports of wheat and wheat flour were above average in 1943. Taking population growth into account, the per capita Bengal food availability index was 9 percent higher in 1943 than 1941.

The Bengal famine was essentially a rural phenomenon. Urban areas, especially Calcutta, were substantially insulated from rising food prices by means of subsidized distribution schemes. Agricultural wages rose about 15 percent between 1941 and 1943, compared with over 300 percent on the open market for food.

The rise in fish prices in mid-1942 may have been "a consequence of the 'boat denial' policy carried through for military reasons. By Orders issued in May boats capable of carrying more than ten passengers were removed from a vast area of river-based Bengal to 'deny' them to the possibly-arriving Japanese." There was also a "rice denial" policy by which "rice stocks were removed from certain coastal districts." The worst affected groups were agricultural and other laborers, fishermen, and craftsmen. The least affected were peasant cultivators and share-croppers (Sen 1981, pp. 67, 71–2).

The increase in the price of rice was the result of inflationary pressure in a war economy. Bengal saw unprecedented military and civil construction financed to a great extent by printing currency. While the famine was killing millions, Bengal was producing the largest rice crop in its history in 1943.

The refusal of the British Government to address the problem was evident on several fronts: the boat and rice denial policies, rice shipments between Indian provinces, including between the relatively low-price provinces to the high-price Bengal, and the much-criticized refusal to permit more food imports into India by the reallocation of shipping.

"One curious aspect of the Bengal famine was that it was never officially 'declared' a famine, which would have meant an official obligation to organize work programmes and relief operations specified by the 'Famine Code' [of] 1883." Bengal Governor Sir T. Rutherford explained: "The Famine Code has not been applied as we simply have not the food to give the prescribed ration. And anyway, the general supply of food did not suggest a famine. In fact, India was expected to be, and was, a major supplier of food and industrial products to other theatres of war" (Sen 1981, p. 79).

Governments are normally very interested in the well-being and morale of their citizens in war-time. Prime Minister Winston Churchill broadcast "the goal of ensuring to Britain all the nutrition necessary to the war effort," and cited the importance of "civilian morale" (Mukerjee 2011, pp. 39, 44–5).

With regard to India, however, he urged a scorched-earth policy, "involving the ruthless destruction of any territory we might have to surrender," such as the coastal areas of Bengal, explaining the rice and boat denial policies and the destruction of stores of food that might fall into the hands of the Japanese. How different from the situation along the southern coast of England depicted in *Dad's Army*. Didn't they want the support of the Indian population, or had they given up on it from the beginning?

THE ETHIOPIAN FAMINES OF 1972–74 AND 1983–85

The especially harsh Ethiopian famines of 1972–73 (primarily in the northern province of Wollo, the land of the Afar pastoralists in particular) and 1973–74 (primarily in the southern province of Harerghe) stemmed initially from rain and harvest failures in mid-1972 and spring 1973. By early 1973, crowds asking for food had marched to the capital in Addis Ababa and lined the main Wollo highway. Despite early warnings from the Ministry of Agriculture, the seriousness of the famine was minimized in its early stages by the Government, cutting into international relief efforts.

The Ministry conducted a survey of production of the main crops in 1972–73 and found normal production in 65 percent of districts, 21 percent below normal, 14 percent above normal, and 7 percent below normal overall – hardly a devastating food availability decline. Some surveys even found above-average food production and calorie consumption. "Indeed, no picture of a sharp fall in food consumption per head ... for Ethiopia as a whole in the famine year 1973 emerges, [although] there was clearly a shortage of food in the province of Wollo ... There was not merely a decline in the food to which the Wollo population was directly entitled out of its own production, but also a collapse of income and purchasing power and of the ability of the Wollo population to attract food from elsewhere" (Sen 1981, pp. 90–94).

Transportation difficulties as a significant explanation of the famine must be dismissed, Sen argues, because the preponderance of Wollo's population, as well as in the relief camps, lived near the main roads through the region. There were in fact reports of food moving out of Wollo. Nor did food prices in Wollo rise significantly because demand (income) in the region fell in line with the supply of food (Sen 1981, p. 95). So there was no inducement for supplies from private sources, and international and domestic charitable activities were late and meager.

Hardest hit were the nomadic pastoralists, whose animals died and fell in price relative to grains, although the majority of the afflicted were agriculturists, small land-holders and tenants. Emperor Haile Selassie finally visited the afflicted areas in November 1973, but had already analyzed the problem:

> Rich and poor have always existed and always will. Why? Because there are those that work ... and those that prefer to do nothing .... We have said wealth has to be gained through hard work. We have said those who don't work starve. (Sen 1981, p. 164)

The Ethiopian government was a dictatorship centered on Haile Selassie, who ruled his backward country seemingly by whim, treating his parliament, consisting of feudal lords, the military, and senior civil servants, as sources of information and suggestions. He had been in power since 1916, maintaining a balance between the major interests, assisted by his godlike status among a substantial part of the population, who were treated primarily as sources of taxes to support the center. The lack of government assistance in the 1970s fit a long-time pattern of insensibility which might have been one of the factors causing Haile Selasse's overthrow in 1974 and assassination the next year. His policy of denial was continued by the military regime that succeeded him (Gilkes 1975, pp. 15, 21, 64; Keneally 2011, pp. 101–26; Markakis 2011, pp. 131–60).

The diverse country of more than 80 ancient, individualist, and often violent nationalities was kept together by force. Famines were sometimes consequences of neglect and/or incompetence, and sometimes an instrument of rule, directed at difficult, rebellious regions. Food supplies were maintained at reasonable prices in the cities, especially the capital. Foreign aid was parceled out on political grounds. The failure of rains in 1972–73 caused almost immediate disasters in the pastoral lowlands towards the Sudanese border in the west, and the grazing grounds of the east bordering Somalia, and also in the farming highlands. Roadblocks were set up to prevent the starving from flocking to the cities.

Ethiopia received 137,000 tons of donations and foreign relief, 70 percent of which went to Wollo and Tigray even though their problems were almost over, and 8 percent to Harar and the Ogaden, where famine was at its height – perhaps because the Ogadenians were Muslims and sometimes troublesome with more in common with the Somalis.

Haile Selassie's Marxist–Leninist successors increased his policies of centralization and control by breaking up local groups and practicing Soviet-style collectivization, called resettlement and villagization, to integrate, move and politically rehabilitate troublesome peoples – even pastoralists who historically had moved significant distances over the course of the year or in search of rain. Over 60 percent of Ethiopia's territory was occupied by nomads with little or no revolutionary or patriotic feelings. Six million people were relocated, many to work for official Peasant Associations (Keneally 2011, pp. 101, 183, 201).

Land was the basis of the Ethiopian economy and power. It was a feudal society in which all land was theoretically (and often actually) owned and controlled by the emperor, collecting rents and services, and maintaining power by overseeing the distribution of land among the aristocratic landlords.

Rights to land were complicated and sources of conflict, which in 1974 the new government promised to rectify. The *Provisional Military Government*'s list of planned reforms included:

4. Law on land tenancy, which will particularly satisfy the common farmer whose livelihood depends on agriculture and will increase the country's agricultural produce, will be urgently acclaimed and implemented. Until such time, all tenants will have a guarantee that they will be able to live on and benefit from the land on which they are settled and which they cultivate.

Within a fortnight it was thought necessary to provide a supplement to explain #4:

We have discovered that some tenants, not having studied and understood the provisional decision and having been instigated by some mischief-makers, have interpreted the words "have a guarantee and benefit" as meaning that they owned the land and had the right to benefit from it forever, and accordingly have been trying to deny some landlords the right to their land.

The emperor was wealthy considering the poverty of the country and the difficulty of collecting taxes, but provided minimal social services and funding for schools (Gilkes 1975, pp. xv, 93, 175). State intervention "lagged far behind in the lowlands and integration made little progress there. Simply put, the regime found the cost of integrating the lowlands uneconomical." As a British colonialist said of the Northern Frontier District of Kenya: "it is useless to put schemes of expenditure in an area which is costing … a great deal and yielding practically no revenue" (Markakis 2011, p. 134). Taxes were impossible to collect in the ordinary way. Neither the police nor civil servants would live in significant numbers on the torrid, fever-ridden lowlands. The area – the torrid zone – was said to be the hottest inhabited place on earth, the temperature often exceeding 120°F, although until recently the inhabitants were limited to a few pastoralists.

"In 1950 the government imposed a *zelan* (nomad) tax at the rate of 0.50 birr (12US¢ in 1970) per camel, 0.25 per cattle, horse, mule, and donkey, and 0.05 per goat and sheep." Sparsely manned police posts and finance offices were established to collect taxes, but "rifles [were] the most valuable household asset and every man's indispensable accessory ..." a harassed official complained to the provincial Governor General:

> You see only three or four policemen in every police station as our district is very vast, and most of its inhabitants are pastoralists who move from place to place with their herds of cattle .... I explained to them that people are considered loyal to their government only if they paying the tax levied on them .... As long as they have firearms these people will not willingly pay their tax, so one thing is clear, they should be disarmed .... Otherwise, they don't show the slightest interest in paying the outstanding or the current tax .... I wanted to use force against them in order to make them pay ... but it would have been meaningless since they possess more firearms than the police force. (Markakis 2011, p. 133)

Not being able to live on the plains, "officials stayed on the heights, and seldom ventured below." Demands for tribute came from these highland posts, which if refused were followed by a raid.

"The isolation and virtual autonomy of the Afar region came to an ... end" in the 1950s with the development by foreign firms of commercial agriculture in the Awash River Valley, supported by the Government at Addis Ababa over local protests. The companies were subsidized by tax breaks and high tariffs on sugar. "The displacement of pastoralists from their land commenced when the local Gilo Oromo herders were forced out of the Wonji plain due to land clearing for the plantation." The operation expanded and 50 years later, the almost uninhabited plain was home to 30,000 workers and their families.

In addition, "Responding to the lure of tourism, the government proceeded at the same time to designate vast tracts of land in the Awash Valley for national parks, game reserves and protected areas .... The stated purpose of designating protected areas was to 'exclude human interests in the form of grazing, farming, mining.' The policies were successful as the loss of land and its rising price made the herders, primarily Muslims in a predominantly Christian country, more susceptible to drought" (Markakis 2011, pp. 134–41).

Successive governments bought no significant improvement, certainly to the rural populations, and the 1983–85 famine was the worst of the century, resulting in the deaths of 1.2 million people, 400,000 fleeing the country, and 2.5 million internally displaced. The famine was initially blamed on drought but according to the Human Rights Watch, it was a man-made tool used by the government to control the population. The famine has been viewed as a tactic to squash insurgency.

The food provided by international aid organizations did little to help the starving people in Ethiopia, which was under a military dictatorship led by Mengistu Haile Mariam. The donated food was seized and controlled by the state instead of being distributed directly to the starving people, much of it being used to feed the army. Government-run food distribution centers were established in locations which forced people to migrate. The resettlement program forced people who lived in "affected/infertile areas" in the North to relocate to the South, which was largely a means by which the state seized land and cattle, and transformed the peasant-run agricultural system into a state-run system.

CLOSING COMMENT

Sen's assertion that famines cannot occur in democracies because of their free press and political accountability has inspired an outpouring of criticism based on observations that, if not famines, a good deal of hunger is found in apparently democratic countries (Sen 1999; Rubin 2009; Banik 2007; Stewart 2011). "Food insecurity" in the U.S.A., especially among minority groups, is wide-spread and well-known. "There has not been a large-scale loss of life [in democratic India] since 1947 [but] there have been many incidents of large-scale food crises that, while not resulting in actual famines, have led to many, many deaths" (Banik 2007).

Part of the apparent conflict might be due to differences between under-standings of "democracy," which is literally rule (*kratos*) by the people (*demos*, some would say "mob"), or "government of the people, by the people, and for the people," as Lincoln said at Gettysburg, presumably through their freely elected representatives. Lincoln associated such a government with "a new birth of freedom," although others have not always been so sure. The nation's founders, for example, although willing to replace the possibly more efficient (but more remote and incompetent because less representative) mon-archies by democracies, feared the latter's (majority rule) threats to liberty/ freedom. Almost the primary concern of the U.S. Constitution was to protect minorities from the majority. The three branches of government and Bill of Rights were both intended to obstruct the will of the majority. Democracies (if properly limited) may be the best form of government, but they are not the end, which is liberty.

So how are government actions decided? One answer points to compro-mises between interests according to their political powers. In a closely related resolution of political conflicts, the United States routinely broke its treaties with Indian tribes when they no longer suited their interests (à la Machiavelli), and the tribes lacked the powers to enforce them. And changes in the form of governments do not necessarily change their actions. For example, a spokes-man for the Institute of Development Studies at Sussex University, "who specializes in food security in Africa," said "more than a half-dozen countries in Africa face a famine threat, including such democracies as Ethiopia, [where] conditions are as bad as in 1984, when famine deaths were estimated at one million. Ethiopia was then ruled by a Marxist dictator [and before that by an absolutist monarch]. Today it is democratically governed, but as many as six million people remain dependent on food aid from abroad" (Massing 2003).

"Democracies are often run by ethnically based groups prepared to do terrible things to other ethnic groups," said professor of development studies Frances Stewart. "Or they can be very corrupt, dominated by elites." Democracies or not, genuine or not, more than nominal gains (real applications of laws) require real (vote getting) political power. Does anyone believe that the *Occupy Wall Street* ("We are the 99%") protests will have any effect on bailouts?

10. Endless wars

> After 16 years of war, the United States and its Afghan partners "have turned the corner" and "momentum is now with Afghan security forces," the top U.S. general there told reporters. Gen. John Nicholson … said the Trump administration's plan to beef up the U.S. battlefield presence is a "game-changer" that puts Kabul's battered forces "on a path to a win."
> –Department of Defense briefing, November 27, 2017

THE NEW WAY OF AMERICAN WAR

American wars since World War II are listed in Table 10.1. U.S. troops engaged foreign forces (government or guerrilla) during 41 of the 70 years between 1950 and 2020, the longest being in Afghanistan 2003–21. In addition to length, there have been several further troublesome aspects of these wars. Some have no end in sight, or any idea what an end would be like. Their connections to American security have been unclear. War has not been declared, but entered into by presidents with subsequent grudging financial support from Congress. They have not been popular, and the willingness to commit large or long-term forces has been limited to what the unenthusiastic American taxpayer would allow. They have been increasingly capital-intensive to spare American lives.

The U.S. has been accused of ignorance of the opposition. Nationalist movements have been underestimated, and sometimes opposed as we supported our colonialist European allies. The U.S. supported France's efforts to retain its Vietnam colony for several years after World War II. Religious differences and their threats to national unity and peace have not been understood. The lessons of history have also been overlooked, including the difficulties of fighting dedicated populations in their own countries, such as the American War of Independence, the Boers in South Africa, and the Spanish vs. Napoleon in the Peninsular War. The outside countries had larger, better-trained, and better-equipped forces than their native opponents, but were unwilling to commit the resources necessary for victory, whatever that was. How and why did the United States of the twentieth century become like the British Empire of the eighteenth century, and the Federal Reserve's support like the Bank of England's?

General discussions of the American way of war include Harlan Ullman, *Anatomy of Failure* (which considers officials' lack of knowledge of history and diplomacy); Andrew Bacevich (2016a), *American War for the Greater Middle East*, "massive but undefined"; *The Nation* (2018), "How to challenge the elite consensus for endless war, there's only one way. We have to harness the energy of millions of fed-up workers"; and *Cato Letter* (2016b), "We've attacked symptoms not causes. Bush asked nothing of the American people and had no strategic plan." (See also the other citations given with quotations below.) Some of these wars (all undeclared) beginning with the 1961 Cuban Bay of Pigs invasion are summarized below.

The rest of the chapter offers explanations of this unsettled state of affairs, including especially the undemocratic separation of government from the populace, with the central bank's assistance in avoiding accountability. It is another example, in addition to monetary policy, of government by the politically advantaged.

The Bay of Pigs invasion was an attempted overthrow of Fidel Castro's government by landing 1,400 Cuban exiles, with the promise of American air support, on a supposedly remote corner of Cuba in April 1961. The plan was to sneak ashore unopposed, take an airfield, and fly in a government-in-exile which would then call for direct U.S. support. They were also counting on a mass anti-Castro uprising.

Everything went wrong. Security had been breached, Cuban forces, outnumbering the invaders 10 to 1, were waiting for them, the U.S. withheld air support, and there was no uprising by the population. As CIA Director Allen Dulles later stated, planners believed that once the troops were on the ground, President Kennedy would authorize any action required to prevent failure – as Eisenhower had done in Guatemala in 1954 after that invasion looked as if it would collapse (Reeves 1963). The invaders surrendered and the episode was soon over.

Opponents of the invasion within the administration were dismissed by hubris-driven advocates as "soft." Arthur Schlesinger, Jr., special assistant and "court historian" to the president also disapproved but interestingly failed to use as evidence the mixed outcomes of invasions dependent on local uprisings; such as Henry Tudor (Henry VII) whose 1483 attempt failed before he overthrew Richard III at Bosworth Field in 1485; the failure of the Duke of Monmouth in 1685, even with some domestic support and an unpopular James II; the short-lived republic of Venezuela before Francisco de Miranda was deposed and imprisoned by royalist forces; and the failure of a French-supported 1797 invasion of South Wales (Battle of Fishguard) by mostly Irish that was defeated principally by the local population.

The Vietnam War originated with France's attempt, supported financially by the U.S., to regain its Asian colonies after Japan's defeat in 1945, but was given up after the defeat of French forces at Dien Bien Phu in 1954. The Geneva Accords of 1954 divided French Indochina into the countries of

Cambodia, Laos, and Vietnam, the last divided into North and South Vietnam, with the North headed by the nationalist/communist Ho Chi Minh and the South by nationalist Ngo Dinh Diem, with U.S. support. Agreed unification with elections in two years did not take place. The North supported resistance to Diem's regime in the South while the U.S.A. first provided military "advisors" to Diem, and from 1965, combat troops whose number peaked at 549,000 in 1969. The U.S.A. had stepped into a decades-long civil war. Diem's control of the South was tenuous and the U.S.A. arranged his assassination but never found a replacement capable of mounting effective resistance to the North.

Lyndon Johnson's administration (1963–69) tried to sell the Vietnam War to the American people as part of its worldwide war on communism, arguing that the fall of South Vietnam to the North would be a precursor – the domino theory – to more falls. However, South Vietnam was unable to defend itself, and the North would not yield to massive American bombing.

The Gulf of Tonkin incident of August 1964 was the U.S. government's false claim of North Vietnam aggression in order to gain public support for direct U.S. involvement. The misinformation campaign about South Vietnamese capabilities and the progress of the war were ultimately unsuccessful, evidenced by public protests, draft resistance, and Congress's withholding of funds. American experts were deficient in just about every respect possible, especially ignorance of the history and current political conditions of Vietnam and the lack of clarity of American aims and commitment, making planning and effective military action impossible. The government did not involve the public (Halberstam 1972, p. 655), and was perceived as deceiving it, a failure of democracy.

The end of the Cold War opened the door for a multiplicity of regional conflicts, including the *Balkans.* In March 1992, Bosnia and Herzegovina, a former Ottoman, multi-ethnic (44 percent Muslim, 32.5 percent Serb, and 17 percent Croat) state, declared its independence from Serb-dominated Yugoslavia. Fighting between the ethnic groups has been called alternatively a civil war and a war of conquest by Serbia. European NATO countries, with various ties to the combatants, were reluctant to become involved. U.S. military forces brought the sides to the bargaining table, although after a lengthy period due to a reluctance to bear the political costs of casualties arising from the use of ground troops, the December 1995 Dayton Agreement ended the fighting and preserved the multiethnic Bosnia and Herzegovina, sort of, and peace has been maintained by a peacekeeping force without settling long-term problems. "As successful as Dayton was at ending the violence, it also sowed the seeds of instability by creating a decentralized political system that undermined the state's authority" (McMahon and Western 2009).

U.S. intervention for famine relief in Somalia in December 1992, ended after the killing of 19 U.S. troops and 73 wounded at Mogadishu in October 1993.

The American withdrawal was ridiculed by al-Qaeda, who may have been responsible for the training of fighters who downed the American helicopters. In the aftermath of the battle, dead American soldiers being dragged through the streets by Somalis was shown on American television. Fear of a repeat has been cited as a reason for American reluctance to become further involved in the region, and may have affected the Clinton administration's decision to not intervene in the Rwandan genocide.

Afterwards, the Shabab spread across the country, pledging allegiance to al-Qaeda in 2012, and threatening Somalia's fragile government. In response, the Pentagon ramped up American drone strikes and Special Operations raids. At the end of 2020, as President Trump hoped to withdraw some of the 7,000 American troops on the African continent, the war in Somalia had become a version of Afghanistan.

Special Operations troops patrol in mine-resistant vehicles, heavily armed gunships patrol the night sky and, despite a torrent of attacks and militant body counts championed in Pentagon news releases, the Shabab remains firmly entrenched in the countryside (Gibbons-Neff 2019). Although the majority of drone attacks miss their target, as the primary American attack weapon they conserve American lives. The U.S.A. is willing to engage in peace-keeping efforts if they are not too costly in American lives.

The Persian Gulf War. In August 1990, Iraq invaded and occupied Kuwait ostensibly because of the latter's violation of OPEC agreements. The U.N. Security Council authorized the use of force to expel Iraq from Kuwait, and a U.S.-led coalition quickly demolished Iraqi forces.

President George H.W. Bush was criticized for limiting the coalition to the letter of the U.N. resolution, allowing Saddam Hussein to remain in power for another 12 years. He was not the first president to fail to be re-elected after arranging a peace. John Adams's support in Congress (mainly Federalists) increased (unusually for the president's party) in the mid-term elections of 1798, when war with France threatened, but he lost the 1800 election after his peaceful settlement with France. Republicans captured both houses of Congress in 2002, after the 9/11/01 terrorist attacks and the U.S. invasion of Afghanistan.

The *Invasion of Iraq* in March 2003, for the avowed purpose of neutralizing Saddam's nonexistent Weapons of Mass Destruction, was a rapid success in disposing of Saddam, but was followed by insurgency, civil war, and the crumbling of the Iraqi army (again), requiring a "surge" of fresh U.S. troops in 2007, who left in 2011, to return in 2014 after ISIS (Islam State of Iraq and Syria) gained control of much of the country. U.S. troops regained control in 2018, and the Iraqi Parliament voted for them to leave in January 2020. Much of the violence following the American victory in 2003 was due to the inadequate occupation force, understood in advance but suppressed in discussion because it implied costs which Congress might not wish to bear (Woodward 2002). Secretary of Defense Donald Rumsfeld rationalized the approach by what became known as the *Rumsfeld doctrine* – use as small a force as possible. "Shock and awe ... and its over" – perhaps justifying what Congress would finance. In fact, political instability and widespread violence continued.

Afghanistan was invaded by the U.S.A. and its NATO allies in October 2001; the Taliban, who had provided safe havens for terrorists, "collapsed," and major conflict ended in 2003. A new constitution was adopted and elections were held in 2004. The Taliban began to regain influence in 2006, NATO forces were increased to 149,000 during 2007–11 (100,000 American) but reduced as the lack of progress became increasingly apparent, and finally withdrawn in 2021, and the Taliban moved in.

At the core of *Obama's Wars* (2010), Bob Woodward wrote, is the unsettled division between the civilian leadership in the White House and the United States military as the president is thwarted in his efforts to craft an exit plan for the Afghanistan War. "So what's my option?" he asked his war cabinet, seeking alternatives to the Afghanistan commander's request for 40,000 more troops in 2009. "You have essentially given me one option ... It's unacceptable."

"Well," Secretary of Defense Robert Gates finally said, "Mr. President, I think we owe you that option."

It never came, and Obama's surge of 30,000 troops and pledge to start withdrawing U.S. forces by July 2011 did not end the skirmishing, although General David Petraeus, the new US/NATO commander in Afghanistan, thought time could be added to the clock if he showed progress. More and more observers, including Niall Ferguson (2005), were coming to believe that the American Empire would not fulfill its commitments. It did not understand that many wars, and the problems causing them, are unending. Realistic (credible) goals are necessary for success, but have often, as in "nation building" been unspecified. Six years later, General Nicholson became at least the eighth commander to have "turned the corner," although toward what destination was never made clear even to those whose mission was presumably its accomplishment.

Table 10.1   U.S. military actions since 1950

Dates	Action in which U.S.A. officially participated	Major combatants
1950–53	Korean War	U.S.A. with U.N. and S. Korea vs. N. Korea and China
1960–75	Vietnam War	U.S.A. and S. Vietnam vs. N. Vietnam
1961	Bay of Pigs Invasion	U.S.A. vs. Cuba
1983	Grenada	U.S. intervention
1989	U.S. Invasion of Panama	U.S.A. vs. Panama
1990–96	Persian Gulf War and occupation	U.S.A. and Coalition vs. Iraq
1993	Aborted attempt to bring peace to Somalia	U.S.A. and rival Somalian groups
1995–96	Intervention in Bosnia and Herzegovina	U.S.A. with European allies
1999	Serbia, Albania, Kosovo	Peacekeeping with NATO
2001–present	Invasion of Afghanistan	U.S.A. and Coalition vs. Taliban
2003–11	Invasion of Iraq	U.S.A. with Coalition vs. Iraq
2004–present	Northwest Pakistan	U.S.A. vs. Pakistan, mainly drone attacks
2007–present	Somalia and Northeastern Kenya	Coalition vs. al-Shabaab militants
2009–16	Operation (Indian) Ocean Shield	NATO vs. Somali pirates
2011	Intervention in Libya	NATO vs. Libya
2011–17	Lord's resistance army	Coalition vs. Lord's resistance army in Uganda
2014–present	U.S.-led interventions in Iraq and Syria	Coalition vs. Islamic State, al-Qaeda, ISIS, and Syria
2014–present	Yemini civil war	U.S.A. and Saudi vs. Houti rebels

Note: Plus many smaller incidents around the world.
Source: Compiled by the author.

THE MEANING OF WAR

War is often understood as violent conflicts between nations' organized military forces. As an example, an historian counted 23 wars, totaling 130 years, between England and France during the interval 1202–1815. Most if not all these wars arose from disputes over land and/or commercial rights.

This definition has at least two problems. First, it does not include extra-governmental (unofficial) conflicts such as the War on Terror following the 9/11 attacks. Second, it often confuses the temporary ends (or lulls) in military hostilities with the settlement of disputes, neglecting the Prussian General Carl von Clausewitz's (1832) statement that "War is the continuation of politics by other means."

Many "peace" treaties are better thought of as truces. The declaration of peace by the 1802 Anglo-French Treaty of Amiens settled no important differences, and war resumed in 14 months. Britain had taken Canada and secured India during the Seven Years' War (1756–63), and William Pitt, the effective head of the British Government, wanted to add to their gains. Too many, however, might sow the seeds for retribution, and Lord Bute, the new King George III's (1760–1820) choice to lead the government, arranged a "mild settlement." He hoped for a lasting peace, and feared that if he took too much, the whole of Europe would unite in envious hostility against Great Britain. The French Foreign Minister, the Duc de Choiseul, however, had no desire for a permanent peace, and, when France went to war with Great Britain during the American Revolution, the British found no support among the European powers. France's defeat had led to military reforms, with particular attention to the artillery. The origins of the famed French artillery that played such a prominent part in Napoleon's victories can be traced to the military reforms begun in 1763 (Marston 2001, p. 90; Dull 2005).

The continuous enmity between France and Germany, especially 1870–1945, was intense. France's foreign policy after losing the Franco-Prussian War of 1870, in which it lost Alsace-Lorainne and incurred a large indemnity, was one of revenge. The Dreyfuss Affair, lasting from 1894 to 1906, in which Captain Alfred Dreyfuss was convicted of treason for allegedly passing secret French documents to the Germans, stemmed from French fears of Germany. Alliances, an arms race, and war plans were developed, with the Central Powers (Germany, Austria-Hungary, the Ottoman Empire, and Bulgaria) ranged against the Allies, or Entente Powers (United Kingdom, France, and Russia).

The spark that started the war was the assassination of the Archduke Ferdinand, heir to the Austro-Hungarian throne, by a Serbian nationalist. Backed by Russia, Serbia refused an Austro-Hungarian ultimatum, which was backed by Germany, troops were mobilized and war was on. The Central Powers lost, were deprived of territories and had to pay reparations imposed by the 1919 Treaty of Versailles, which added to Germany's feelings of revenge leading to the rise of Hitler and the resumption/continuation of what has been called the second Thirty Years War.

FINANCING WARS

Wars nearly always involve substantial government borrowing and debasement of the coinage. In the time of King Alfred the Great (871–99), a troy ounce of silver was worth 20 English pennies, 24 pennies at the beginning of the Hundred Years War (1346), and 40 pennies in 1464 as English kings financed their wars by debasing the coinage. Henry VIII (1509–47) went further with 266 pennies per ounce of silver in 1551, but it was partially restored to 60 pennies per ounce in 1552, where it approximately remained until Great Britain switched to the gold standard in 1816, and the gold value of the pound remained unchanged (except for temporary suspensions related to world wars) until 1931 (Feavearyear 1931). The period from 1552 to 1931 in England and its dependent or associated regions was one of the longest periods of stability in the history of currencies, and might be attributed to the growth of capitalism and the importance of property, whose agents were typified by Sir Robert Peel and Alexander Hamilton, who wielded significant political power.

Table 10.2   *Central Government receipts (R) and expenditures (E), World War I, millions*

	France (Fr)		Germany (DM)		UK (£)		US ($)	
	R	E	R	E	R	E	R	E
1913	5,092	5,067	2,095	3,521	198	192	714	715
1914	4,549	10,065	2,399	9,651	227	559	725	726
1915	4,131	20,925	1,769	26,689	337	1,559	683	746
1916	5,259	28,113	2,045	28,780	573	2,198	761	713
1917	6,943	35,320	7,682	53,262	707	2,696	1,100	1,954
1918	7,621	41,897	6,830	45,514	889	2,579	3,645	12,677
1919	13,282	39,970	9,712	54,867	1,340	1,666	5,130	18,493
Billions	$\Delta R/\Delta E=3/111=3\%$		$\Delta R/\Delta E=12/147=8\%$		$\Delta R/\Delta E=1.9/8.6=22\%$		$\Delta R/\Delta E=7.6/31=25\%$	

Note: U.S. fiscal year ending June 30. U.S.A. 1917–19; others 1914–18. Excesses over 1913 (1916 for U.S.A.).
Source: Compiled by the author.

Even during these years banks financed governments when needed, especially in wartime. The Bank of England was established in 1694 to help finance England's war with Louis XIV. Its reputation – even its paper credit during a temporary suspension of convertibility – gave England a financial edge in another war with France a hundred years later (Bordo and White 1991).

In 1803, the British and Dutch merchant bankers, Barings and Hope, facilitated the Louisiana Purchase which doubled the area of the U.S.A. This was accomplished even though Britain was at war with France, and the sale helped finance Napoleon's war effort. In 1818, the French Foreign Minister called Barings "the sixth great European power," after England, France, Prussia, Austria, and Russia.

The military call-ups at the beginning of World War I meant that nearly every family in France and Germany suffered painful separations and financial loss. The French government quickly responded with family allowances, and was slow to raise taxes. Other countries also took steps to boost home morale and their support of the war. The war was everywhere largely financed by borrowing, expected to be repaid out of reparations on the enemy. Table 10.2 shows the small increases in central government receipts (mainly taxes) relative to spending during the war: 3 percent in France, 8 percent in Germany, 22 percent in the U.K., and 25 percent in the U.S.A.

FINANCING U.S. WARS

Table 10.3 shows federal Government revenues and spending during American wars. Revenue increases (mainly taxes) relative to spending tended, with exceptions, to be larger in smaller wars, such as the Spanish American (1897–99, 70 percent) and Korean (1950–54, 92 percent). Revenues actually fell during wars that were unpopular in large sections of the country – the War of 1812 (1811–14) and the Mexican War (1845–47). Revenues also fell (with the Bush tax cut) between 2000 and 2003, and rose only 15 percent relative to spending between 2000 and 2011, before the pullbacks in Afghanistan. The relatively small revenues during the large Civil War (1850–65) and World War I (1916–18), compared with World War II (1938–45), must be due partly to the lack of a sophisticated income tax system in the former. The 60 percent and 63 percent revenue/spending figures for the Vietnam War expansion (1965–68) and Reagan military buildup (1980–86) were determined not by special efforts to pay for the military spending but by ordinary increases in income. The differences between taxes and spending were made up by borrowing, after 1913 with the help of the Federal Reserve.

Table 10.3   U.S. budgets before and at the peaks of war spending, $ millions ($ billions from1916)

Year	Receipts	Spending	Military	ΔR/ΔS %
1811	14.4	8.1	4.0	
1814	11.2	34.7	27.7	
1845	30.0	22.9	18.1	
1847	26.5	57.3	46.2	
1860	56.1	63.1	27.9	
1865	333.7	1,297.6	1,031.3	22
1897	347.7	365.8	83.5	
1899	516.0	605.1	293.8	70
1916	716.5	713.0	337.0	
1918	3,645.2	18,492.7	11,011.4	16
1938	5.6	6.8	1.2	
1945	50.2	98.3	80.5	49

Year	Receipts	Spending	Military	ΔR/ΔS %
1950	40.9	39.5	13.4	
1954	69.7	70.9	40.6	92
1965	116.8	118.2	50.6	
1968	153.0	178.1	81.9	60
1980	517.1	590.9	134.0	
1986	769.2	990.4	273.4	63
2000	2,025.2	1,789.0	294.4	
2003	1,782.3	2,159.5	404.7	
2011	2,303.5	3,603.1	705.6	15

Note: The Gulf War (1990–91) has been omitted as military spending fell after 1989 because of the fall of the Soviet Union (although spending in other major areas increased).
Sources: Compiled by the author from United States Census Bureau, *Historical Statistics of the U.S., Economic Report of the President.*

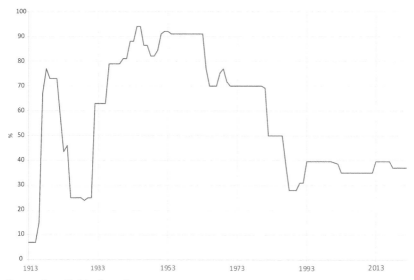

Source: Compiled by the author.

Figure 10.1   History of top U.S. personal income tax rates

Referring to Figure 10.1, the highest federal income tax rate jumped from 15 percent in 1916 to 67 percent in 1917 and 77 percent in 1918. In 1913, the top tax bracket was 7 percent on all income over $500,000 ($11 million in today's dollars); and the lowest tax bracket was 1 percent. Tax rates dropped precipitously after the war.

Congress raised taxes again in 1932 during the Great Depression from 25 percent to 63 percent on top earners. In 1944, the top rate peaked at 94 percent of taxable income over $200,000 ($2.5 million in today's dollars). Tax rates were lowered after World War II, then raised during the Korean War, which uniquely in American experience, largely due to the penny-pinching Harry Truman, was financed without a deficit. Rates remained high until the Kennedy (Keynesian demand) tax cut. The *Economic Recovery Tax Act of 1981* (Reagan supply side) slashed the highest rate from 70 percent to 50 percent, and indexed the brackets for inflation.

The *Tax Reform Act of 1986*, a so-called two-tiered flat tax, expanded the tax base and dropped the top rate to 28 percent. The supporting argument was that the broader base contained fewer deductions, but would bring in the same revenue. Further, lawmakers claimed they would never have to raise the 28 percent top rate. That promise lasted three years.

During the 1990s, the top rate jumped to 39.6 percent (President Clinton). *The Economic Growth and Tax Relief and Reconciliation Act of 2001* dropped the highest income tax rate to 35 percent (George W. Bush). *The American Taxpayer Relief Act of 2012* raised the highest income tax rate to 39.6 percent again, and the *Patient Protection and Affordable Care Act* made it 43.4 percent (Obama), to be reduced to 40.8 percent in 2018 (Trump). A turning point in U.S. war finance had been demonstrated by the failure to raise taxes during the Vietnam War (except for the brief and small 1968 surcharge, to be discussed below) or the Reagan military expansion, or the Bush tax cut of 2001.

Administrations have also tried to lighten the perceived costs of wars by underpredicting and underreporting them. In 2003, officials projected Iraq as a $50–60 billion war, but by 2008 the total cost to the United States was closer to $3 trillion. Federal spending for the post-9/11 wars through 2020 exceeded $6 trillion, far beyond direct Congressional war appropriations. The approximately $2.1 trillion in Congressional appropriations for Overseas Contingency Operations – which include combat in the post-9/11 war zones as well as international assistance through the State Department and USAID – do not include related additions to the Pentagon "base" budget, which total over $900 billion through financial year 2020. And while the U.S.A. paid for past wars by raising taxes and selling war bonds, the current wars have been paid for almost entirely with borrowed money.

The federal Government also committed itself to a series of I.O.U.s – medical and disability payments for veterans and administrative overhead costs – that will total another estimated $1.5–$1.7 trillion or more from 2001 to 2050. Finally, among the costs of these wars are increases in Homeland Security spending, intended to avert the threat of a terrorist attack and respond to and recover from attacks. Totaling these expenses and Congressional requests through financial year 2020, the U.S. federal Government had spent and obligated over $6.4 trillion on the post-9/11 wars (Stiglitz and Bilmes 2008; Crawford 2019).

VIETNAM, THE PRESIDENT, AND THE FEDERAL RESERVE

The Vietnam War period provides a good example of Government–central-bank cooperation and conflict. Setting the stage, monetary policy had been directed by the Executive from the inauguration of Franklin Roosevelt in March 1933 to the *Treasury-Federal Reserve Accord*, which in March 1951 allowed the Fed "to minimize monetization of the public debt." The Treasury bill rate had been fixed at 0.375 percent between June 1942 and June 1947, along with less than 2½ percent for long-term U.S. bonds, to allow a low-interest war, and then minimize the deficit and stimulate the economy.

Interest rates were freed a little as the Fed pressed the Treasury after the war, although long rates had not risen and T bills were still low at 1.375 percent in 1951, even though Korean War (which began in June 1950) demands brought consumer price inflation of 7.9 percent per annum in 1951. (Inflation averaged nearly 6 percent between 1946 and 1952.) According to the Accord, the Fed regained the independence written into the Federal Reserve Act of 1913, and experienced between 1922 and 1933, with the help of a Congress worried about inflation and ineffectively resisted by a president made unpopular by the Korean War.

Inflation was steady around an average of 1.4 percent per annum between 1953 and 1965, as the conservative Fed under the chairmanship of William McChesney Martin, Jr. (1951–70), preferred price stability to the easy-money stimulation desired by Keynesian critics whose primary goal was full employment. The latter complained of the tight-money behavior of Martin, who reminded them that the long period of almost continuous (although small by later standards) inflation was record-breaking for the U.S.A. The Fed's sound-money preference eroded in the 1960s with presidents Kennedy and Johnson (LBJ) pro-Keynesian governors' appointees and growing federal deficits as LBJ sought to fight two wars – against poverty and the Viet Cong. Neither war was popular enough to induce Congress to raise taxes for their expansion.

Johnson kept U.S. actions and his plans secret, as much as he could, which prevented him from sharing them with Congress except in special appropriations and continuing resolutions. Certainly no tax increases. He had to borrow, preferably at low interest rates, and for this he needed the Federal Reserve. After the Martin Fed raised the discount rate in late 1965, LBJ summoned

Martin to his Texas ranch, leading to the famous confrontation in which the president pushed the smaller Martin against a wall and complained that "my boys are dying in Vietnam, and you won't print the money I need."

The primary American monetary difference before and after World War II was the nearly continuous inflation afterwards. The price level in 1933, when the U.S.A. departed from the gold standard, was about the same as 100 years earlier. Inflations during the Civil War and World War I had been offset by subsequent deflations. Price rises after 1945 were small but nearly continuous as they rose more than thirteen-fold by 2020, about 3.45 percent per annum. Federal deficits were also nearly continuous. An associated fiscal phenomenon has been the persistent fall in personal income tax rates (see Figure 10.1).

The Kennedy tax cut of February 1964 (actually accomplished during the presidency of Lyndon Johnson) saw an approximately 20 percent across-the-board reduction in individual income tax rates (the highest bracket from 91 percent to 70 percent), and a cut in the corporate tax rate from 52 percent to 48 percent. Johnson was unable to get Congress to reverse the change during the Vietnam War, and also found the Federal Reserve reluctant to supply the credit he wanted. Even so, Martin's last five years at the Fed, 1965–70, the years of expanding American military involvement in Vietnam, saw a tripling of inflation to 4.2 percent.

Allegations of North Vietnamese attacks on U.S. vessels in neutral waters in August 1964 persuaded Congress to pass the Gulf of Tonkin Resolution, which authorized the president to "take all necessary measures, including the use of armed force" against any aggressor in the Vietnam conflict, but not necessarily the funds to carry them out. When in 1965, President Johnson decided on a major increase in American troops despite doubts regarding the public's support, he chose to keep his plans secret.

The chairman of the Council of Economic Advisors (CEA) remembered that "There was a period of a couple of months – six weeks maybe – in the summer in which there was, I think, a deliberate effort not to let anybody know what was going on. But the people in Defense knew it, and the people in Budget and the Council did not know it" (Hargrove and Morley 1984, p. 249). Whatever they knew, they promised not to tell the Fed. Budget Director Charles Schultze memoed the president: "I have instructed my staff not to discuss the budgetary outlook with the Fed. Quite apart from security considerations I am afraid that the budgetary outlook would be used as an excuse to tighten up on monetary policy" (Meltzer 2009, p. 449).

Johnson later said the reason for secrecy was to prevent the Soviet Union and China from increasing their support of North Vietnam (Johnson 1971, p. 149; Meltzer 2009, p. 149). Word got around, however, including to Martin, who had connections in Congress and the Defense Department. He confronted the president several times, and warned that interest rates might have to rise.

In fact, they were rising with inflation. One wonders how Johnson thought his projects would be financed if neither by taxes nor by investors attracted by market returns. The answer lay with the central bank.

News of the 1965 increase in government spending inspired a Martin speech on June 1 that "shocked both the administration and the financial community." He saw "the threat of another Great Depression .... We find disquieting similarities between our present prosperity and the fabulous twenties."

Not unusually, spenders wanting finance found allies in those who denied money's influence on inflation. CEA Chairman Gardner Ackley (1964–68, a cost-push devotee) told LBJ that "It is hard to know what Bill was really driving at in his speech" (Ackley 1971, pp. 5–6; Kettl 1973, p. 103), believed inflation was "deeply imbedded in the economic structures of modern western societies," and described his job as "President Johnson's principal agent in attempting to hold down wages and prices by 'jawboning.'" This resembled Federal Reserve Board Chairman Jerome Powell's later (2021–22) denial of the Fed's and money's effect on inflation. It also raises a question regarding the direction of influence between advisors and advised.

Board member Sherman Maisel was encouraged by what turned out to be empty Treasury and Council offers "to coordinate monetary and fiscal policies." Ackley and the Secretary of the Treasury "told me" that the administration was considering fiscal restraint, and promised that "if fiscal policy were not tightened, they would urge President Johnson to call for a tighter monetary policy in his State of the Union message" (Maisel 1973, pp. 74–5). Nothing of the kind was done, and Martin continued to warn the president of the need to restrain spending, by increased taxes preferably, or if not, by tighter monetary policy. Martin explained the FOMC's failure to act (dates at the beginning of quotations refer to the minutes of the FOMC):

10/12/65. As Chairman, he had the responsibility for maintaining System relations within the Government – for getting the thinking of the President and members of the Administration, and for apprising them of the thinking within the Committee – and he had made that one of his principal concerns during the fourteen years he had held his present office. Last week he had given the President a paper expressing his personal views [that tightening might have to occur]. [H]e had talked with the Chairman of the Council of Economic Advisors, with Treasury officials, and with the President. They had all expressed the view that it would be unwise to change monetary policy now. The President had not taken a rigid position on the matter [according to Martin's generous interpretation] – he had not suggested that the [FOMC] Committee should abdicate its responsibility for formulating monetary policy .... With a divided Committee and in the face of strong Administration opposition he did not believe it would be appropriate for him to lend his support to those who favored a change in policy [tightening] now.

So what was the Fed to do? The Federal Reserve Act had assigned the Fed responsibilities for an elastic currency, its gold value, and bank supervision, but its primary objective soon became the monetization of the federal debt (during World War I and again during World War II). The gold standard was abandoned in 1933 and the executive took control of the Fed without the benefit of legislation. The Fed regained substantial but uncertain control in 1951, although the Employment Act of 1946 declared it to be "the continuing policy and responsibility of the Federal Government to coordinate and utilize all its plans, functions, and resources ... to promote maximum employment, production and purchasing power."

Whether the law implies an independent Fed focused on price stability or a monetary-and-fiscal policy coordinated by the executive depends on one's macroeconomic model: the classical neutrality of money, with costly inflation, according to Martin, or the interventionist Keynesianism of the Employment Act. The Fed might take its cues from Congress, whose creature it is, although that body has many spokespersons and interpretations of its wishes in the absence of legislation, or even with it.

Federal deficits might be interpreted as violations of democracy, that is, spending more than the taxes voted by [or reasonably expected to be voted by] Congress, the elected representatives of the people (Wood 2009, pp. 69–71; Keech 1996, pp. 160–61). So the Fed's occasional resistance to presidents could have been due as much to defenses of the Constitution, particularly Article I, Section 7.1, as differences in economics:

> All Bills for raising Revenue shall originate in the House of Representatives; but the Senate may propose or concur with Amendments as on other Bills.

Taking this power seriously means that Section 8.2, which gives Congress the power "To borrow Money on the credit of the United States," implies that borrowing is in anticipation of taxes. In any case, Federal Reserve purchases of government debt, although implied by congressional decisions, are not directly considered or voted on by Congress. Legislators are enabled to benefit politically from spending without paying the political costs of taxes.

As 1965 approached its end, having given up on the administration's promises and unimpressed with its studies which found nothing to worry about, Martin stiffened. "He was finally ready," in Allan Meltzer's words, "to accept the challenge." He knew the government's spending plans had continued to grow, notwithstanding the president's claims to the contrary, and so were inflationary pressures. When on October 6, Martin told Johnson that a rate increase was necessary, the latter said: "I'm scheduled to go into the hospital tomorrow for a gall bladder operation. You wouldn't raise the discount rate while I'm in the hospital, would you?" Martin replied: "No, Mr. President, we'll wait until you get out of the hospital." After considerable lobbying by Martin and New York Fed President Alfred Hayes, on December 3, the Board voted 4 to 3 to recommend increases in discount rates, and the Reserve Banks raised their rates from 4 percent to 4½ percent (Meltzer 2009, p. 453). Martin warned of the risk to the System's independence if it acted against the president's wishes, but said: "There is a question whether the Federal Reserve is to be run by the administration in office."

The Board also raised the maximum rate payable on bank time deposits, which threatened to fall below market rates and cause deposit drains. The *Banking Act of 1933* had included Regulation Q, which prohibited interest on demand deposits and directed the Fed to fix ceilings on time deposits. The maximum rate payable on savings deposits was 2½ percent from 1935 through 1956, when the Fed began to raise it in line with market rates (Federal Reserve Board 1975, p. 673; Wood 2005, p. 32).

The 12 (usually equal) Federal Reserve Bank discount rates are decided (recommended) by their Boards of Directors subject to the approval of the Federal Reserve Board, which at full strength is the majority of the FOMC. President Hayes led off November's roundtable discussion:

11/23/65. Most of the directors of the New York Bank have felt for some time that an increase in the discount rate is overdue. Indeed, on a number of occasions some of them have urged that the Bank take the initiative in this area. I am now prepared to recommend that they vote a 1/2 per cent discount rate increase within the next week or so.

Most of the rest of the FOMC were on the fence, and Martin gave them a pep-talk.

He commented that over the past two years he had been proud to preside over the Federal Reserve System because, despite continuing differences of opinion, the debates had been on a consistently high level. Having said this, he would also say that he considered it unfortunate that the System had been divided and continued to be divided. He had always felt that when the System was united it occupied a strong position within the ranks of the Government. When divided, the System was in a less strong position.

We could debate full- and less-than-full employment forever,

But, Chairman Martin said, he wanted to make his own point of view clear this morning. He thought the time for decision had arrived, and he wanted the record to reflect his opinion that it was not possible to run away continually from making a decision. [I]t was necessary to make fundamental judgments, [which] was easy for him … because he believed the country was in a period of creeping inflation already… [H]e thought the economy was going too fast at the moment. This was where one came up against the basic problem – to which he did not know the answer

– relating to the economics of full employment. Here there were different schools of thought. Personally he felt that at some point, if the economy went too fast, the possibility of achieving sustainable full employment would be destroyed. And he thought the situation was about at that point now.

He commented additionally that it must be remembered that the Open Market Committee did not set the discount rate, just as it did not fix reserve requirements or margin requirements. The Committee meetings were used as a forum for discussion of System policy generally, but no commitment could be made with respect to the discount rate. The Board would have to act on that, and he could not anticipate how the Board would act. He had merely wanted to make it clear that for his part, as one member of the Board – and assuming a continuation of present conditions – if any Reserve Bank should come in with an increase in the discount rate he would be prepared to approve.

The Fed continued its pressure into 1966, and short-term market rates began to exceed the legal maximum rates on bank deposits. Deposits fell, banks restricted credit, and on September 13, 1966, Hayes told the FOMC "that the financial community was experiencing growing and genuine fear of a financial panic." However, the Committee stayed with the directive of "firm but orderly conditions." Martin was "impressed by its high degree of agreement on policy."

> 10/4/66. The directive continued "firm but orderly conditions in the money market; provided, however, that operations shall be modified in the light of unusual liquidity pressures or of any significant deviation of bank credit from current expectations."

What actually happened was monetary expansion. The president got his way. Money and prices accelerated. Martin said later that the Fed's ease had partly stemmed from the disappointed hope that the temporary income tax surcharge pried from Congress would suppress demand (more on this below). In Meltzer's words, "Martin had shown courage and determination by refusing to back down under intense pressure from the president. Then he retreated" (Meltzer 2009, p. 493).

In July 1966, the Board disapproved several Reserve Bank requests for rate increases. Governor Dewey Daane explained his position: "Every economic ground said to increase the rate; his reluctance was because such an action would be harmful to relationships with the administration" (Meltzer 2009, p. 505). Martin later explained his reluctance to take action against inflation:

> 10/24/67. Large deficits in the budget are rapidly generating inexorable forces that might prove more important than any decisions the committee would take.

However, he resisted the president's pressures to ease. Unable to obtain a permanent tax increase, LBJ asked in his State of the Union message of January

1967, for a temporary income tax surcharge. The hesitant Congress gave him a bill to sign in July 1968, which imposed a one-year, 10 percent surcharge (later extended for a year at 5 percent). In addition to providing revenue for the Vietnam War, the tax was expected to slow inflation-driven private spending and allow the easing of interest rates which the administration's economists expected the Fed to accommodate.

They, as well as some of the Board's staff and governors, forecast economic slowdowns, but Martin was buying none of it. In his judgment, the present inflationary difficulties

> 8/17/68. … were largely traceable to the long delay in introducing fiscal restraint and to the fact that monetary policy had moved toward restraint too slowly. He now thought that the discount rate should have been raised to the current 5½ per cent level considerably earlier than it had been. The Chairman remarked that July evidently was a good month for business and he was not as pessimistic as the staff was about the economic outlook for the rest of the year.

The September meeting saw admissions by the Board's Director of Research and Statistics, Daniel Brill, that his and the administration's forecasts had been mistaken. A "study" by the Treasury, Budget Bureau, CEA, and Brill and his staff, who were generally in favor of ease and at odds with Martin, had recommended no tightening in monetary policy at least until the publication of the federal budget in January, given that "a step-up in federal spending [was] unlikely," even though Martin knew (and he knew they knew) the opposite was more likely (Bremner 2004, p. 206). Economists later pointed out that the small effect of the temporary tax surcharge on spending was unsurprising in light of the permanent income hypothesis as income earners spread the tax's effect over their lifetime consumption (Eisner 1969). Martin repeated his previous month's skepticism, and in December, a month after Richard Nixon's election, the Fed tightened, and Brill resigned soon thereafter:

> 1/14/69. Martin reported that he had told the new president that inflation was the primary economic problem now facing the nation, and the administration would have to deal with it effectively from the beginning if it were not to get out of control. He told the Committee that it would be better to risk overstaying, rather than understaying, a policy of restraint.

Nixon was wary of Martin, whom he blamed for his defeat in the 1960 presidential election. The economy had peaked in April 1960 and bottomed in February 1961. In his book *Six Crises*, Nixon (1962) described his friend Arthur Burns's advice in March 1960 that monetary policy should be eased to avoid an "economic dip just before the elections." However, neither Eisenhower nor Martin could be persuaded to change course. Nixon offered Martin, whose term as chairman extended to February 1970, the job of Secretary of the Treasury in order to open the Fed chairmanship to Burns, but Martin said he would serve out his term (Bremner 2004, pp. 260–61).

The president and his Council of Economic advisors hoped to reduce inflation with a minimal increase in unemployment. Council Chairman Paul McCracken referred to their plan as "gradualism." A little bit of monetary tightening would slowly lower inflation toward price stability, which, when achieved, would promote the return to full employment. This fine-tuning exercise in small, smooth, temporary movements along static, well-behaved curves did not take account of spenders' expectations, Martin believed. The failure of the income-tax surcharge to slow spending was another case of the futility of temporary measures. He was not a gradualist. The market had to be shocked.

> July 15, 1969. Martin observed that the go-around discussion of economic conditions revealed sentiment for shading monetary policy in both directions depending on the effects of the current policy of restraint. His personal view was that policy should not be changed, primarily because he did not favor fine-tuning to the degree to which some apparently were inclined. He did not agree with those who argued that it was necessary only for the System to pull the right levers to do an effective job of stabilization.
>
> Shading towards ease, for example, because of the risk that it would be interpreted as a more significant move toward ease than would be intended. Inflationary psychology remained the main economic problem. It would be a mistake to take any action that might reinforce inflationary expectations just at the time they might be weakening. The System had been overly hasty in moving toward ease in the summer of 1968, after the credit crunch and in response to the administration's promise of fiscal restraint.
>
> Accordingly the Committee voted unanimously for a directive which included: System open market operations ... shall be conducted with a view to maintaining the currently prevailing firm conditions.

Martin informed Congress and the public of the Fed's determination. "There is no gadgetry in monetary mechanisms ... that will save us from our sins," he told a group of bankers. Expectations of inflation were deeply embedded, and their elimination would require "a good deal of pain and suffering." The Fed had indicated, "perhaps unwisely," after the 1966 credit crunch that "we don't want a recurrence." However, "if you don't take some risk in policy you never get any result." Martin strongly implied that the Fed would not back down again even in the event of increased unemployment, the *New York Times* reported (U.S. Congress 1969, pp. 648–51, 668–9; Matusow 1998, p. 25; Bremner 2004, p. 253).

The Fed persisted until Burns replaced Martin in February 1970, after which the Treasury bill rate, which had risen from 3½ percent in 1967 to 8 percent in January 1970, was reduced to 3½ percent, and inflation, which had increased from 1.1 percent during 1966 to 2.2 percent during 1969, jumped nearly to double digits in 1973.

Vietnam was not the last time, as we have seen; in fact it marked the new practice, that Congress has permitted but chosen not to pay for a war, with savers, helped by the Fed, expected to make up the difference, and the soaring national debt is almost certain to go unpaid, as Smith (see Chapter 1) would almost certainly have said.

THE ALL-VOLUNTEER ARMY

WASHINGTON (Army News Service, July 2, 2012) – When newly elected President Richard M. Nixon requested the Department of Defense to eliminate the draft and create an all-volunteer force, Army leaders knew there would be some hurdles. Instead of drafting young men to fill the ranks, the Army would need to spend money to ramp up recruiting efforts and portray military service as an attractive career choice.

Comfortable furniture soon filled the open-bay barracks, which were divided into sleeping rooms. Beer, once prohibited, became a popular beverage, and grooming standards relaxed. But Army leaders soon realized some changes caused more problems than they solved, and new initiatives began that focused on instilling professionalism and building pride for the Army.

Sgt. Major Ray Moran, now retired, thinks the all-volunteer force initiative has proven a success – and he was proud to have been part of it. "We built a volunteer Army that really proved itself in Desert Storm," said Moran, in a 2011 interview. "They were just a marvelous bunch of Soldiers, and they have done it right through to Iraq and Afghanistan today. We are very proud of the all-volunteer Army."

"Everybody in the Army wants to be in the Army," said Major General Thomas Seamands, director of army personnel management.

There were several reasons for the end of the draft:

- *Demographics.* The size of the eligible population reaching draft age each year was so large relative to the needs of the military that the draft was no longer universal or regarded as fair.
- *Cost.* Obtaining enough highly qualified volunteers was possible at acceptable budget levels.
- *Moral and economic rationale.* Conservatives and libertarians argued that the state had no right to impose military service on young men without their consent. Liberals asserted that the draft placed unfair burdens on the underprivileged members of society, who were less likely to get deferments.
- *Opposition to the war in Vietnam.* The growing unpopularity of the Vietnam War meant the country was ripe for a change to a volunteer force.
- *The U.S. Army's desire for change.* The Army had lost confidence in the draft as discipline problems among draftees mounted in Vietnam.

These views were reinforced by the Gates Commission, set up in 1969 by President Nixon to advise him on establishing an all-volunteer force, and the end of the draft was announced in January 1973.

Thoughts on Bringing Back the Draft

Arguments for the draft are mainly social, such as: It's unfair for a tiny percentage of Americans – less than 1 percent – to shoulder the burden of fighting wars; the draft could rehabilitate young criminal offenders; and, by bringing Americans of different backgrounds together, contribute to the "melting pot" that makes America great. A truly American military, inclusive of all social classes, might cause politicians and voters to be more selective in choosing which battles are worth fighting and at what expense. It would also have the significant effect of getting the majority of the country behind those wars in which we do engage (Epstein 2015; Fallows 2015). Perhaps the lack of discipline among draftees was more serious during the Vietnam War than less unpopular wars.

Most Americans, however, are reluctant to compel their fellows to face the horrors of war. A Vietnam medical corpsman commenting on the above views found his experiences so horrific that he "would never subject our young men and women to the draft." According to a 2011 Pew survey, recent veterans oppose a draft even more than civilians do: "More than eight-in-ten post-9/11 veterans and 74% of the public say the U.S. should not return to the draft at this time."

In the 1990s the House twice voted to defund the Selective Service Commission but funding was restored by the Senate. The only proposal to reinstate the draft, in 2004, was defeated 402 to 2.

The recent *National Commission on Military, National, and Public Service* reflected these views as its 2020 report supported "a culture of voluntary service," with "mandatory military service" reserved for national emergencies.

EXPLAINING THE ENDLESS WARS

America's foreign intervention failures have had several well-known causes, including inadequate specifications of objectives, lack of commitment, ignorance of conditions on the ground – of histories, governments, and populations – and lack of accountability, of the consequences of failure:

> [Y]ou can't lose a reputation fighting a losing war for the United States. If you want proof of that, just check out the photo that *Guardian* columnist Julian Borger recently highlighted. It's a smile-a-thon of self-satisfaction that happens to include former National Security Advisor and Secretary of State Henry Kissinger (think: Vietnam,

Cambodia), former National Security Advisor and Secretary of State Condoleeza Rice (think: the invasions of Afghanistan and Iraq), and former CIA director and Secretary of Defense Robert Gates (think: America's twenty-first-century forever wars), [with UK PM Tony Blair and Australian PM John Howard, who committed troops to Iraq, and Indian PM Narendra Modi, who moved troops into Kashmir and rounded up Muslims]. All three are still admired and have kept their reps in Washington, which should tell you what you need to know about what passes for American foreign policy and the top officials of the national security state in 2019. (Bacevich 2019)

The latter-day crusade in pursuit of Saddam Hussein's non-existent weapons of mass destruction was one of the most disastrous mistakes in history, unleashing a cascade of violence that killed well over half a million people and ushered in an era of extreme violence in the Middle East that continues today. The fact they are still feted as foreign policy sages suggests that once you reach a certain level in global diplomacy, you can only fail upwards. (Borger 2019)

The American goal in South Vietnam was a non-communist government. It was feared that a fall to the communist North Vietnam in their civil war, according to the Domino Theory, would lead to more communist take-overs in the area. The American involvement was part of its world-wide war against communism that had begun in 1945, whereas the objective for most Vietnamese had long been the riddance of foreign domination, especially by China, in a conflict exceeding a thousand years. American pressure drove North Vietnam into the arms of the Chinese for support, contrary to the interests of both.

The United States was on record as a supporter of nationalist resistance to colonialism, but its concern for communism took precedence. Cuban patriots' desires to be free of their giant neighbor to the north were also misunderstood.

American foreign policy has failed to take nationalist movements into account, which is surprising in light of its own revolutionary experience, when a sizeable committed part of the population outlasted the British effort, whose forces were superior but never sufficient to pacify the country. The British eventual decision that its military efforts were not worth the cost was a wise one, and anticipated by the substantial anti-war groups in and out of Parliament. It is very difficult to defeat and maintain control of a committed population. Massive American bombing was ineffective and might even have hardened North Vietnam's effort, although Secretary of Defense Robert McNamara (1995) was surprised by the "unintended consequences" of the policy.

The British were faced with a similar war against a population in the Boer War of 1899–1902, in which it tried to limit citizens' assistance to insurgent guerilla forces by isolating groups in inhumane concentration camps, bringing much domestic and international condemnation. Britain eventually claimed a formal victory, but pulled its forces out of what became an independent country although South Africa became a member of the "free and equal" British Commonwealth of Nations.

Numbers of American troops in Vietnam were limited by lukewarm public support and rising criticisms of the purposes and conduct of the war – which was just enough to keep the corrupt, unpopular, and ineffective South Vietnamese government afloat. Nixon won the 1968 presidential election on the promise to end the war, and began to reduce American forces, finally leading to withdrawal and the government's collapsed. Years later, Vietnam's relations with the United States are healthy and it is commonly seen as an ally in conflicts with China's ambitions in the area.

The American military presence in Afghanistan was intended to deprive terrorists of bases in that country, which was understood to mean the establishment of a viable anti-terrorist government and military. After its initial defeat, the Taliban (supporters of terrorist groups) regained control of substantial portions of the country, the American-supported government grew progressively weaker and more corrupt, and the U.S. military left in 2021.

This departure of a sizable American force is associated by the press, and often in government statements, with the end of the war in Afghanistan. This attitude suggests confusion of what the war was about, and indeed of war in general. If the purpose of American involvement was American security, that is, the prevention of the country's use as a base for anti-American terrorism, the presence of a few thousand troops in that tribally dominated mountainous country was bound to be insufficient, as the many failures of past invaders had demonstrated. Propping up a government in the capital city was certainly insufficient for the purpose. The same can be said for nation-building and human rights, especially when the cooperation of Afghans is limited by the lack of confidence in American commitment.

American security is, of course, a never-ending objective. Sizeable troop deployments in Kabul and elsewhere may be irrelevant, compared with strike forces and surveillance. Defeats of local groups are temporary. The military owes the president a plan, perhaps an imaginative plan, for the neutralism of anti-American activity, not just successive calls for more troops. However, neither the military nor successive administrations have specified realistic goals or means of achieving them for several reasons; for example, ignorance of history and local conditions (as in Vietnam), and the lack of accountability to a disinterested public.

The public's willingness to accept repeated expensive failures may be attributed to its lack of interest, which is odd in view of their normal interest in and support of the military. However, several steps have been taken to separate the public from government decisions. The purposes of those interventions have not been clear enough for administrations to risk calls for declarations of war, or for strong, unified, long-term support. Marking strong deviations from the past, the Vietnam War and other wars since then have not been associated with tax increases. President George W. Bush (2001–09) assured Americans that they would not be inconvenienced personally or financially by his military ventures, which would be fought by volunteers and financed by borrowing assisted by the central bank. This is where the Federal Reserve comes in. By assisting government borrowing, it joins the All-Voluntary Military as a way of lessening taxpayers' and other citizens' scrutiny of government borrowing. It is a violation of the fundamental principles of democracy, of the public's oversight of government, by which the public decides government activities and enables and limits those activities by taxing themselves to pay for them, now or definitely planned for the future. Costs should be attached to benefits.

11. Summary: government and the public

Nature is more powerful than education.
–Disraeli 1832, pt. i, ch. Xiii

There have been many academic studies of and proposals for optimal monetary policies in support of presumed public welfares (e.g., Friedman 1960; Walsh 2017; Taylor 1993), as well as legislated rules or guides (e.g., gold ties in the 1844 Bank Act; an elastic currency in the Federal Reserve Act; promotion of maximum employment, production, and purchasing power in the Employment Act of 1946; and inflation targeting contracts since the 1980s). Most of these have been paid lip-service by central bankers from time to time, but none has been able to withstand the pressures from interests desiring otherwise, particularly governments and a public which desire easy money (although they dislike inflation).

In October 2021, for example, when the Federal Reserve's stated inflation goal was an average of 2 percent per annum (changed from a constant 2 percent when it rose above that number), inflation was in fact 11 percent at an annual rate (6.2 percent the previous 12 months and rising). The money stock had risen 12 percent the past year (38 percent since early 2020). Fed Chairman Jerome Powell expected inflation to ease eventually, but was "frustrated" that getting people vaccinated and arresting the spread of the Covid delta variant "remains the most important economic policy that we have":

> It's also frustrating to see the bottlenecks and supply chain problems not getting better – in fact at the margins apparently getting a little worse .... We see that continuing into next year probably, and holding up inflation longer than we had thought. (Senate Banking, Housing and Urban Affairs Committee, September 28, 2021)

This was standard Fed practice of denying responsibility for inflation while satisfying the president's desire for easy money (even though the expected effectiveness of the increase in money as an offset to the lockdowns was not explained). It might nevertheless be called a success because Powell was reappointed as chairman in November 2021.

Chairperson Cecilia Rouse "attributed the increase in prices to disruptions caused by the pandemic, including supply-chain disruptions .... As supply chains ease, as people get back to work, as we normalize our economy, the price pressures will start to ease" said Rouse, who's on leave from her post

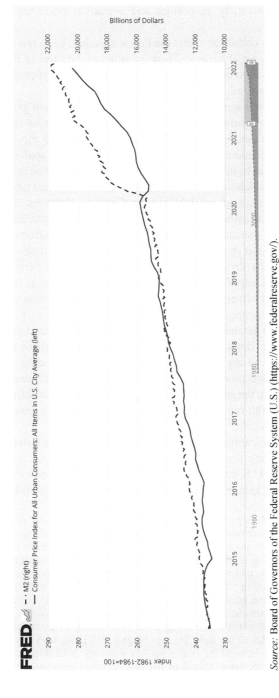

Source: Board of Governors of the Federal Reserve System (U.S.) (https://www.federalreserve.gov/).

Figure 11.1 U.S. money and prices, 2014–21

as a Princeton University economics and education professor (Cook and Dmitrieva 2021).

In any case, it is unthinkable that the Fed will undertake to reduce inflation such that its average will become 2 percent either in the short or the long run. Its recent and long-term behavior conforms to the readiness of central banks to supply requests (demands?) for government finance.

There seemed little appreciation by the Fed, or Government generally, that health and economic policies are interrelated in their effects on the spread of Covid-19. The various forms of lockdown or isolation had mostly negative consequences for economic activity, but governments have applied stimuli of unprecedented scale to offset those losses, "strongly supported by ultra-loose monetary policy, which included sharp cuts of nominal interest rates and large scale purchases of government debt by central banks." However, these actions "might also have had a non-negligible effect on pandemic dynamics .... It is far from obvious how monetary policy should react beyond its efforts to preserve financial stability and (possibly) support" appropriately calibrated financing, thus minimizing the drop in economic activity. However, "engineering an aggregate demand expansion can prove counterproductive in times of the pandemic since" it offsets "an intentional and desired reduction in economic activity." Optimal aggregate demand management has to resolve a trade-off between aggregate demand and health risks (Brzoza-Brzezina et al. 2021).

Federal Reserve Bank of St. Louis President James Bullard (2020) said it is inappropriate to argue for "economic stimulus" intending to ramp up production or create new demand in this situation, as that would work at cross-purposes with the goal of reducing the level of economic activity in order to meet public health objectives. A better concept is that we should strive to "keep everybody whole."

On the other hand, although "Federal Reserve Chair Jerome Powell was once on the verge of being fired by President Donald Trump for not doing enough to turbocharge the U.S. economy," a journalist observed, he now (9/20) stands a decent chance of keeping his job no matter who is elected president:

> Powell's extraordinary pledge to spend trillions of dollars to support the economy and keep borrowing rates at historic lows during the pandemic has helped stock prices roar back to pre-Covid levels – Trump's favorite barometer of his performance. Maintaining market stability would be a major consideration for Democrat Joe Biden, too. But under Powell's leadership, the Fed has also unveiled a sweeping new policy promoting "broad-based and inclusive" job gains, a major acknowledgment that the central bank should help disadvantaged Americans – in line with a call by Biden's campaign for the Fed to directly tackle racial inequality.
>
> Powell, who will testify before Congress three times this week, has also cultivated allies on both sides of the aisle. He met roughly 250 times with lawmakers from when he took the helm of the central bank in February 2018 through July [2020], according to his personal calendars. He has garnered bipartisan praise for his

actions during the pandemic – including from Trump, who has called him the "most improved player" in government, a remarkable turnabout from a president who publicly abused him for more than a year for not cutting interest rates.

"He's done a fantastic, very smart job," Rep. Patrick McHenry (R-N.C.), the top Republican on the House Financial Services Committee, said of Powell. (Guida 2020)

In his nomination speech of November 22, 2021, President Biden said:

I'm confident that Chair Powell and [vice-chair nominee] Dr. Brainard's focus on keeping inflation low, prices stable, and delivering full employment will make our economy stronger than ever before. Together, they also share my deep belief that urgent action is needed to address the economic risks posed by climate change, and stay ahead of emerging risks in our financial system. Fundamentally, if we want to continue to build on the economic success of this year we need stability and independence at the Federal Reserve – and I have full confidence after their trial by fire over the last 20 months that Chair Powell and Dr. Brainard will provide the strong leadership our country needs.

The next week, however, Powell told the House Financial Services Committee that the risks of persistent elevated inflation have "clearly risen," and monetary policy would evolve in response. "We've seen inflation be more persistent. We've seen the factors that are causing higher inflation to be more persistent."

Powell told the Senate Banking Committee (11/30/21) it would be "appropriate" to discuss whether the central bank should wind up its asset purchases at a faster pace given heightened inflation risks. He also said he wanted to retire the word "transitory" to describe price increases, and that inflation pressures will "linger well into next year." "The inflation that we're seeing is still clearly related to pandemic-related factors. "I would also add … that it has spread more broadly in the economy and I think that the risk of persistent higher inflation has clearly risen."

Powell's avoidance of any mention of "money," whose full effect is yet to be realized, was remarkable for a central banker. The more than one-eighth increase in money during the first quarter of the pandemic (II/20, Figure 11.2) was not immediately reflected in inflation because money-holding increased (from 0.7 to 0.9 of annual GDP, Table 11.1), but began to be effective a few months later, and looked likely to be a source of significant inflation if and when money holdings returned to pre-pandemic values.

Table 11.1   *The demand for money 2019–21, $ billions (GDP annual rate, M average)*

	GDP	M	M/GDP
I/2019	21,002	14,488	0.6898
	21,289	14,675	0.6893
	21,505	14,940	0.6947
	21,694	15,243	0.7026
I/2020	21,481	15,630	0.7276
	19,477	17,701	0.9088
	21,139	18,432	0.8719
	21,478	18,945	0.8821
I/2021	22,038	19,657	0.892
	22,741	20,323	0.8937
	23,187	20,801	0.8971

Source: Compiled by the author.

We see that little has changed in the fundamentals of central banking over the last two centuries beyond the abandonment of the constraints of the gold standard which has allowed more political pressures on monetary policies in the forms of government finance and bailouts and other subsidies to the big banks. Examples of these influences include suspension of the gold convertibility of the pound in 1797, enabling the Bank of England to finance the Government's wartime deficits and allowing prices to rise 50 percent by 1810. Parliament had voted in 1803 to restore the pound's convertibility within six months of the end of the war, but was delayed a few times afterwards.

In 1815, the paper pound was trading at a 10 percent discount from its 1797 par, and there was insufficient will to incur the monetary restriction necessary to resume the prewar par. "[T]he Bank had found itself comfortable under the Suspension, and felt no enthusiasm for a return to a system which did not guarantee it against being asked to pay its debts at a possibly inconvenient moment; and the Government and Parliament were as slack as they usually are after a great war" (Cannan 1919, pp. xxix–xxx).

Even so, the Government was committed to stability, social and economic, in the long run in the interests of its property-owning electorate. Tory Prime Minister Lord Liverpool's (1812–27) father had been a leading advocate of price stability, and inflation was seen as an attack on property (Woodward 1938, p. 107). On the other hand, the economic losses of creditors due to inflation, political reformer Thomas Attwood (1817, p. 163) argued, would be more than offset (for the general interest) by the preservation of employment.

The Government had to go along with several delays in resumption until finally, following the recommendations of Commons and Lords committees,

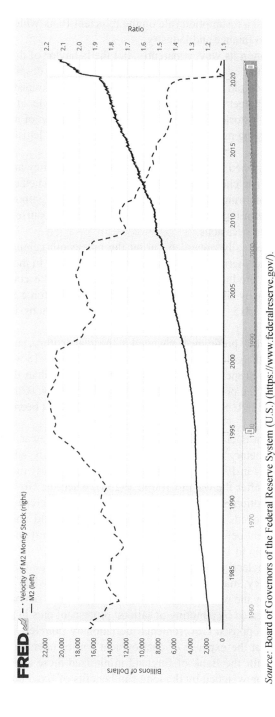

Source: Board of Governors of the Federal Reserve System (U.S.) (https://www.federalreserve.gov/).

Figure 11.2   Money and its velocity/demand, 1980–2021

Parliament imposed a resumption rule on the reluctant Bank which feared the risks of deflation to finance and industry.

Property had gotten its way, apparently, but the behavior of the Bank over the next 20 years turned out to be unsatisfactorily volatile despite its forced conformance to the gold standard. Its erratic behavior, combined with peace and government budget surpluses, caused the loss of some of the Bank's privileges, but the historic preference for the monopolization of money led to the Bank's notes being made the sole legal tender, tied by a legislative rule to its gold.

As critics had warned, a loss of gold restricted the currency and provoked a financial crisis. The choice facing the Government was whether to enforce the rule, with its long-run stable-price promise, or allow its temporary suspension in the short-term interests of the economy. The latter course was chosen in 1847 and on later occasions.

So property eventually prevailed during the nineteenth century, although with significant short-term concessions to the wider public. In the developing free-trade system, producers depended on and had to make concessions to labor, explaining why the Bank of England hesitated to force tight money on business after 1815, and was willing to relax restrictions in 1847 and afterwards.

This order of policy preferences changed in the next century, such as during the resumption of the gold value of the pound after the 1914–18 war. The gold standard had been suspended in 1914, U.K. prices more than doubled, and the dollar value of the pound, normally $4.86, fell below $4. (Currencies had begun to be valued in U.S. dollars, whose gold value had not been changed by the war.)

The Government declared its intention to restore the prewar value of the pound, and a monetary policy of restraint was accordingly adopted, U.K. prices fell from 264 in 1920.IV (based on 100 in 1914.III; easy money continued for two years after the war) to 166 in 1925.II, when the Government felt the pound's resumption of $4.86 was due, even though 10 percent of the labor force was unemployed. Prices fell a further 14 percent and unemployment surpassed 20 percent before the Government gave up its quest and suspended (involuntarily) again in 1931.III.

The Bank of England and party leaders never admitted the futility of their exchange-rate policy, made possible by international borrowing, until its collapse was forced by the withdrawal of foreign lending and a run on the pound, most notably instigated by a mutiny of sailors' protests of cuts in pay.

Labour leaders opposed Governments' deflationary policies, including its budget-balancing at the expense of employment and of unemployment benefits. Spokesmen for the Bank of England minimized these short-run costs, saying they were outweighed by the long-run benefits of fixed rates, the gold standard, and the City's contributions to the economy – positions accepted by party leaders.

Labour and the short run prevailed, however, with the collapse of the gold standard, although monetary conservatives might point to the long-run consequences of fiat money – including a 20-fold increase in prices, meaning a 95 percent loss of the pound's purchasing power, during the second half of the twentieth century, compared with the near equality of prices at the beginning and end of the 1822–1913 continuous gold standard.

The story was much the same in the United States, where the implications of the gold standard for prices were not understood by Treasury or Federal Reserve officials. In a world of deflation forced by overvalued currencies, American prices fell slightly in the 1920s and then more rapidly after 1929. Farmers and others complained about the deflation, and urged price increases and the relaxation of gold and other restraints on the Federal Reserve, blocked by political leaders until President Franklin Roosevelt's inflation policy, including the gold devaluation of the dollar, began in March 1933.

Returning to the nineteenth century in the United States, the uneven resumption of the gold standard after the inflation that came with the War of 1812 had much in common with the contemporary U.K. Arguments for and against restraint and resumption were the same, and the mobilization of political support for monetary orthodoxy took time. Furthermore, those eventually in charge of resumption, including Prime Minister Lord Liverpool and Member of Parliament and economist David Ricardo in the U.K., and Treasury Secretary William Crawford in the U.S.A., knew what they were doing. They understood their monetary environment and the probable consequences of their actions.

The administrators of the lengthy post-Civil War resumption also understood the economic effects of monetary policies but were responsible to the electorate. The American Congress took an explicit role in resumption, freer than on other occasions because of the absence of an official central bank. The money markets, especially New York, were the center of the distribution of the nation's financial resources, and Congress, especially the House of Representatives, paid close attention to banking and finance.

Sound-money economists and officials, including the Secretary of the Treasury, wanted a quick resumption, but the vocal majority who feared its deflationary implications resisted forced gold increases in the dollar until finally, after 13 years, the economy and demand for money had grown into the existing money supply.

The United States had no official national or central bank between 1833, when President Andrew Jackson ordered the withdrawal of federal deposits from the Bank of the United States, and the Federal Reserve System established in 1913. American money and prices would thereafter be determined not by the gold standard and/or Congress working with the money-center banks, but by a presidentially appointed Federal Reserve Board in Washington, D.C. The Federal Reserve Act directed the continuation of the gold standard but gave the System unlimited power over money and made it subservient to the Executive.

After World War II, the Bank of England was assigned to suppress private borrowing in favor of nationalized industries and the value of the pound. The Federal Reserve adopted a stable-price stance while yielding to government pressures for finance and a 60 percent increase in prices between 1950 and 1970, followed by a more-than-doubling over the next ten years.

The Great Inflation of the 1970s made inflation a significant political issue, reinforced by the end of the Cold War and the realization (if only temporary) that easy money is not economically beneficial. However, the Great Moderation between the mid-1980s and early 2000s made possible by low inflation was ended by the Great Recession of 2006–09 caused by the collapse of the government-subsidized housing bubble and the Treasury–Federal Reserve panic response.

Practice has changed less than theory. Keynesian influences on post-World War II American fiscal and monetary policies have been exaggerated. Whether because of ideology, inattention, or sluggishness, government budgets have seldom been used to moderate fluctuations in economic activity, while monetary expansions have continued to be concessions to wartime or politically inspired government deficits.

The superior attention to the politically advantaged during the Great Recession, which was at least as pronounced as during the Great Depression, was particularly embarrassing, demanding more than the usual apologies, claiming that Wall Street's bail-out was for the benefit of Main Street. In summary, changes in finance and monetary policy have been more technical than fundamental. Monetary policy theories have undergone near constant change, but there has been little change in the practice of monetary policy. It has consistently been determined by interests, governments' in the forefront, and then property.

Monetary authorities whose interests have overlapped the public's, such as the pre-1914 Bank of England and the U.S. Independent Treasury, have adapted to those interests. The political remoteness of the Federal Reserve which was written into its founding, on the other hand, has continued, and those believing in its advertised goal of stability have blamed perceived errors either on inconstant discretions or faulty rules of behavior.

The Fed has often stated fairly explicit rules, such as the reserve positions of money-market banks (the Strong rule) before 1933, leaning against the wind between 1951 and 1970 (Martin) and the dual (inflation-output) mandate of the 1970s. Only the single low-inflation goal during the Great Moderation deserves high marks, although Martin also did well considering the political pressures with which he had to deal.

The unequalled American price stability of the 1920s was coincident with balanced budgets, the low (by later standards) but continuous inflation of 1951–70 with small but repeated budget deficits, and the larger inflation of the 1970s accompanied larger budget deficits. The return to low inflation in the 1990s, with budget surpluses, followed the end of the Cold War.

Some of the more famous perceived failures (if that is what they were) of rules have been explained within the frameworks of those rules. For example, the Fed's confusion of low interest rates and little commercial bank borrowing from the Fed with expansive monetary policy during the Great Depression should have been corrected, one might have thought, by observations of deflation and unemployment.

Similarly with the stagflation of the 1970s. Monetary "policy during the 1970s was … a systematic, activist, forward-looking approach such as is often identified with good policy advice in theoretical and econometric policy evaluation research," Anthanasios Orphanides (2002) wrote. "This points to the unpleasant possibility that the policy errors of the 1970s occurred despite the use of a seemingly desirable policy approach."

One might have thought at the time, again, that a look at the data – inflation near 10 percent and unemployment 8 percent – would have suggested that something was wrong. The eventual correction came not from the Fed, however, or even from the economics profession, but from the public through the political process. It seems to take a lot of inflation to overcome (or modify) the remote and interest-driven behavior of the monetary authority, as we have seen in 1951, 1979, and 2021. Otherwise, inflation has been continuous and almost unnoticed, certainly unaddressed.

President Jimmy Carter (1977–81) was forced to recognize inflation as a significant problem, his "inflation czar" (Alfred Kahn) became a leading administration spokesman, and he appointed a tight-money figure (Paul Volcker) with freedom to act to the Fed's chairmanship – although inflation was not brought down to acceptable levels until 1983, too late to help Carter.

These events bear similarities to the Great Depression, which was probably ended in the U.S.A. by a reform administration elected to replace one determined to maintain historical relations (Hoover's subsidies to particular firms were no more helpful than those of Bernanke and Paulson during the Great Recession).

The failures to adjust rules which are obviously mistaken from plausible public welfare standpoints is due to the precedence of more important objectives, such as the needs of Government finance and the politically powerful, as well as policymakers' emotional and informational distances from the public.

Adam Smith's thesis that the public interest is best served by individuals pursuing their own interests, which requires the information most, or even uniquely, available to those affected by policies, is a necessary as well as a sufficient condition for their true optimality.

References

PRIMARY SOURCES

United Kingdom

Bank of England. 2013. Governors of the Bank of England. https://www.bankofengland.co.uk/about/people/governors.

British Parliamentary Papers [BPP]. 1969. Irish University Press.

British Parliamentary Papers [BPP]. 1801–99. Irish University Press. https://www.crl.edu/irish-university-press-series-british-parliamentary-papers.

Callaghan, James. 1976. *Leader's Speech*, Blackpool. http://www.britishpoliticalspeech.org/speech-archive.htm?speech=174.

House of Commons (HC). 1803–. *Parliamentary Debates*. T.C. Hansard. https://hansard.parliament.uk/.

House of Commons [HC]. 1813. *Parliamentary History of England from the Earliest Period to the Year 1803*. T.C. Hansard.

House of Commons [HC]. 1819. *Second Report from the Secret Committee of the Bank Resuming Cash Payments*. BPP, Monetary Policy, General 1.

House of Commons [HC]. 1832. *Committee on the Bank Charter. Minutes of Evidence*. BPP, Monetary Policy, General 4 [available in T.E. Gregory. 1929. *Select Statutes, Documents & Reports Relating to British Banking, 1832–1928*. Oxford University Press].

House of Commons [HC]. 1840. *Select Committee on Banks of Issue* [available in T.E. Gregory. 1929. *Select Statutes, Documents & Reports Relating to British Banking, 1832–1928*. Oxford University Press].

House of Commons [HC]. 1840, 1841. *Select Committees on Banks of Issue*. BPP, Monetary Policy, General 5–6.

House of Commons [HC]. 1841. *Report from the Select Committee on Banks of Issue*. Q1362.

House of Commons [HC]. 1848. *First Report from the Secret Committee on Commercial Distress*. BPP, Monetary Policy, Commercial Distress 1–2 [available in T.E. Gregory. 1929. *Select Statutes, Documents & Reports Relating to British Banking, 1832–1928*. Oxford University Press].

House of Lords. 1848. *Report from the Secret Committee to Inquire into the Causes of the Distress Which Has for Some Time Prevailed among the Commercial Classes, and How Far it Has Been Affected by the Laws for Regulating the Issue of Bank Notes Payable on Demand*, July 29.

Montagu, Charles (Lord Halifax). 1696. "Exchequer bills," MS Memorandum 65, Goldsmith Library, University of London [available in B.L. Anderson and P.L. Cottrell. 1974. *Money and Banking in England: The Development of the Banking System, 1694–1914*. David & Charles].

Oxford Dictionary of National Biography [ODNB]. 2004. Oxford University Press. https://www.oxforddnb.com.

United States

Annals of Congress. https://memory.loc.gov/ammem/amlaw/lwac.html.
Federal Reserve. 1926. *Governors Conference*, March.
Federal Reserve Board. 1943. *Banking and Monetary Statistics 1914–41.*
Federal Reserve Board. 1959. *All-Bank Statistics, 1896–1955.*
Federal Reserve Board. 1975. *Banking and Monetary Statistics, 1941–70.*
Federal Reserve Board. 1977. *Industrial Production.*
Federal Reserve Board. 2020. *Federal Reserve Bulletin.*
Library of Congress Digital Collections. Nelson W. Aldrich Papers.
United States Census Bureau. 1975. *Historical Statistics of the U.S.*
U.S. Comptroller of the Currency. *Annual Reports*. Washington, D.C.
U.S. Congress. 1922. *Credit.* Report of the Joint Commission for Agricultural Inquiry, Part II. 67th Congress, 1st session.
U.S. Congress. 1927. *Stabilization.* Hearings before the House Committee on Banking and Currency. 69th Congress, 1st session.
U.S. Congress. 1932. *Stabilization of Commodity Prices.* Hearings before the Subcommittee of the House Committee on Banking and Currency (Goldsborough Committee) on H.R. 10517. For *Increasing and Stabilizing the Price Level and for Other Purposes*, 72nd Congress, 1st session.
U.S. Congress. 1969. *The 1969 Economic Report of the President.* Hearings, Joint Economic Committee. 91st Congress, 1st session.
U.S. Congress. 1991. *Hearings, Implications of the Too Big to Fail Policy.* House Subcommittee on Economic Stabilization of the Committee on Banking, Finance and Urban Affairs, 102nd Congress, 1st session.
U.S. Congress. 2008. *U.S. Financial Markets and the Sale of Bear Stearns.* Hearings, Senate Committee on Banking, Housing, and Urban Affairs, 112th Congress, 2nd session.
U.S. Treasury. 1820. *Report on Currency* (Sec. Wm. Crawford), for the House of Representatives, February 24.

SECONDARY SOURCES

Ackley, Gardner. 1971. "Stemming world inflation," *Atlantic Papers*, 2.
Acres, Marston. 1931. *The Bank of England from Within, 1694–1900.* Oxford University Press.
Acworth, A.W. 1925. *Financial Reconstruction in England, 1815–22.* P.S. King & Son.
Aldrich, Nelson W. [1910] 2009. *An Address before the Economics Club of New York on the Work of the National Monetary Commission.* Published by the NMC in 1910.
Alesina, Alberto F. and Andrea Stella. 2011. "The politics of monetary policy," in Benjamin M. Friedman and Michael Woodford, eds., *Handbook of Monetary Policy*, vol. 3B. Elsevier.
Allison, John A. 2013. *The Financial Crisis and the Free Market Cure.* McGraw-Hill.
Anderson, B.L. and P.L. Cottrell. 1974. *Money and Banking in England: The Development of the Banking System, 1694–1914.* David & Charles.

Andreades, A. 1924. *History of the Bank of England, 1640–1903*, 2nd edn., trans. Christabel Meredith. Frank Cass.

Andrew, A. Piatt. 1908. "Substitutes for cash in the panic of 1907," *Quarterly Journal of Economics*, 22(4): 497–516.

Angelides, Phil [chairman]. 2011. *Report on the Causes of the Financial and Economic Crisis in the United States*, Financial Crisis Inquiry Commission, pursuant to public law 111–21, USGPO.

Antoniades, Adonis. 2015. "Commercial bank failures during the Great Recession: the real (estate) story," European Central Bank Working Paper no. 1779.

Armantier, O., S. Kreiger and J. McAndrews. 2008. "The Federal Reserve's Term Auction Facility," Federal Reserve Bank of New York *Current Issues*, 14(5). https://www.newyorkfed.org/medialibrary/media/research/current_issues/ci14-5.pdf.

Arpac, Ozlem and Graham Bird. 2009. "Turkey and the IMF: a case study in the political economy of policy implementation," *Review of International Organization*, 4(2): 135–57.

Ashcraft, Adam B. 2006. "New evidence on the lending channel," *Journal of Money, Credit and Banking*, 38(3): 751–75.

Ashworth, William. 1960. *An Economic History of England, 1870–1939.* Methuen.

Ashton, T.S. 1948. *The Industrial Revolution, 1760–1830.* Oxford University Press.

Attwood, Thomas. 1817. *Prosperity restored; or, Reflections on the Cause of the Public Distresses, and on the Only Means of Relieving Them.* Baldwin, Cradock and Joy.

Attwood, Thomas. 1828. "Famine," *The Globe*, June 11, 1828. [Reprinted in Attwood, 1832, *The Scotch Banker*, 2nd edn., James Ridgway; Forrest H. Capie, 1993, *History of Banking*, Pickering.]

Ayotte, Kenneth and David A. Skeel, Jr. 2010. "Bankruptcy or bailouts," *Journal of Corporate Law*, 35(3): 469–98.

Bacevich, Andrew J. 2016a. *America's War for the Greater Middle East*. Random House.

Bacevich, Andrew J. 2016b. "Endless war in the Middle East," *Cato Letter*, 14(3), 1–6.

Bacevich, Andrew J. 2018. "How to challenge the elite consensus for endless war," *Nation*, July 16.

Bacevich, Andrew J. 2019. "Why those endless wars must never end," *TomDispatch*, October 31.

Bagehot, Walter. 1872. *The English Constitution*, 2nd edn. H.S. King.

Bagehot, Walter. 1873. *Lombard Street.* H. S. King. [Reprinted 1920, E.P. Dutton].

Banik, Dan. 2007. Starvation and India's Democracy. Routledge.

Baring, Francis. [1797] 2015. *Observations on the Establishment of the Bank of England and on the Paper Circulation of the Country.* Minerva Press. [Reprinted 1967 with *Further Observations*, Augustus M. Kelley.]

Baum, L. Frank. 1900. *The Wonderful Wizard of Oz.* Geo. M. Hill.

Beckett, J.C. 1969. *The Making of Modern Ireland, 1603–1923.* Faber and Faber.

Ben-Ishai, Stephanie and Stephen J. Lubben. 2011. "A comparative study of bankruptcy as bailout," *Brooklyn Journal of Corporate, Financial, and Commercial Law*, 6(1). https://brooklynworks.brooklaw.edu/bjcfcl/vol6/iss1/3.

Benston, George J. and George G. Kaufman. 1986. "Risks and failures in banking," Federal Reserve Bank of Chicago Memorandum.

Bernanke, Ben. 2002. *Remarks* at the Conference to Honor Milton Friedman at the University of Chicago, November 8. Federal Reserve Board.

Bernanke, Ben. 2008. "Opening remarks," Maintaining Stability in a Changing Financial System. Federal Reserve Bank of Kansas City. https://www.kansascityfed.org/documents/3159/2008-Bernanke031209.pdf.

Bernanke, Ben. 2015. *The Courage to Act: A Memoir of a Crisis and its Aftermath.* W.W. Norton.

Bernstein, George L. 1995. "Liberals, the Irish Famine and the Role of the State," *Irish Historical Studies,* 29(116): 513–36.

Berrospide, Jose M. and Rochelle M. Edge. 2010. "The effects of bank capital on lending: what do we know and what does it mean," Federal Reserve Board, working paper, August 17.

Best, Gary D. 1972. "Financing a foreign war: Jacob H. Schiff and Japan, 1904–05," *American Jewish Historical Quarterly,* 61: 313–24.

Beveridge, William. 1944. *Full Employment in a Free Society.* Allen & Unwin.

Bew, John. 2011. *Castlereagh.* Quercus Publishing.

Birkenhead, Earl of. 1961. *The Professor and the Prime Minister.* Houghton.

Blaine, James G. 1886. *Twenty Years of Congress.* Henry Bill.

Blinder, Alan S. 1979. *Economic Policy and the Great Stagflation.* Academic Press.

Bloomfield, Arthur. 1959. *Monetary Policy under the International Gold Standard, 1880–1914.* Federal Reserve Bank of New York.

Bloomfield, Arthur. 1963. *Short-term Capital Movements Under the pre-1914 Gold Standard.* Princeton: Princeton University, Department of Economics and Sociology, International Finance Section.

Bolles, A.S. 1894. *The Financial History of the United States,* 4th edn. D. Appleton [Reprinted 1969, A.M. Kelley.]

Bordo, Michael D. and Hugh Rockoff. 1996. "The gold standard as a Good Housekeeping Seal of Approval," *Journal of Economic History,* 56(2): 389–428.

Bordo, Michael D. and Eugene N. White. 1991. "A tale of two currencies: British and French finance during the Napoleonic Wars," *Journal of Economic History,* 51(2): 303–16.

Bordo, Michael D., Angela Redish and Hugh Rockoff. 2015. "Why didn't Canada have a banking crisis in 2008 (or 1930, or 1907, or …)?" *Economic History Review,* 68(1): 218–43.

Borger, Julian. 2019. "Masters of war: architects of modern conflicts say cheese for the camera," *The Guardian,* October 23.

Bourne, Edward G. 1885. *The History of the Surplus Revenue of 1837.* G.P. Putnam's Sons.

Boyle, Andrew. 1967. *Montagu Norman.* Cassell.

Brand, Donald. 2016. "Populism is Congress's next big threat," *Fortune,* November 9. https://fortune.com/2016/11/09/election-2016-populism-congress-donald-trump/.

Bremner, Robert P. 2004. *Chairman of the Fed: William McChesney Martin, Jr., and the Creation of the Modern American Financial System.* Yale University Press.

Brittan, Samuel. 1969. *Steering the Economy.* Martin Secker & Warburg.

Brock, W.R. 1967. *Lord Liverpool and Liberal Toryism, 1820–1827.* Archon.

Brooks, David. 2018. "The strange failure of the educated elite," *New York Times,* May 28.

Brown, George A. 1971. *In My Way.* St. Martin's Press.

Browning, Andrew H. 2019. *The Panic of 1819.* University of Missouri Press.

Browning, Peter. 1986. *The Treasury and Economic Policy, 1964–85.* Longman.

Brunner, Karl and Allan H. Meltzer. 1964. *The Federal Reserve's Attachment to the Free Reserves Concept*, Subcommittee on Domestic Finance, Committee on Banking and Currency, House of Representatives, 88th Congress, 2nd session.

Bryan, William Jennings. 1896. *The First Battle: A Story of the Campaign of 1896.* W.B. Conkey.

Bryant, Arthur. 1950. *The Age of Elegance, 1812–22*. Harper and Brothers.

Brzoza-Brzezina, Michal, Marcin Kolasa and Krzysztof Makarski. 2021. *Monetary Policy and Covid-10*, IMF working paper 21274.

Buchanan, James M. and Richard E. Wagner. 1977. *Democracy in Deficit: The Political Legacy of Lord Keynes*, Academic Press.

Bullard, James. 2020. "Expected U.S. macroeconomic performance during the Pandemic Adjustment Period," Federal Reserve Bank of St. Louis, *Economy Blog*, March 22. https://www.stlouisfed.org/on-the-economy/2020/march/bullard -expected-us-macroeconomic-performance-pandemic-adjustment-period.

Bullock, Alan. 1960. *The Life and Times of Ernest Bevin, Vol. I, Trade Union Leader, 1881–1940.* William Heinemann.

Burnet, G. 1724–34. *History of His Own Time*. J. Hyde, R. Gunne, R. Owen, and E. Dobson.

Callaghan, James. 1987. *Time and Chance*. Collins.

Calomiris, Charles W. and Gary Gorton. 1991. "The origins of banking panics: models facts and bank regulation," in R. Glenn Hubbard, ed., *Financial Markets and Financial Crises*, pp. 109–74. University of Chicago Press.

Calomiris, Charles W., Gary Gorton and Stephen Haber. 2014. *Fragile by Design: The Political Origins of Banking Crises*. Princeton University Press.

Cannan, Edwin. 1919. *The Paper Pound of 1797–1821: A Reprint of the Bullion Report with an Introduction.* P.S. King & Son.

Capie, Forrest H. 1993. *History of Banking*. Pickering.

Capie, Forrest H. and Forrest Webber. 1985. *A Monetary History of the United Kingdom, 1870–1982, Vol. 1, Data.* George Allen and Unwin.

Carney, Brian M. 2008. "Bernanke is fighting the last war: interview with Anna Schwartz," *Wall Street Journal*, October 18.

Carosso, Vincent P. and Richard Sylla. 1991. "U.S. banks in international finance," in Rondo Cameron and V. Borrykin, eds., *International Banking, 1870–1914*, pp. 48–71. Oxford University Press.

Cassel, Gustav. 1922. *Money and Foreign Exchange after 1914*. Macmillan.

Catterall, Ralph C.H. 1902. *The Second Bank of the United States.* University of Chicago Press.

CBS News. 2008. Bernanke defends Bear Stearns bailout. April 3. https://www .cbsnews.com/news/bernanke-defends-bear-stearns-bailout/.

Chandler, Lester V. 1958. *Benjamin Strong, Central Banker*. Brookings Institution.

Chandos, Lord (Oliver Lyttleton) 1967. *Memoirs.* Bodley Head.

Chapman, Richard A. 1968. *Decision Making: A Case Study of the Decision to Raise the Bank Rate in September 1957*. Routledge & Kegan Paul.

Churchill, Winston S. 1956. *History of the English-Speaking Peoples*. Cassell & Co.

Clapham, John H. 1926. *An Economic History of Modern Britain*. Cambridge University Press.

Clapham, John H. 1944. *The Bank of England*. Cambridge University Press.

Clarke, Stephen V.O. 1967. *Central Bank Cooperation, 1924–31.* Federal Reserve Bank of New York.

Clausewitz, Carl Von. 1832. *On War*, trans. Howard Michael and Peter Paret, 1976–84. Princeton University Press.

Clay, Henry. 1957. *Lord Norman*. Macmillan.

Cochrane, John H. 2020. "Bailouts v. bankruptcy," *The Grumpy Economist*, blog, March 27. https://johnhcochrane.blogspot.com/2020/03/bailouts-v-bankruptcy.html.

Coghlan, Erin. 2018. "What really caused the Great Recession?" *Policy Review* for University of California, Institute for Research on Labor and Employment, WP 133–12.

Connell, K.H. 1965. "Land and population of Ireland, 1780–1845," in D.V. Glass and D.E.C. Eversley, eds., *Population in History*. Aldine.

Coogan, Tim Pat. 2012. *The Famine Plot: England's Role in Ireland's Greatest Tragedy*. Palgrave Macmillan.

Cook, Chris and John Stevenson. 2014. *A History of British Elections since 1689*. Routledge.

Cook, Nancy and Katia Dmitrieva. 2021. "Top Biden economist: 'I really do believe' inflation will ease,'" *Bloomberg*, December 16. https://www.bloomberg.com/news/articles/2021-12-16/top-biden-economist-i-really-do-believe-inflation-will-ease.

Cookson, J.E. 1975. *Lord Liverpool's Administration: The Crucial Years, 1815–1822*. Anchor Books.

Cottrell, Allin F., Michael S. Lawlor and John H. Wood. 1995. "What are the connections between deposit insurance and bank failures"? in Allin F. Cottrell, Michael S. Lawlor and John H. Wood, eds., *The Causes and Costs of Depository Institution Failures*, pp. 163–98. Kluwer Academic Publishers.

Cox, Christopher. 2008. "Letter to Basel Committee in support of new guidance on liquidity management," March 20. https://www.sec.gov/news/press/2008/2008-48.htm.

Crawford, Neta C. 2019. *United States Budgetary Costs and Obligations of Post-9/11 Wars through FY2020: $6.4 Trillion*. Watson Institute of International and Public Affairs.

Croker, John W. 1884. *Correspondence and Diaries*, ed. L.J. Jennings. Charles Scribner's Sons.

Crossman, Richard H.S. 1975. *Diaries of a Cabinet Minister*. Hamish Hamilton and Jonathan Cape.

Crouzet, Françious. 1982. *The Victorian Era*. Columbia University Press.

Dangerfield, George. 1952. *The Era of Good Feelings*. New York: Harcourt, Brace and World.

Darling, Alistair. 2012. *Back from the Brink: 1000 Days at Number 11*. Atlantic.

Davis, Joseph and Marc D. Weidenmier. 2017. "America's first great moderation," *Journal of Economic History*, 77(4): 1116–43.

Day, A.C.L. 1964. "The myth of four per cent," Westminster Bank Review, November: 2–13.

Demsetz, Rebecca S., Marc R. Saidenberg and Philip E. Strahan. 1996. "Banks with something to lose: the disciplinary role of franchise," Federal Reserve Bank of New York Economic Policy Review. https://www.newyorkfed.org/medialibrary/media/research/epr/96v02n2/9610dems.pdf.

DeVroey, Michel and Lugo Pensieroso. 2006. "Real business cycle theory and the Great Depression," *Contributions to Macroeconomics*, January.

Dewey, Davis R. 1922. *Financial History of the United States*, 8th ed. Longmans, Green.

Dewey, Davis R. and Martin Shugrue. 1922. *Banking and Credit*. Ronald Press.

Disraeli, Benjamin. 1832. *Contarini Fleming*. John Murray.

Disraeli, Benjamin. 1844. *Coningsby* [Reprinted 1911, J.M. Dent & Sons (Everyman).]

Dornbusch, Rudiger and Jacob A. Frenkel. 1984. "The gold standard and the Bank of England in the crisis of 1847," in Michael D. Bordo and Anna J. Schwartz, eds., *A Retrospective on the Classical Gold Standard, 1821–1931*, pp. 233–75. University of Chicago Press.

Douglas, Roy. 1999. *Taxation in Britain since 1660*. Macmillan.

Dow, J.C.R. 1964. *The Management of the British Economy, 1945–60*. Cambridge University Press.

Dull, Jonathan R. 2005. *The French Navy and the Seven Years' War*. University of Nebraska Press.

Eggertsson, Gauti B. 2008. "Great expectations and the end of the depression," *American Economic Review*, 98(4): 1476–516.

Eichengreen, Barry. 1985. "Introduction," in Barry Eichengren and Marc Flandreau, eds., *The Gold Standard in Theory and History*, 2nd edn., pp. 1–30. Methuen.

Eichengreen, Barry. 1992. *Golden Fetters*. Oxford University Press.

Eichengreen, Barry and Jeffrey Sachs. 1985. "Exchange rates and economic recovery in the 1930s," *Journal of Economic History*, 45(4): 925–46.

Einzig, Paul. 1932. *Montagu Norman*. Kegan Paul, Trench, Trubner.

Eisner, Robert. 1969. "Fiscal and monetary policy reconsidered," *American Economic Review*, 59(5): 897–905.

Elliott, John E. 1994. "Joseph A. Schumpeter and the theory of democracy," *Review of Social Economy*, 52(4): 280–300.

Epstein, Joseph. 2015. "How I learned to love the draft," *The Atlantic*. https://www.theatlantic.com/magazine/archive/2015/01/how-i-learned-to-love-the-draft/383500/.

Falkender, Lady (Marcia Williams). 1975. *Inside No. 10*. Weidenfeld and Nicolson.

Fallon, Ivan. 2015. *Black Horse Ride: The Inside Story of Lloyds and the Banking Crisis*. Robson.

Fallows, James. 2015. "The tragedy of American foreign policy," *The Atlantic*, January/February.

Fay, Stephen. 1997. *The Collapse of Barings*. W.W. Norton.

Feavearyear, A.E. 1931. *The Pound Sterling*. Clarendon Press.

Federal Deposit Insurance Corporation. 1998. *A Brief History of Deposit Insurance in the U.S.* https://www.fdic.gov/bank/historical/brief/brhist.pdf.

Feinstein, C.H. 1972. *The Development of American Commercial Banking: Statistical Tables of National Income, Expenditure and Output of the U.K., 1855–1965*. Cambridge University Press.

Fenstermaker, Joseph Van. 1965. *The Development of American Commercial Banking, 1782–1837*. Bureau of Economics and Business Research, Kent State University.

Ferguson, Niall. 2005. *Colossus: The Rise and Fall of the American Empire*. Penguin.

Fforde, J.S. 1992. *The Bank of England and Public Policy, 1941–58*. Cambridge University Press.

Fisher, Irving. 1911. *The Purchasing Power of Money*. Macmillan.

Fisher, Irving. 1920. *Stabilizing the Dollar*. Macmillan.

Fleming, Michael J. and Asani Sarkar. 2014. "The failure resolution of Lehman Brothers," Federal Reserve Bank of New York *Economic Policy Review*, December. https://www.newyorkfed.org/research/epr/2014/1412flem.html.

Fligstein, N. and A. Goldstein. 2014. "The transformation of mortgage finance and the industrial roots of the mortgage meltdown," University of California, Institute for Research on Labor and Employment, working paper 133–12.

Friedman, Milton. 1960. *A Program for Monetary Stability*. Fordham University Press.

Friedman, Milton and Anna J. Schwartz. 1963. *A Monetary History of the United States, 1867–1960*. Princeton University Press.

Friedman, Milton and Anna J. Schwartz. 1970. *Monetary Statistics of the United States: Estimates, Sources, Methods*. National Bureau of Economic Research. https://www.nber.org/books-and-chapters/monetary-statistics-united-states-estimates-sources-methods.

Frontline. 2009. "Inside the meltdown – you have a weekend to save yourself." https://www.pbs.org/wgbh/pages/frontline/meltdown/etc/script.html.

Gallatin Albert. 1831. *Considerations on the Currency and Banking System of the United States*. Carey and Lea.

Gallatin Albert. 1841. *Suggestions on the Banks and Currency of the Several United States*. Wiley and Putnam. [Reprinted 1879 in Henry Adams, ed. *Writings*; Reprinted 1960, Antiquarian Press.]

Gardner, Bruce L. 2002. *American Agriculture in the 20th Century*. Harvard University Press.

Gardner, Richard N. 1956. *Sterling-Dollar Diplomacy*. Oxford University Press.

Gash, Norman. 1972. *The Life of Sir Robert Peel after 1830*. Longman.

Gash, Norman. 1977. "From the origins to Sir Robert Peel," in Lord Butler, ed., *The Conservatives*. George Allen & Unwin.

Gibbons-Neff, Thomas. 2019. "The American Intervention against ISIS is Just Another Chapter of an Endless War," *New York Times*, March 15.

Gilbart, J.W. 1856. *A Practical Treatise on Banking*, 6th edn. Longman, Brown, Green, and Longmans.

Gilkes, Patrick. 1975. *The Dying Lion: Feudalism and Modernization in Ethiopia*. Julian Friedman.

Glass, Carter. 1927. *An Adventure in Constructive Finance*. Doubleday, Page.

Glock, Judge. 2021. *The Dead Pledge: The Origins of the Mortgage Market and Federal Bailouts, 1913–39*. Columbia University Press.

Goldenweiser, E.A. 1925. *Federal Reserve System in Operation*. McGraw-Hill.

Goodfriend, Marvin and Jeffrey M. Lacker. 1999. "Limited commitment and central bank lending," Federal Reserve Bank of Richmond, *Economic Quarterly*. https://www.richmondfed.org/publications/research/economic_quarterly/1999/fall/lackergoodfriend.

Gorton, Gary. 1988. "Banking panics and business cycles," *Oxford Economic Papers*, 40(4): 751–81.

Gouge, William M. 1833. *A Short History of Paper Money and Banking in the United States*. Grigg & Elliott. [Reprinted 1968, Augustus M. Kelley.]

Gregory, T.E. 1929. *Select Statutes, Documents & Reports Relating to British Banking, 1832–1928*. Oxford University Press.

Grellier, J.J. 1810. *The History of the National Debt, from the Revolution in 1688 to the Beginning of the Year 1800*. J. Richardson.

Grigg, P.J. 1948. *Prejudice and Judgment*. Jonathan Cape.

Grossman, Richard S. 1994. "The shoe that didn't drop: explaining bank stability during the Great Depression," *Journal of Economic History*, 54(3): 654–82.

Guida, Victoria. 2020. "Powell's pandemic response gets him bipartisan praise – and a possible second term," *Politico*. https://www.politico.com/news/2020/09/21/fed-powell-trump-another-term-419679.

Halberstam, David. 1972. *The Best and the Brightest*. Random House.

Hall, Robert L. 1991. *Diaries, 1947–53*, ed. Alec Cairncross. Unwin Hyman.

Hall, Robert L. and C.J. Hitch. 1939. "Price theory and business behavior," *Oxford Economic Papers*, May. [Reprinted 1951 in Thomas Wilson and P.W.S. Andrews, eds., *Oxford Studies in the Price Mechanism*. Clarendon Press.]

Hammond, W. Bray. 1957. *Banks and Politics in America from the Revolution to the Civil War*. Princeton University Press.

Harding, W.P.G. 1925. *The Formative Period of the Federal Reserve System*. Houghton Mifflin.

Hargrove, Edwin C. and Samuel A. Morley. 1984. *The President and the Council of Economic Advisors: Interviews with CEA Chairmen*. Westview Press.

Hawtrey, R.G. 1962. *A Century of Bank Rate*, 2nd edn. Frank Cass & Co.

Hays, Tom. 2008. "Ex-Bear Stearns managers arrested at their homes," https://eu.pjstar.com/story/news/2008/06/19/ex-bear-stearns-managers-arrested/42343272007/.

Healey, Denis. 1989. *The Time of My Life*. Michael Joseph.

Henderson, David. 2008. "Are we ailing from too much regulation?" *Cato Policy Report*. https://www.cato.org/sites/cato.org/files/serials/files/policy-report/2008/11/cpr30n6-1.pdf.

Hennessy, Elizabeth. 1995. "The governors, directors and management of the Bank of England," in Richard Roberts and David Kynaston, eds., *The Bank of England: Money, Power and Influence, 1694–1994*. Clarendon Press.

Hepburn, A. Barton. 1903. *History of Coinage and Currency in the United States and the Perennial Contest for Sound Money*. Macmillan.

Hetzel, Robert L. 2012. *The Great Recession: Market Failure or Policy Failure?* Cambridge University Press.

Hill, Christopher. 1961. *The Century of Revolution, 1603–1714*. Thomas Nelson and Sons.

Hilton, Boyd. 1977. *Corn, Cash, Commerce: Tory Governments 1815–30*. Oxford University Press.

Hilton, Boyd. 2006. *A Mad, Bad, and Dangerous People? England, 1783–1846*. Clarendon Press.

Hirsch, Fred. 1968. "Influences on gold production," *IMF Staff Papers*. https://www.elibrary.imf.org/view/journals/024/1968/003/article-A002-en.xml.

Hirsch, Fred. 1977. "The Bagehot problem," *Manchester School of Economic and Social Studies*, 45(3): 241–57.

Hoppit, Julian. 1986. "Financial crises in eighteenth-century England," *Economic History Review*, 39(1): 39–58.

Hori, M. 1996. "New evidence on the causes and propagation of the Great Depression," PhD dissertation, University of California, Berkeley.

Horsefield, J. Keith. 1960. *British Monetary Experiments, 1650–1710*. Harvard University Press.

Howson, Susan. 1973. "'A Dear Money Man'? Keynes on monetary policy, 1920," *Economic Journal*, 83(330): 456–64.

Howson, Susan. 1975. *Domestic Monetary Management in Britain, 1919–38*. Cambridge University Press.

Howson, Susan. 1993. *British Monetary Policy, 1945–51*. Oxford University Press.

Humphrey, Thomas. 2010. "Lender of last resort: what it is, whence it came, and why the Fed isn't it," *Cato Journal*, 30(2): 333–64.

Hussman Funds. 2008. "Weekly market comment: why is Bear Stearns trading at $6 instead of $2?". https://www.hussmanfunds.com/wmc/wmc080324.htm.

Hutchison, T.W. 1968. *Economics and Economic Policy in Britain, 1946–66*. Routledge.

Irwin, Douglas A. 2012. "The French Gold Sink and the Great Depression of 1929–32," *Cato Papers on Public Policy*. https://www.cato.org/sites/cato.org/files/serials/files/cato-papers-public-policy/2013/6/cppp-2-1.pdf.

Isaac, W.M. 2010. *Senseless Panic: How Washington Failed America*. Wiley.

Jastram, Roy W. 1977. *The Golden Constant*. Wiley.

Jenkinson, Charles. 1805. *A Treatise on the Coins of the Realm*. Cadell and Davies.

Johnson, H. Clark. 1997. *Gold, France, and the Great Depression, 1919–32*. Yale University Press.

Johnson, Lyndon B. 1971. *The Vantage Point: Perspectives of the Presidency, 1963–69*. Holt, Rinehart and Winston.

Johnson, Paul. 1991. *The Birth of the Modern: World Society 1815–30*. HarperCollins.

Jones, A.H.M. 1974. *The Roman Economy*. Basil Blackwell.

Jones, Kit. 1994. *An Economist among Mandarins: A Biography of Robert Hall, 1901–88*. Cambridge University Press.

Joplin, Thomas. 1822. *An Essay on the General Principles and Present Practice of Banking*. Baldwin, Craddock, and Joy.

Kane, Thomas P. 1922. *The Romance and Tragedy of Banking: Problems and Incidents of Governmental Supervision of National Banks*. Bankers Publishing Co.

Kaufman, George G. 1990. "Are some banks too large to fail? Myth and reality," *Contemporary Policy Issues*, 8(4): 1–14.

Kaufman, George G. 1992. "Bank contagion: theory and evidence," Federal Reserve Bank of Chicago Working Paper 92–13, June. https://www.chicagofed.org/publications/working-papers/1992/1992-13.

Kaufman, George G. 2000. "Banking and currency crises and systemic risk: a taxonomy and review," *Financial Markets, Institutions, and Instruments*, 9(2): 69–131.

Kaufman, George G. 2007. "Deposit insurance," *Concise Encyclopedia of Economics*. Liberty Fund.

Keech, William R. 1996. *Economic Politics*. Cambridge University Press.

Keeley, Michael. 1990. "Deposit insurance, risk, and market power in banking." *American Economic Review*, 80(5): 1183–200.

Keneally, Thomas. 2011. *Three Famines: Starvation and Politics*. Public Affairs.

Kennedy, Liam. 2016. *Unhappy the Land: The Most Oppressed People Ever, the Irish?* Irish Academic Press.

Kennedy, Liam, Paul S. Ell, E.M. Crawford and L.A. Clarkson. 1999. *Mapping the Great Irish Famine*. Four Courts Press.

Kettl, Donald F. 1973. *Leadership at the Fed*. Yale University Press.

Keynes, J.M. 1971–89. *Collected Writings*, ed. D.E. Moggridge. Macmillan.

Keynes, J.M. 1923. *Tract on Monetary Reform*. Macmillan.

Keynes, J.M. 1925. "The economic consequences of Mr. Churchill," *Evening Standard*, July 22–25 (Writings, ix).

Keynes, J.M. 1930. *A Treatise on Money*, Vol. II. Macmillan.

Keynes, J.M. 1936. *The General Theory of Employment, Interest, and Money*. Macmillan.

Kindleberger, Charles P. 1973. *World in Depression, 1929–39*. University of California Press.

King, Mervyn. 2017. *The End of Alchemy*. W.W. Norton.

Kinsley, Michael. 2015. "Ben Bernanke's 'the courage to act,'" *New York Times*, October 8. https://www.nytimes.com/2015/10/25/books/review/ben-bernankes-the-courage-to-act.html.

Klamer, Arjo. 1984. *Conversations with Economists*. Rowman & Littlefield.

Koch, Adrienne and William Peden. 1944. *The Life and Selected Writings of Thomas Jefferson*. Modern Library.

Kolko, Gabriel. 1963. *The Triumph of Conservatism: A Reinterpretation of American History, 1900–1916*. Macmillan.

Konishi, Toru, Valerie A. Ramey and Clive W.J. Granger. 1993. "Stochastic trends and short-run relationships between financial variables and real activity," NBER Working Paper No. 4275, February. https://www.nber.org/papers/w4275.

Krooss, H.E. 1969. *Documentary History of Banking and Currency in the United States*. Chelsea House.

Kydland, Finn and Edward C. Prescott. 1977. "Rules rather than discretion: 'The inconsistency of optimal plans,'" *Journal of Political Economy*, 85(3): 473–92.

Kynaston, David. 1995. "The Bank and the Government," in Richard Roberts and David Kynaston, eds., *The Bank of England: Money, Power and Influence, 1694–1994*. Clarendon Press.

Lane, Frederic C. 1937. "Venetian bankers, 1496–1533: a study in the early stages of deposit banking," *Journal of Political Economy*, 45(2): 187–206.

Larson, Martin A., ed. 1981. *Jefferson, Magnificent Populist*. R.B. Luce.

Leffingwell, Russell C. 1921. "The discount policy of the Federal Reserve Banks: discussion," *American Economic Review*, 11: 30–36.

Levy, Peter B. 1996. "No new taxes," *Encyclopedia of the Reagan–Bush Years*. Greenwood Press.

Link, Arthur S. 1956. *Wilson: The New Freedom*. Princeton University Press.

Litton, Helen. 2006. *The Irish Famine: An Illustrated History*. Wolfhound Press.

Livingston, James. 1986. *Origins of the Federal Reserve System: Money, Class, and Corporate Capitalism, 1890–1913*. Cornell University Press.

Loyd, Samuel Jones. 1840. *Remarks on the Management of the Circulation, and on the Condition and Conduct of the Bank of England and of the Country Issuers during the Year 1839*. Pelham Richardson.

Loyd, Samuel Jones. 1844. *Thoughts on the Separation of the Departments of the Bank of England*. Pelham Richardson. [Reprinted 1993, Capie.]

Lucas, Robert E., Jr. 1987. *Models of Business Cycles*. Blackwell.

Macaulay, Thomas Babington. 1855. *The History of England from the Accession of James the Second*. Longman, Green, Longman, Roberts & Green.

Macey, Jonathan. 2008. "The government is contributing to the panic," *Wall Street Journal*, October 11. https://www.wsj.com/articles/SB122367942018324645.

Macey, Jonathan and Geoffrey P. Miller. 1992. "Double liability of bank shareholders: history and implications," *Wake Forest Law Review*, 27: 31–62.

Macroeconomic Advisors. 2008. Policy Focus. "Is monetary policy still working?", February 29.

Maisel, Sherman J. 1973. *Managing the Dollar*. W.W. Norton.

Malthus, Thomas R. 1808. "Spence on commerce," *Edinburgh Review*, 22: 429–48.

Markakis, John. 2011. *Ethiopia: The Last Two Frontiers*. James Currey.

Marshall, John. 1807. *The Life of George Washington*. C.P. Wayne. [Reprinted 1983, Chelsea House.]

Marston, Daniel. 2001. *The Seven Years' War*. Osprey.

Martynova, Natalya, Lev Ratnovski and Rasvan Vlahu. 2014. "Franchise value and risk-taking in modern banks," De Nederlandsche Bank Working Paper No. 430. https://www.dnb.nl/en/publications/publicatieoverzicht/research-publications/working-papers-2014/430-franchise-value-and-risk-taking-in-modern-banks/.

Massing, Michael. 2003. "Does democracy avert famine?" *New York Times*, March 1. https://www.nytimes.com/2003/03/01/arts/does-democracy-avert-famine.html.

Matusow, Allen J. 1998. *Nixon's Economy*. University Press of Kansas.

Mazumder, Sandeep and John H. Wood. 2021. "The cause of the Great Depression: the decision to resume the gold standard on prewar terms," *Independent Review*. https://www.independent.org/pdf/tir/tir_26_1_12_mazumder.pdf.

McCloskey, Deirdre. 2010. *Bourgeois Dignity: Why Economics Can't Explain the Modern World*. University of Chicago Press.

McCloskey, Deirdre and J. Richard Zecher. 1976. "How the gold standard worked, 1880–1913," in Jacob A. Frenkel and Harry G. Johnson, eds., *The Monetary Approach to the Balance of Payments*, ch. 16. University of Toronto Press.

McDonald, Lawrence G. and Patrick Robinson, 2009. *A Colossal Failure of Common Sense*. Crown Business.

McKinley, Vern. 2008. *Financing Failure*. Independent Institute.

McMahon, Patrice C. and Jon Western. 2009. "The death of Dayton: how to stop Bosnia from falling apart," *Foreign Affairs*, 88(5): 69–83.

McNamara, Robert S. 1995. *In Retrospect: The Tragedy and Lessons of Vietnam*. Times Books.

Meade James E. and P.W.S. Andrews. 1938. "The significance of the rate of interest." [Reprinted 1951 in Thomas Wilson and P.W.S. Andrews, *Oxford Studies in the Price Mechanism*. Clarendon Press.]

Meltzer, Allan H. 2003, 2009. *A History of the Federal Reserve*, 2 vols. University of Chicago Press. [Volume 1, 2003; Volume 2, 2009.]

Merry, Robert W. 2017. *President McKinley: Architect of the American Century*. Simon & Schuster.

Mikesell, Raymond F. 1954. *Foreign Exchange in the Postwar World*. Twentieth Century Fund.

Milesi-Ferreti, Gian M. 1995. "The disadvantage of tying their hands: on the political economy of planned economies," *Economic Journal*, 105(433): 1381–402.

Mill, J.S. [1848–71] 1909. *Principles of Political Economy with Some of Their Applications to Social Philosophy*, ed. W.J. Ashley. Longmans Green.

Miller, Marion M., ed. 1913. *Great Debates in American History*. Current Literature.

Milward, Alan S. 1992. *The European Rescue of the Nation State*. University of California Press.

Miron, Jeffrey A. 2009a. "In defense of doing nothing," *Cato's Letter*. https://www.cato.org/sites/cato.org/files/pubs/pdf/catosletterv7n2.pdf.

Miron, Jeffrey A. 2009b. "Bailout or bankruptcy," *Cato Journal*. https://www.cato.org/sites/cato.org/files/serials/files/cato-journal/2009/1/cj29n1-1.pdf.

Mishkin, Frederic S. 2006. *The Economics of Money, Banking, and Financial Markets*, 7th edn. Pearson.

Mishkin, Frederic S and Adam S. Posen. 1997. "Inflation targeting: lessons from four countries," Federal Reserve Bank of New York *Economic Policy Review*, August. https://www.nber.org/papers/w6126.

Mitchel, John. [1873] 2005. *The Last Conquest of Ireland (Perhaps)*. Lynch, Cole & Meehan [Reprinted 2005, Dublin University Press.]

Mitchell, B.R. 1962. *Abstract of British Historical Statistics*. Cambridge University Press.

Mitchell, Waldo F. 1925. *The Uses of Bank Funds*. University of Chicago Press.

Moggridge, D.E. 1969. *The Return to Gold, 1925*. Occasional Paper, University of Cambridge, Department of Applied Economics.

Moggridge, D.E. 1972. *British Monetary Policy, 1924–31: The Norman Conquest of $4.86*. Cambridge University Press.

Montagu, Charles (Lord Halifax). 1696. "Exchequer bills," MS Memorandum 65, Goldsmith' Library, reprinted in B.L. Anderson and P.L. Cottrell, 1974, *Money and Banking in England: The Development of the Banking System, 1694–1914*. David & Charles.

Mooney, Chase C. 1974. *William H. Crawford*. University Press of Kentucky.

Morawetz, Victor. 1909. *The Banking and Currency Problem in the United States*. North American Review Publishing Co.

Morley, John. 1903. *The Life of William Ewart Gladstone*. Macmillan.

Mukerjee, Madhusree. 2011. *Churchill's Secret War: The British Empire and the Ravaging of India during World War II*. Basic Books.

Mundell, Robert. 1993. "Debt and deficits in alternative macroeconomic models," in Mario Baldassarri, Robert Mundell and John McCallum, eds., *Debt, Deficit, and Economic Performance*, pp. 5–129. St. Martin's Press.

Nelson, Bill, Francisco Covas, Greg Baer and Jeremy Newall. 2021. "What does a bank's franchise value tell about its risk to the taxpayer?" *Bank Policy Institute*. https://bpi.com/what-does-a-banks-franchise-value-tell-us-about-its-risk-to-the -taxpayer/.

Nevin, Edward. 1955. *The Mechanism of Cheap Money: A Study of British Monetary Policy, 1931–39*. University of Wales Press.

Nicolson, Harold. 1946. *The Congress of Vienna: A Study in Allied Unity, 1812–22*. Harcourt, Brace and Co.

Nicolson, Harold. 1952. *King George V*. Constable.

Nixon, Richard M. 1962. *Six Crises*. Doubleday.

North, Douglass C. and Barry W. Weingast. 1989. "Constitutions and commitment: the evolution of institutions governing public choice in seventeenth-century England," *Journal of Economic History*, 49(4): 803–32.

O'Gorman, Frank. 1989. *Voters, Patrons, and Parties: The Unreformed Electoral System of Hanoverian England, 1734–1932*. Clarendon Press.

Ó Gráda, C. 1979. "The population of Ireland 1700–1900: a survey," *Annales de Démographie Historique Année*: 281–99. https://www.jstor.org/stable/44385954.

Ó Gráda, C. 1981. "Agricultural decline, 1860–1914," in Roderick Floud and Donald McCloskey, eds., *The Economic History of Britain since 1700*, Vol. 2. Cambridge University Press.

Ó Gráda, C. 1999. *Black '47 and Beyond: The Great Irish Famine in History, Economy, and Memory*. Princeton University Press.

Ogg, David. 1955. *England in the Reigns of James II and William III*. Clarendon Press.

Olsen, Henry. 2010. "Populism, American style," *National Affairs*. https://www .nationalaffairs.com/publications/detail/populism-american-style.

Orphanides, Anthanasios. 2002. "Monetary policy rules and the Great Inflation," *American Economic Review*, 92(2): 115–20.

Page, William. 1919. *Commerce and Industry: A Historical Review of the British Empire from the Peace of Paris in 1815 to the Declaration of War in 1914 Based on the Parliamentary Debates*. Constable.

Palgrave, R.H.I. 1903. *Bank Rate and the Money Market in England, France, Germany, Holland, and Belgium, 1844–1900*. John Murray.

Panić, M. 1993. *European Monetary Union: Lessons from the Classical Gold Standard*. Macmillan.

Parker, Charles S., ed. 1899. *Robert Peel from his Private Correspondence*, 2nd edn. John Murray.

Parker, Randall E. 2002. *Reflections on the Great Depression*. Edward Elgar Publishing.

Paulson, Henry M., Jr. 2010. *On the Brink*. Business Plus.

Peden, G.C. 1983. "Sir Richard Hopkins and the Keynesian revolution in employment policy, 1929–45," *Economic History Review*, 36: 281–96.

Peltzman, Sam. 1970. "Capital investment in commercial banking and its relationship to portfolio regulation," *Journal of Political Economy*, 78(1). https://www.journals .uchicago.edu/doi/abs/10.1086/259597.

Perkins, Bradford. 1964. *Castlereagh and Adams: England and the United States, 1812–1823*. University of California Press.

Petty, William. 1682. *Quantulumcunque Concerning Money*. [Reprinted 1963, Charles Hull, ed., *Economic Writings of William Petty*. A.M. Kelley.]

Polanyi, Karl. 1944. *The Great Transformation*. Farrar & Rinehart.

Pollack, Alex J. 2016. "'Commercial' bank is a misnomer: 'real estate' bank is more apt," *American Banker*. https://www.americanbanker.com/opinion/commercial -bank-is-misnomer-real-estate-bank-is-more-apt.

Pressnell, L.S. 1956. *Country Banking in the Industrial Revolution*. Clarendon Press.

Prest, John. 2009. "Sir Robert Peel, second baronet," *Oxford Dictionary of National Biography*. https://www.oxforddnb.com.

Radcliffe, Lord. 1959. *Report of the Committee on the Working of the Monetary System*. HMSO.

Redish, Angela. 2001. "Lender of last resort policies: from Bagehot to bailout," ms. University of British Columbia.

Reeves, Richard. 1993. *President Kennedy: Profile of Power*. Simon & Schuster.

Reichert, John and Jim Sheriff. 2017. "Weighing the benefits of a state charter," BankDirector.com. https://www.bankdirector.com/issues/weighing-benefits-state -charter/.

Reinhart, Carmen M. and Kenneth S. Rogoff. 2010. *This Time is Different: Eight Centuries of Financial Folly*. Princeton University Press.

Robinson, E.A.G. 1964. "The Times review of industry," *London and Cambridge Economic Bulletin*, June.

Rockoff, Hugh. 1986. "Walter Bagehot and the theory of central banking," in Forrest Capie and Geoffrey Wood, eds., *Financial Crises and the World Banking System*. Macmillan.

Rockoff, Hugh. 1990. "The *Wizard of Oz* as a monetary allegory," *Journal of Political Economy*, 98(4): 739–60.

Rolnick, Arthur J. and Warren E. Weber. 1983. "New evidence on the free banking era," *American Economic Review*, 73(5): 1080–91.

Romer, Christina D. 1992. "What ended the Great Depression?" *Journal of Economic History*, 52(4): 757–84.

Rothbard, Murray. 1962. *The Panic of 1819*. Columbia University Press.

Rubin, Oliver. 2009. "The Niger famine: a collapse of entitlements and democratic response," *Journal of Asian and African Studies*. https://doi.org/10.1177/ 0021909609102899.

Salter, Arthur. 1932. *Recovery: The Second Effort*. Century Co.

Sampson, Anthony. 1961. *Anatomy of Britain*. Hodder & Stoughton.

Sarin, Natasha and Lawrence H. Summers. 2016. "Have big banks gotten safer?" *Brookings Papers on Economic Activity*. https://www.brookings.edu/bpea-articles/have-big-banks-gotten-safer/.

Saunders, A. and M.M. Cornett. 2012. *Financial Markets and Institutions*, 5th edn. McGraw-Hill/Irwin.

Saul, S.B. 1969. *The Myth of the Great Depression, 1873–96*. Macmillan.

Sayers, R.S. 1951. "The development of central banking after Bagehot," *Economic History Review*, 4(1): 109–16.

Sayers, R.S. 1956. *Financial Policy, 1939–45*. Longmans.

Sayers, R.S. 1976. *The Bank of England, 1891–1944*. Cambridge University Press.

Schumpeter, Joseph A. 1942. *Capitalism, Socialism, and Democracy*. Harper and Row.

Schwartz, Anna J. 1992. "The misuse of the Fed's discount window," Federal Reserve Bank of St. Louis *Economic Review*, 74(5). https://research.stlouisfed.org/publications/review/1992/09/01/the-misuse-of-the-feds-discount-window/.

Seeking Alpha. 2008. *Bear Stearns Bondholders Win Big*. https://seekingalpha.com/article/70098-bear-stearns-bondholders-win-big.

Seldon, Anthony. 1981. *Churchill's Indian Summer: The Conservative Government, 1951–55*. Hodder & Stoughton.

Selgin, George and Lawrence H. White. 1999. "A fiscal theory of government's role in money," *Economic Inquiry*, 37(1): 154–65.

Selgin, George, William D. Lastrapes and Laurence H. White. 2012. "Has the Fed been a failure?" *Journal of Macroeconomics*, 34(3): 569–96.

Sen, Amaryta. 1981. *Poverty and Famines: An Essay on Entitlement and Deprivation*. Oxford University Press.

Sen, Amaryta. 1990. "Public action to remedy hunger," Tanco Memorial Lecture, *Interdisciplinary Science Reviews*, 16(4): 324–36.

Sen, Amaryta. 1999. *Development as Freedom*. Knopf.

Shaw, William A. 1906. "The Treasury order book," *Economic Journal*, March.

Shonfield, Andrew. 1958. *British Economic Policy Since the War*. Penguin.

Skidelsky, Robert. 1967. *Politicians and the Slump: The Labour Government of 1929–31*. Macmillan.

Skidelsky, Robert. 1983, 1992, 2000. *John Maynard Keynes*, 3 vols. Penguin.

Smith, Adam. [1776] 1937. *An Inquiry into the Nature and Causes of the Wealth of Nations*, W. Strahan and T. Cadell.

Smith, David L. 1999. *The Stuart Parliaments, 1603–89*. Oxford University Press.

Smith, Paul. 1987. "Disraeli's politics," *Transactions of the Royal Historical Society*, 37: 65–85.

Smith, Walter B. 1953. *Economic Aspects of the Second Bank of the United States*. Harvard University Press.

Sorkin, Andrew R. 2009. *Too Big to Fail*. Viking Press.

Southern, Pat. 2001. *The Roman Empire from Severus to Constantine*. Routledge.

Speck, W.A. 1988. *Reluctant Revolutionaries: Englishmen and the Revolution of 1688*. Oxford University Press.

Sprague, O.M.W. 1910. *History of Crises under the National Banking System* (National Monetary Commission). U.S. Government Printing Office.

Stanton, T.H. 2012. *Why Some Firms Thrive While Others Fail: Government and Management Lessons from the Crisis*. Oxford University Press.

Stasavage, David. 2006. "Partisan politics and public debt: the importance of the Whig supremacy for Britain's financial revolution," ms. New York University.

Stewart, Frances. 2011. "Inequality in political power: a fundamental (and overlooked) dimension of inequality," *European Journal of Development Research*, 23(4): 541–5.

Stiglitz, Joseph E. and Linda Bilmes. 2008. *The Three Trillion Dollar War*. W.W. Norton.

Strong, Benjamin. 1930. *Interpretations of Federal Reserve Policy*, ed. W.R. Burgess. Harper & Row.

Studenski, Paul and Herman E. Krooss. 1952. *Financial History of the United States*. McGraw-Hill.

Sumner, Scott. 2015. *The Midas Paradox: Financial Markets, Government Policy Shocks, and the Great Depression*. Independent Institute.

Tanner, J.R. 1928. *English Constitutional Conflicts of the 17th Century, 1603–1689*. Cambridge University Press.

Tarr, David G. 2010. "Lehman Brothers and Washington Mutual show too big to fail is a myth," SSRN. https://papers.ssrn.com/sol3/papers.cfm?abstract_id=1533522.

Taus, Esther R. 1943. *Central Banking Functions of the U.S. Treasury, 1789–1941*. Columbia University Press.

Taylor, A.J.P. 1965. *English History, 1914–45*. Oxford University Press.

Taylor, John B. 1993. "Discretion versus policy rules in practice," *Carnegie-Rochester Conference Series on Public Policy*, 39: 195–214.

Taylor, John B. 2009. *Getting Off Track: How Government Actions and Interventions Caused, Prolonged, and Worsened the Financial Crisis*. Hoover Institution Press.

Taylor, John B. and J.C. Williams. 2009. "A black swan in the money market," *American Economic Journal of Macroeconomics*, 1(1): 58–83.

Temin, Peter. 1969. *The Jacksonian Economy*. W.W. Norton.

Temzelides, T. 1997. "Are bank runs contagious?" Federal Reserve Bank of Philadelphia *Business Review*. https://fraser.stlouisfed.org/files/docs/historical/frbphi/businessreview/frbphil_rev_199711.pdf.

Thatcher, Margaret. 1993. *The Downing Street Years*. HarperCollins.

Thomas, S. Evelyn. 1934. *The Rise and Growth of Joint Stock Banking*. Pitman.

Thornton, Daniel L. 2011. "The effectiveness of unconventional monetary policy: the Term Auction Facility," Federal Reserve Bank of St. Louis *Review*. https://research.stlouisfed.org/publications/review/2011/11/01/the-effectiveness-of-unconventional-monetary-policy-the-term-auction-facility.

Thornton, Henry. 1802. *An Enquiry into the Nature and Effects of the Paper Credit of Great Britain*. [Reprinted 1939, George Allen & Unwin; and 1965, Augustus M. Kelley.]

Timberlake, Richard H. 1993. *Monetary Policy in the United States*. University of Chicago Press.

Tooke, Thomas. 1826. *Considerations on the State of the Currency*. John Murray.

Tooke, Thomas. 1838–57. *A History of Prices and the State of the Circulation from 1793 to 1837*, 2 vols. Longman, Orme, Brown, Green and Longmans (1838). [Vol. 3, 1840; Vol. 4, 1848; Vols. 5 and 6 (with William Newmarch), 1857.]

Torrens, R. 1837. *A Letter to the Right Honourable Viscount Melbourne on the Cause of the Recent Derangement in the Money Market and on Bank Reform*. Longman, Rees, Orme, Brown, & Green.

Trevelyan, Charles E. 1848. "The Irish crisis," *Edinburgh Review*, 87(175): 229–320.

Triffin, Robert. 1968. *Our International Monetary System*. Random House.

Ullman, Harlan K. 2017. *Anatomy of Failure: Why America Loses Every War it Starts*. Naval Institute Press.

Unger, Irwin. 1959. "Business men and specie resumption," *Political Science Quarterly*, 74(1): 46–70.

Unger, Irwin. 1964. *The Greenback Era: A Social and Political History of American Finance, 1865–79*. Princeton University Press.

Vanhaute, Eric, Richard Paping and Cormac Ó Gráda. 2006. *The European Subsistence Crisis of 1845–1850: A Comparative Perspective*. IEHC.

Veitch, George S. [1913] 1965. *The Genesis of Parliamentary Reform*. Archon Books.

Walsh, Carl E. 2017. *Monetary Theory and Policy*, 4th edn. MIT Press.

Walter, John R. 2005. "Depression-era bank failures: the Great Contagion or the Great Shakeout?" Federal Reserve Bank of Richmond *Economic Quarterly*. https://www .richmondfed.org/publications/research/economic_quarterly/2005/winter/walter.

Warburg, Paul M. 1907. "A plan for a modified central bank," *Proceedings of the Academy of Political Science in the City of New York*, 4(4): 26.

Warburg, Paul M. 1930. *The Federal Reserve System: Its Origin and Growth*. Macmillan.

Ward-Perkins, C.N. 1950. "The commercial crisis of 1847," *Oxford Economic Papers*, 2(1): 75–94.

Webb, Beatrice. 1985. *Diary*, vol. 4, ed. Norman and Jeanne MacKenzie. Belknap Press.

Webb, Sidney and Beatrice Webb. 1963. *The Development of English Local Government, 1689–1835*. Oxford University Press.

Wechsberg, Joseph. 1966. *The Merchant Bankers*. Simon & Schuster.

Wedgwood, C.V. 1955. *The King's Peace, 1637–41*. Collins.

Weiler, Peter. 1993. *Ernest Bevin*. Manchester University Press.

Wessel, David. 2010. *In Fed We Trust: Bernanke's War on the Great Panic*. Three Rivers Press.

West, Robert C. 1977. *Banking Reform and the Federal Reserve, 1863–1923*. Cornell University Press.

Whale, P. Barrett. 1944. "A retrospective view of the Bank Charter Act of 1844," *Economica*, 11(43): 109–11.

Wheelock, David C. 2010. "Lessons learned? Comparing the Federal Reserve's responses to the crises of 1929–33 and 2007–2009," Federal Reserve Bank of St. Louis *Review*. https://files.stlouisfed.org/files/htdocs/publications/review/10/03/ Wheelock.pdf.

White, Eugene N. 2010. "'To establish a more effective supervision of banking': how the birth of the Fed altered bank supervision," in Michael Bordo and William Roberds, eds., *The Origins, History, and Future of the Federal Reserve*, pp. 7–54. Cambridge University Press.

Wicker, Elmus R. 1965. "Federal Reserve monetary policy, 1922–33: a reinterpreta-tion," *Journal of Political Economy*, 74(4). https://doi.org/10.1086/259034.

Wicker, Elmus R. 1966. *Federal Reserve Monetary Policy, 1917–33*. Random House.

Wicker, Elmus R. 1996. *Banking Panics of the Great Depression*. Cambridge University Press.

Wilding, Norman and Philip Laundy. 1971. *An Encyclopedia of Parliament*, 4th edn. St. Martin's Press.

Williams, David. 1963. "London and the 1931 Financial Crisis," *Economic History Review*, 15(3): 513–28.

Willis, H. Parker. 1923. *The Federal Reserve System*. Ronald Press.

Wilson, Harold. 1971. *The Labour Government 1964–70: A Personal Record*. Michael Joseph.

Wilson, Woodrow. 1966–94. *Papers*, ed. Arthur Link. Princeton University Press.

Wilson, Woodrow. 1885. *Congressional Government*. Houghton Mifflin.

Wood, John H. 2003. "Bagehot's lender of last resort: a hollow hallowed tradition," *Independent Review*, 7(3): 343–51.

Wood, John H. 2005. *A History of Central Banking in Great Britain and the United States*. Cambridge University Press.

Wood, John H. 2009. *A History of Macroeconomic Policy in the United States*. Routledge.

Wood, John H. 2015. *Central Banking in a Democracy*. Routledge.

Wood, John H. 2020. *Who Governs?* Palgrave Macmillan.

Wood, John H. and Norma Wood. 1985. *Financial Markets*. Harcourt Brace Jovanovich.

Woodham-Smith, Cecil B. 1962. *The Great Hunger: Ireland, 1845–49*. Hamish Hamilton.

Woodward, Bob. 2002. *Bush at War*. Simon & Schuster.

Woodward, Bob. 2010. *Obama's Wars*. Simon & Schuster.

Woodward, E.L. 1938. *The Age of Reform, 1815–70*. Clarendon Press.

Woolrych, Austin. 1958. "The collapse of the Great Rebellion," *History Today*, 8(9). https://www.historytoday.com/archive/collapse-great-rebellion.

Wraxall, N.W. 1818. *Historical Memoirs of My Own Time*, 3rd edn. Lea and Blanchard.

Yonge, Charles D. 1868. *The Life and Administration of Robert Banks Jenkinson, Second Earl of Liverpool*. Macmillan.

Ziegler, Philip S. 1988. *The Sixth Great Power: A History of One of the Greatest of all Banking Families, The House of Barings, 1765–1929*. Knopf.

Index